We Remember

U.S. Cavalry Association

TURNER PUBLISHING COMPANY

TURNER PUBLISHING COMPANY
412 Broadway, P.O. Box 3101
Paducah, KY 42002-3101
Phone: (502) 443-0121

Turner Publishing Company Staff:
Douglas W. Sikes, Publishing Consultant
Herbert C. Banks II, Designer

US Cavalry Association Staff:
BG Philip L. Bolte, USA (Ret.) President
Patricia S. Bright, Executive Director

Ed Daily, Author

Library of Congress Catalog Card Number:
96-61446
ISBN: 1-56311-318-X

Additional copies may be purchased
directly from Turner Publishing Company.

Printed in the United States of America.

Limited Edition.

TABLE OF CONTENTS

DEDICATION

This book is dedicated to Colonel James R. Spurrier, USA (Ret.), for establishing the United States Horse Cavalry Association (now called the U.S. Cavalry Association). He served as the first Chairman of the Board of Trustees 1976-78 and the first President 1976-1995. We thank him for his inspiration, long hours and hard work. We praise him for his devotion to duty, honor and country.

FOREWORD

"If men could learn from history, what lessons it might teach us!"
Samuel Taylor Coleridge, 1772-1834

"Charge the bastards! Ride them down, boys!"
Henry "Light Horse Harry" Lee, 1756-1818

This book, published in the twentieth year since a small group of dedicated former horse cavalrymen set about to preserve the history and spirit of the U.S. Cavalry, tells the story of the establishment and growth of an organization dedicated to the preservation of a unique part of American military history. The story of the U.S. Cavalry Association, like that of the U.S. Cavalry, is the story of an effort to overcome the odds, to accomplish worthwhile tasks, and to prevail over obstacles.

The record of the U.S. Cavalry is interwoven with the growth of the United States. From a small body of cavalrymen in the Revolution, through the performance of cavalry militia in the War of 1812, the establishment of the Regiments of Dragoons to protect westward expansion, the performance of the Regiment of Mounted Riflemen in the War with Mexico, the trials of the Civil War, the years of Indian Wars, and in the wars of the Twentieth Century, the cavalryman has written in his sacrifice and dedication to duty a significant part of the history of this nation. Now the mount has changed from horse to vehicle, land or air, but the spirit of the Cavalry remains.

The U.S. Cavalry Association is dedicated to the maintenance of that Cavalry spirit through the preservation of U.S. Cavalry history. It is an effort that takes many forms: from support of the U.S. Cavalry Museum to the encouragement of mounted memorial units, from the identification of a cavalry bibliography to the collection of Cavalry artifacts, and from the providing of assistance to researchers to encouraging the camaraderie of a like-minded membership.

This book is a salute to the U.S. Cavalry of all generations and to the U.S. Cavalry Association members who support the preservation of the Cavalry spirit.

Philip L. Bolte
BG, USA, Ret
President

6

A CAVALRYMAN'S EULOGY

History has it that a cavalryman's life was often very hard; thus the legend of "Fiddler's Green" was created. "Fiddler's Green" is a place where a cavalryman stops during his hereafter travel to his ultimate destination.

Fiddler's Green is where a cavalryman meets his comrades who have gone before him, at an old canteen, surrounded by a broad meadow, dotted with trees and crossed by many streams. Here the cavalryman stops, unsaddles his horse, and joins his comrades for a visit with many stories, reminiscences, and camaraderie, before continuing his journey. Soldiers of no other branch of service may stop at Fiddler's Green, they must continue to march.

Today we honor trooper (name), who has served with distinction as a cavalryman, and is now ready to make his trip to Fiddler's Green. We wish him a safe and speedy journey and a happy reunion with his cavalry comrades, who await him. In a final tribute we present him with this symbol of his honored service as a cavalryman (a small guidon). We wish him God's speed.

FIDDLER'S GREEN

Halfway down the trail to Hell,
In a shady meadow of green,
Are the Souls of all dead troopers camped
Near a good old-time canteen,
And this eternal resting place
Is known as Fiddler's Green.

Marching past, straight through to Hell,
The Infantry are seen,
Accompanied by the Engineers,
Artillery and Marine,
For none but the shades of Cavalrymen
Dismount at Fiddler's Green.

Though some go curving down the trail
To seek a warmer scene,
No trooper ever gets to Hell
Ere he's emptied his canteen,
And so rides back to drink again
With friends at Fiddler's Green.

And so when man and horse go down
Beneath a saber keen,
Or in a roaring charge of fierce melee
you stop a bullet clean,
And the hostiles come to get your scalp,
Just empty your canteen
And put your pistol to your head
And go to Fiddler's Green.

101st NY.N.G. Mounted Band followed by H.Q. Troop in Washingtons Bi-Centenial parade 1932. The costumes for the Band and H.Q. Troop were supplied by the city of New York -Mayor Jas. Walker reviewed , with other notables. The Band is shown on 5th Avenue in N.Y.C. facing the Washington Arch at Washington Square. The Band was formed at the Brooklyn Armory in 1928 (Col. Jas. Howlett Comdg.) and attached to H.Q. Troop for administration. (Courtesy of Ed Daily)

Author's Note: Many designated cavalry units from its origin as horse cavalry have experienced peace and have fought in World War II, Korea, Vietnam, and the Persian Gulf War. The author apologizes for those cavalry units that were not expressed or mentioned herein. Due to limited space, it was impossible to cover all the history of the many gallant cavalry units. More emphasis was shown to those existing cavalry units of today's modern Army, which gives a faithful picture of events and those aspects of military history as they participated. In conclusion, the author is hopeful that the reader of this book will have a better understanding of those contingency cavalry forces throughout the history of America's Army. Edward L. Daily, author

UNITED STATES CAVALRY
HISTORY

INTRODUCTION

This book will attempt to illuminate the fascinating and remarkable history of cavalry in the United States Army. To do this we must first briefly examine its European roots which saw their greatest periods of development during the Seven Years War (1756-63) and the Napoleonic Wars (1804-15). Napoleon had a picturesque quality that belied his ruthless methods and led to a tremendous service record. Handsome General Lasalle, who said that no French Hussar ought to live beyond the age of 30; Marulaz, who had 26 horses killed under him; and Murat, the inn-keeper's son who became a king are a few examples of this period's heroes.

In the early 17th century, the decline of feudalism, together with economic development, the forming of powerful centralist states and the advent of firearms, led to a diminishing role for the established form of the knight's armored cavalry in many countries of Western Europe, and to the forming of professional mercenary armies that would reach their peak during the Thirty Years War (1618-48). The first standing armies that had all the structure of modern armed forces came into existence toward the middle of the 17th century. Military administration was set up, the standardization of uniforms began and barracks for the troops were built. Instead of depending on local sources, the Army now got its supplies from warehouses. It was also during this period that the foundations of the medical corps and the military judicial system were laid, and the first decorations and medals handed out. The Officer Corps was recruited from the ranks of the nobility and the aristocracy. Due to the growth in manpower and the division into various arms, the organizational structure of the armies improved. Permanent military formations such as the troop, company, squadrons, battalion and regiment appeared. From the major fighting impact that cavalry began to have, its significance and structure developed at the pinnacle of its usage, a fighting art that many consider to be the most prestigious of all warrior disciplines. Many cavalry units received designated names (i.e. Cossacks, Grenadiers, Musketeers, Dragoons, Hussars) and each had a distinctive trait. An example of such extraordinary prestige came during the reign of Austrian Empress Maria Theresa (1717-80), whose Hungarian Hussars were regarded as the best light cavalry in Europe.

The new system of replacement and the greater effectiveness of firearms had an influence on the ratio of cavalry to infantry in the armies. Infantry troops, armed with muskets and bayonets, became the most important and largest arm of the military. Artillery also became a separate branch of the military, with formations of its own. However, cavalry remained the principle maneuvering force, especially in the period of rigid infantry line tactics. It was still divided into heavy cavalry for battle, light cavalry for reconnaissance, protection and pursuit and dragoons, who were progressively losing their role as mounted infantry and turning into combat cavalry.

The need of European armies for horses increased commensurably with their growth. To ensure fast and adequate replacement of mounts, special stables were founded from the 17th century on; and in the middle of the 18th century the remocent service was established. Selective breeding resulted in new stock, adapted fot conditions of service in the military. The first standards for military horses were introduced at the same time as the first veterinarian services. Riding schools were instituted.

The Thirty Years War and the English Civil War (1642-49) signaled the definitive demise of the knights and gentry of the Middle Ages, the armored horsemen on their big, heavy mounts, whose charge for glory and riches was the consummation of victory and usually the final phase of the battle. The battle formation of individual combatants adorned with colorful flags and decorated with plumes and coats of arms shattered when faced with the wall of fire of disciplined infantry, or the equally disciplined ranks of horsemen armed with pistols. Many saddles were emptied in a none too chivalrous manner before the fighting had begun in earnest.

The appearance of firearms and their rapid development greatly changed the way war was waged. Muskets became more accurate and their bullets deadlier; and perhaps most important, the length of time between two shots was shortened. Military leaders realized that speed of movement on the battlefield was becoming a crucial factor in combat. The opponent had to be given as little chance of shooting as possible, in order to "conserve the more sabers for the final showdown." Further strengthening of the horses' and riders' armor would be costly, and would also necessitate heavier and slower horses, whose breeding would also add to the cost. And even such a tank on four legs couldn't offer certain protection from the effects of firearms. The solution was to do away with superfluous armor, thus increasing the horses' speed.

It had originally taken Western Europe 500 years to breed a large and heavy horse strong enough to bear its armor and an armored rider and withstand a collision with a similar one-ton monster. Strength and weight were then given more consideration than speed and maneuverability. But as the strategy changed, rulers and generals started searching for lighter and faster horses for their mounted troops. Development of cavalry organization, equipment, uniforms and tactics enabled cavalry to move faster and more effectively through reforms and improved training. By the second half of the 17th century, great cavalry masses were formed and grouped into divisions and corps. The new age of the cavalry had begun.

Guidon of the Sweedish dragoons, about 1660.

Saxon cavalry standard made in 1709.

Russian two-headed eagle, common symbol used by cavalry regiments in tzarist Russia.

English standard of the Royal Regiment of Horse; beginning of the 18th century.

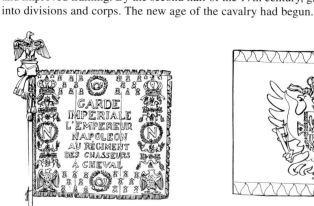

French standard of the Chasseurs a Cheval de la Farde Imperiale in 1805.

Austrian cavalry standard, 1806-1816.

THE CAVALRY BEGINS IN AMERICA

The situation in Europe had not changed much as a consequence of the Seven Years War, but the relations among the colonial powers had been altered. Great Britain had profited the most. Making use of the large number of its colonies, Britain drove Holland and France out of America. But the 13 colonies, experiencing a period of rapid growth, wanted more independence from the mother country in matters of economy and politics. Great Britain, on the other hand, wanted them to remain only sources of raw materials and a market for its industrial products. Open conflicts between the colonists and regular English troops started in 1775 and marked the beginning of the American War of Independence.

During the Seven Years War in Europe, between the drawn-out maneuvers of large armies that waited for favorable occasions to take up battle, frittering away their time in long sieges, a whole series of smaller clashes took place which were not conducted according to the rules of engagement valid for large-scale, orderly battles. Line tactics and constant drilling on the exercise fields were designed to eliminate a soldier's initiative and make of him an automaton who was supposed to execute orders without thinking. Nevertheless, short, surprise clashes and skirmishes demanded speed of reaction, initiative and a large degree of improvisation. The English military authorities realized this, and formed seven regiments of Light Dragoons who were free from rigid line tactics and the accompanying harsh discipline.

As the situation in America grew more serious, the 16th and 17th Light Dragoons were sent over. They became a model of cavalry observed by George Washington's Militia; although the first Colonial cavalry unit used in the war was a troop of German mercenaries and veterans of the Seven Years War named the Pennsylvania Hussar Company. They were, however, disbanded after only a few weeks because they were too expensive.

At the end of 1776, when war between the British and Americans was gaining intensity, Washington wrote to Congress: "From the experience I have in this campaign of the utility of horse, I am convinced there is no carrying on the war without them, and I would therefore recommend the establishment of one or more corps." On the strength of this recommendation Congress allowed the equipping of 3,000 light horsemen. Four regiments of Continental Light Dragoons were formed from provincial militia detachments at the beginning of 1777. Bland's Virginia Light Horse became the 1st Regiment; the second, commanded by Colonel Elisha Sheldon, became known as Sheldon's Dragoons; and the third and fourth were known, respectively, as Baylor's Dragoons and Moylan's Dragoons. Following English practice, a regiment was divided into six troops; each of which was supposed to have 280 men at full complement. In reality, they rarely had more than 150. Owing to lack of equipment and armaments, each horseman carried the weapons that he had managed to procure for himself. It was definitely not unheard of for American dragoons to be armed with Indian spears and tomahawks. The colors of coats for each regiment had been set forth in principle, and were as follows: tan with green facings for the 1st, blue with buff facings for the 2nd, white with blue facings for the 3rd and red with blue facings for the 4th.

Instead of grouping his four new cavalry regiments into a larger fighting formation, Washington split the Continental Light Dragoons up into a number of smaller units with the tasks of scouting, maintaining communications and patrolling on "no-man's land." In the following years, a series of lesser conflicts, with never more than a few hundred horsemen taking part on both sides, was recorded. One of the biggest of these happened in 1781 at a place in South Carolina called Cowpens. American General Morgan, commanding 800 infantrymen, 80 horsemen of the 4th Continental Light Dragoons, under Colonel William Washington, and 45 horsemen of McCall's Mounted Militia, defeated British General Tarleton, at the head of 700 infantrymen, 200 green-uniformed dragoons of the British Legion, 50 horsemen of the 17th Light Dragoons and a battery consisting of two artillery pieces. The battle was decided when Washington's 80 dragoons, previously hidden from the enemy, charged and broke the green dragoons and forced the already demoralized English to lay down their arms. Tarleton succeeded in escaping with 150 of his men; all the others were killed or captured. In 1783, America gained its independence, the Army was disbanded and the horsemen went home.

John Churchill, Duke of Marlborough (1650-1722), the greatest cavalry commander in the beginning of the 18th century. Contemporary painting.

Gebhard Leberecht Blucher (1742-1819), one of the best-known Prussian commanders, served as a hussar in his youth.

Michael Kovats de Fabriczy was born in Hungary in 1724. He served under Frederick the Great. Decorated for bravery with the highest Award Pour Le Merit, he was the commander of the Free Gersdorf Hussars. He volunteered his services through Benjamin Franklin, then American Envoy to the Court of Versailles. Washington assigned him as Master of Exercise to the newly formed cavalry and he was commissioned by the Continental Congress as a Colonel and later became Commandant of the new Cavalry. In the August 4, 1778 issue of the Maryland Journal, the editor gave a very high mark to the cavalry… "distinguished not only by its splendid uniforms and standardized equipment from the rather poorly clad and depressed revolutionary troops but also by its good training and exemplary discipline. And in his work, the lion's share belongs to Kovats who had by far the most peacetime and battle experience in organizing independent units, as well as training and commanding them." After two years of intensive campaigning under General George Washington, Col. Kovats fell mortally wounded May 11, 1779 in the battle of Charleston, South Carolina. His English opponent, Brigade Major Skelly, paid him the greatest tribute at the requiem at his grave. He said: "The best cavalry the Rebels ever had." The Citadel, at Charleston, S.C. has an important display of memorabilia in its Museum to preserve the memory of his heroism.

EUROPEAN CAVALRY CHANGES

At the end of the 18th century, cavalry consisted of four basic types; although in some armies this division was not so apparent. The heavy cavalry consisted of cuirassiers, carabiniers and some guard regiments that traditionally had other names. Like the knights of the Middle Ages, the heavy cavalry had the task of administering the coup de grace to a shaken enemy, to breach his battle formation and create an opening for the infantry, which was supposed to finish the opponent off, and the light cavalry, whose task was to pursue the remnants of his force.

Dragoons made up the medium type of cavalry. Due to their versatility, they were the most numerous of the cavalry troops. With the appearance of firearms, a mounted foot soldier became a dragoon. At the time of the greatest expansion of cavalry, he lost nearly all his original characteristics. In modern times, he would remain the only mounted soldier and revert to his original role - a foot soldier on horseback. Dragoons were trained to fight like cuirassiers, but also to reconnoiter and patrol like light horsemen; as they were armed with carbines, musketoons and bayonets, they could play the part of infantry, too. They lacked, however, the impact of the heavy cavalry, the speed of the light cavalry and the fire-power of infantry. Also, dragoons presented the most variations among armies. Where there was no heavy cavalry, dragoons were the real battle cavalry.

Reconnaissance, patrolling, pursuit of the enemy, cutting of his communication lines, capturing and guarding inhabited places or bridges until the arrival of infantry, as well as foraging, were the tasks of the light cavalry - Hussars (Polish), Jagers zu Pferde (Lancers), Chevauxlegers (Sabers), Chasseurs (Muskets) a Cheval or Light Dragoons (mounted infantry with short muskets). Most of the other light cavalry units were cheaper alternatives to the Hussars, whose richly decorated uniforms were extremely expensive. For an army, it was easiest and most economical to equip a light horseman who did not need so much training as a cuirassier or a dragoon. At the beginning of the 19th century, a cuirassier's horse in France cost 300 francs, and a light cavalryman's horse only 100 francs. Horses of very high quality, for officers or guards units, could cost in excess of 500 francs (today about $800 US).

The fourth and youngest of the cavalry units combined the speed of light cavalry with the force and impact of the heavy cavalry. These were the uhlans, light horsemen armed with a spear, who had been a part of the Polish and Lithuanian armies since the 16th century. Their names derives from the Turkish word "oglan," meaning "young man;" they were dressed in traditional Polish costume, with the characteristic "czapka" on their heads, and a double-breasted uniform coat called the "durtka." Countries that were frequently at war with Turkey, or else bordered on Poland, appreciated the worth of these riders, and took them into their service. Friederich II had Bosniaks in his cavalry in 1793 when Prussia occupied part of Poland. In 1784 Austria formed its first regiment of uhlans; and in 1803, Russia changed its Odesky hussars into uhlans.

At the end of the 18th century, the cost of equipping and training a horseman in Austria was 2,200 crowns for a Jager zu Pferd; 2,800 crowns for a hussar; and 3,300 crowns for a cuirassier. In comparison, a musket cost 10 crowns, a pair of shoes two, a 12-pound gun 460 and a dragoon horse 80 crowns. The cost of equipping and training a foot soldier was 200 crowns, which also gives us an idea of how expensive cavalry was.

Horses were bought, or sometimes simply requisitioned in the field, with the issuing of a paper stating that the state would pay this debt at some future time. In peacetime, the criteria for the acquisition of horses were very strict; but during war, because of high losses, every horse was a good horse.

AMERICAN EXPANSION

After the War of Independence, the American economy developed rapidly, with farming and industry predominate in the North, and a more plantation oriented economy in the South. The Constitution of 1787 marked the creation of the United States of America, with Congress as the legislative body. At that time, the United States had approximately four million inhabitants; about 500,000 of them were black, and a further 400,000 were native Indians living in several hundred tribal communities throughout America. Economic expansion and a great influx of immigrants forced the United States to expand toward the south and west, thus displacing and destroying the Indian tribes, which put up a stiff resistance. The first steps in this direction were the purchases of Louisiana, from Napoleon, in 1803, for the sum of 15 million dollars, and Florida, from Spain, in 1819. With these acquisitions, the territory of the USA stretched from the Atlantic Ocean to beyond the Mississippi, and from Canada to the Gulf of Mexico. Canada, to the north, belonged to Great Britain and harbored refugees from the losing side in the War of Independence; Mexico, to the south, considered Texas, New Mexico, and all territories west of the Rocky Mountains its own.

Napoleon's accession to power and related events on the other side of the Atlantic did not leave America unaffected. In 1807, Great Britain placed an embargo on American trade with European countries that Napoleon had occupied; the same year, the United States Government responded by closing its ports to foreign shipping. British support of the Indians, who fought against the USA

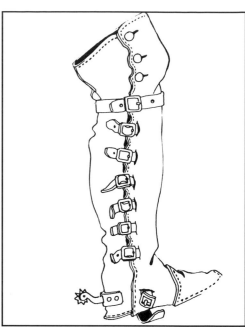

Dragoon's leather gaiters similar to the cloth gaiters of the infanty; from the time of the Seven Years War.

Napoleon Bonaparte (1769-1821) in the uniform of a chasseur a cheval of the Guard. Painting by J. Chabord.

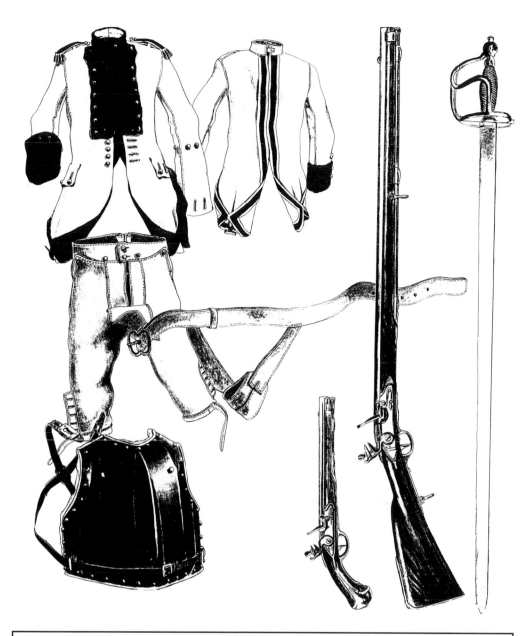

Mexican General Santa Anna with his cavalry, 1848. Comtemporary etching.

under the leadership of Chief Tecumseh, worsened the situation. In 1812 war broke out; for the most part, it took place at sea and along the Canadian border. Congress voted to increase the standing Army to 35,000 men and empowered the president to raise a further 30,000 volunteers and 100,000 men in the state militias. In practice, however, the Regular Army never numbered more than 10,000 during the whole war, while the militia was undisciplined and unreliable. On the other hand, because of the European wars, Great Britain could never afford to have more than 6,000 regular soldiers and 2,000 militiamen in America.

In an act dating back to 1799, Congress had allowed for the mobilization of 24 infantry and three cavalry regiments in case of war. Equipment for 3,000 horsemen was bought and stored in war reserves for such a contingency. When relations with Great Britain deteriorated, one regiment was brought up to full complement and another one raised. Thus, in 1808, the United States Cavalry consisted of the 1st and 2nd Regiments of US Light Dragoons. Each regiment had eight companies, with 400 men at full complement. Following the precedent set during the War of Independence, the blue-uniformed dragoons were divided into smaller formations that took part in the expeditions into British territory.

In 1813 Colonel Richard M. Johnson, a popular congressman, was granted permission by the Secretary of War to raise two battalions of mounted volunteers for four months' service. The force numbered 1,200 men in 14 companies. For several months Johnson's Volunteers patrolled and carried out reconnaissance along the border. During pauses Johnson trained his men to charge in line; and in order to accustom them and their horses to the sound of gunfire, he would dismount part of the troops and have them play the enemy by firing blanks. These exercises also served to help the men conquer their fear of charging the British infantry.

In autumn of 1813, 800 Redcoats of the British 45th Foot clashed with Johnson's Volunteers by the Thames River, about 90 miles east of Detroit. The British, accustomed to the accurate fire of enemy light infantry, took up an extended order in two lines, so as to present a smaller target. Johnson saw his opportunity in this, ordered his men to develop in line and commanded the first battalion to charge. Five hundred riders armed with tomahawks, hunting rifles and knives could not be stopped by two volleys. They rode through the British lines at full gallop, swinging away with their tomahawks, stopped, dismounted and opened fire. The British, under fire from the back and faced with the charge of 500 more horsemen from the front, surrendered immediately.

At the beginning of 1814 Congress disbanded one of the dragoon regiments in order to cut expenses. At the end of the year, the war ended after several inconclusive battles. The Peace Treaty of Ghent restored the status quo ante. The remaining dragoons were discharged at the end of 1815, with the explanation that they were too expensive.

As more traders and settlers moved west, the east bank of the Mississippi became a constant battleground between whites and Indians. This was why Congress adopted the Removal Act in 1830, which envisaged moving all Indian tribes to the west bank of the river. In 1832 Congress, in order to protect the settlers, keep open the caravan trail to Santa Fe and guard against any attempt by the Indians to come back, approved the creation of the US Mounted Ranger Battalion, made up of volunteers organized in six companies with 100 privates each. Each volunteer, together with his own horse and equipment, enlisted for a year, and was paid one dollar a day.

The Rangers faced Indian warriors in the open and wild country between the river and Great Plains. The Comanche, whose equestrian skills and knowledge of horses rivaled that of the Mongols and Tartars, were the best-known of them. After the Spanish conquerors arrived in Mexico, the Indians quickly realized the value of horses and started providing themselves with them, either by capture in war or by simple theft.

The combination of brave warriors and horses descended from the excellent Spanish breeds resulted in hard mounted fighters. Even though the Rangers did not lag behind the Indians in fighting qualities, they lacked reliability, good organization and discipline. That was why Congress decided, in 1833, to form a regular unit, the US Regiment of Dragoons, which consisted of 10 companies, marked with the letters A-K and with a total complement of 750 men.

In Florida, which America had acquired from Spain, the government, after 1821, took a similar policy towards the Seminole Indians as toward those on the east bank of the Mississippi. In 1835, Osceola, chief of the Seminoles, led his tribe into war against the white settlers. As the militia and volunteer units could not stand up effectively to the Indians, Congress decided in 1836 to approve the creation of the 2nd US Regiment of Dragoons.

The dragoons were armed with a saber, two pistols and a carbine. Fifty new Colt six-shot revolving rifles were distributed to the best shots in the regiment in 1838. Their uniforms were dark blue, except those of the units stationed in the subtropical climate of Florida, which were light-col-ored and made of cotton. Every company had a red-and-white guidon with the regiment's mark and the letter of the company.

The constant skirmishes with the Great Plains Indians, the war with the Seminoles, which would last for nearly seven years, and the Texas declaration of independence from Mexican rule in 1836 complicated the situation along America's southern border. As Mexico still considered Texas a part of its territory, America's annexation of Texas in 1845 was taken as a declaration of war.

On April 24, 1846, 1,600 Mexican horsemen crossed the border at the Rio Grande and surprised two companies of the 2nd Dragoons. Eleven Americans were killed, and the remaining 52 captured. General Zachary Taylor informed the president that war had begun, and moved toward the Mexicans. At Palo Alto, 800 Mexican lancers attempted to attack Taylor from the right flank; but they were stopped by the sudden assault of a company of Texas Rangers, armed with one or two Colt revolvers. When two companies of the 2nd Dragoons arrived, also armed with Colts, the Mexicans retreated in panic. They lost 257 men, Taylor only 55. The cavalry clash at Palo Alto demonstrated a new dimension of mounted warfare. The 120 American soldiers taking part could fire about 800 shots from their revolvers without reloading. The results of this impressive firepower were the five times greater Mexican losses. From this time on, firearms supplanted swords and lances as the principal weapons in hand-to-hand combat.

For the war with Mexico, Congress allowed the raising of 50,000 volunteers, including additional mounted units from Kentucky, Tennessee, Missouri, Arkansas and Texas. The structure of both regular and irregular regiments remained the same

Uniform of a U.S. Dragoon in 1850. (Courtesy of Ed Daily)

Charge of the Union cavalry at Cedar Creek 1864. Contemporary painting.

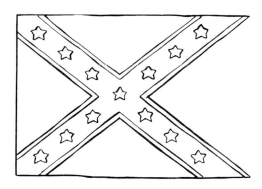

Confederate Cavalry guidon, 1861.

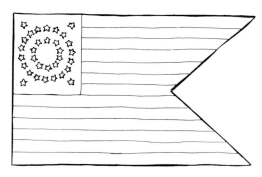

U.S. Cavalry guidon, 1863.

Left: *General "Jeb" Stuart of the Confederate States Army. He ws noted as one of the most important cavalry leaders of the Civil War and he was mortaly wounded in a vicous melee at Yellow Tavern in 1864.* **Right:** *General Nathan Bedford Forrest of the Confederate States Army. His cavalry raids during the Civil War disrupted many Federal supplies. (Courtesy of Ed Daily)*

- 10 companies designated by letters. Some of the volunteer regiments, though, though, numbered over 1,000 men.

The Mexican army had 15 infantry regiments, four artillery brigades, 15 regiments of regular cavalry and five regiments of militia cavalry. The basic horseman of the Mexican army was armed with a lance, saber and carbine, and rode a lighter horse than the dragoons.

The Mexicans were fighting against what probably was the best cavalry of the time. Armed with rapid-fire revolvers, with officers educated at the US Military Academy at West Point, privileged in the choice and quality of equipment and horses, and with 10 years of experience in the war with the Indians, the US Dragoons were a formidable troop of the highest quality. Also, among the im migrants from Europe there were German cuirassiers, Prussian uhlans and English dragoons and hussars who volunteered for the US Dragoons.

In February 1847, at Buena Vista, Taylor waged a defensive battle against the vastly superior forces of General Santa Anna. General Torrejon's Lancer Brigade threatened the Americans' rear; but in a near-replay of Palo Alto, 100 troopers of the 1st Dragoons attacked and broke the Mexicans. Santa Anna had to retreat. Both sides suffered heavy losses.

Meanwhile General John Charles Fremont, with his mounted frontiersmen and immigrants, and with the help of the naval fleet, captured California; and Colonel Phil Kearny took New Mexico. After landing at Vera Cruz, General Winfield Scott, with the regular Regiment of Mounted Rifleman, made his way to Mexico City and captured it. At the beginning of 1848, Mexico was forced into a peace settlement and had to cede the territories of California, New Mexico, Texas, Utah and Nevada. With these gains, the USA stretched from the Atlantic to the Pacific, and south to the Rio Grande.

Progress was always important to America, and Americans were quick to take up on new developments. America was the second country in the world (after Great Britain) to open a railway line in 1830. The pace of expansion of the railroad network was so fast that at mid-century there were already 15,000 kilometers (9,000 miles) of track in the United States. Following the first public demonstration of the telegraph in 1837, the nation was soon covered with telegraph poles and wires. A breech-loading rifle built according to Von Dreys's construction was produced in 1854; it increased firing speed twice, and extended the useful range to 600 paces. The practical uses of mass production of steel opened the way for higher quality in weapons' production. In 1860, Williams presented the first machine gun, and Spencer and Winchester the rapid firing rifle. All these advances would lead to changes in the way war was waged and a different role for cavalry.

THE CIVIL WAR

The growth of the American economy led to increased differences between the North and the South. From the mid-19th century, the abolitionist movement in the North gathered steam. Significant moments in the fight against slavery were the armed conflict between farmers and slave owners in Kansas and John Brown's uprising. The influence of the Republican Party, founded in 1854 and opposed to slavery, increased. Abraham Lincoln, a Republican, was elected president in 1860. The 11 states of the South - South Carolina, North Carolina, Mississippi, Florida, Alabama, Georgia, Louisiana, Texas, Virginia, Arkansas and Tennessee - whose ruling circles had decided to preserve slavery at any cost, seceded from the Union and formed the Confederate States of America. Richmond was chosen as the capital of the Confederacy, and Jefferson Davis elected president. The attempts by the North to preserve the Union without bloodshed became hopeless when Confederate forces took Fort Sumter, near Charleston, on April 14, 1861. War between the 22 states of the North, with 23 million inhabitants, and the 11 states of the South, with nine million inhabitants, including 3.5 million Negro slaves, became inevitable.

At the middle of the 19th century, the US Army was mainly involved in combat with the Indians. Nearly four-fifths of its forces were in the border area. At the end of 1855, the US Army had 15,752 men. That same year, Congress decided to raise two more regiments, simply called the 1st and 2nd US Cavalry, whose structure was the same as the Dragoons'.

"Cavalry" finally became an official branch of the US Army in 1855 with the creation of the 1st and 2nd Cavalry Regiments. (These regiments later would be redesignated the 4th and 5th Cavalry in 1861, after the 1st and 2nd Dragoons and the Regiment of Mounted Rifleman became the new 1st, 2nd and 3rd Cavalry.) More and more wagon trains loaded with pioneer settlers were rolling west and being attacked by Indians. And the Army had a huge area to cover and protect in the new state of Texas. A fast, mobile, high-spirited strike force was needed.

The day after the fall of Fort Sumter, President Lincoln called up 75,000 volunteers for a period of three months, and immediately after that, 42,000 more for the Regular Army and Navy, for a period of three years. As a part of these measures, another regular cavalry regiment was formed, as well as two regiments of mounted volunteers. The general opinion was that the war would soon be over and that no more cavalry would need to be raised and trained.

In Northern Virginia, the Confederacy gathered two rebel armies - 20,000 men under General P.T. Beauregard at Manassas, and 11,000 men under General Joseph E. Johnston at Harper's Ferry. Before the beginning of operations, the Union assembled 30,000 men under General Irwin McDowell on the Potomac, near Washington, DC and 25,000 men under General Robert Patterson at the mouth of the Shenandoah River. McDowell, at the head of his still unprepared army, headed for Manassas on July 16, but was defeated at Bull Run.

The defeated Yankees were pursued by the gray-uniformed 1st Virginia Cavalry of Colonel James Ewell Brown Stuart (better known as J.E.B. Stuart) and other rebel cavalry units.

After the battle of Bull Run, Congress empowered President Lincoln to call up 500,000 more volunteers. A similar mobilization of industrial and humane resources would be repeated in the First and Second World Wars. The country would demonstrate the ability to quickly organize large and effective armies, the standards of which would be accepted by many armies with longer traditions and more experience. Lincoln switched on what was later to be called the US war machine.

The six existing regiments were renamed, the 1st Dragoons becoming the 1st US Cavalry, the 2nd Dragoons the 2nd US Cavalry, and so on by seniority. Twenty-eight new regiments were formed and named after the places where they were recruited, e.g., 7th New York Cavalry, 5th Pennsylvania Cavalry, etc. The number of companies in a regiment was increased to 12; and they were renamed troops, with about 100 troopers each. Theoretically, each regiment should have numbered 1,200 men; but in practice they rarely exceeded half that number. The 6th US Lancers were formed in Pennsylvania, and they carried lances until 1863.

Views on the role of cavalry had not changed much after the Napoleonic Wars. Military authors still held to the belief, the development of firearms notwithstanding, that cavalry was the branch of the Army most useful in decisive operations, especially on large battlefields. It could play an important part in the preparation of the battle, in its conclusion, in covering a retreat, or in pursuing the enemy. The introduction of rifled guns and breech-loading rifles increased not only the infantry's firepower, but the cavalry's as well. Horsemen, therefore, had to learn to fight as well on foot as on horseback. That is why nearly all the cavalry in the Civil War was of dragoon type, armed with single-shot rifles or carbines, revolvers and a heavy saber.

The Union was faced with many problems in realizing its ambitious plan of raising and equipping an Army of half a million men. Over 100,000 horses with equipment had to be procured immediately. The old acquisition system did not work any more, so the first depots for buying and equipping horses were formed. With the forming of the Cavalry Bureau on July 28, 1863, under General George Stoneman, the new system began to function properly. The Bureau oversaw six large depots: Giesboro, District of Columbia; Greenville, Louisiana; St. Louis, Missouri; Nashville, Tennessee; Harrisburg, Pennsylvania; and Wilmington, Delaware. Each of these could hold 5,000-10,000 horses in specially constructed stables and stockyards. These depots also served for the treatment of sick, wounded and exhausted horses. Soldiers were trained in camps that were just as well organized. The federal war machine succeeded in increasing the cavalry forces from 5,000-60,000 battle-ready troopers in less than two years.

The South, chronically short of war equipment and armaments, had a numerous class of landed gentry and farmers, whose way of life was linked with horses, and who represented a source of excellent riders and high-quality horses. Regiments were organized territorially, and consisted of 10 companies, with 60-80 men in each. At first, every man brought his own horse and armed himself with what he could find. At Bull Run, Stuart's Virginians had hunting rifles, shotguns, pistols, revolvers and a few sabers of obscure origin. Regiments were named after their place of recruitment - 6th

Texas Cavalry or 10th Virginia Cavalry, and so on. As the officers of both sides were schooled at West Point, the cavalry drill was similar. Cavalry maneuvered a column of fours, and changes were executed in a double line. A double line was also foreseen as for attack, but this practice was abandoned in 1863 in favor of the single line. For dismounted action, one man in four was detached as a horse holder.

The events at the beginning of the war demonstrated the importance of the training and discipline of the troops. Large and quick operations could not be executed with untrained troops, which at first constituted the majority on both sides. Unprepared commanders, especially in the North, and lack of organization in the higher staffs were further obstacles in the carrying out of planned operations.

The Civil War demonstrated that frontal attacks on strong enemy positions seldom succeeded. Maneuvering became paramount in importance, and this was an opportunity for cavalry. The difficulties of supply and movement over great distances, which had frustrated Napoleon in Russia, were lessened by the use of rail transport. Railroads became vital communications links. Many complex operations depended on the proper running of the railway system for their success, so the rail network was a permanent target for the enemy. If the success and effectiveness of cavalry was not

apparent in the well-known battles of the Civil War, it was in the raids and expeditions into the opponent's rear army, executed by forces ranging in size from a single troop to several thousand men, and equipped with batteries of horsemen. One of the most successful cavalry raids was undertaken by Confederate forces under J.E.B. Stuart (by then a general) between June 12 and 15th, 1862, and is known as "ride around McClellan."

Of his 1,200 men, Stuart lost only one. He circled the whole Army of the Potomac, gathered important information, which would influence the outcome of future operations to the advantage of the rebels, and took 165 prisoners. Later on the night of August 23, Stuart and his riders burned down the transport trains in Catlett's Station on the Orange & Alexandria Railroad, capturing 300 Yankees and 220 horses, and all the personal baggage of General John Pope and his staff. Two days later, he was joined by General Jonathan "Stonewall" Jackson and 1,200 men in a raid on the Orange & Alexandria Railroad; and on August 26 he destroyed a Union supply dump at Manassas Junction, demolished the bridge across the Broad Run and destroyed two trains.

General Bragg, the Confederate commander in Tennessee, sent General Nathan Bedford Forrest with 3,000 troopers and General John Hunt Morgan with 3,900 men and seven cannons behind Grant's army, with the task of destroying railroads

and trains. Morgan's assignment was to demolish the networks in Nashville and Louisville. Among his men he had 400 of them unarmed, whom he was hoping to equip with captured weapons. They started out on December 22, 1862, and arrived in Glasgow, Kentucky on the 24th, after a 144 kilometer (90 mile) march. On the 25th they clashed with a smaller formation of Union infantry. On the 26th, the road was cut at Upton, and a Union patrol captured. Elizabethtown was taken on the 37th with the help of cannon and the 650 men of its garrison made prisoners. Muldraugh's Hill was taken on the 28th, two small forts destroyed with cannon and 700 men captured, as well as two big bridges on the track to Nashville and Louisville demolished.

The expedition clashed with the forces of Colonel Harlan on the 29th, crossed the Rolling Fork at Lebanon on the 31st and returned on January 2. It had achieved the destruction of the tracks at several points, the capture of 2,000 men and weapons, with losses of 66 dead and 24 wounded.

After two years of effort, the North succeeded in putting a formidable cavalry arm in the field in 1863 with the creation of the Cavalry Corps of the Army of the Potomac under the command of General George Stoneman. It consisted of three cavalry divisions - 1st, commanded by General John Buford; 2nd, commanded by General Judson Kilpatrick; and 3rd, headed by Colonel David Gregg - totaling 9,000 men. Divisions consisted of two or three brigades, each with three or four cavalry regiments and two batteries of horsemen. General Alfred Pleasonton was soon appointed to command the Cavalry Corps. With well-armed, well-equipped, well-dressed and well-mounted Yankee riders, he was ready to tackle the hitherto invincible men of J.E.B. Stuart.

The first two years of the war brought advantage to neither side. But as the Union's strength grew, the South's deteriorated. Fewer ships from Europe were making it through the Union blockade; the Confederacy's financial resources were running out; and General U.S. Grant had come down the Mississippi and in June 1863 laid siege to Vicksburg, the key position on the Confederacy's west flank. General Braxton Bragg's Army of Tennessee, faced the forces of General William Stark Rosecrans, and Lee's 89,000 men in Virginia faced General Joseph Hooker's 130,000 troops. Lee, one of the greatest generals in modern history, after the victory at Chancellorville, near Fredericksburg on May 3, 1863, had several options: stay on the defensive and protect Richmond from behind fortified positions; send some of his forces to help Bragg in Tennessee; or, characteristically, attack, and try to decide the war with one great battle. Lee decided on attack. The site of the historic battle was Gettysburg, Pennsylvania.

On June 2, Lee headed from Virginia toward Pennsylvania with an Army of 76,000 men, with 272 cannons. Hearing that Lee was moving north, Hooker prepared to defend Washington and Baltimore with 111,500 men and 362 cannons. Stuart, whose riders had been the eyes and ears of the Southern armies in previous campaigns, was ordered to take his 8,000 veteran horsemen and prevent the enemy from reconnoitering Lee's movements, while gathering information about their intentions at the same time. Pleasonton was given an equal assignment on the other side - find out Lee's intentions at any cost and stop Stuart from spying on the Union Army. These tasks were akin to those Murat had given his chasseurs and other light cavalry.

In order to protect Lee's troop concentration at Culpeper County, Virginia, Stuart guarded the crossings over the Rappahonnock with his five brigades and artillery. Hooker, informed of the arrival of Lee's forces, ordered Pleasonton to cross the river at Brandy Station with his cavalry corps, and, by aggressive reconnaissance, find out the possible concentration and intentions of the rebels. Pleasonton sent Buford's division across Beverly's Crossing, to the north, with the support of an infantry brigade and three batteries of horsemen. The divisions commanded by General Alfred Duffie (who had replaced the wounded Kilpatrick) and Gregg crossed 10 km (6 miles) to the south, also backed by an infantry brigade and two batteries of horsemen.

On the morning of June 9, the 8th New York Cavalry, including the van of Buford's division, crossed the river and encountered a company of the 6th Virginia Cavalry guarding the crossing. The defensive action of the Virginians gave enough time for the rest of the regiment to arrive, together with the 7th Virginia Cavalry. The two regiments held Buford back for an hour and enabled Stuart to concentrate his four brigades and artillery at St. James's Church. Stuart thus achieved a nearly 2-1 superiority of which he decided to take advantage. Buford put up a stubborn resistance, particularly the 6th Pennsylvania Cavalry, half of whom died in a frontal charge on a rebel horse battery.

About noon Stuart received word from Robertson, the commander of his fifth brigade positioned to the south, that a mass of Yankee horsemen had crossed the river at Kelly's Crossing, threatening the flank and rear of the Southern position. At first, Stuart did not take this information seriously. Only an artillery bombardment at Brandy Station, behind his back, forced him to intervene. He sent two brigades, which clashed with Gregg's division in successive charges. Gregg's 1st New Jersey Cavalry beat back the 12th Virginia Cavalry, which headed the arriving Confederate forces. Charges succeeded one another as the regiments arrived until exhaustion prevailed on both sides. The Union troops withdrew, together with Duffee's division, which was securing the direction to Stevensburg. Stuart had narrowly escaped defeat, even though he had lost 450 men to the Yankees' 850.

Fifteen thousand men had taken part in the Battle at Brandy Station, the largest cavalry clash of the Civil War. The battle was the introduction for a whole series of conflicts in the next month while Lee's operation lasted: Aldie, Middleburg, Upperville and Paris. At Fairfield, VA, the 6th US Cavalry shattered the 7th Virginia Cavalry but suffered heavy loses itself from freshly arrived rebel reinforcements.

On July 1, just west of Gettysburg, Pennsylvania, two Union horse brigades dis-

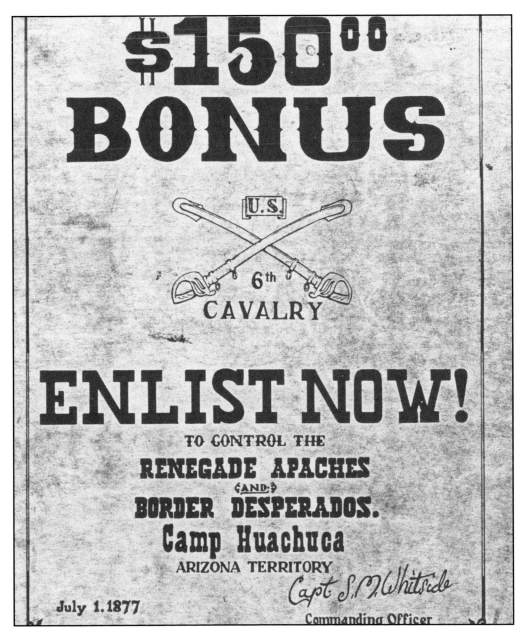

$150.00 BONUS

U.S.

6th CAVALRY

ENLIST NOW!

TO CONTROL THE
RENEGADE APACHES
(AND)
BORDER DESPERADOS.
Camp Huachuca
ARIZONA TERRITORY

Capt. S. M. Whitside

July 1, 1877

Commanding Officer

mounted and held back with their fire a whole division of southern infantry for several hours in order to enable the development of their units. On July 3, at the height of Lee's efforts to break the Union's defensive lines at Gettysburg, Stuart started out with four brigades and three batteries of horsemen - about 6,000 riders, in all - to penetrate the enemy's rear, prevent the arrival of supplies and gather information. Receiving information of Stuart's intentions, Gregg, with three brigades attacked the front. After a pitched cavalry battle lasting over two hours, Stuart had to withdraw.

The Union cavalry, which had prevented diversion in its rear and stopped Stuart from gathering key information that could have changed the course of the battle, was one of the main factors of Lee's failure at Gettysburg. Soon, Lee would receive news that the Confederacy had lost Vicksburg on July 4, 1863. The defeat of the South was now only a matter of time.

In May of 1864, Grant gave General Philip Henry Sheridan the opportunity to raid Richmond with 10,000 riders and accompanying artillery. On the 11th of the same month, Stuart was killed at Yellow Tavern while trying to stop Sheridan with one-half the forces. In a raid lasting a month, the Yankees, some of them already armed with seven-shot Spencer carbines, wrought chaos and destruction in the South's rear lines with the loss of some 600 men. The South had increasing trouble in replacing losses in men, weapons and horses. From the second half of 1864 to May 1865, when the war ended, the blue cavalry dominated the battlefields and was one of the key elements in military operations of the North.

The Union fielded three million soldiers during the Civil War, the Confederate States one million. Americans were to remember the Civil War as the bloodiest in their history: over 500,000 men died. Some elements of future conflicts were foreshadowed in this war: the use of railroads and the telegraph, destruction of enemy rear lines, construction of field fortifications for economy of forces, and the use of light cavalry and effectiveness of infiltration of enemy lines and disruption of their operations.

THE INDIAN WARS

During the Napoleon Wars, the corps was established as the largest organizational form for cavalry units, especially in large-scale battles. Reconnaissance and the pursuit of enemy units could be effected without the need to form great cavalry masses. The reason that the corps was formed lies in the need to dispose of a large number of horsemen who could be the decisive factor in the defense of one's position, or in an attack on the opponents.

In the American Civil War, cavalry was rarely seen on the field during great battles. The explanation for this lies in the fact that the infantry's and artillery's firepower had greatly increased, and that the erection of fortification and obstacles on the battlefield had become a matter of course, enabling units to shelter themselves from cavalry charges.

The cavalry corps remained the highest organizational form, but with an added quality; it had become an army unto itself, capable of independently carrying out a whole series of tasks. As we have seen, 10,000 horsemen could set out on a month-long raid, during which they would cover 670 miles without re-supplying from their rear lines. Such a corps took care of itself, the protection of its supply train and wounded men, of the

Captain S.M.Whiteside, Company and staff, 6th Cavalry, Camp Huachuca, Arizonia Territory ca. 1880. (Courtesy of S.M. Whiteside.)

Quartermaster and Commissioning Building built in 1882. Porched in 1930s, loading docks in rear. Horses belong to Fort Clark Guest Ranch.

Commanding Officer's Quarters No. 29 built in 1874. General Ranald MacKenzie was the first occupant. General Wainwright aslo stayed here.

*Left: Colonel Ranald MacKenzie in 1880s. (Courtesy of National Archives). **Right:** Colonel Lapham Bullis in 1880s. (Courtesy of Institute of Texas Cultures)*

Interior barracks of 1880s. (Courtesy o fEd Daily)

On parade in 1890s. (Courtesy of Ed Daily)

prisoners it had taken of its artillery, and even of the timber needed to build improvised bridges over swollen streams. General John Hunt Morgan, CSA, even used several telegraph machines during his raid, creating great confusion by its use in counter-intelligence.

In the second half of the 18th century, infantry and artillery became the dominant branches of the military. The horse was increasingly just a means of transport, and cavalry, the "mechanized" units. From the forming of the first regular regiments until the end of the American Civil War, the individual successes of cavalry units in battle were just exceptions to a general rule. As the end of the 19th century neared, cavalry exploits and charges became episodes to remember. In Europe, however, events demonstrated that cavalry regiments were no longer of much battle value, and owed their existence largely to prestige and wrong military doctrine.

From 1865—1891, US troops undertook 13 expeditions against the Indian tribes, best known of which were the Cheyenne, Sioux, Navajo, Apache, Commanche, Cherokee, Kiowa, Pawnee and Delaware. These people were mainly warriors and hunters. Unlike the Indian tribes of South and Central America, the North American Indian lived in numerous smaller tribal groups. Only a few tribes were united in tribal communities, the federation of which encompassed 50 related tribes. Armed with bows and arrows, tomahawks, spears and clubs, the Indians made their livelihood by hunting and fishing. Most of the several hundred tribes were perpetually at war with each other, most often over the problems of rights to hunting grounds. Disunited, and spread out over an enormous space, they were in no position to put up an effective and organized resistance to the European colonizers. Starting in the 17th century, the European settlers pushed back and exterminated the Indians in the process of expanding their colonies, although the Indians resisted as best as they could.

After the end of the Civil War, in order to pacify the Wild West, protect the settlers from Indian attacks and introduce law and order among them, the US government formed four more regiments: the 7th, 8th, 9th and 10th US Cavalry. In 1876, after destroying several camps of the Cheyenne, Arapaho, Kiowa and Sioux Indian in previous campaigns with the 7th Cavalry, General George Armstrong Custer was defeated by a combined force of several thousand Indians in the Battle of Little Bighorn. He was killed along with 210 of his men. The 7th Cavalry's total casualties on the day of June 25, 1876, were 276 dead and 53 wounded.

In the 16th century, Spaniards had brought the first horses to America. In time, the Indians, too, came into possession of horses. Spanish horses had a lot of Arabian blood, and most of the properties bred into horses during hundreds of years in the arid climate of North Africa. Such a horse, called a pony by the Indians, gained a new quality in America - the ability to survive in even the harshest conditions. The ponies were out in the open all the time, day or night, rain or shine, and they could withstand all of nature's caprices. It was no coincidence that Americans chose ponies for the male line from California to the East. The Indians also mastered the skill of riding bareback, which required considerable dexterity. Only a well organized and equipped cavalry, employing the services of scouts from friendly tribes, could effectively oppose the Indians and their hit-and-run tactics.

The cavalry on the western frontier traced its

Noncommissioned staff of the Ninth Cavalry.

origins to the Regiment of Dragoons (later First Regiment of Dragoons), established in 1833. Within a few years, the Second Regiment of Dragoons and the Regiment of Mounted Rifleman had been formed. They fought in the Mexican War. They also protected forty-niners traveling overland to the California gold fields and immigrant wagon trains bound for Oregon.

During the Civil War, the southwest Texas frontier was left relatively unprotected and Indian depredation, particularly by Indians using Mexico as a sanctuary, became wide spread and devastating. After the war, attempts by federal troops to curtail Indian raids were only partially successful, until 1873, when Colonel Ranald S. Mackenzie and the US 4th Cavalry were ordered to Fort Clark to replace Lieutenant Colonel Wesley Merritt and the 9th Cavalry. Citizens' appeals to Washington brought Secretary of War W.W. Bellknap and General Philip Sheridan to Fort Clark for secret talks with Mackenzie. As a result, on May 17, 1873, Mackenzie led six companies of the 4th Cavalry across the border into Mexico on a punitive expedition against Kickapoo and Lipan Apache Indians at Remolino. Despite Mexico's protests, other sorties followed. Mackenzie and the 4th were later replaced by Lieutenant Colonel William Rufus Shafter, destined to become the most successful of Fort Clark's Indian fighting commanding officers.

Under Colonel Shafter, Fort Clark became the garrison for the 10th Cavalry and the 24th and the 25th Infantry. These were mounted regiments of Blacks, known as Buffalo soldiers by the Indians, who although mostly unacclaimed, left a distinguished record of service in ridding the Indian menace from southwest Texas. Mackenzie's raid in '73 had stopped Indian activity, but within a year there were new raids into Texas by Lipan and Mescalero Apaches. Shafter, a large beefy man with the sobriquet "Pecos Bill," conducted an extensive campaign on the Pecos River and in Mexico a number of times in pursuit of these marauding Indians and their chief, Whasha Lobo.

Especially significant during the Indian Wars were the Seminole-Negro Indian scouts who served at Fort Clark from 1872 until 1914. Not to be confused with the black "Buffalo soldiers," the Seminole-Negro Indian scouts had spent 20 years (1850-70) protecting the northern Mexican frontier state of Coahuila before being recruited by the US Army to serve as scouts. Under Lieutenant John L. Bullis,

*Left: Sitting Bull, Lakota (Sioux) spiritual leader, guided his people for nearly 40 years during the Indian Wars. Photo by David F. Barry, 1884. **Right:** Lt. Col. George Armstrong Custer, the famous comander of the 7th Cavalry during the Indain wars. Photo by Jose Maria Mora, 1876 and taken just prior to his death at The Battle of The Little Bighorn. Note the short length of his hair. (Courtesy of Ed Daily)*

who served as their commander from 1873-81, the Seminole-Negro Indian scouts played a decisive role in the Indian campaigns under both Colonels Mackenzie and Shafter. Among the roster of scouts are four who were awarded the Congressional Medal of Honor.

"Forty miles a day on beans and hay," the frontier cavalrymen used to sing. In the main, theirs was a harsh, thankless life - long days and weeks of drudgery and hardship, interrupted by occasional bursts of action. If a soldier were lucky, he might enjoy a few moments of glory in a long career. If unlucky, he might be buried on a lonely prairie without so much as a headstone to mark his place of rest.

After Appomattox a war-weary Congress slashed the size of the Army, leaving posts undermanned and their units too thinly spread for the peacekeeping mission they were assigned. Underpaid, under-appreciated officers and men did their best, against heavy odds, to bring Indian troubles to an end.

With few exceptions, western forts were roughly built of natural materials close at hand - adobe, stone, logs, or pickets with the gaps plastered with mud. Buildings were drafty and cold or stifling and hot. It was said that poor food and bad water killed more soldiers than Indians did.

For a private soldier, the pay was $13 a month in paper money, discounted when he spent it at the sutler's store, or in the rowdy whiskey villages and "hog ranches" that always seemed to spring up like a pestilence just beyond the post commander's jurisdiction.

Officers lived only marginally better than the enlisted men. On the march they shared their troops' discomforts. A frontier army wife described the existence as "glittering misery," its military pomp and ceremony offset by dirt, mud, pain and privation.

As if to add insult to injury, the soldiers were held in low regard by many of the citizens they were sent to protect. In Texas, where the Army battled fierce Commanches and Kiowas, most residents were ex-Confederates who resented the troops, viewing them as Yankee invaders. Even in western states loyal to the Union, the general public often derided them as misfits and ne'er-do-wells who had joined the Army as a last resort. They hooted when a cavalry troop came in empty-handed after an Indian chase but were quick to call upon the soldiers when they saw or imagined they saw a feather.

Given the hardships, and lack of support by both the public and a penny-pinching Congress, the Army of the west accomplished an amazing feat in the 20 or so years between the end of the Civil War and the closing of the Indian wars. Though there is ample cause to question the rightness of its assignment - the subjugation of the Native Americans and their confinement to soul-killing reservations - the Army faithfully carried out that mission against formidable odds.

In the early years, most officers and noncommissioned soldiers were veterans of combat in the Civil War. This was a mixed blessing because the challenge they faced on the frontier was much different and the enemy's fighting style a far cry from that of the Confederate Army. It took many officers years to understand the Indian's approach to warfare, and some never did.

There were no fixed battle lines, no front and no rear. To the Plains Indian, war was a way of life, with no beginning and no end. Rarely did he ride into battle bent on total extermination of his adversaries. In a strong sense, he looked upon war as a blood sport, a rough game played for glory and honor. When he had fought a good fight and decided he had won enough honor for the day, he was likely to withdraw and celebrate, letting some, or even all, of his enemies survive to fight him again.

The Indian did not share the white man's dogged determination for full and final victory. If he annihilated all of his enemies, who would be left for him to fight? How could the young men prove themselves in the eyes of their people if not through combat? The Indian was often confused and dismayed when the soldiers continued to press him relentlessly, even after winning a good victory, or after being badly battered by the warriors' hit-and-run, slash-and-burn tactics.

Who were these blue-clad horsemen who persevered despite the danger, the suffering, the public ingratitude?

The officers were mostly graduates of West Point, established by President Thomas Jefferson in 1802 to educate the Army's leadership in engineering and science, as well as military tactics. A notable exception to the West Point tradition was General Nelson A. Miles, Commander of the Army in the 1890s. He stood proud for having fought his way up through the ranks, sometimes subjecting troops and Indians to unnecessarily harsh treatment to prove that he was as good as any graduate of the Point and better than most.

In the Army's severe down-sizing after the war, most officers had to accept a drastic demotion from their temporary brevet ranks. Some who had commanded as generals gave up their stars to wear the insignia of captains and majors. The scrambling and fevered competition to hold any place at all, led to rivalries and feuds that could be detrimental to operations. Sometimes good field officers were overruled by superiors whose rank was of higher order than their judgment. That they managed as well as they did was a tribute to their courage and determination to serve, regardless of their own feelings and the personal cost.

The enlisted men were a varied lot. Some were young fellows who fancied the West as a place of romance, adventure and glory. Here and there might be found a former cadet who did not make the grade at West Point, but hoped to fight his way up through the ranks as Miles had done. Hard times, such as the money panic of 1873, brought a rush of unemployed seeking any job they could find that would feed and clothe them.

A significant percentage of enlisted personnel were immigrants - Irish in particular, Germans, French, and English as well, some of them veterans of service in European armies and already at home in the military life. There were ex-Confederate soldiers who found nothing left for them in the war-battered South, and, of course, there were men who enlisted under assumed names and to whom the Army was a refuge from the law, from debts, or from family troubles.

Seldom did reality live up to the promises of the recruitment officers. Often the soldiers found themselves carrying picks, shovels, trowels and hammers as much as, or more, than rifles. They built new posts to which they were assigned or renovated older ones because the money-short Army chose not to pay the higher wages of civilian artisans.

Much ammunition issued in the West was years old, surplus from the war, and misfired when soldiers needed it most. Its scarcity and price made the Army frugal in its use. Some frontier troops were obliged to do their target practice with empty rifles because their officers would have to pay for the ammunition out of their own pockets. The first shot some enlistees ever fired was in a fight with Indians.

Moreover, the Indians sometimes faced them with better rifles than those the Army issued.

Nevertheless, most soldiers welcomed the opportunity to go on an extended campaign because it carried them away from the manual labor, the monotony, the tiresome garrison drills. It offered them at last a chance for action and excitement, and occasionally they got it; the hostiles' young men were always eager to demonstrate their valor. They loved nothing better than to rush a soldier encampment at night, shouting, waving blankets or buffalo robes and driving off as many horses as they could stampede.

Often they dogged a column, watching for a chance to pick off stragglers or to hit supply wagons that lagged behind the main body. They could strike like a whirlwind and be gone in moments. They had the advantage of knowing the land; its hiding places and its water holes. They knew where they could lose their tracks and disappear like wisps of smoke.

For this reason, the Army on the march usually took along civilian scouts, who presumably knew the country almost as well as the Indians. Some were veteran mountain men who had trapped and hunted over it and had learned to know not

7th Cavalry, Troop K.

only the terrain but also the ways of the native people who lived on it.

Often, too, the Army used trusted Indian scouts, usually of a tribe hostile to the one the soldiers sought. Crows, Shoshonis and Pawnees in particular often allied themselves to the whites to fight traditional enemies such as the Sioux, Cheyennes and Arapahoes. Tonkawas and Seminole-Negro scouts were especially efficient in tracking down Commanches and Kiowas on the lower plains.

General George Crook believed it took an Apache to catch an Apache, and he used intratribal enmities to set scout of one band of hostilities against another.

Ironically, many officers and men saw the Indian side and sympathized with their foe, even as they carried out orders from a higher authority which did not share their sympathy.

Some of the better officers, such as Crook and Ranald Mackenzie, took no pleasure in killing Indians and made an effort to limit casualties, though they did what they had to do to bring them under the power of the US Government.

Buffalo hunters by 1873 had finished off most of the bison along the Arkansas and Republican Rivers, so they turned their attention southward toward the Texas herd. Alarmed Commanches, Kiowas and Southern Cheyennes banded together for a massive dawn attack upon the hunters' trading post at Adobe Walls on June 27, 1874. To their dismay, they failed to overwhelm the determined defenders and settled for raiding scattered hunting camps.

This triggered a stern Army pincers movement against the Indians of the southern plains that fall. It was decisive, and much less bloody than Custer's wild sachet on the Washita. The 4th Cavalry struck the first and hardest blow. It was commanded by irritable, hard-driving Colonel Ranald Mackenzie, who had to fight against constant pain from unhealed Civil War wounds.

In 1872 he had led a successful secret mission into Mexico to punish the Kickapoo raiders and stop their incursions into Texas from sanctuary across the Rio Grande.

At daylight on September 28, 1874, Mackenzie gazed down into the bottom of the deep Palo Duro canyon at a three-mile-long winter encampment, mostly Commanches and Kiowas, some Cheyennes and Arapohoes. His men led their horses single file along a narrow game trail down the steep canyon wall. They surprised and routed the hostiles with only four Indian dead that Mackenzie knew about and one of his own men wounded. He destroyed the camp and captured most of the horses, setting the Indians on foot. Quietly but relentlessly dogged by soldiers, they had little choice but to walk to the reservation. Except for a few scattered outbreaks, Commanche, Kiowas, and Southern Cheyenne resistance was broken.

Like their allies to the south, the Indians on the northern plains were vanquished, except for occasional outbreaks, such as those by Cheyennes under Dull Knife and Little Wolf in 1878, and the tragic Ghost Dance movement, which climaxed in the massacre of the Sioux at Wounded Knee in 1890. In the northwest, the Nez Perce made a break for freedom under Chief Joseph in 1877. They traveled a zigzag course totaling some 1,700 miles, fighting repeated engagements with pursuing troops and suffering heavy loss of life, only to be stopped 30 miles short of the Canadian border and the sanctuary they sought. It was there that Joseph made his heartbroken surrender declaration: "From where the sun now stands, I will fight no more forever."

THE SPANISH-AMERICAN WAR

Most Americans can remember at least a few sketchy history lessons dealing with the "splendid little war" that erupted in Cuba in 1898. The battleship *Maine* blew up in Havana Harbor in February of that year, and two months later the United States declared war on Spain.

What they don't remember, Richard Wormser writes in the *Yellowlegs,* is that cavalry did not win this three-month conflict:

"Most of what is popularly remembered of the Spanish-American War is that cavalry regiment, usually called Teddy Roosevelt's Rough Riders. Roosevelt, a very aristocratic New Yorker, had been a rancher on the Plains; he recruited the regiment from the West and from Long Island; almost every man in it was either a cowboy or a polo player."

Wormser, whose book is entertaining and enlightening reading for any student of cavalry, notes that "Leonard Wood, who had entered the Army as a surgeon, was colonel of the regiment and Roosevelet was its lieutenant colonel. The outfit was really Wood's Rough Riders and never really rode except in practice and on parade. No troop horses were taken to Cuba; only high-ranking officers, including Roosevelt, rode. The cavalry fought dismounted, so the war is really no concern of a cavalry history."

A junior captain named John Joseph Pershing led dismounted troops of the black 10th Cavalry Regiment's 2nd Squadron during the famous charge up Kettle and San Juan Hills at Santiago, Cuba. Despite his low rank, Pershing was nearly six years older than many officers of equal rank. He had earned a law degree before he was accepted at West Point, and by 1898 he was a seasoned veteran of cavalry combat. Serving initially with the 6th Cavalry Regiment, he had battled Sioux and Geronimo's Apaches, captured white horse thieves, led a detachment of Sioux scouts during the Ghost Dance War, rounded up Cree Indians in Montana who had fled murder charges in Canada and taught military tactics at West Point.

After fighting in Cuba, Pershing quickly grew

Cavalry camp and crap game.

Pyramid of troopers taking a hurdle.

dissatisfied with desk duty in Washington, DC. In 1899 he sought the chance to get back into the saddle and back into action. In those days, many units of the cavalry, the Army's glamour service, were going off to a new war half-way around the world: the Philippine Insurrection. Pershing spent most of the next 15 years in the Far East.

The United States had taken control of the Philippines after the Spanish-American War; now, America was caught up in an all-out fight with Filipino guerrillas. The insurgents had started rebelling against the Spanish in 1896. Three years later, they wanted no part of American rule.

The rebel's leader, Emilio Aguinaldo, declared independence and organized a powerful army of 30,000 guerrillas. The United States responded by sending a total of 74,000 troops, including a number of cavalry regiments, and created a total of 639 garrisons in the islands. The mounted troopers and infantrymen pursued the insurgents through the hills and rural area, but the guerrillas, at first, held the upper hand. They often enjoyed popular support in parts of the countryside and could blend in with groups of field workers before or after launching an attack. Their tactics frustrated many field commanders, who were hemmed in by political as well as military constraints dictated both from Manila and Washington.

"The objective was to tire the Americans and make their occupation of the Philippines as costly as possible," John Morgan Gages has pointed out in *Schoolbooks and Krags: The United States Army in the Philippines, 1898-1902*. "Guerrillas were not expected to fight pitched battles, but they were to constantly harass the Americans by raids on supply trains, patrols and small detachments."

The insurrection finally ended in 1902, after Aguinaldo was captured and the US changed to tactics that more resembled all-out war. The cavalry and infantry regiments moved out of their many small garrisons and relentlessly pursued the guerrillas in force, giving them no time to rest or replenish.

Yet, despite many fierce battles, the Philippine Insurrection was hardly noticed by most Americans. To them it was simply a strange war in a strange and distant land. "This obscurity is ironical," Frank N. Magill has stated in *Great Events from History*, "for the three-year Philippine Insurrection was more severe and bloody than the Spanish-American War. It cost the lives of more than 4,000 American soldiers, between 16 and 20,000 rebels, and through disease and starvation, approximately 200,000 civilians."

While Pershing in 1901 was sizing up the Filipino insurgents at close range and relishing his long-awaited promotion to captain, a new regiment, the 12th Cavalry, was being organized halfway around the world at Fort Sam Houston, Texas. This new unit, created on February 8, 1901, eventually would become the final cavalry regiment to join the 1st Cavalry Division. It would not become part of the division until 1933. In the interim, its troopers would compile outstanding records of service in the Philippines in 1903 to 1905 and 1909 to 1911, along the Mexican Border starting in 1914 and in Mexico against the rebel leader, Pancho Villa, and in the Panama Canal Zone.

In 1898 the 5th Cavalry Regiment traveled from San Antonio to Florida to go to war and spent virtually the entire Spanish-American conflict bottled up in the embarkation congestion at the port of Tampa. The 5th's troopers finally got into the fight in a new setting more than 2,000 miles from their home ranges.

The Spanish surrender in Cuba did not immediately end four centuries of Spanish colonial rule in Puerto Rico. More than 17,000 US troops, including the 5th Cavalry Regiment, were dispatched to seize the island. The invasion force landed at the small port of Guanica, 15 miles west of Ponce on the island's southwest coast, in July 1898. It was split into four columns of infantry and cavalry and in early August began fanning out across the mountainous countryside. The majority of Puerto Ricans warmly welcomed the Americans, but there were scattered, and sometimes sharp, skirmishes with some of the 8,000 Spanish defenders.

Troop A of the 5th Cavalry Regiment saw much of the action. It was part of a 2,800-man force sent north under the command of Brigadier General Theodore Schwan. Schwan's column, known as the Independent Regular Brigade, covered 92 miles in eight days, capturing nine towns and 192 Spanish prisoners.

Troop A performed well in short battles at the small towns of Las Marias and Hormingueros, seven miles south of Mayaguez. The 1,400 Spanish defenders resisted briefly but suffered 50 casualties. The Americans lost one killed and 16 wounded, and Schwan's brigade quickly took Mayaguez as the Spanish hastily retreated.

In the victories at Las Marias and Hormigueros, the 5th Cavalry Regiment earned the right to display the Maltese Cross at the top of its regimental shield.

The Spanish finally turned Puerto Rico over to the United States on December 10, 1898. The 5th Cavalry remained on the island until early in 1899, then returned to San Antonio. In 1901 it sailed for the distant Philippines to help put down that bloody insurrection. Two years later, back in the United States, troopers of the 5th Regiment found themselves being spread through Arizona, Colorado, New Mexico and Utah. Some of them fought small actions against rebellious Navajo Indians in Arizona and Utah. The regiment, however, was then called to help strengthen the US military presence in the new territory of Hawaii.

The 7th Cavalry also went to the Philippines twice prior to 1906, then patrolled the Mexican border and battled Pancho Villa's Villistas in 1916.

The 8th Cavalry likewise became a well-traveled outfit between the Spanish-American War and World War I. In 1898 it rode from South Dakota to

The main entrance to Fort Brown, Texas.

Fort Brown, Brownsville, Texas.

Alabama, then embarked for Cuba. The troopers arrived too late to fight the Spanish, but they stayed to help secure the peace. Four years later from 1902 to 1905, they kept watch on the US border with Mexico. A two-year assignment in the Philippines followed. There, the cavalrymen patrolled supply and communication lines and sources of water on the islands of Luzon and Jolo. A five-year stint at Marfa, Texas, was next. In 1912 the 8th Cavalry Regiment returned to the Philippines. This time, the troopers fought rebellious Moro tribesmen on the island of Mindanao, in the Sulu Archipelago, in the Battle of Bagsak Mountain, June 1913, a total of 51 members of the 8th Cavalry's Troop "H" joined other soldiers in a violent battle with hundreds of Moro warriors on Jolo. The American force, led by Brigadier General John J. Pershing, killed an estimated 300 Moros while suffering only light losses. Oddly, this lopsided victory greatly assisted Pershing in his job as Governor of Moro Province. The manner in which he fought and sought peace settlements showed the Moro that he understood their Moslem values and culture. This helped lead to more peaceful times in that part of the Philippines.

PANCHO VILLA

In World War I, airplanes and tanks would emerge as the glamour weapons of the future, but military tradition and battlefield need died hard. Not all of America's military thinkers had been dissuaded by the cavalry's limited successes amid the slaughter of trench warfare.

There still would be needs for horses and horse warriors in the United States Army after 1918.

Cavalry, for instance, remained the fastest and most effective force for patrolling the desert Southwest and Mexican border. Aviation and mechanized armor still were in their awkward, unpredictable infancies. They were hardly suited for ranging across rugged countryside, setting up ambushes, riding stealthy reconnaissance missions and fighting fast-moving skirmishes.

Somebody else, however, managed to stir up the most trouble between the US and Mexico. On March 9, 1916, the Mexican rebel leader, Pancho Villa, led a raid on the small border town of Columbus, New Mexico. Villa and a band of followers, estimated at between 500 and 1,000, slipped into the sleeping town at about 4:00 a.m., but the 13th Cavalry's sentries were awake - rumors had been afloat for months that Villa might strike somewhere on the border. The troopers engaged the raiders in a sharp firefight along the town's main street.

In their desire to wreak destruction, the Villista, shouting "Viva Villa" and "Mueran los gringos," rashly set fire to several wooden buildings, including the hotel. The fires caused damage, but also illuminated the Villistas with their big sombreros and their bandoleers of ammunition, and they became easy targets. The dismounted troopers and their officers quickly set up a well-organized crossfire and mowed down the Villistas by the dozen until the survivors fled. Sixty-seven dead raiders were found after daybreak and were burned in a huge funeral pyre. The American losses were seven soldiers and eight civilians killed, plus a handful of wounded.

Angered and under pressure to retaliate, President Woodrow Wilson ordered a punitive expedition to go into Mexico and chase down Villa. The

General John J. Pershing. 1922.

Bridge at Fort Riley, Kansas.

British trooper and his horse protected against mortal gas during the First World War.

difficult assignment was handed to General John J. Pershing at Fort Bliss in El Paso.

From the outset, Pershing was hampered by severe political and military restrictions designed to keep the two nations from going to war, and his heart was not completely in the expedition.

An *Associated Press* writer later would recall that Pershing "looked across the Rio Grande and said, "The people yonder need school, not soldiers; bread, not bullets." Still, he was a professional soldier, and he had his orders. On March 15 at noon, six days after Villa's raid, Pershing led his force, one that eventually would grow to 15,000 men, across the river and into Mexico.

Military historian Frank J. Vandiver has called the punitive expeditionary force "the most unusual American Army committed to the field." In addition to cavalry regiments, field artillery and mule-drawn pack trains, Pershing had to deal with a few new fangled and unreliable innovations, as well as the Army's first motorized truck company, a squadron of eight JN-4 "Jennies" (canvas and wood biplanes that kept breaking down or crashing while trying to take off or land in the rough Mexican countryside), field telephones and machine guns. Pershing felt weighted down by some of these frills, not to mention hampered by the severe restriction and delicate politics that surrounded his mission. "Every commander has a segment of service dearer, hence, clearer to him than others," Vandiver wrote in his book, *John J. Pershing.* "Cavalry was Pershing's own beloved branch of the service. He used it in Mexico better than anything else. That was logical, Cavalry alone had any chance to hurt Villa."

Villa and his bandidos moved about and fought much like Indians. Vandiver has noted in his compelling study of Pershing's career. "Over the years they had become excellent light cavalry and mobility must be the key to catching them. Cavalry would have to do most of the hard work of pursuit. For that reason, there were more troopers than other components with Pershing."

Another veteran of this expedition, Douglas A. MacArthur, had long nurtured a special affinity for cavalry. As the son of a career military man, he had grown up listening to stories about Civil War cavalry battles and to the tales told by the troopers

just back from fights with Apaches. MacArthur, too, had seen action in the Philippines Insurrection, killing two guerrillas with his pistol, and in Mexico on a daring and violent reconnaissance mission, during the American occupation of Vera Cruz in 1914. He had become a military engineer, however, not a cavalryman. Yet years later, in World War II and Korea, he would repeatedly single out the 1st Cavalry Division for important assignments.

Destiny rode with the punitive expedition in yet another way. One young cavalry officer at Pershing's side was a man, 1st Lieutenant George Smith Patton Jr., an officer of the 8th Cavalry Regiment and a brash believer in action. He was especially fond of pistols, was a good, quick shot, and became one of Persing's aides-de-camp. Impatient with the slow progress of the expedition, Patton personally rode out in search of Villa. He did not find the elusive Mexican raider, but Patton did track down Villa's bodyguard, Julio Cardena, in the town of Miguel and killed him in a shootout.

That was the closest the 11-month American punitive expedition would come to getting Villa. Yet the mission was not a failure. The cavalrymen fought a number of skirmishes with Villa's men and scattered them all over the Mexican countryside. Never again would they be a threat to the US border towns.

In the expedition's most significant action by a cavalry unit, the 7th Regiment, led by Colonel George A. Dodd, surprised and inflicted heavy losses on a large group of Villistas.

"Pershing's campaign certainly added two or three important landmarks to American military annals," one of Villa's biographers, Haldeen Braddy, declared in *Cock of the Walk: The Legend of Pancho Villa.* "For the first time in combat, America employed overhead machine guns, rounded up their adversaries in motor passenger cars and dropped supplies to stranded platoons from airplanes."

Frank X. Tolbert, of *The Dallas Morning News,* uncovered another little-known sidelight to the punitive expedition - Pershing's rescue of hundreds of Chinese merchants living in northern Mexico in 1917. Tolbert wrote, "Chinese peddlers, food merchants and cafe operators helped supply the US Army which Pershing led into Chihuahua on that punitive expedition." Villa had been practicing a scorched-earth policy, which forced Pershing to rely on long supply lines, and the help of the Chinese was invaluable. Villa learned of this, of course, and swore to kill every Chinese who had aided the Gringos.

Villa and his men did in fact massacre many Chinese before Pershing's forces led the survivors to safety. One Chinese merchant who afterward owned a fine store in San Antonio recalled to Tolbert that "Black Jack tell that all who want to get out of Chihuahua to follow the army back to Columbus, New Mexico. We load everything in mule carts, and we walk all the way from Cas Grande to New Mexico. That General Pershing! Oh, he was a nice man! He did everything he could to help us."

Lieutenant George Patton, for his forthright, if unorthodox, actions, received from Pershing a "battlefield" promotion to captain. After that, Patton's biographer, Ladislas Fargo, has pointed out, his military career "skyrocketed so fast that it amazed even him."

Pershing finally was ordered to turn the force around in January 1917, after leading his men more than 400 miles into Mexico and enduring rising political pressures on both sides of the Rio Grande.

When he crossed back into the United States on February 5, 1917, he had no idea that he had just led what one historian would term "the last campaign of the old cavalry." He also had little notion of the dramatic fate that awaited him. The cavalryman soon would lead the American Expeditionary Force, the half million Yanks dispatched "Over There" by President Woodrow Wilson. This great force would help break the savage stalemate in the trench war in Europe.

WORLD WAR I

From 1871—1914, while the United States was busy with wars and territorial expansions, Europe slowly became a dangerous powder keg. During those yeas, the continent grew increasingly preoccupied with political intrigues, secret alliances, nationalism, colonialism and building great armies and navies.

The Powder keg finally blew up on June 28, 1914. A young Serbian nationalist shot and killed Austrian Archduke Francis Ferdinand and his wife. Austria delivered an ultimatum to Serbia, and dissatisfied with the small Slavic nation's reply, invaded on July 29, 1914. Within days, Germany, France, Britain and Russia, too, were in the war.

In its main theater, World War I soon settled into a grim stalemate that would remain unbroken for more than three years. On the Western Front, the trenches and barbed wire stretched more that 450 miles, from Switzerland through France to the North Sea.

The slaughter was incredible along the static trenches, as well as on battlefronts in other parts of the world. By war's end in 1918, more than 65,000,000 men had been mobilized by 23 nations and virtually half of them had been killed, wounded, captured or declared missing.

The great cavalries of Europe suffered grievously early in the war when they tried gallant charges across battlegrounds heavily laced with barbed wire and raked by machine gun fire and quick-reloading artillery. The mounted regiments soon found themselves reduced to secondary roles: reconnaissance, diversion, transportation of messages and supplies, and plugging small breaks in defensive lines.

Unlike conflicts of the past, World War I was primarily an infantryman's war and a war for inventors. New weapons appeared on, and over, the battlefields: machine guns, tanks, poison gas, improved artillery pieces, dirigibles and airplanes.

Soon after the tank made its debut in 1915, debates began to rage anew over the future of horse cavalry. Some believed the horse could never be replaced, and others were convinced that a regiment of tanks could be fashioned into a mechanical cavalry that would be an unstoppable juggernaut. The arguments would last for more than 20 years, and they would have direct influence on the shape and future missions of America's Cavalry.

Traditional horse cavalry did have at least two moments of glory on World War I battlefields, and these victories, too, had bearing on how long cavalry horses and pack mules remained an important part of the United States Army.

Beginning late in 1917, British General Demund Allenby swept through Turkish-held Palestine with an odd expeditionary force that included cavalry units from India, Australia and New Zealand, plus Australian mounted riflemen and English Yeomanry regiments. The yeomen were proud horsemen who considered themselves a cut above common cavalry. They usually bought their own mounts and only select men were granted admission to their ranks. The traditions of yeomanry dated back to medieval times when countrymen rode to battle in private armies raised by rich nobles.

Allenby made masterful use both of cavalry's mobility and the open desert terrains as he scored victory after victory against the Turks, who were being helped by the Germans and Austrians. Military observers trying to decide if horse cavalry finally had become an anachronism were both amazed and confused by Allenby's successes. At Beersheba, for instance, when a bold attack seemed in jeopardy of being lost to darkness, stiff resistance and the horses' need for water, Australian cavalrymen broke through and routed the Turks with an old-style, flashing-saber charge. In nearly a dozen other battles, Allenby's cavalry boldly charged and overran enemy positions held by well-entrenched riflemen and machine gunners. Traditional cavalry tactics that were not working well in Europe suddenly were being vindicated in splendid fashion in the Middle East.

"It was in some ways a tragedy that Allenby was so successful in Palestine," James D. Lunt has argued eloquently in *Charge to Glory!* "That big, bluff, bullying cavalry general of the old school was the last commander to win a campaign by the bold use of horse cavalry; but by doing so, he put back the military clock by nearly 20 years and may have contributed indirectly to the defeat of the British and French armies in 1940.

Allenby's skill with cavalry, Lunt contended, caused many armies to resist too long the inevitable need to mechanize. While they tarried, Germany embraced the tank and perfected other armored vehicles that would help spearhead its "blitzkrieg" in World War II.

Horse cavalry had one final moment of glory in Europe in March 1918. The importance of this victory may also have helped prolong the future of horse-mounted troopers a few more years. At Moreuil Wood in France, squadrons of Canadian cavalry, on horseback and foot, seized a vital ridge from the Germans and stopped a breakthrough that could have altered the entire course of World War I. Had the Germans held the ridge long enough to move up reinforcements, they could have poured through Paris, routed the French and driven the British back to the channel.

When it became apparent that US forces would be sent to help the beleaguered Allies, many American cavalrymen confidently expected to ride into the thick of the European fighting, but only one US Cavalry regiment, plus scattered troopers from other units, would be assigned to the provisional cavalry unit hastily thrown together in 1918 and would actually ride into action, pursuing a few retreating Germans shortly before the end of the war.

The regiments that remained in the United States were far from idle, however, as the Great War raged halfway around the world. The troopers were getting into frequent, small-scale combats with raiders, smugglers and Mexican revolutionaries along the Rio Grande River that divides the United States and Mexico.

Tensions along the border had heated up after revolution broke out in Mexico in 1910. The fighting continued to flare inside that country through 1920, with thousands of casualties. During that decade, many border incidents occurred that required a strong cavalry presence. The total US forces along the border including cavalry, infantry, artillery and supporting units, rose to about 150,000 men by 1916.

Troop A, 105th Cavalry, 1932.

Troop B, 11th Cavalry, Capt. E.R. Touseh, Commanding. (Courtesy of Albert L. Hettrich)

U.S. Cavalry Machine Gun Troop showing Vickers-Maxin watch cooled machine guns.

One incident, that took place while the Punitive Expedition still was in Mexico searching for Pancho Villa, strained relations between the two neighbors. On January 17, 1917, German Foreign Secretary Alfred Zimmerman sent a secret message to the German minister stationed in Mexico. The message, historians now call "The Zimmerman Note," gave the minister in Mexico special instructions in case the United States and Germany went to war. He was to propose to Mexico's leaders that they declare war on America and "reconquer the lost territory in New Mexico, Texas and Arizona." The message was intercepted by British intelligence, but not released to the public until March 1, 1917, after Pershing and his men were safely out of Mexico. The Zimmerman Note and the unrestricted sea war waged by German submarines helped lead the United States into World War I in April of that year.

Troopers of the 8th Cavalry, who were transferred to Camp Marfa in the Big Bend Country of Texas in mid-1917, clashed on several occasions with bands of Mexicans who crossed the Rio Grande to steal cattle or create other troubles. Led by Colonel George T. Langhorne, the cavalrymen also skirmished with members of various Mexican revolutionary groups who conducted raids across the border.

In one unusual occurrence that foreshadowed the future of the 1st Cavalry Division, the troopers were called upon to quickly reinforce the garrison at Presidio, 68 miles away, after a large Mexican force crossed the border. The cavalrymen climbed into automobiles driven by citizens of Marfa and

United States Army Horseshow Team, 1935.

The Georgia Hussars in full dress uniform on parade on the 200th Anniversary of Georgia in Feb. 1933. The unit behind is in Pulaski Legion uniforms. The Hussars were with Pulaski in his fatal charge at the Battle of Savannah on Oct. 9, 1779 at which he was mortally wounded. (Courtesy of Lindsey P. Henderson, Jr.)

Armor car, M-1.

Brig. Gen. W.C. Short, 2nd Cavalry Brigade, Fort Bliss, TX. Sept. 1, 1921-May 2, 1922 and Sept. 18, 1928-Oct. 1, 1933. (Courtesy of Ed Daily)

Col. S.R.H. Tompkins, 7th U.S. Cavalry. (Courtesy of Ed Daily)

Aerial view of Fort Riley, KS, 1936.

covered the distance in a speedy three and a half hours.

Another incident, recounted in Carlysle Graham Raht's 1919 book, *The Romance of the Davis Mountains and Big Bend Country*, further illustrates the changes that were coming to cavalry operations. Raht's account also reveals the occasionally chaotic nature of the border skirmishes: "At eleven o'clock, Christmas morning, 1917, Mr. Luke Brite telephoned Colonel Langhorne that his headquarters ranch was being raided. In 18 minutes after the troops were notified, the first of them left the Army camp at Marfa in citizens' automobiles, followed by others within a few minutes. In the meantime, troops were ordered from Ruidosa to march up the river to intercept the bandits. The troops, ranchers, sheriffs, and civilians reached Brite's ranch within an hour."

The troopers who arrived in automobiles borrowed horses and saddles at the ranch, and they and the troopers from Ruidosa caught up with the bandits the next day in Mexico, killing 20 in a sharp fight.

In one skirmish in June 1919, four American units destined to become part of the 1st Cavalry Division - the 5th and 7th Cavalry regiments, the 8th Engineer Battalion (Mounted) and the 82nd Field Artillery Battalion (Horse) - saw new action against Pancho Villa's Villistas. On the evening of June 15, Mexican snipers fired across the Rio Grande and killed a member of the 82nd who was standing picket duty. That same night an American force composed of cavalry, infantry, artillery, engineer, signal and ambulance units crossed the Rio Grande in hot pursuit. The next morning at Cinecue, near Juarez, the troopers and horse artillery engaged a column of Villista and opened fire. Airbursts of shrapnel knocked dozens of Villa's men out of their saddles. Others holed up to make a stand in an adobe hut, but also died when the horse artillery scored direct hits. The remaining Villistas were scattered before the American expedition returned to its side of the border.

In the aftermath of World War I, certain military thinkers confidently declared the cavalry's thousands of years as "the Queen of battle" at last were over. Modern weapons made cavalry units an utterly obsolete concept, they declared.

History, as usual, would prove them wrong, again and again. Soldiers on horseback would fight successfully in battles as late as World War II and Korea. Armored and airmobile cavalry would carry the traditional concepts of shock action, mobility and shifting fire power, and the capability for fast reconnaissance from the jungles of Vietnam to the diverse needs of the 1980s.

The history of cavalry was not finished in 1918. In many ways, it was just the beginning. Cavalry was about to be transformed and revitalized.

BETWEEN THE WORLD WARS

The 1st Cavalry Division assembled for its first division maneuvers in 1923 at Camp Marfa, Texas. The times were not especially happy ones for the US Army. Peacetime manpower reductions and cuts in military spending were the order of the day. Maneuvers could be scheduled only when meager funds permitted, and most units were armed and equipped with obsolete hardware, relics of World War I and earlier. The Regular Army was limited to a total of 125,000 men and 12,000 com-

missioned officers. The new 1st Cavalry Division rode at only a fraction of full strength.

Over the next four years, elements of the division were stationed at Camp Marfa and Fort Bliss in West Texas and at Fort Clark in south-central Texas, halfway between San Antonio and the Mexican border. The troopers' main duties consisted of riding in maneuvers or saddling up for long, hot, dusty patrols through desolate countryside. When they saw any action, it was against small bands of smugglers or bandits who operated along the border.

A precursor of the future, however, joined the division in 1928 - the 1st Armored Squadron. This new and experimental unit had been organized and trained at Aberdeen Proving Ground, in Aberdeen, Maryland. It traveled across the country to assume its new duties with the 1st Cavalry in November of that year. Over the next 15 years, the armored car squadron went through several reorganizations and transformations. Finally, designated the 91st Reconnaissance Squadron, it left the division in 1943 in time to join the fighting against the Germans and Italians in North Africa.

Major General Kenyon A. Joyce, Commander , 1st Cavalry Div. in 1939. (Courtesy of National Archives)

The 5th Cavalry marching in 1938. (Courtesy of Ed Daily)

Brig. Gen. Wainwright and Staff at Balmorhea Maneuvers in 1939. (Courtesy of Daughters of the Republic of Texas Library)

Half section races at Fort Riley.

Polo game at Fort Riley.

Fort Riley hunt.

Troop B, 101st Cavalry, 1st Army manuevers. Plattsburgh, NY. (Courtesy of Ed Daily)

Fort Riley horse exercise.

Pfc. Allen A. MacDonald at Fort Bliss, TX, 1937. (Courtesy of Allen MacDonald)

Also in 1928, the 8th Engineer Battalion moved from Fort Bliss to Fort McIntosh in Laredo. Major changes were ordered in the 1st Cavalry Division's organization, according to *A Brief History of the First Team*, prepared by the 14th Military History Detachment. "Lettered troops of the regiments were decreased from six to four. Troops A and B each regiment formed the 1st Squadron, and E and F formed the 2nd Squadron. Also, separate machine gun squadrons and troops were eliminated, and the machine gun squadron troop was returned to the regiment. The new regimental organization was designed to reduce overhead, increase firepower, and retain mobility. Reduction in wagon and pack animals in the new regiment was offset by the addition of three one and one-half ton trucks and three stripped, modified automobiles, called light cross-country cars."

"Many famous old cavalry units were dangerously near being lost to the Army because of these organizational changes," the 14th Military History Detachment's account continues. "but the policy of retraining surplus units on the rolls of the Army in an inactive status was established, permitting units to be preserved for future use rather than being disbanded or redesignated.

Between 1928 and 1939, cavalry regiments typically had 690 men. The headquarters troop had 78; the regimental band had 28; the four rifle troops each had 119 men and 108 men were assigned to a machine gun troop.

On March 3, 1929, new tensions erupted along the United States southern border after the Escobar Revolution broke out in Mexico. A group of dissident politicians and military men wanted to put General Jose Gonzalo Escobar into power as Mexico's president. When fighting flared up in northern Mexico, elements of the 1st Cavalry Division soon were spread along the United States border from El Paso to Douglas, Arizona, as a precaution. The revolt ended less than two months later with virtually no border incidents. More than 2,000 people were killed in Mexico, and most of the rebel leaders took refuge in the United States.

The Depression in the 1930s brought an unusual and decidedly "uncavalry" assignments to the division. The Civilian Conservation Corps was created on March 31, 1933, to provide paying jobs to unemployed males between the ages of 18 and 25. More than 1,300 work camps were established across the United Sates, 310,000 young men were assigned to them in less than two months. From 1933—1936, the 1st Cavalry's 3,300 troopers provided training and leadership for 62,500 members of the Civilian Conservation Corps in the Arizona-New Mexico District. The young CCC workers performed a wide variety of tasks in forest lands in the two states.

Nationally, the CCC helped pump money back into the beleaguered American economy, but it proved to be a mixed blessing for the Army. For one thing the young civilian workers received $30 a month, versus $18 a month for an Army private. Troop training came virtually to a standstill while the young civilians were shepherded, but most of the workers got their first exposure to military discipline in the CCC camps. When World War II broke out, many who had been in the CCC were well prepared for the rigors of basic training.

During the twenties and thirties, however, many cavalry officers found themselves without regimental assignments. Some found outlets for their skill by helping train National Guard Cavalry and Cavalry Reserve units. Other turned with great enthusiasm to mounted sports such as polo, fox

Sgt. Charlie Atwell on a government mount at Camp Furston, KS, prior to attending the NGNCO class at the Cavalry School. Sept. 15, 1939-Dec. 14, 1939.

West Riding Hall decorated for a show at Fort Riley, KS. (Courtesy of Ed Daily)

hunting, steeplechase and horse shows. "All these sports kept the officers fit and alert, and furnished a welcome antidote to the routine of garrison life; and, with the color and splendor of mounted reviews and parades, furnished glamour to service in the cavalry lacking in the other services," wrote Major General John Knowles Herr in his book, *Story of the U.S. Cavalry*. "The Chief of Staff, General Peyton L. March, and his successor, General Pershing, were both enthusiasts for these mounted sports and wholeheartedly supported them. Polo was officially approved as a sport which developed the qualities so valuable to combat officers in war, and wisely so, for it graduated such men as Patton, Truscott, Wainwright, Terry Allen, Paddy Flint and many others who later became outstanding leaders in battle."

In January 1933, another Chief of Staff, General Douglas MacArthur (who also organized the CCC), announced new policies that spelled dramatic changes for all US Cavalry forces. MacArthur was beginning to attract worldwide attention as a military thinker. According to William Manchester in *American Caesar*, MacArthur believed the next war would be "total war" - with airplanes, tanks and submarines emerging as the supreme weapons. The conflict would be, MacArthur predicted, one of "maneuver and movement," Consequently, MacArthur decreed that every branch of the Army should mechanize as much as possible as soon as possible.

"The horse," MacArthur declared in his directive to cavalry forces, "has no higher degree of mobility today than he had a thousand years ago.

L toR: Ronald Reagan and 2nd Lt. Robert Ferguson, Presidio of Monterey, CA. 1937. taken during the making of the movie "Sgt. Murphy."

W.B. Fraser and his horse Arrojo, Fort Bliss, TX, 1934. Fraser was a member of B Troop, 8th Cavalry, 1st Cavalry Divison.

1st Cavalry Division parade, Fort Bliss, TX, ca. 1940s.

Sparta, WI, Aug. 1-31, 1940. Camp McCoy. 2nd Army Maneuvers. Gen. George C. Marshall and Lt. Gen. Stanley H. Ford with men who slept in culvert all night. (Courtesy of Wisconsin National Guard.)

1st Lt. Eben R. Jones and his horse King, Fort Riley, KS. (Courtesy of Eben Jones)

Sgt. Kermit Lay and horse Klondike, 6th Troop, 14th Cavalry. Fort Riley, KS. July 7, 1941.

31

The time has therefore arrived when the Cavalry arm must either replace or assist the horse as a means of transportation, or else pass into the limbo of discarded military formations. There is no possibility of eliminating the need for certain units capable of performing more distant missions than can be efficiently carried out by the mass of the Army," MacArthur wrote. "The elements assigned to these tasks will be the cavalry of the future, but manifestly the horse alone will not meet its requirements in transportation.

Mechanized cavalry thus was born with the mission to cover wide areas quickly. Mechanized regiments were to be equipped with combat vehicles, such as light tanks, trucks and scout cars, instead of horses. The mechanized cavalry was not expected to take and hold objectives for extended periods - unless it could get quick support from infantry or horse cavalry units and artillery.

The 1st Cavalry Division was one of the units that was reorganized to take advantage of the maneuverability, speed and striking power of modern vehicles. The 1st Cavalry gained a tank company and a small quadroon of biplanes for air observation. The division also developed a horse porte concept using large 4 by 4 trucks with slatted bodies. The special trucks were used to transport (porte) horses and men long distances so they would be fresh for mounted duties and combat. The division's 82nd Field Artillery Battalion (Horse) already had been restructured, in 1932, into the 82nd Field Artillery Regiment. The 12th Cavalry had joined the Division in 1933. The division's war strength was increased to 465 officers and 8,840 enlisted men.

By 1938 the entire Army was expanding and gaining new equipment, thanks to improved financial support from Congress. Faster light and medium tanks were created and adopted both by cavalry and infantry units. The mobile, 105mm howitzer became the chief artillery piece of the Army divisions. There also was a new urgency in the air - from Washington to the most isolated cavalry camps in the desert Southwest. Japan, which had invaded Manchuria in 1931, continued to pour more troops into its savage conquests in China. Now, Nazi Germany had annexed Austria and was threatening to seize Czechoslovakia.

Against this background of rising international tensions, the 1st Cavalry Division's maneuvers in the mountains near Balmorhea, Texas, in 1938 took on deeper meanings. They included more units, such as the 1st Signal Troop, the 27th Ordinance Company and the 1st Medical Squadron, which had joined the expanding 1st Cavalry Division. The division's second maneuvers at Balmorhea were made even more memorable and intense by their timing; they coincided with Germany's shocking invasion of Poland on September 1, 1939, and with Britain's and France's declarations of war.

Officer and men of the 1st Cavalry Division began to prepare mentally and physically for battle. They had no way of knowing that their first crack at combat would not arrive for another four and a half years.

The next major assignment for the troopers, their horses and vehicles, was slogging through the difficult swamps of Louisiana in 3rd Army maneuvers in 1940. Then, the division, less the 1st Cavalry Brigade, returned to Fort Bliss and became a labor force. Sweating in the desert heat, the troopers constructed cantonments, or temporary housing, for 20,000 soldiers undergoing antiaircraft training.

The Germans in the meantime were scoring dramatic victories in Europe, and the Japanese were becoming increasingly militaristic throughout Asia. Despite strong isolationist sentiments in the United States, it seemed only a matter of time before America would join the war.

The 1st Cavalry Division quickly began to grow bigger. In 1940 Troops "C" and "G" in each regiment were reactivated. In 1941, as war clouds loomed closer and closer, the authorized strength of the division was nearly tripled to 10,100 men. The 61st Field Artillery Battalion was created, and the Texas National Guard's 56th Cavalry Battalion was attached to the division for training and operations.

The 1st Cavalry Brigade was headquartered at Fort Clark, near Brackettville, Texas, under the command of General Jonathan Wainwright, who was about to embark on his fateful reassignment to the Philippines. The 5th Cavalry Regiment was at Fort Clark; Fort Brown, the home of 12th Cavalry Headquarters and the 12th's 1st Squadron, was near Brownsville and the mouth of the Rio Grande; the 2nd Squadron, 12th Regiment was at Fort Ringgold, near Rio Grande City and the 8th Engineer Squadron was at Fort McIntosh near Laredo.

Late in 1940 the 1st Cavalry Brigade was ordered to rejoin the main division at Fort Bliss. Later, the division took part again in maneuvers in Louisiana, this time with a force that was 70 percent new or replacement troopers. The rugged maneuvers also marked the first time in American military history that one field army had been pitted against another in war games.

Germany's rapid conquest of Poland in September 1939 demonstrated the power and speed of German armor. In the spring of 1940, panzer units of the German war machine were on the move again, this time rolling westward through the low countries and France. Also, during the US Army maneuvers of 1939-40, it had been evident to armor enthusiasts that development of mechanization under cavalry and infantry was not being given enough consideration. The German successes and the Army maneuvers helped armor leaders to convince the War Department of the value of armor and the urgency of establishing similar units in the US Army. On July 10, 1940, the Armored Force was created with Chaffee, promoted now to brigadier general, as its first chief. Since there was no

Col. Tupper Cole last regimental commander of the 2nd Calvary horse-mounted regiment. Fort Riley, KS 1941-42.

1st Lt. Whiteside Miller on Donnavan Field, Schofield Barracks, HI 1934.

Congressional authorization for a separate armored branch, it was established technically "for purposes of service test."

With authorization of 530 officers and 9,329 enlisted men, the new organization was built around the 7th Cavalry Brigade (Mechanized) and the 6th Infantry (Armored) at Fort Knox, and the approximately seven infantry tank battalions in the three infantry (tank) regiments of the Provisional Tank Brigade at Fort Benning. From these units the Armored Force was assembled and by mid-1942 its assigned strength reached 148,192. Also under command of General Chaffee was the I Armored Corps, activated on July 15, 1940, and consisting of the 1st Armored Division (successor of the 7th Cavalry Brigade) at Fort Knox and the 2nd Armored Division (organized from the Provisional Tank Brigade) at Fort Benning. Other elements of the Armored Force were the 70th Tank Battalion at Fort Meade, the Armored Force Board, and an Armored Force School and Replacement Training Center.

Inheriting fewer than 1,000 mostly obsolete tanks and other vehicles, the Armored Force was hampered from the beginning in its efforts to equip its units. One armored division alone, to be fully equipped, required 3,243 vehicles of which 1,140 were of the combat type. To speed manufacture of new vehicles of all types, current designs were placed in mass production, but it was not until 1943 that the equipment shortage began to ease.

The devastating firepower and speed of the US Army's armored divisions of World War II was largely the result of the genius of American industry. When Germany invaded western Europe in 1940, the US Army had only 28 new tanks - 18 medium and 10 light - and these were soon to become obsolete, along with some 900 older models on hand. The Army had no heavy tanks and no immediate plans for any. Even more serious than the shortage of tanks was industry's lack of experience in tank manufacture and limited production facilities. Furthermore, the US was committed to helping supply its Allies. By 1942 American tank production had soared to just under 25,000, almost doubling the combined British and German output for that year. And in 1943, the peak tank production year, the total was 29,497. All in all, from 1940 through 1945, US tank production totaled 88,410.

The National Guard, before any of its units were inducted into federal service during 1940-41, had four cavalry divisions, the 21st through the 24th. All four were broken up and none entered federal service, although many of their elements did. Also, conversions and reorganizations of 17 National Guard cavalry regiments before induction resulted in the organization of seven horse-mechanized cavalry regiments, as well as several field artillery regiments, coast artillery regiments and separate battalions, and an antitank battalion. Thus, after the reshuffling, seven partially mechanized regiments and a brigade of two horse cavalry regiments entered federal service. The horse-mechanized regiments were the 101st (New York), 102nd (New Jersey), 104th (Pennsylvania), 106th (Illinois), 107th (Ohio), 113th (Iowa) and the 115th (Wyoming); the horse brigade was the 56th (Texas) consisting of the 112th and 124th Cavalry (Texas). While in federal service, all of the horse-mechanized regiments were completely mechanized and split up to form groups and separate squadrons, similarly to those of the Regular Army. The horse regiments, the 112th and 124th were dismounted, withdrawn from the 56th Cavalry Brigade and reorganized as infantry with much the same composition as regiments of the 1st Cavalry Division. Finally in mid-1944, the Headquarters and Headquarters Troop, 56th Cavalry Brigade, became the 56th Reconnaissance Troop, Mechanized.

Then, without warning, the Japanese devastated the American fleet at Pearl Harbor on December 7, 1941. Troopers rushed back to the 1st Cavalry Division from all over the United States. They prepared their horses, their vehicles and their weapons to join the war against the Axis.

The troopers, however, would have to wage a different and utterly unexpected battle over the next two years and three months. They would have to fight to get into World War II, and they would have to leave behind the fast and sturdy cavalry horses

Sgt. Walter Schweizer on Big Cain, Fort Ord, CA. 1942. Troop C, 107th Cavalry.

Fort Ord, CA. 1942. Troop C, 107th Cavalry.

Col. Lindsey P. Henderson, Jr., Troop A, 108th Cavalry. (Courtesy of Lindsey P. Henderson, Jr.)

and stubborn pack mules that had served them so well.

Once in combat, the 1st Cavalry's troopers would prove that dismounted cavalrymen can fight, and fight well, with tanks, jeeps, amphibious vehicles and trucks - and no steeds except their own two feet.

WORLD WAR II

Dark days followed the disaster at Pearl Harbor. The Japanese made quick conquests across vast areas of the Pacific. By June 1942 they had captured many Allied installations. They were threatening many more - from Australia to Alaska and as far away as India.

Until the Japanese attacked Hawaii, America had been reluctant to join the war in Asia and Europe. Consequently, US military forces were ill-prepared to go on the offensive. The Army and Army Air Corps were deployed primarily to defend the continental United States. Most American units were not properly trained for the battlefields of the Pacific or Europe. Much of their equipment was obsolete, and ammunition was in critically scarce supply.

Late 1941 and early 1942 found Cavalry troopers ready, willing and eager to charge into battle anywhere in the world. Traditional cavalry had not fared well in the opening days of World War II. When Poland's proud lancers charged at the invading Germans in September 1939, they were slaughtered by tanks, machine guns, heavy artillery and planes of the Luftwaffe. In Burma in March 1942, a group of Sikh cavalrymen led by a British officer spurred their mounts straight at a force of Japanese they suddenly encountered. Their classic charge quickly was snuffed out by concentrated small arms and machine gun fire.

The last US Army riders to see combat as traditional horse soldiers had fared somewhat better. In December 1941, troopers of the 26th Cavalry Regiment (Philippine Scouts) joined the unsuccessful fight to keep the Japanese from expanding their beachheads on Luzon. Then, in January 1942, the 26th Cavalry troopers finally were forced to slaughter their horses. The meat helped keep Bataan's defenders alive and fighting a little longer. The Japanese paid a heavy price for their conquest, but Bataan fell on May 6.

It was during this fateful defensive campaign that Lieutenant Edward P. Ramsey led his outnumbered platoon of 27 Filipino scouts in a successful charge on the advancing Japanese infantry at Morong, Philippine Islands. As it had for centuries, the shock of a mounted charge overwhelmed the Japanese and caused them to flee in confusion back into the river and swamps. This engagement at Morong on January 16, 1942, was the last mounted Cavalry charge in US Military history.

By now, American infantry, artillery, airborne and armor units finally were beginning to reach combat readiness and a few were shipped overseas.

New orders did not arrive for the frustrated men of the 1st Cavalry Division, and they remained assigned to the Southern Defense Command. Cavalrymen seemed fated to spend yet another war patrolling the long and dusty border with Mexico and guarding bridges of the Southern Pacific Railroad.

Their desire to fight was strong, however. Early in 1942, the division commander relayed to higher channels the troopers' willingness to swap their horses for light trucks, if doing so would help them get a combat assignment.

At first, nothing happened. Once more, the

115th Cavalry Regiment (Horse-Mechanized).

Water call.

troopers rode in Louisiana maneuvers, and once again they demonstrated impressively that they were a crack fighting force.

On paved roadways, the troopers' horses could not keep pace with the trucks that now hauled infantrymen forward. Out in the flanks and rough terrain, the 1st Cavalry's abilities startled even the staunchest critics of horse soldiers. In one 20-hour march during war games, the division moved more than 40 miles, forded a treacherous river and attacked and wiped out the opposing force's communications. In another war games' march, the mounted troopers covered more than 70 miles in 35 hours, crossed a swollen river and established an effective bridgehead for an armored force.

Despite these displays, American military planners decided that motor vehicles and armor were the future. In March 1942, the War Department abolished the Army's office of Chief of Cavalry. The days of horses and mules in the US Army were numbered. Motor vehicles and armor were

the future. Douglas MacArthur's campaign had prevailed. "The constant trend in the modern world is toward greater and greater speed," he had written.

Horses and pack animals did not vanish entirely from the US Army, however. The Cavalry School at Fort Riley, Kansas, was to remain open until October 31, 1945. Horses and mules did not disappear from the front lines of World War II; in fact, in other armies, mounted soldiers played bigger roles in World War II than they did in World War I. The Germans, who created fearsome tanks and effectively exploited the capabilities of mechanized armor, also fielded several divisions of horse-mounted soldiers, mostly on the Eastern Front. From 1939—1945, the Wehrmacht used nearly three million horses as mounts or pack animals - twice the number the German army employed in World War I. German cavalry rode against the Soviet Army, which by 1942 had nearly 20,000

SYNOPSIS OF CAVALRY ARTILLERY

At the beginning of World War II, the 1st Cavalry Division was still a "square" division with horses, and had not been reorganized under the new "triangular" concept. The division had a general support artillery battalion and there were two cavalry brigades each with two cavalry regiments, each of which had in turn two cavalry squadrons. Each brigade was supported by one light artillery battalion.

Then a decision was made in regard to the fate of the division and this decision did not include horses. Also, would be the change of the cavalry uniform from lace boots, breeches and campaign hat to combat boots, new pot helmet with separate liner, and the olive drab fatigue uniform more suitable to the new wartime environment.

The changeover from horses to vehicles came in February 1943, when the 1st Cavalry Division received orders assigning it overseas. Under the command of Major General Innis P. Swift, it arrived in Australia on July 26, 1943, to prepare for six months of jungle and amphibious training at Camp Štrathpine, near Brisbane, for eventual warfare against the Imperial Japanese Army.

This is a condensed version of an article submitted by Major General William A. Becker, USA (RET). He is currently the chairman of the Board of Governors, 1st Cavalry Division Association.

mounted soldiers in 35 cavalry divisions. At the end of the war, the Russians would have 50 divisions of horse soldiers. Red cavalrymen slashed repeatedly at the Germans, and often with great success. Their nimble, sturdy mounts kept going through mud that trapped tanks, wheeled vehicles and foot soldiers alike. When winter temperatures dropped so low that engines would not start, Red cavalry units swarmed over the immobilized Nazis. In the right circumstances and terrain, the Russians proved that horse cavalry remained a superb mobile striking force, even on a "modern" battlefield. After the Red Army held on at Stalingrad, for instance, and mounted an offensive in November 1942, fast-moving Soviet cavalrymen closed the encirclement that sealed the doom of the German Sixth Army.

In the sweeps through North Africa, Sicily, Italy and Belgium, and the final Allied drive across Europe, mechanized forces functioned in the traditional cavalry role. Armor, as the ground-mobility arm functioning like cavalry, emerged from World War II with a large share of credit for the Allied victory, and cavalry's postwar role was envisioned as an amplification of its traditional role, using mechanization and armor. General George S. Patton's breathtaking sweeps through North Africa and Sicily, and later through Europe, were nothing if not cavalry maneuvers. Patton, with his pistols on his hips, was nothing if not a cavalryman who understood that some of the mounts had changed. His high speed, high-powered 6th Cavalry Group Army Information Service - popularly known as Patton's Household Cavalry - performed like a reincarnation of Jeb Stuart in supplying information necessary for the success of the final Allied drive in Europe.

While no horses went overseas in World War II, troopers drilled on horseback daily until they shipped out, and saber charges were practiced. Requests for horse cavalry arrived throughout the war from field commanders who knew best the conditions under which they were fighting and after the war, General Patton joined many who believed that the mounted trooper had not outlived his usefulness, adding, had we possessed an American cavalry division with pack artillery in Tunisia and Sicily not a German would have escaped. Nor did the military use of horses end with the demise of the 26th Cavalry in the Philippines. In the jungles of Burma and India, a unit under Brigadier General Frank D. Merrill, nicknamed Merrill's Marauders, used approximately 340 horses and 360 mules.

In Sicily the 3rd Infantry Division organized the Provisional Reconnaissance Troop, Mounted, which served in the mountains during the invasion of Italy and included 143 horses and 349 mules in September 1943.

The 1st Cavalry Division's long-awaited orders finally arrived in February 1943. They were a shock. The division was instructed to turn in its horses and cavalry equipment and proceed as soon as possible to Australia for infantry training. To many of the cavalrymen having to become foot soldiers was a hard and emotional blow. They had chosen cavalry because they loved to ride and because they firmly believed there was still a place for the unique capabilities and traditions of horse warriors. They were going to war, and they were leaving the familiar desert to fight in the muggy jungle of the Pacific.

The troopers' belief in cavalry and their reticence to surrender their mounts would be vindicated several times during World War II; however. In North Africa, Sicily, Italy and other areas of rough countryside, many US field commanders repeatedly would wish aloud for units of horse soldiers to send ahead of their infantry and armor to pursue retreating enemy troops. In the wilds of Burma, horses and mule would help "Merrill's Marauders" operate effectively behind Japanese lines.

In Australia, the troopers neared the end of their intensive training, they were inspected and pronounced ready by General MacArthur - the man who had helped cause them to be dismounted. They had disliked him when they lost their horses, but now MacArthur was their boss and the commander of Allied operations in the Southwest Pacific. At Camp Strathpine, he welcomed them warmly and strongly by declaring: "I want the elan of the cavalry."

During its training in Australia, the First Cavalry Division was reorganized partly under infantry and partly under cavalry tables of organization. Special allowances of heavy equipment and other components were supplied to tailor the division for combat in the Southwest pacific. It contained, in addition to two brigades of four infantry-type cavalry regiments, four 105mm artillery battalions, a tank company, and various normal combat support elements that brought its special authorized strength to 13,258, almost the same as an infantry division. Later in the Philippines, on 25 July 1945, it was reorganized wholly as an infantry division, but retained the cavalry unit designations.

The initial commitment of the First Cavalry Division was in the Admiralty Campaign when a task force built around the 2nd Squadron, 5th Cavalry, landed on 29 February 1944 on Los Negros. Additional troops of the division arrived until by 9 March both brigades and all four regiments were ashore. By 30 March, the division had made its sixth amphibious landing in the campaign. Hard fighting continued until total victory and the campaign was officially terminated on 18 May.

By the fall of 1944, MacArthur was ready to fulfill his promise to return to the Philippines. Lead elements of the First Cavalry Division landed on Leyte as part of X Corps, fighting a grueling campaign for the rest of the year on Leyte and Samar. With landings on Luzon in late January, the division began its last campaign of the war, driving for Manila. The campaign lasted until the end of June.

Although the First Cavalry Division was the only cavalry division to survive the war, the Army also contained a lesser-known Second Cavalry Division. This division was activated at Fort Riley on 1 April 1941 as a racially mixed formation, with the 3rd and 4th Cavalry Brigades, the 4th Brigade being Negro. It contained some of the oldest and proudest cavalry regiments of the Regular Army. The lack of a requirement for horse-mounted units lead to the deactivation of the Second Cavalry Division on 15 July 1942. The 3rd Brigade was redesignated the 9th Armored Division Train, but the 4th Brigade remained active and formed the nucleus of the new Second Cavalry Division (Colored), which was reactivated at Fort Clark, TX, on 25 February 1943. The division arrived in North Africa during March 1944, but was inactivated there in May. Its personnel were used to form logistic units in the theater.

The formation of the first armored divisions in the U.S. Army absorbed several cavalry regiments as the First Cavalry Regiment (Mechanized) in July 1940 was redesignated the 1st Armored Regiment, a major element of the 1st Armored Division; the 2nd Cavalry Regiment (Horse) became in July 1942 the 2nd Armored Regiment; and the 3rd Cavalry Regiment (Horse) in July 1942 became the Third Armored Regiment. Other nondivisional cavalry regiments changed their peacetime mounts from horse to vehicles and were designated as Cavalry Regiments (Mechanized), retaining their historic numerical designations.

As the U.S. Army organized and trained the mighty force necessary for the invasion of Northwest Europe and the campaign to defeat Germany, most of the cavalry regiments were converted to mechanized cavalry groups. The group organization provided more flexibility than the fixed organization of the traditional cavalry regiment and was designed to meet the challenges of the modern battlefield.

Each cavalry group (mechanized) consisted of a small group headquarters and two mechanized cavalry squadrons..

A cavalry squadron was formed of a headquarters troop, three reconnaissance troops, an assault gun troop, and a light tank company.

Each reconnaissance troop had a headquarters platoon and three reconnaissance platoons. The reconnaissance platoons each consisted of three teams, each of one armored car, one machine gun 1/4-ton truck (Jeep), and one mortar 1/4-ton truck. The armored car had a turret-mounted 37mm gun and a caliber .30 machine gun. The assault gun troop had six assault guns, which were 75mm howitzers mounted on a light tank chassis. The troop was divided into three sections of two guns each.

12th Cavalry early in WW II.

A Cavalry unit making a river crossing.

A Cavalry platoon in line of Squads in column.

A Platoon from Machine Gun Troop on the move.

A Squad from Machine Gun Troop on the move.

The light tank company had seventeen tanks, two in headquarters and five in each of three platoons. Initially, the company was equipped with M5A1 tanks, each armed with a 37mm cannon and three caliber .30 machine guns. These were later replaced with M24 tanks, each armed with a 75mm gun, one caliber .50 machine gun, and two caliber .30 machine guns.

These cavalry groups were designed to perform the traditional roles of cavalry on the modern battlefield. Once the invasion had succeeded and the Northwest Europe campaign underway, they usually operated under corps control and performed such missions as reconnaissance, screening, and security. They were often used as economy of force elements and in attacks, as well. There were thirteen cavalry groups deployed to Northwest Europe in 1944 and 1945.

The 2nd Cavalry Group (Mechanized), including the 2nd and 42nd Cavalry Reconnaissance Squadrons, was redesignated from the 2nd Cavalry Regiment (Mechanized) at Fort Jackson, SC, on 22 December 1943. It deployed to England in April 1944 and landed in France on 19 July 1944. Initially, it protected lines of communication from Cherbourg to the Carentan, but was committed to combat on 2 August. It drove to the Loire River and joined XII Corps at Le Mans on the tenth, protecting its right flank. On 18 September, it fought against the 11th Panzer Division at Luneville. It was attached to the 26th Infantry Division in October and November. The group entered Germany on 5 December, but returned to France two days later. It crossed into Luxembourg on 23 December and guarded the right flank of XII Corps along the Moselle River until 1 March 1945, then entering Germany at Wasserbilling on the West Wall. It reached the Rhine on 16 March and crossed on the 25th. On 5 May, the group entered Czechoslovakia, where it ended the war.

The 3rd Cavalry Group (Mechanized), with the 3rd and 43rd Cavalry Reconnaissance Squadrons, was redesignated from the 3rd Cavalry Regiment (Mechanized) at Camp Gordon, GA, on 3 November 1943. After participating in maneuvers in Tennessee, it was deployed to England, arriving in June 1944. It landed in France on 9 August and was first committed to combat on 10 August with XX Corps in the Le Mans area. Its 3rd Squadron was used as infantry to assault Fort Driant at Metz. The group was reunited and protected the north flank of XX Corps. It held defensive positions along the West Wall and then entered Germany 28 February 1945, operating in front of or on the flanks of XX Corps. It crossed the Rhine on 29 March and entered Austria on 5 May, where in ended the war.

The 4th Cavalry Group (Mechanized), with the 4th and 24th Cavalry Reconnaissance Squadrons, was redesignated from the 4th Cavalry Regiment (Mechanized) in England on 21 December 1943. It assaulted Normandy on 6 June 1944 under VII Corps and participated in the capture of Cherbourg. It was attached to the 2nd Armored Division during the St. Lo battle. Protecting the south flank of VII Corps, it entered Belgium and Germany in November. Moving into the Huertgen Forest, it maintained contact between the 2nd Armored Division and the 8th Infantry Division during the German Ardennes Offensive. Moving back to Belgium 22 December, it fought at Aachen and entered Germany and crossed the Roer in February 1945. The group crossed the Rhine at Bonn and helped seal the Ruhr Pocket.

The 6th Cavalry Group (Mechanized), with the 6th and 26th Cavalry Reconnaissance Squadrons, was redesignated from the 6th Cavalry Regiment (Mechanized) in Ireland on 1 January 1944. It landed in France on 9 July, where it was used as an information service for Third Army until 1 December. It was then committed to combat at St. Avold, France. It entered Luxembourg on 31 December to locate German forces in the Bastogne vicinity and then reduced German units between the 26th and 35th Infantry Divisions in the Lintage-Saar area, where it remained until 13 January 1945. It crossed into Germany with VIII Corps on 25 February, attacking through Bauler, Waxweiler, ans Lasel. Protecting the VIII Corps southern flank, it mopped up along the Berlin autobahn.

The 11th Cavalry Group (Mechanized), with the 36th and 44th Cavalry Reconnaissance Squadrons, was activate at Camp Young, CA, on 5 May 1943. It arrived in England 10 October 1944 and landed in France on 26 November. It went into the line in Germany on 12 December, protecting the Roer River sector. Crossing into the Netherlands on 3 February 1945, it entered Germany 27 February on the left flank of the 84th Infantry Division. Under XIII Corps, it held a defensive line along the Rhine near Dusseldorf and then crossed the Rhine on at Wesel on 1 April. It then screened the north flank of XIII Corps and saw action during the battle at Munster and the seizure of the Ricklingen Bridge over the Leine River.

The 14th Cavalry Group (Mechanized), with the 18th and 32 Cavalry Reconnaissance Squadrons, was activated at Fort Lewis, WA, on 12 July 1943. It arrived in England on 3 September 1944 and landed in France on 27 September. Crossing into Luxembourg, it was committed to combat on the West Wall on 20 October. Crossing into Belgium, it suffered heavy losses near Manderfield when the Germans launched their Ardennes Offensive. The group attacked the Roer River line on 28 January and crossed into Germany on 6 February, where it helped eliminate the Ruhr Pocket.

General Patton presents J.H. Polk the Legion of Merit award in Austria. (Courtesy of J.H. Polk)

The spoils of war.

The 15th Cavalry Group (Mechanized), with the 15th and 17th Cavalry Reconnaissance Squadrons, was redesignated from the 15th Cavalry Regiment (Mechanized) on 15 March 1944 in England. It landed in France on 5 July and was committed to combat near Avranches on 2 August for the assault on Brest. It remained at St. Nazaire and Lorient until relieved by the 66th Infantry Division, thereafter performing screening missions for Ninth Army. Attached to XIV Corps, it entered the Netherlands on 16 February 1945 and Germany on 3 March.

The 16th Cavalry Group (Mechanized), with the 16th and 19th Cavalry Reconnaissance Squadrons, was redesignated from the 16th Cavalry Regiment (Mechanized) at Fort Devens, MA, on 22 November 1943. It arrived in England on 27 November 1944 and France on 27 February 1945. It was assigned to Third Army and went into line alongside the 3rd cavalry Group on 8 March. Entering Germany the next day, it was actively engaged in the Saar-Moselle triangle near Trier and protected the left flank of XX Corps during the drive into Germany. It crossed the Rhine near Mainz on 29 March and was transferred to Fifteenth Army on 7 April.

The 101st Cavalry Group (Mechanized), with the 101st and 116th Cavalry Reconnaissance Squadrons, was redesignated from the 101st Cavalry Regiment (Mechanized) on 21 December 1943. It arrived in England on 12 November 1944 and France on 31 January 1945. Assigned to XV Corps, it entered Germany on 9 February, where it attacked along the Saar River line on 14 March. It then moved to protect the lines of communication of XXI Corps and screened the advance of the 4th Infantry Division through March and later those of the 12th Armored Division.

The 102nd Cavalry Group (Mechanized), with the 38th and 102nd Cavalry Reconnaissance Squadrons, was redesignated from the 102nd Cavalry Regiment (Mechanized) in England on 2 January 1944. It landed in France on 8 June with the mission of protecting the V Corps left flank. It operated in Belgium, Luxembourg, and Germany in the fall and held positions along the West Wall during the German Ardennes Offensive. It returned to Germany on 31 March 1945 and screened the left flank of V Corps, fighting at Colmar and reaching Czechoslovakia on 8 May.

The 106th Cavalry Group (Mechanized), with the 106th and 121st Cavalry Reconnaissance Squadrons, was redesignated from the 106th Cavalry Regiment in England on 14 March 1945. It landed in France on 2 July and mopped up German forces in Normandy under VII Corps. It helped seal the Falaise Pocket and fought as infantry in the Foret de Parroy alongside the 44th and 79th Infantry Divisions. In November, it helped capture Strasbourg. Entering Germany on 20 March 1945, it captured Salzburg in Austria by the end of the war.

FORT CLARK, TEXAS

For 21 years, from 1920 to November 1941, Fort Clark was home for the 5th Cavalry Regiment. Colonel George S. Patton Jr. served here in 1938 as its regimental commander. At the outbreak of World War II, the 112th Cavalry Division of the Texas National Guard under the command of Colonel Julian Cunningham was assigned to Fort Clark, where they trained until their deployment for combat duties in the Pacific. In 1942 Colonel William C. Chase and the 113th Cavalry spent a short stay guarding the Southern Pacific Railroad. On February 25, 1943, the 2nd Cavalry Division, the Army's last horse-mounted unit, was activated under command of Major General Henry H. Johnson, with more than 12,000 troops stationed here until their deployment in February 1944. The war added another feature to the history of Fort Clark, that of having a German Prisoner of War sub-camp on the 4,000 acre reservation.

Many famous officers served at Fort Clark and a number of the streets and buildings on the Fort honor their names: Colonel R.S. Mackenzie, one of the truly great Indian fighters in the Southwest; General Wesley Merritt, who later commanded the Philippine Expedition; General William R. Shafter, Commander of the Cuba Expedition; General John L. Bullis, who won fame and acclaim as commander of the Seminole Scouts; General George C. Marshall, US Chief of Staff in World War II; General Jonathan M. Wainwright, hero of Bataan and Corregidor and General George S. Patton Jr., famous for his mighty mobile armored operation North Africa, Sicily and across France into Germany. Many combat decorations and honors were awarded to Fort Clark veterans.

By the end of World War I the technological advancement of modern arms signaled the obsolescence of the horse cavalry. Yet it was not until June 1944 that full mechanization of the cavalry caused the government to close Fort Clark, one of the last horse-cavalry posts in the country. The fort was officially inactivated in early 1946, and later that year it was sold to Brown & Root Company for salvage and later used as a guest ranch.

CPL George Snedeker, 1941. (Courtesy of Donald Snedeker)

The 113th Cavalry Group (Mechanized), with the 113th and 125th Cavalry Reconnaissance Squadrons, was redesignated from the 113th Cavalry Regiment (Mechanized) in England on 1 February 1944. Landing in France on 2 July, it was committed to combat at St. Jean de Haye two days later and attacked St. Lo with the 35th Infantry Division on 28 July. It joined the 2nd Armored Division at Percy and protected the XIX Corps to Mortain, helping to seal the Falaise Gap. It entered Belgium on 5 September, the Netherlands on 13 September, and Germany on 26 November. During the German Ardennes Offensive, it moved to the northern edge of the Huertgen Forest. It then assaulted the Roer River and screened between XIX and XIII Corps during the Rhine crossings. In April, it assisted in sealing the Harz Mountains.

The 115th Cavalry Group (Mechanized), with the 104th and 107th Cavalry Reconnaissance Squadrons, was redesignated from the 115th Cavalry Regiment (Mechanized) at Fort Lewis, WA, on 1 January 1944. It landed in France on 15 January 1945 and relieved the 15th Cavalry Group at St. Nazaire. Its initial combat was on 10 February and it entered Germany on 22 April, protecting the right flank of VI Corps from Stuttgart to Innsbruck, entering Austria on 3 May.

There were three cavalry groups that did not serve overseas. The 104th Cavalry Regiment (Mechanized) was redesignated the 104th Cavalry Group (Mechanized), with the 104th and 119th Cavalry Reconnaissance Squadrons, at Salem, OR, on 1 January 1944. It served at Fort Lewis, WA, and Camp Gruber. OK, under XVI Corps. The 107th Cavalry Regiment (Mechanized) was redesignated the 107th Cavalry Group (Mechanized), with the 45th and 115th Cavalry Reconnaissance Squadrons, at Santa Rosa, CA, on 1 January 1944 and moved to Camp Polk, LA, under XXI Corps. The 29th Cavalry Group (Mechanized), with the 127th, 128th, and 129th Cavalry Reconnaissance Squadrons, was activated 1 May 1944 at Fort Riley, KS, and formed from the assets of the 29th Cavalry Regiment. It was assigned to the Replacement and School Command. The Cavalry Replacement Training Center operated throughout the war.

In addition to the squadrons of the mechanized cavalry groups, each armored division had an organic cavalry reconnaissance squadron. These were somewhat larger than the squadrons of the cavalry groups, but were essentially similar and performed similar functions for their respective divisions. With several exceptions, the squadrons were numbered from the 81st for the 1st Armored Division, 82nd for the Second Armored Division, etc.

Besides the group and armored division cavalry reconnaissance squadrons, there were several separate such squadrons. The 91st was attached to Fifth Army and fought in the campaigns in North Africa, Sicily, and Italy, while the 117th was attached to Seventh Army in Europe. The 115th was attached to Fourth Army within the United States.

Each infantry division included a cavalry reconnaissance troop. These troops were equipped with armored cars and 1/4-ton trucks and included no light tanks or assault guns.

Two separate Texas National Guard cavalry regiments, the 112th and the 124th, were reorganized as special light infantry regiments and fought in the South Pacific. The 112th initially performed mounted non-combat service in New Caledonia, arriving in August 1942, under the First Island Command, prior to being reorganized in Australia in May 1943. The regiment established an excellent combat record in hard jungle fighting. During much of its combat, it was attached to the First Cavalry Division.

Armor, as the ground arm of mobility, emerged from World War II with a lion's share of the credit for the Allied victory. Indeed, armor enthusiasts at that time regarded the tank as being the main weapon of the land army. But demobilization quickly followed the end of hostilities and, in essence, the armor strength was destroyed. By mid-1948 the Regular Army divisions of all types

R.C. Barham on "Little Boy." (Courtesy of B.B. Smith)

VMI Cadet Horse Cavalry Troop cantering on the VMI Parade Ground with cadet barracks and Old Library in the background. (Courtesy of Leonard L. Lewane)

were reduced to 10; the 2nd Armored Division remained as the lone division organized as armored until 1951, when the 1st Armored Division was again activated. Furthermore, the Armored Center at Fort Knox was inactivated on October 20, 1945, and most of its functions were assumed by the Armored School.

Between mid-1940 and mid-1941 the cavalry strength of the active army more than quadrupled, from slightly under 13,000 to over 53,000. By May 31, 1945, it reached 91,948, its peak strength during the war.

Even after the end of World War II, however, there was unusual need for mechanized organizations in the requirements of the occupational forces in Europe. Highly mobile security forces with flexible organizations and a minimum of personnel were needed, and armor and cavalry units were more readily adaptable to the task than infantry. Consequently, the US Constabulary in Europe absorbed most of the elements of the 1st and 4th Armored Divisions. These units were gradually reorganized and redesignated as Constabulary organizations, the US Constabulary becoming fully operational on July 1, 1946.

In addition to its headquarters and special troops, the Constabulary consisted of the 1st, 2nd and 3rd Constabulary Brigades and the 1st, 2nd, 3rd, 4th, 5th, 6th, 10th, 11th, 14th and 15th Constabulary Regiments. Most regiments had the usual three squadrons. Each regiment, to carry out its peculiar peacetime duties, had a light tank troop, a motorcycle platoon (25 motorcycles) and a horse platoon (30 horses).

By early 1947 the Constabulary strength reached nearly 35,000, but continuing turnover in personnel was one of its major problems. On November 14, 1950, Headquarters and Headquarters Company, US Constabulary, was inactivated; most of its units were assigned to the newly activated 7th Army. The last of the units, the 2nd Constabulary Brigade and the 15th and 24th Constabulary Squadrons, continued to operate until inactivated on December 15, 1952.

Since the Armored Force had been created as a temporary measure for World War II, armor was not a permanent arm to which officers could be assigned. The officers retained their basic branch while serving with armored (tank) units. To prevent the loss of identity of armored officers, the War Department began action in early 1947 to assign them to the Cavalry. At the same time, announcement was made of expected eventual statutory approval of an Armored Cavalry arm to replace Cavalry. Pending that action, all qualified armored (tank) officers were to be detailed in Cavalry, unless they objected. Cavalry officers not qualified in and not desiring to serve with armor could be transferred to or detailed to other arms and services.

As late as August 1949, official publications listed Armored Cavalry, instead of Cavalry, as a branch of the Army. Described as "an arm of mobility, armor protected firepower, and shock action," Armored Cavalry was to engage in all types of combat actions in co-ordination with other arms and services. Reconnaissance types of missions were usually to be performed by light Armored Cavalry units, which were to avoid sustained offensive or defensive combat.

Use of the term armored cavalry was a compromise between those who wanted the word armored in the new branch name and those who were as reluctant to discard the term cavalry as they had been to part with their horses. To others, especially those who had not served with horse cavalry, armor was a new medium, and that term best described the branch. On the other hand, proponents for the continued use of the term cavalry contended that armor, or whatever it might be called, still was the mounted branch - regardless of its mode of transportation - teaching the same principles of mobility, firepower and shock action. The combination term, armored cavalry, was not popular with either group, but the matter was finally resolved, at least legally, when Congress in its Army Organization Act of 1950, designated Armor as the new branch name and further provided that it would be "a continuation of the Cavalry."

The armored division after World War II was larger and heavier than it had been during the war. Its authorized personnel strength was increased in 1948 from 10,670 to 15,973; its tank strength was increased from 272 to 373, most of the additional tanks being in the medium and heavy classes. The reserve command received additional officers, men, and equipment, placing it on a par with the two combat commands and enabling it to function as a third combat command when needed. Also added to the division were a battalion of heavy tanks, a battalion of heavy artillery, and a battalion of infantry; infantry companies were increased from three to four in the battalions, boosting the total infantry companies for the division from nine to 16.

The 1st Cavalry Division, serving on occupation duty in Japan, continued to be the only division bearing the cavalry designation. In the 1949 reorganization, however, only the division and its cavalry regiments survived the change to infantry designations, the squadrons becoming battalions and the troops becoming companies. The 1949 reorganization deleted one cavalry regiment, leaving the division with three, the 5th, 7th and 8th; the 12th was inactivated and withdrawn.

Except for the cavalry units in the US Constabulary and those in the 1st Cavalry Division, there were no other active cavalry regiments in the Regular Army until the 3rd Armored Cavalry was organized in 1948. Later that year three other armored cavalry regiments, the 2nd, 6th and 14th, were organized, their elements consisting of converted and redesignated units of the US Constabulary.

The armored cavalry regiment of late 1948, with three reconnaissance battalions as its principal elements, had an authorized strength of 2,883 and was equipped with 72 light and 69 medium tanks.

One of the most difficult problems facing the National Guard after World War II was preservation of the historical continuity of its units. While in federal service during the war, most National Guard units had undergone many redesignations, reorganizations and inactivation. After the war the types of units allotted to the National Guard often varied considerably from the types inducted during the war. To keep from losing the histories of units traditional to certain geographical areas, the Department of the Army permitted the postwar units to retain the histories of the pre-war units. Thus, in most instances, units allotted after the war perpetuated histories of pre-war units.

Heading the post-World War II list of National Guard armor and cavalry units were the 49th and 50th Armored Divisions of Texas and New Jersey, respectively. Non-divisional units included five armored groups, three cavalry groups, 31 tank battalions and 15 cavalry reconnaissance squadrons. Each of the 25 National Guard infantry divisions had a mechanized cavalry reconnaissance troop and a tank battalion, and each infantry regiment had a tank company. The National Guard had no horse cavalry units.

In the Organized Reserves, cavalry and tank units activated in late 1946 were the 19th Armored Division, the 301st through the 304th Cavalry Groups, the 75th Amphibian Tank Battalion, the 782nd Tank Battalion, the 314th and 315th Cavalry Reconnaissance Battalions and the 83rd Reconnaissance Troop. In early 1948 the Organized Reserve became the Organized Reserve Corps and in 1952 this component became the Army Reserve.

With swift advances during the postwar period in the development of atomic and recoilless weapons, rockets and guided missiles, the tank appeared to many to be obsolete. Although emphasis upon armor did decline, efforts continued toward development of a tank with a greater firepower and armor protection without losing mobility. But costs were increasing sharply. For example, the initial price of equipping an armored division rose from 30 million dollars in 1944 to about 200 million in 1950. A single light tank costing $27,000 in 1939 increased to about $225,000 in 1950.

Because of rising costs and the trend toward atomic weapons and missiles, the modern Army's requirement for tanks was not sufficient to command all the funds for the tank development many advocated. Some progress, however, was made. In late 1948 the M-46 Patton was introduced. Named for General Patton, the M-46 was a modified version of the M-26 of late World War II. Still mounting a 90mm gun, but with increased power and speed, the M-46 was capable of 30 miles per hour. The Army also developed a replacement for the M-24 light tank, the M-41, mounting a 76mm guns.

KOREA

It happened before dawn, June 25, 1950. Less than five years after the terrible devastations of World War II, a new war broke out. This time, trouble had come to a distant land whose name means "Morning Calm."

Around the world many were shocked and surprised as invading North Korean troops shattered the morning calm of South Korea. But the only real surprise, an American intelligence expert later would testify, was the conflict's timetable. A Korean War was known to be festering. Its warning signs had been visible for at least a year. The seeds for conflict had been germinating since 1945.

Led by Soviet-made T-34 tanks supported by infantry, the Reds struck simultaneously at six major points on the 200-mile border. Their amphibious forces swept ashore at four key locations on South Korea's east coast. They were out to conquer the rest of Korea.

While the United Nations Security Council tried unsuccessfully to arrange a cease-fire, the Reds drove relentlessly against the out-gunned South Koreans. The Republic of Korea (ROK) forces included a well-trained army of 100,000 men. But they were armed with few weapons heavier than machine guns. South Korea had no tanks, no armored ships in its tiny navy, virtually no artillery pieces or antitank weapons and only a handful of outdated planes that were quickly destroyed.

By contrast, the North Koreans, with a population less than half that of South Korea, had a well-equipped 200,000 man force, many new Russian tanks, a bigger navy and an air force nearly 20 times the size of its opponent's.

If South Korea was to survive and stay free, it desperately needed quick help from its friends.

America's fateful decision came less than two days later, after the fast-moving North Koreans broke through the ROK defenses and sent tanks roaring into the capital city of Seoul, 35 miles south of the demarcation line. President Harry S. Truman ordered the Navy and Air Force to go immediately to South Korea's aid.

The Army Chief of Staff in 1950, General J. Lawton Collins, later noted in his book, *War in Peacetime*, that the 1st Cavalry Division in Korea "was officered chiefly by former cavalrymen or armored tankers, who took pride in their cavalry heritage and instilled the same spirit in their men. Its commander was Major General Hobart R. Gay. He had been Chief of Staff to General George S. Patton Jr. in the North African, Italian and European campaigns of the Third Army and was imbued with Patton's hell-for-leather spirit."

The 7th, 24th and 25th Infantry Divisions and the 1st Cavalry Division (organized as infantry), all on occupation duty in Japan, had assigned to them the 77th, 78th, 79th and 71st Tank Battalions, respectively. But only one company (A) of each battalion had been organized, and those companies had only M-24 light tanks. Heavier tanks, it was feared, would damage Japanese roads and bridges.

Although the rugged terrain in Korea had been considered generally unsuitable for tank employment, Russian-made T-34s were used with success by the North Koreans during the early days of the war. American tanks were rushed to the scene in support of the United Nations and engaged in their first combat on July 10. For several weeks they were outnumbered, and it was not until late August that the tank balance in Korea was tipped in favor of the United Nations. By then more than 500 US tanks were in the Pusan Perimeter, outnumbering the enemy's there by over five to one. For the remainder of the war, tank units of battalion size and smaller were in most combat actions.

Tank battalions in the early Korean fighting of July and August 1950 were the 6th, 70th, 72nd, 73rd and 89th, averaging 69 tanks each. The 6th was equipped with M-46 Pattons; the other battalions were about equally divided between M-26 Pershings and M4A3 Shermans. The 64th Tank Battalion entered the war in early November 1950 with the 3rd Infantry Division. By early December, the U.S. had shipped 1,188 medium and 188 light tanks to Korea.

No armored divisions were sent to Korea, although six armored divisions, the 1st, 2nd, 3rd, 5th, 6th and 7th were soon active. Actually only two, the 1st and 2nd, were organized as armored, the others being principally training organizations and only the 2nd went overseas, going to Germany in 1951.

The 8th Cavalry Regiment, reinforced by Division Artillery and other units, landed first and moved by train, truck and jeeps to relieve the 24th Infantry Division's 21st Infantry Regiment near Yongdong. The 5th Cavalry's Regimental Combat Team marched quickly toward Taejon. Four days later after Typhoon Helene pounded the Korean coastline, the 7th Cavalry Regiment and the remainder of the division's troops arrived ashore.

Ferrying the 1st Cavalry from Japan had been tense duty for the convoy sailors led by Rear Admiral James H. Doyle. Once the First Team was deployed in Korea, Doyle revealed that Navy sonarmen had detected submarines, presumably Russian, "all around us" while the LSTs and screening ships crossed the Sea of Japan.

The 1st Cavalry Division arrived one-third under-strength, short on supplies and largely using equipment left over from World War II. Quick enemy advances already had changed its original mission, a behind-the-lines amphibious assault on the port city of Inchon. But morale was high. The Division's fighting spirit desperately was needed to help reverse the Allies' retreat. The war was in immediate danger of being lost.

The enemy used many tactics. Some of its soldiers attacked wearing American uniforms. The North Koreans cruelly herded refugees across mine fields, then followed with tanks and infantry. Enemy soldiers disguised themselves with the long, flowing robes of refugees and carried weapons and explosives behind troopers' positions. The wary cavalrymen soon learned to use mine detectors to catch "refugees" carrying arms.

The 1st Cavalry Division was assigned to defend a 35-mile-long sector of the Naktong River Line, extending from three miles north of Waegwan southward to the area defended by the 24th Infantry Division. To the 1st Cavalry's stretched American and ROK forces, under the command of Lieutenant General Walton C. Walker, could not cover all the river's extended frontage. So Walker positioned a minimum of troops in the key hills overlooking the places where the Reds were most likely to try to cross. The bulk of Walker's forces, meanwhile, were held in reserve, ready to counterattack and drive the North Koreans back into the river. It was a classic river-line defense tactic, but its success hinged both on Walker's timing and his ability to muster enough troops from his under-strength Eighth Army.

On August 1, the First Team was ordered to set up defensive positions near Kumchon on the rail route from Taegu to Pusan. The 5th and 7th Cavalry Regiments accomplished this and the 5th Cavalry also screened the withdrawal of the 25th Infantry Division. This allowed the establishment of a new defensive line to the rear.

For more than 50 days, between late July and mid-September, First Team troopers and other UN soldiers performed the difficult, bloody task of holding on to the vital Pusan Perimeter. The UN sector was roughly 50 miles wide, from the Naktong River to the Sea of Japan, and about 100 miles deep. The North Koreans, who now held the rest of the country, kept probing all along the perimeter, looking for places where their main force could break through, split the defenders and take the UN's last stronghold.

The 7th Cavalry came under attack from Hills 490 and 518 and finally was forced to withdraw after repulsing human waves of enemy. The Reds lost 425 killed. The 61st, 77th and attached 9th Field Artillery batteries stayed on the move, dodging counter-fire. But they also unleashed 3,800 rounds in delivering 154 fire missions.

The First Team pulled back some forward positions and tightened its defenses. The 5th Cavalry withstood two more punishing attacks, but the North Korean push finally ground to a halt on September 8, seven miles short.

The North Koreans fiercely resisted the breakout from their positions on key hills. The 5th Cavalry ran into tough fighting along the Taegu-Waegwan highway and railroad, especially at Hill 203. The 8th Cavalry started up the "Bowling Alley" on September 20, but after 1,000 yards began receiving heavy crossfire. The regiment took heavy casualties and finally had to withdraw to its original positions. But this was to be the last major enemy resistance on the perimeter.

Also on September 20, the 7th Cavalry, which was being held in reserve, began preparing to join the break-out. The regiment (less the 2/7 Cavalry which was in Eighth Army Reserve) was organized into two battalion combat teams under Task Force 777 by Lieutenant Colonel William A. Harris. Harris had assumed command after leading the 77th Field Artillery Battalion. Task Force 777 took its name from the 7th Cavalry and the 77th Field Artillery. The 1/7 Cavalry Battalion Combat Team, meanwhile, was named Task Force Witherspoon for its commander Major William Witherspoon. The 3/7 Cavalry's Battalion Combat Team was called Task Force Lynch, taking its name from Lieutenant Colonel James H. Lynch. Each task force had a battery from the 77th Field Artillery Battalion, plus a company from the 8th Engineer Battalion, elements of the 70th Tank Battalion, a platoon each from the regimental heavy weapons company, and an air liaison team. Task Force 777 contained the rest of the organic and attached units, and Task Force Lynch was named the lead element for the break-out operation.

September 27 was a day the Spirit of the Cavalry rejoiced. With skillful employment of mobility, shifting firepower and shock action, the hallmarks of traditional cavalry, First Team troopers once again had achieved a long thrust into enemy lines, cutting off and demoralizing Red units. This allowed quick mop-up by First Team units following to consolidate the gains. North of Osan a sign soon appeared, "This drive from Taegu to Osan, a distance of 196 road miles and 166 air miles, marks the longest advance in the history of the American Army through enemy held territory.

From MacArthur came new orders for the 1st Cavalry and other UN forces: Cross the 38th Parallel. The Reds had lost an estimated 200,000 men in South Korea and more than 40,000 of their troops had been captured. With their new defeats and heavy losses, their defenses were crumbling rapidly.

After a tough fight at Hokkyo-ri, halfway up the highway, the capital city fell on October 19. Troopers of the 1st Cavalry, once again upholding the hard-earned reputation of the First Team, were the first UN forces to enter the city. Members of Company F, 5th Cavalry Regiment, arrived 18 minutes ahead of the South Korean 1st Division. Meanwhile, North Korea's government hastily relocated closer to Manchuria. The 187th Airborne Regiment parachuted 2,800 men about 30 miles north of Pyongyang and trapped more enemy troops.

With the harsh Korean winter setting in, ROK and UN units pushed north toward the Yalu River. Part of the 1st Cavalry at first remained in Pyongyang, refitting and mopping up resistance. The 8th Cavalry's 1st Battalion and the 70th Tank Battalion moved out and made contact with the paratroopers near Sunch'on.

On October 28, orders came from I Corps to saddle up the rest of the Division and move north. The Korean War seemed to be nearing its conclusion. North Korean forces were being squeezed into a shrinking perimeter along the Yalu and the borders of Red China and Manchuria. By now, more than 135,000 Red troops had been captured and the North Korean army was virtually destroyed.

Barely four days later, however, the Korean War took a grim new turn. The UN Forces, including the 1st Cavalry, were hit broadside by masses of Red Chinese troops. The sudden move caught the UN troops heavily outnumbered and dangling at the end of long, precarious supply lines. A bloody second chapter had come to the "limited" war.

The fortunes of war began to change swiftly for the UN forces on October 25, 1950. On that day, the worst fear of the front-line troops came to life. The North Koreans gained the aggressive support of a formidable ally. Masses of Red Chinese soldiers from General Lin Piao's 4th Field army suddenly attacked the ROK II Corps below the Yalu and sent the South Koreans reeling. Undetected, the Red Chinese had slipped more than a quarter of a million fresh, well-trained soldiers into North Korea. Leaving behind their heavy equipment, the Chicoms had moved at night or beneath canopies of smoke, deliberately setting at least 10 forest fires to hide their southward advance. To avoid detection by UN reconnaissance planes, they also had spent the daylight hours resting in perfectly camouflaged encampments or in huts, buildings, mine shafts and rocky ravines.

"Each Chinese soldier going into action was a self-sufficient unit," General Matthew B. Ridgeway wrote in his book, *The Korean War*. A Red Chinese infantryman was "equipped with cooked food (they wanted no fires to betray their positions) in the form of rice, beans, corn, and sufficient small-arms ammunition to last four or five days - after which he would either be relieved or would retreat to his main battle line and be replaced by fresh units, depending on the course of battle."

But the Chinese were attacking in force with waves of soldiers, and a favorite, and fearsome, weapon of the Soviet army, 82mm Katyusha rockets. Against the South Koreans, the Chinese also were making effective use of horse-mounted cavalry, and irony of modern war that would not be lost on the 1st Cavalry Division's dismounted troopers.

During the morning of November 1, patrols from the 8th Cavalry's 1st and 2nd Battalions clashed with soldiers clearly identified as Red Chinese. Still, General Gay did not receive orders to withdraw until 11:00 p.m., after the Chicoms had mauled three South Korean divisions, rushed south of the 8th Cavalry's right flank, cut the main road below Unsan, and were preparing for encirclement. By then, an orderly, safe pullback was not possible. The troopers prepared for heavy combat.

In the darkness, the cavalrymen heard bugles, horses, shrill whistles and American obscenities shouted with Chinese accents. Then the Chicoms charged, in a wild massive assault that swept forward in human waves. Ignoring horrible casualties, the Reds climbed over piles of their own dead and kept coming as the outnumbered cavalrymen pumped frantic fire into their ranks.

With the Chinese readying their final attack, some 200 men and a half-dozen surviving officers tried a heroic but desperate dash. They fought their way through a hole in the enemy lines and reached the nearby mountains. But they soon were surrounded again. Splitting into small groups, they tried to filter out, but most were killed or captured. "On November 6," General Collins wrote, "the 3rd Battalion, 8th Cavalry Regiment, ceased to exist as a unit. It died gallantly. More than 600 officers and men of the 8th Cavalry Regiment were lost at Unsan, most from the 3rd Battalion."

On January 22, 1951, the First Team's revitalized 3rd Battalion, 8th Cavalry, rebounded from its tragedy at Unsan and moved back into action. It conducted a reconnaissance mission against light resistance.

Three days later, led personally by Ridgway, the 8th Army returned to the offensive, and the 1st Cavalry Division was to play key roles in the new operation.

Chief – The last living Cavalry horse, Fort Riley, KS, 1963.

On February 14, heavy fighting erupted around an objective known as Hill 578, which finally was taken by the 7th Cavalry after stiff Chinese resistance. During this action, General MacArthur paid a welcome visit to the First Team.

Seoul fell to parts of the Eighth Army on March 15. To the east, meanwhile, the 1st Cavalry joined units of X Corps and advanced through the center of Korea toward Chunchon. A day earlier, the 3rd Battalion, 8th Cavalry had crossed the Hangchon River under Chinese fire.

After Chunchon was taken on March 19, X Corps and ROK III Corps continued to drive the Chinese back across forbidding terrain and through the valley of the Pukhan River. The new objectives were to keep the Chinese from rebuilding and resupplying their forces and to advance to the "Kansas Line."

The Kansas Line roughly followed the 38th Parallel and the winding Imjin River. Part of the line, however, was the Hwachon Reservoir, which was above the demarcation line and about 60 miles north and west of Seoul. Most of the Kansas Line was secured by April 9. But the countryside and the enemy kept X Corps' advance elements from reaching the vicinity of the reservoir until April 11.

On April 22, 1951, a massive enemy force, 21 Chinese and nine North Korean divisions, slammed into the Kansas Line. Their main goal was to recapture Seoul. The UN troops withdrew through previously established delaying positions to a defense line just noth of Seoul. The 1st Cavalry Division joined the defense line and the bitter battle to keep the Reds out of the South Korean capital. This time, the enemy was stopped.

Next, the Reds tried to go around Seoul's defenders with an attack that began after dark, May 15. They pushed 30 miles south in five days, but were hit hard with artillery fire and counterattacks. Their large forces were no match for concentrated firepower and prepared defenses. Before they could withdraw to regroup, the Eighth Army moved forward and rolled almost all the way back to the Kansas Line. Later, the First Team cracked deeper into North Korea, reaching the towns of Yonchon and Chorwon, at the base of the "Iron Triangle," on June 9, 1951. The Iron Triangle was an enemy resupply area encompassing three small towns.

From June 9 to November 27, the 1st Cavalry took on various roles in the UN's summer-fall campaign. On July 18, 1 year after it had entered the war, the division was assigned a reserve status, but this duty did not last long. The war was settling into a pattern of patrols, ambushes, artillery duels and firefights along lines that remained mostly static. Big battles, however, still remained.

On the nights of September 21 and 22, the 7th Cavalry's 2nd and 3rd Battalions repulsed waves of Red Chinese with hand-to-hand fighting. But harder work soon followed, when Operation Commando was launched. The mission was to push the Chinese out of their winter defense positions south of the Yokkok River. The 1st Cavalry drew the task of blasting almost an entire Chinese army from caves, reinforced bunkers and elaborate trenches in the steep hills.

The Chinese defense line had been given the name "Line Jamestown." On October 3, the 1st Cavalry moved out from Line Wyoming and immediately ran into Red fire. For the next two days, hills were taken, lost and retaken. On the third day, however, the Red lines began to crack in front of the 7th Cavalry. Also, on October 5, the 8th Cavalry captured Hill 418, a flanking hill on which the northern end of Line Jamestown was anchored.

The Chinese counterattacked twice, unsuccessfully, against the 7th Cavalry on October 10-11. Two days later, the 8th Cavalry took the central pivot of the line, Hill 272. Line Jamestown's southern sector held out longer despite heavy strikes by B-26 bombers. But it, too, eventually fell to the determined troopers. So did a hill called "Old Baldy."

The troopers did not yet know it, but Line Jamestown was to be their last major combat in the Korean War.

In December 1951, the 1st Cavalry Division's 549 days of combat in the Korean War came to a well-earned and welcome end. Orders arrived transferring the division to defensive duties on Hokkaido, Japan's northernmost and second-largest island.

The Korean War, the "limited" war, would drag on in bloody stalemate until July 27, 1953. The First Team had performed tough duties with honor, pride, valor and distinction, and it had won new "firsts" for its continuing record book.

The decade following the Korean armistice was marked by two major reorganizations of US Army divisions, both of which influenced the structure of armor units: First to come was the pentomic plan of 1957-59, then the Reorganization Objective Army Divisions (ROAD) plan of 1962-64. Underlying these reorganizations were developments in nuclear weapons that made wide dispersion, high mobility and great flexibility - without loss of massed firepower - mandatory characteristics for military forces. Combat areas of future nuclear wars were viewed as much broader and deeper than battlefields of the past, requiring small, self-contained, fast-moving units. Speed was imperative not only in the concentration of forces for attack but also in dispersion for defense. On the other hand, the Army had to retain its ability to fight limited or non-nuclear wars, where the requirements for mobility or dispersion were not as important.

Tests of new division organizational concepts for atomic warfare, begun in early 1955, culminated in late 1956 in the pentomic organization, and by mid-1958 the new scheme had been applied to all armored divisions. Since combat commands already provided much of the flexibility that was sought, little change was made in the basic structure of the armored division. The greatest change was in firepower, the division artillery being given an atomic capability. The division still had its four tank battalions, and all were authorized 90mm gun

tanks (one battalion had previously been authorized 120mm gun tanks). Armored infantry and field artillery battalions also remained at four each. A small increase in tanks brought the full-strength total to 360 - 306 mounting 90mm guns and 54 mounting 76mm's. Strength of the new division stood at 14,617, only 34 fewer than its former number.

From 1951-55 the Regular Army had two active armored divisions - the 1st and the 2nd. In 1955 the 3rd and 4th were added. Three continued as active divisions for the remainder of the 1953-68 period; the 1st Armored Division was reduced to a single combat command from 1957-62.

By late 1955 the Army National Guard armored divisions had been increased from two to six by converting four infantry division, the 27th, 30th (the portion in Tennessee), 40th and 48th. The North Carolina portion of the 30th Infantry Division became a full infantry division and retained "30th" also as its numerical designation. As of mid-1967, Army National Guard had the following armor units: six armored divisions, two armored brigades (separate), seven armored cavalry regiments, an armored cavalry squadron and 16 separate tank battalions. Also, the 17 infantry divisions of the National Guard had 34 tank battalions and 17 cavalry squadrons.

The second major reorganization of Army divisions, know as ROAD, was completed in 1964. Under this plan the Army was to have four types of divisions: airborne, infantry, armored and mechanized. The base upon which each was built, being essentially the same. All had their usual types of organic reconnaissance, artillery and support units. The main differences came in the maneuver elements (tank and infantry battalions) which varied with mission and other factors. All had three brigade headquarters, which, in the armored division, corresponded to its former combat commands. Thus while the organization of all divisions became more flexible, the change in the armored division was less than in other types.

For example, a ROAD armored division with a composition of six tank and five mechanized infantry battalions would have a full-strength total of 15,966. Since each tank battalion was equipped with two light and 54 medium gun tanks and each

mechanized infantry battalion had two light gun tanks, this combination of maneuver battalions gave an armored division 40 light and 324 medium-gun tanks, including the 18 light tanks of its armored cavalry squadron.

Concurrent with the division reorganizations, another major change having far-reaching effect upon the organization of most combat type units was the Combat Arms Regimental System, or CARS. Arrival of the atomic era with its new weapons and tactical doctrine had rendered the regiment, the traditional fighting unit of the Army, obsolete - it was too large.

Even during World War II armored regiments, except those of the 2nd and 3rd Armored Divisions, were broken up to form separate battalions and many old cavalry regiments had been dismembered to form new units. With approval of the CARS plan early in 1957, the old cavalry and armored regiments could be revived, at least in name, to continue their regimental histories.

As illustrated in Chart No. 1, the plan provided an average of approximately 15 battalions that could be organized to perpetuate the lineage and honors of a single regiment. The regimental headquarters was placed under Department of the Army control, and the other regimental elements were used to form separate battalions or squadrons as needed. Within these battalions and squadrons the organic elements were new.

Parent regiments for use under CARS were carefully selected. Except for the 2nd, 3rd, 6th, 11th and 14th Armored Cavalry Regiments, the 1st through the 17th Cavalry Regiments were included. Armor parent regiments were the 32nd through the 35th, the 37th, 40th, 63rd, 64th, the 66th through 70th, and the 72nd, 73rd, 77th and 81st. A subsequent decision by the Department of the Army that CARS cavalry regiments would contain reconnaissance-type units instead of tank battalions caused the redesignation of three cavalry regiments, the 13th, 15th and 16th, as the 13th, 15th and 16th Armor. Not affected by this decision were those elements of the 5th, 7th and 8th Cavalry assigned to the 1st Cavalry Division which, remained organized as infantry. When the CARS reorganization was completed, cavalry had nine regiments and armor had 20. Elements of these parent regiments were organized in both the Regular Army and the Army Reserve. Army National Guard parent regiments were selected from National Guard units.

Under the 1963 reorganization of the armored cavalry regiment, its organic elements reverted to the traditional cavalry designations of squadrons and troops and an aviation company was added. There was little change in the personnel or tank totals for the regiment. Under the 1965 tables, the regiment's full strength rose to 3,349, an increase of 550, and an air cavalry troop replaced the aviation company. The 1965 regiment had 48 helicopters, while its tanks numbered 132, an increase of 10.

In an era abundant with new weapons and organizations for the modern Army, yet another new military concept dawned in the mid-1950s when air vehicles were included in cavalry units. As part of a training maneuver, Operation Sagebrush, during the winter of 1955-56, tests were made of an organization, called Sky Cav, that had light tanks, reinforced infantry and helicopters. Among its special equipment were electronic, photographic and other devices for detecting an enemy at night as well as during the day. Initially, the idea stemmed from a broadening of the term communications to cover "not only the transmission of information

Officers, 2nd Squadron, 10th Cavalry, Unchoni, Korea. Northernmost U.S. Camp in Korea, 1961. (Courtesy of C.M. Ferguson, Jr.)

within Army units but also the acquisition and relay of combat intelligence on enemy activities, including observation and reconnaissance." It was in the nature of this reconnaissance phase of communications that "Sky Cav," combining both air and ground elements in the same unit, was born. First to be authorized a unit of this type was the airborne division, its airborne reconnaissance troop of 1956 being authorized 12 helicopters (10 light cargo and 2 observation). In 1957, with the advent of CARS, Troop B, 17th Cavalry, was organized in the 101st Airborne Division and was soon followed by Troop A, 17th Cavalry, in the 82nd Airborne Division.

By late 1957 the feasibility of armed helicopters had been accepted by the Department of the Army, and a third dimension was added to the Army battlefield. In September 1959 a provisional unit, called an aerial reconnaissance and security troop, was organized for test purposes within the 2nd Infantry Division. It was equipped with 27 helicopters, 17 of which were armed.

When the divisions were reorganized under ROAD, the 1963 tables of organization and equipment provided for an air cavalry troop in the armored cavalry squadron in all types of divisions. The mission of air cavalry troop was described as being the extension, by aerial means, of the squadron's reconnaissance and security capabilities. The troop's principal elements were an aero scout platoon, an aero rifle platoon, a service platoon, a flight operations section, and an aero weapons section. At full strength, it was equipped with 26 helicopters. In the airborne division, the air cavalry troop had greater fire power and a few more men.

When the 120mm gun tank was eliminated in late 1955, more emphasis had been placed upon the medium-gun tank as the Army's main battle tank. By mid-1959 the first of the new M-60 series, in the medium tank class was placed in production. Mounting a 105mm gun and having a diesel engine, the M-60 had more firepower and greater operational range than its predecessor, the M-48. It also had improved crew protection and slightly less over-all weight.

The development of an entirely new weapons system, known as the Shillelagh, to provide a direct fire, surface-to-surface, guided missile that could be vehicle mounted, was hailed in 1961 as the initiation of a program to produce a "radical, new main battle tank." Four years later the Shillelagh system was installed on a revolutionary new tank, the XM551 General Sheridan, and for the first time a guided missile became part of a combat vehicle's main armament. Its 152mm gun launcher had the dual capability of firing conventional rounds and launching missiles; the conventional ammunition represented another first with its fully combustible cartridge case. Also, with aluminum armor, the new tank weighted only about 16.5 tons combat loaded and had a maximum speed of over 40 miles per hour. The General Sheridan not only had greater firepower and ground mobility than any other current US Army tank but also had both amphibious and airdrop capabilities. Moreover, its Shillelagh missile system was adaptable for installation on existing tanks in the M-60 series. Changes in tactics and doctrine were in process to keep pace with the combat potential of the remarkable new tank and weapons system. Despite these giant strides in the development of armor vehicles and weapons, a program for yet another new main battle tank for the 1970 Army was already under way in a co-operative effort of the United States and West Germany. After three years of development, the first

prototype of this joint undertaking, the MBT-70, described as the most advanced military track laying combat vehicle in existence, was unveiled in October 1967.

During the summer of 1965 the 1st Cavalry Division was reorganized as still another type of division, called airmobile, and was dispatched to the Republic of Vietnam when the US Army began deploying major combat forces to help that country in its struggle for independence. The airmobile principle emphasized the use of Army aircraft to increase the division's battlefield mobility.

VIETNAM

It was not one man's dream - the notion of using helicopters as the fast, new steed of modern cavalry. The efforts and ideas of many went into the formation of the world's first air assault division. More than a decade of experiments, debates, evaluations and developments of hardware and tactics preceded the conversion, in 1965, of the 1st Cavalry Division to the air assault configuration.

As these early experiments began, the mid-50s were rife with international tensions in Europe and Asia. The "Cold War" simmered dangerously near the boiling point, new weapons and organizations to evaluate and perfect - just in case. The climate was right for trying out unorthodox tactics, as well.

Tests were conducted both with troop helicopters and with helicopters, carrying a variety of machine guns and rockets.

At Fort Benning, Georgia, in the mid-50s, General John Tolson, later a commander of the First Team in Vietnam, developed a tactical doctrine for the use of helicopters in combat, and became one of the early pioneers of modern air-mobility.

Two additional organizations and two men played vital parts in the development of the air assault concept: the Rogers Board, the Howze Board, Secretary of Defense Robert S. McNamara, and Major General Harry William Osborne Kinnard.

Several other military figures also played key roles in the development of missions, configurations and weapons for air cavalry in the mid-50s and early 60s.

Lieutenant General James M. Gavin, the Department of the Army's G-3, pushed for helicopter units that could take over, extend, and add great speed to the traditional roles of horse cavalry. Soon, at the Aviation School at Fort Rucker, Alabama, a colorful colonel named Jay D. Vanderpool, who had no official resources, threw together a "Sky Cav" platoon, using borrowed equipment and borrowed personnel. The "Sky Cav" began giving impressive, and occasionally hair-raising, demonstrations of the roles that helicopter units could fill in combat. Heralding the era of sleek gunships, the "Sky Cav" lashed a variety of weapons and rockets to its helicopters and test-fired them.

In the spring of 1962, Secretary of Defense Robert S. McNamara ordered a panel of distinguished military leaders and civilian experts to re-examine the Army's aviation needs. McNamara worried that the Army's request for aircraft, and

3rd Armored Cavalry, D Troop, 1/3 ACR
Baumholder, Germany, May-June 1967.

its plans for using them, were too conservative, given the growing troubles in several "hot spots" overseas.

The 18-member "Howze Board" commissioned by McNamara was headed by Lieutenant General Hamilton H. Howze, a man with significant links to the 1st Cavalry Division. Himself a cavalryman, Howze also was the son of the man who had been the First Team's first commanding general in 1921, Major General Robert Lee Howze.

The 1st Cavalry Division (Airmobile) arrived in Southeast Asia in 1965 and was in combat almost immediately as the enemy tested the new arrivals. Its first major action occurred in November when it struck an enemy stronghold in the highlands of Pleiku Province. Fierce combat ensued. Attacking into the Ia Drang Valley, the 1st Battalion, 7th Cavalry landed squarely in the midst of two North Vietnamese regiments. In desperate fighting, with the 1st Cavalry taking heavy losses, the enemy was decisively beaten and the 1st Cavalry blooded and proven. The heroic, successful campaign earned the division the Presidential Unit Citation, the first awarded for action in Vietnam.

In the first 17 days of 1966, the 1st and 2nd Brigades were airlifted west of Pleiku and Kontum for Operation Matador. Contact was light after the air assaults, but the search-and-destroy missions near the Cambodian border proved successful and significant in several other ways. Enemy logistics was disrupted in two provinces, more than a half million pounds of supplies were captured, and for the first time, enemy soldiers were clearly observed

escaping across the border to sanctuaries in Cambodia. Another "first" also was scored by the First Team. For the initial time in combat, troop ladders were lowered from Chinooks. The big choppers hovered above a canopy of heavy forest, and engineers scrambled down the ladders to clear the LZ with chain saws.

During Operation Nathan Hale the 2/7 captured three scrawny miniature Vietnamese horses, about pony size. They had been abandoned by the Viet Cong along a jungle trail.

The 2/7 CO quickly arranged for one of his Cavalry "wranglers" to throw the horses and tie their feet. They were then loaded in empty Hueys going back to An Khe. At 2/7 base they were put to "work" cutting grass and soon became fat and sassy. They also participated in some interesting distractions such as the time when some inebriated troopers decided to ride them through the mess tent.

In the midst of two more operations, Lewis and Clark and Davy Crockett, the First Team received a new commander in Vietnam. On May 6, 1966, during colorful ceremonies and rousing flybys of First Team aircraft, Major General Kinnard turned over his post to his replacement, Major General John Norton. General Norton, a veteran paratrooper, was no stranger to the First Team, nor its unique fighting style. In Korea in 1959-60, he had served with the 1st Cavalry as a battle group commander. Later, as a member of the Howze Board, General Norton had helped pioneer airmobility.

The first phase of Operation Davy Crockett

ended after the Cavalry's 3rd Brigade destroyed the 9th Battalion of NVA's 22nd Regiment. During the second phase of Davy Crockett, which concluded May 16, the First Team made extensive use of a new hunter-killer air assault technique developed by Colonel Harold G. Moore, commanding officer of the 3rd Brigade. The new concept was created out of a need to make better use of airmobility's efficiency. In short, too many troops were being rushed into action each time the enemy was spotted, and too many helicopters were being flown too often. The "hunter" units, small teams of lightly equipped soldiers, were inserted into operational areas to find "Charlie." Then, once an enemy force was located, larger "killer" forces, on alert at a nearby landing zone, were airlifted into action. The hunter-killer concept quickly became part of American's repertoire of tactics in the Vietnam War.

The next major operation arrived quickly for the First Team. Operation Crazy Horse commenced on May 16, amid Vietnam heat that already had soared to 110 degrees during Davy Crockett. Crazy Horse was another search-and-destroy assignment, this time into the heavily jungle hills between the Suoi Ca and Vinh Thanh valleys.

Operation Thayer II lasted from October through the end of 1966. During this operation the 1st Battalion, 7th Cavalry, operated in the Phu My District, working off many landing zones in the area.

The 11th Cavalry arrived in Vietnam in early September 1966. Shortly after its arrival the Mili-

This is what happens when you go off for training and the kids are left alone. Actually the breaks failed. (Courtesy of Jerry Edgin)

tary Assistance Command welcomed its second US Army tank battalion, the 2nd Battalion, 34th Armor, commanded by Lieutenant Colonel Raymond L. Stailey. Part of the 4th Infantry Division before being sent to Vietnam, the battalion was attached to II Field Force in the III Corps Tactical Zone to replace the 1st Battalion, 69th Armor, which had moved to the II Corps area. On September 19, Company B was detached to the 1st Infantry Division at Phu Loi, and on October 5 Company A was detached to the 25th Infantry Division at Cu Chi. Finally, Company C was sent north to I Corps Tactical Zone until December. The practice of parceling out its tank companies was to haunt this battalion throughout its service in Vietnam; seldom did it have more than one tank company under battalion control. This unfortunate practice, so characteristic of the French in Indochina, was symptomatic of a command with few armored units. It reached a new high later in the war when, for a period of several months, the commander of the 2nd Battalion, 34th Armor, again had no tank companies to command. The 11th Cavalry also suffered from the detachment practice, and there were periods when the headquarters controlled only the regimental air cavalry troop.

After Operation Attleboro in September and October 1966, units of the 11th Cavalry returned to Bien Hoa to continue Operation Atlanta, whose mission was to clear and secure lines of communication in three provinces near Saigon and to secure the new Blackhorse Base Camp, 13 kilometers south of Xuan Loc. At first the operation was limited to clearing and securing Route 1 from Xuan Loc to Bien Hoa and Route 2 to the base camp. As Atlanta continued, however, the 11th Cavalry extended its operations away from the roads and throughout the area.

From the standpoint of the number of enemy killed, and, more important, from the number of roads opened to military and civilian traffic, Atlanta was a success. Regimental experience varied from roadrunner and convoy escort duties to cordon and search operations in which the squadrons sealed off an area and then worked, both mounted and dismounted, to drive out the enemy. Throughout, the regiment was able to move at will, both on and off the roads, and experienced little difficulty with the terrain. Areas hitherto considered Viet Cong sanctuaries were entered by armored columns that destroyed base camps, fortifications and supplies.

It was during Operation Atlanta that the 11th Cavalry fought its first major battle. Twice the enemy tried to ambush and destroy resupply convoys escorted by units of the 1st Squadron, but in both attempts was defeated by the firepower and maneuverability of the cavalry. The second of these two ambushes took place on December 2, 1966, near Suoi Cat, 50 kilometers east of Saigon.

At 1600, December 2, 1965, the convoy commander, Lieutenant Wilbert Radosevich, readied his convoy for the return trip to Gia Ray. The column had a tank in the lead, followed by two ACAVs, two trucks, another ACAV, and finally the remaining tank. Lieutenant Radosevich was in the lead tank, and after making sure that he had contact with the forward air controller in an armed helicopter overhead, moved his convoy out toward Suoi Cat. As the convoy passed through Suoi Cat, the men in the column noticed an absence of children and an unusual stillness. Sensing danger, Lieutenant Radosevich was turning in the tank commander's hatch to observe closely both sides of the road when he accidentally tripped the turret control handle.

The turret moved suddenly to the right, evidently scaring the enemy into prematurely firing a command detonated mine approximately 10 meters in front of the tank. Lieutenant Radosevich immediately shouted "Ambush! Ambush! Claymore Corner!" over the troop frequency and led his convoy in a charge through what had become a hail of enemy fire while he blasted both sides of the road. Even as Lieutenant Radosevich charged, help was on the way. Troop B, nearest the scene, immediately headed toward the action. At squadron headquarters, Company D, a tank company, Troop C, and the howitzer battery hastened toward the ambush. Troop A, on perimeter security at the regimental base camp, followed as soon as it was released. The gunship on station immediately began delivering fire and called for additional assistance, while the forward air controller radioed for air support.

When the convoy reached the eastern edge of the ambush, one of the ACAVs, already hit three times, was struck again and caught fire. At this point Troop B arrived, moved into the ambush from the east, and immediately came under intense fire as the enemy maneuvered toward the burning ACAV. Troop B fought its way through the ambush, alternately employing the herringbone formation and moving west, and encountering the enemy in sizable groups.

Lieutenant Colonel Martin D. Howell, the squadron commander, arrived over the scene by helicopter 10 minutes after the first fire. He immediately designated National Highway 1 a fire coordination line, and directed tactical aircraft to strike to the east and south while artillery fired to the north and west. As Company D and Troop C reached Suoi Cat, he ordered them to begin firing as they left the east side of the village. The howitzer battery went into position in Suoi Cat. By this time Troop B had traversed the entire ambush area, turned around, and was making a second trip back toward the east. Company D and Troop C followed close behind, raking both sides of the road with fire as they moved. The tanks fired 90mm canister, mowing down the charging Viet Cong and destroying a 57mm recoilless rifle. Midway through the ambush zone, Troop B halted in a herringbone formation, while Company D and Troop C continued to the east toward the junction of Route 333 and Route 1. Troop A, now to the west of the ambush, entered the area, surprised a scavenging party, and killed 15 Viet Cong.

The squadron commander halted Troop A to the west of Troop B. Company D was turned around at the eastern side of the ambush and positioned to the east of Troop B. Troop C was sent southeast on Route 1 to trap enemy forces if they move in that direction. As Troops A and B and Company D consolidated at the ambush site, enemy fire became intense around Troop B. The Viet Cong forces were soon caught in a deadly crossfire when the cavalry units converged. As darkness approached, the American troops prepared night defensive positions and artillery fire was shifted to the south to seal off enemy escape routes. A search of the battlefield the next morning revealed over 100 enemy dead. The toll, however, was heavier than that. Enemy documents captured in May 1967 recorded the loss of three Viet Cong battalion commanders and four company commanders in the Suoi Cat action.

The success of the tactics for countering ambushes developed during Atlanta resulted in their adoption as standard procedure for the future. The tactics called for the ambushed element to employ all its firepower to protect the escorted vehicles and fight clear of the enemy killing zone. Once clear, the cavalry would regroup and return to the killing zone. All available reinforcements would be rushed to the scene as rapidly as possible to attack the flanks of the ambush. Artillery and tactical air would be used to the maximum extent. This technique was used with success by the 11th Cavalry throughout its stay in Vietnam.

Throughout 1967 and 1968, the 1st Cavalry Division and the 11th Cavalry Regiment conducted a series of offensive actions that put great pressure on enemy elements within South Vietnam.

After the success of operations against enemy sanctuaries in South Vietnam, the next step was sealing the borders, or at least making them reasonably secure. With the growing demands of pacification and the prospect of troop withdrawals, which would limit the resources available, the task naturally fell to mobile units, both ground and air, that could move rapidly and control large areas. Armored and airmobile units became the mainstay of border operations, particularly those in the critical III Corps area north of Saigon.

Based at Phuoc Vinh, the 1st Cavalry Division, with three brigades of airmobile infantry and operational control over the 11th Armored Cavalry, was extended among more than a hundred kilometers of borders from east of Bu Dop to northwest of Tay Ninh City, opposite enemy base area 354. The 25th Infantry Division controlled the western and southern approaches to Saigon, and the 1st Infantry Division commanded the entrances to the Saigon River corridor and the old, now quiet war zones in southern Binh Long and Phuoc Long provinces.

Border operations of the armored cavalry, the air cavalry, and the airmobile infantry of the 1st Cavalry Division illustrate the tactics of both sides in the conflict. As the enemy tried to cross the border in strength, supported from bases beyond South Vietnamese boundaries, the defenders attempted to prevent the crossing with firepower and maneuver. By early 1970 the cavalry and airmobile infantry forces had developed some sophisticated techniques employing Rome plow cutting, sensors and automatic ambush devices to deny the use of trails to the enemy. These techniques were first applied systematically in the northwestern part of the III Corps area from Bu Dop to Loc Ninh along QL-14A and almost immediately produced good results. The 2nd Squadron, 11th Armored Cavalry, controlled this region from Fire Support Base Ruth outside Bu Dop and patrolled east and west along the Cambodian border.

Early on the morning of January 20, 1970, as Lieutenant Colonel Grail L. Brookshire, commander of the 2nd Squadron, and Colonel Donn A. Starry, the regimental commander, conferred at Fire Support Base Ruth, a deluge of mortar and rocket fire descended on the base. Both commanders took off in helicopters, and while Colonel Brookshire gathered his squadron, Colonel Starry requested tactical air, air cavalry, and artillery fire support. Two battalions of the 65th North Vietnamese Regiment and part of an anti-aircraft regiment had occupied a dry lake bed about three kilometers west of the base; it was from near this crescent-shaped opening in the otherwise dense jungle that the indirect fire attack on the base began. Later it was learned that the enemy had hoped to lure the American forces into an airmobile assault into the clearing, where carefully sited antiaircraft guns would have devastated such a force.

As gunship, tactical air, and artillery fire was

brought in, a scout helicopter was shot down, leaving the wounded pilot stranded in a bomb crater. The 2nd Squadron began to move to the location, with the tanks of Company H approaching from the north and the cavalry of Troops F and G from the south. A Cobra pilot, Captain Carl B. Marshall, located the flaming wreckage and spotted the wounded pilot, First Lieutenant William Parris, waving from the bomb crater. Captain Marshall flew in low and landed nearby in a hail of machine gun and mortar fire. Lieutenant Parris raced to the aircraft and dove into the front seat, where he lay across the gunner's lap, legs dangling from the open canopy, as Captain Marshall pulled up, barely clearing the wood line.

Artillery, fighter bombers and gunships descended on the enemy, while Troop F hastened up Highway 14A to link up with Troop G which was already heading north. After crossing a meadow near Bau Ba Linh and a seemingly unfordable stream, Troop G bore into the jungle. Ninety minutes and two kilometers of single and double canopy jungle later, Troop G arrived, joined Troop F, and, on line, the cavalry assaulted. From the helicopter Colonel Starry had meanwhile called for an airdrop of tear gas clusters on enemy bunkers toward the north side of the crescent. Colonel Brookside halted the artillery fire long enough for the drop, which brought the enemy troops out of the bunkers and sent them running north for the

border. Colonel Brookshire then ordered artillery and gunship fire while Troops G and F attacked through the enemy positions. Company H, in position north of the crescent, caught the fleeing enemy with canister and machine gun fire.

The ground forces continued to fight and maneuver until nightfall. Darkness prevented a detailed search, and the next morning the 2nd Squadron pulled out at dawn. The fight had lasted almost 14 hours, with over 600 rounds of artillery fired, 30 tactical strikes employed, and 50 Cobra rocket loads delivered. The 65th North Vietnamese Regiment did not appear again in battle for nearly four months. Colonel Brookshire's search of the crescent was broken off abruptly as he moved to reinforce the regiment's 1st Squadron, fighting near An Loc.

Early on January 21, 1970, 35 kilometers to the west, the 1st Squadron, which was operating in a Loc Ninh rubber plantation, intercepted two North Vietnamese battalions moving south into Loc Ninh District. The 11th Armored Cavalry piled on with Colonel Brookshire's 2nd Squadron racing in from the crescent battleground to the northeast and Lieutenant Colonel George C. Hoffmaster's 3rd Squadron attacking north along Highway 13 out of An Loc. Over half of the regiment converged on the fight in less than three hours and broke the back of the enemy attack. The two North Vietnamese battalions ran for cover in Cambodia, with elements

of the cavalry pursuing them to the border. The pursuit was aided by a map found on the North Vietnamese commander that showed the escape plan. Those fugitives who reached the escape routes were met by tactical air and artillery fire. After these two fights and a few more with the same outcome, the enemy showed reluctance to risk a fight with the cavalry, whose mobility and firepower had been overwhelming.

Operations along Highway 14A were so successful in drying up enemy logistical operations along the jungle trails that it was decided to repeat the scheme in War Zone C. The plan was to stop the supply operations of the enemy's 50th Rear Service Group operating out of the Cambodian Fishhook area into the Saigon River corridor through War Zone C. The American forces were to conduct extensive land clearing operations along Route 246, generally east and west across War Zone C, thus blocking the north and south trails from Cambodia to the Saigon River corridor.

By mid-February Rome plows had cleared a swath of jungle 400 to 500 meters wide along Highway 246 from An Loc in Binh Long Province to Katum in Tay Ninh Province, just south of the border. Along this cut the 11th Armored Cavalry began operations. The 3rd Squadron anchored the east flank near An Loc, the 2nd Squadron held the middle, and the 1st Squadron covered the west in northwestern Tay Ninh Province. Airmobile infan-

Colonel Lee Lewane, Commander, 1st Brigade (saluting mounted on German Riding Academy horse at far left) "Trooping The Line" at mounted armor review of 1st Brigade, 1st Armored Division, stock barracks at Illesheim, Germany with Major Ken White, 4/35 Armor and SP-4 Justo Rodreguez, 4/35 Armor, Color-Bearer. May 1972.

try battalions of the 1st Cavalry Division, operating south in War Zone C, frequently under control of the 11th Armored Cavalry, completed the interdiction force.

Colonel Starry was convinced that to cut enemy supply lines successfully ground had to be held, and that control of the ground followed from constant use of the ground. The operational pattern of the regiment, therefore, was one of extensive patrolling, day and night, and the setting up of an intricate network of manned and unmanned ambushes all along the trail system. The cavalry soon came to know the enemy's trails well, and by clever use of automatic devices reduced logistical operations to a trickle. The ambush net cost the enemy 10 to 30 casualties each night. Every site was checked and electrical devices were moved and reset each day. It was like running a long trapline.

Monitoring enemy radio traffic, the 11th Armored Cavalry learned that enemy units to the south were desperate for food and ammunition. Enemy relief parties were killed in ambushes or by the cavalry units that took advantage of information gleaned from careless enemy radio operators. Enemy messengers sent along the trails were killed or captured; their messages and plans provided information for setting up more traps.

The enemy, reluctant to confront the cavalry, attacked only by fire in War Zone C, and tried to outflank the net of ambushes. The 209th North Vietnamese Army Regiment lost over 200 men when it ran headlong into Captain John S. Caldwell's Troop L, 3rd Squadron, in the Loc Ninh rubber plantation in March. Later, in April, the 95C North Vietnamese Regiment, trying to move west around the ambush system, encountered Lieutenant Colonel James B. Reed's 1st Squadron near Katum. With the cavalry and tanks of the 1st Squadron heavily engaged, Colonel Starry alerted Colonel Brookshire to move two troops from the 2nd Squadron west to join in the fight. The enemy now had two battalions locked in combat with the 1st Squadron, while a third battalion was escaping to the north. Realizing he faced the cavalry regiment, the enemy commander panicked and began broadcasting instructions to his battalions in the clear. As the enemy troops tried to disengage, intercepts of the instructions they were receiving were passed to Colonel Reed. Armed with this information, the 1st Squadron blocked the enemy. In the ensuing melee the cavalry squadrons virtually destroyed the

M2A2 Bradley fighting vehicle. (Courtesy of Ed Daily)

M1A1 Abrams main battle tank. (Courtesy of Ed Daily)

Horse Troop of the 1st Cavalry Division stationed at Fort Hood, Texas, preparing for the charge. 1995. (Courtesy of Ed Daily)

two battalions opposing Colonel Reed. Some of the 3rd Battalion to the north escaped despite air strikes and artillery fire placed along the escape routes.

It was more than six months before the North Vietnamese 95C Regiment fought again. The extensive system of Rome plow cuts and the presence of cavalry and airmobile forces in late 1969 enabled free world forces to choke off enemy supply lines and neutralize bases in War Zone C. More so than at any other period in the war, except when the attacks were made into Cambodia, enemy access to South Vietnam was cut off.

While the First Cavalry Division demonstrated the advantages of air mobility and the 11th Cavalry combined aggressive ground and air offensive action, there were other cavalry units carrying out similar actions. Each infantry division had an organic cavalry squadron and each separate brigade had a cavalry troop.

At this time, the division cavalry squadron was a powerful force and those in Vietnam modified to meet the particular challenges of that war. The squadron had a strength of approximately 1,050 men. The three ground cavalry troops, A. B. and C, were formed of a headquarters and three platoons, each of three tanks and seven armored cavalry assault vehicles (ACAV). The ACAVs were M113 armored personnel carriers mounting one caliber .50 machine gun and two 7.62 mm machine guns, each with a gun shield. The D Troop, an air cavalry troop, had a headquarters and three platoons. The scout platoon has equipped with light observation helicopters; the aero-rifle platoon was an infantry platoon with troop-carrying helicopters; and the weapons platoon had Cobra gunships. The troop had 27 helicopters. The Squadron Headquarters Troop included two flame thrower M113 ar-

AIR CAVALRY OPERATIONS

As a necessary complement to ground armored forces, air cavalry units brought a new dimension to the Vietnam conflict. The first air cavalry unit, the 1st Squadron, 9th Cavalry, 1st Cavalry Division, exploited the concept and literally wrote the book on air cavalry operations. Few other air cavalry units, particularly those with divisional cavalry squadrons, were assigned air cavalry roles at first; instead, they were used to escort airmobile operations—like armed helicopter companies. After the armor study and the assignment of more experienced and innovative commanders, air cavalry troops finally began to operate in air cavalry missions. Quite often, however, rotation of commanders, particularly senior commanders, required that lessons be re-learned time and again. There was thus a continuing discussion on the proper role and the command of air cavalry units.

In units that properly used air cavalry, operations followed a daily pattern. Upon receipt of information indicating enemy activity, an air reconnaissance was conducted by the troop to determine whether or not further exploitation by ground forces was required. If ground reconnaissance was desirable, the troop commander usually committed his aerorifle platoon. A standby reserve force could be called by the troop commander if the situation required. The air cavalry troop commander controlled all reaction forces until more than one company from a supporting unit was committed. At the time control passed to the commander responsible for the area, and the operation was conducted like a typical ground or airmobile engagements, often with the air cavalry remaining in support. Major General John J. Tolson, Commander, 1st Cavalry Division, clearly stated his feeling about air cavalry: "I cannot emphasize how valuable this unit, 1st Squadron, 9th Cavalry, has been to me as division commander. Over 50% of our major contacts have not been initiated by actions of this squadron.

To be successful, air cavalry operations had to be swiftly followed by ground or airmobile elements of the division or regiment. Unfortunately, in many units with air cavalry, reported leads were frequently not followed up. Consequently, many air cavalry units adopted the unofficial practice of developing leads that could be handled by the air cavalry itself.

In October 1967, two air cavalry squadrons, the 3rd and 7th Squadrons, 17th Cavalry, arrived. Because they were the first units of their type to be assigned to US infantry divisions in Vietnam, their integration into the force was accomplished with some difficulty. Most problems reflected a lack of knowledge on the part of the division commander and staff concerning capabilities, limitations and basic support needs of air cavalry squadrons. There was an unfortunate tendency to use the aircraft for command and control and for transportation in airmobile operations rather than for reconnaissance. At the outset, therefore, air cavalry was not used to best advantage, and there was some misuse. Only after commanders became more aware of the capabilities of their air cavalry squadrons was proper employment achieved, and in some cases the process was slow and painful.

Re-enacting the Brandy Station Battle. (Courtesy of Ed Daily)

mored personnel carriers and two mounting 106mm recoilless rifles.

The cavalry troops of the separate brigades were generally organized without tanks. Where tanks were included in cavalry troops, they were initially M48A3 main battle tanks, mounting 90mm guns, a caliber .30 coaxial machine gun, and a commander's caliber .50 machine gun. In some cavalry units, these tanks were later replaced with M551 Sheridans.

The Americal Division, formed overseas as it had been in World War II was a unique division. It was composed of three separate infantry brigades that had deployed independently to Vietnam. Originally formed as Task Force Oregon, when the task force was organized as a division the 1st Squadron, 1st Cavalry Regiment, was sent from the 1st Armored Division at Fort Hood and attached to the Americal as its division cavalry squadron. Because the 11th, 196th, and 198th Infantry brigades of the division each had its own cavalry troop, the 1st Squadron, 1st Cavalry operated generally as a complete unit instead of having its troops often detached to support infantry elements. Operating in the relatively flat ground around the Quang Tin Province capital of Tam Ky, the squadron could apply overwhelming force to any enemy incursions. During the Tet Offensive of 1968, the squadron was instrumental in defending Tam Ky and driving enemy units back into the hills. Later that year, the squadron tangled with a North Vietnamese regiment that approached the capital and in three vicious days of fighting virtually destroyed the regiment. In the spring of 1969, when a North Vietnamese regiment secretly moved to the outskirts of the city, a reinforced troop of the 1st Squadron, 1st Cavalry, in conjunction with South Vietnamese infantry, destroyed the attacking force.

In order to provide the 4th Infantry Division with additional cavalry, the 2nd Squadron, 1st Cavalry, was also detached from its division, the 2nd Armored, at Fort Hood and deployed to Vietnam. The cavalry of the 4th Division spent much of its effort on keeping open difficult routes of communication in the Vietnamese Highlands.

Each infantry division and separate brigade faced unique combat conditions and each adapted to the terrain and the enemy in its area. Cavalry squadrons with their armor and organic helicopter assets were particularly valuable to the divisions, while separate brigades found the mobility and armored fire power of their cavalry troops of great value.

Thus, while the war in Vietnam was primarily an infantry war, both divisional and nondivisional cavalry played a significant role.

PERSIAN GULF WAR

In the perilous autumn of 1990, the country of Kuwait was engulfed with Saddam Hussein menacing the entire Arabian Peninsula, ignoring UN calls for withdrawal. Eventually, this act of aggression would lead to the military operation of Desert Shield and Desert Storm.

Again cavalrymen would be called on, this time to support the Allied Coalition in a planned effort to attack and dislodge the Iraquis.

The substance of the Coalition offensive was to launch holding and secondary attacks against Iraqi forces in the east, while a major "left hook" by two corps would attack across the relatively lightly held western area. The key to success was surprise. A massive, and successful, effort was made by every means, including air strikes and communications deception, to keep the Iraqis from determining the true location of the main attack.

The two corps that would constitute the main attack force were VII Corps, which had deployed from Germany, and XVIII Airborne Corps from the United States. VII Corps included the 1st Infantry Division (Mechanized), the 1st and 3rd Armored Divisions, and the 2nd Armored Cavalry Regiment. The XVIII Airborne Corps included the 101st Airborne Division (Air Assault), the 24th Infantry Division, and the 3rd Armored Cavalry Regiment, plus the French force committed to the Coalition.

Within VII Corps, the plan called for the 1st Infantry Division to create the front line breach and the two armored divisions to attack abreast, led by the cavalry regiment. Within XVIII Airborne Corps, the 24th Infantry Division, with the 3rd Armored Cavalry Regiment attached, would make the major ground thrust, while the 101st Airborne Division air assaulted to cut off the enemy near the Euphrates River. The French force would protect the left flank.

Re-enactors cross Kelly's Ford at Brandy Station. (Courtesy of Jack Johnson)

Cpl. Jack A. Johnson. (Courtesy of Jack Johnson)

The British division, to the right of VII Corps would attack forward and swing to the right behind the Iraqi front lines. The First Cavalry Division (now an armored division) would be part of the deception by making a limited attack forward. The Marines and forces of Arab nations would attack frontally and advance based on their degree of success.

By now, the armored cavalry regiments included, in addition to three ground cavalry squadrons, an aviation squadron. The ground cavalry troops included M1A1 Abrams tanks, armed with a smoothbore 120mm cannon, a caliber .50 machine gun, and two caliber .30 machine guns, and Bradley fighting vehicles armed with a 25mm automatic cannon, a caliber .50 machine gun, and a caliber .30 machine gun. Each squadron included a howitzer battery. The aviation squadron was equipped with light observation helicopters, attack helicopters, and utility helicopters.

In addition to the cavalry regiments, each corps possessed within its divisions, divisional cavalry squadrons, which included ground and aviation assets.

As stated in *Certain Victory*, the official Army story of the Persian Gulf War, on the afternoon of 24 February 1991, G-Day, the beginning of the ground offensive, "Like race horses springing from the starting gate, the 24th Infantry Division and the 3rd Armored Cavalry regiment sped across the border berm to begin their dash to the Euphrates.... The 3rd Armored Cavalry Regiment drove north, continually stretching an arm to the east to maintain contact with the 3rd Armored Division in the VII Corps sector. Both units had already eliminated Iraqi screening forces during the pre-G-Day warmup. For the next three days, they fought time and terrain more than they did Iraqis." By the end of the first day, the force had advanced sixty miles into Iraqi territory.

In VII Corps, the 2nd Armored Cavalry Regiment served as the lead scouts for the corps. The regimental mission was to clear the zone in front of the 1st and 2nd Armored Divisions and, most importantly, to discover the Republican Guard main line of defense so that the armored divisions could aim for it. The corps screen began with a thin line of Bradley fighting vehicles and an aerial picket of Cobra attack helicopters from the 4th Squadron. The 1st and 3rd Squadrons followed on line about 10 kilometers back in a thicker formation of Abrams tanks and Bradley fighting vehicles. The three howitzer batteries of the regiment were augmented with three additional battalions of artillery. Helicopters from the 1st Armored Division augmented the regimental aviation assets and the Air Force supported the regiment with A-10 ground support aircraft.

Crossing the line of departure, the regiment cut a 40 kilometer swath, attacking anything in its way. By the end of the first day, the regiment had eliminated the remnants of an infantry brigade.

Around noon of the second day, the 2nd Armored Cavalry Regiment met a force of T-55 tanks and armored personnel carriers in prepared defensive positions. They were part of the 50th Armored Brigade, 12th Armored Division. The cavalry regiment shifted to the right to allow the 1st and 3rd Armored Divisions to move north against the force.

The regiment then covered the area between the 3rd Armored Division and the British. The 1st Armored Division used its 1st Squadron, 1st Cavalry, and the 3rd Armored Division its 4th Squadron, 7th Cavalry, to lead their advance and screen their flanks.

On February 26, the 2nd Cavalry struck the Republican Guard Tamalkalma Division in what came to be known as the Battle of 73 Easting. The security force it encountered first was destroyed. The captured commander said that he had lost only two of his 39 tanks in the air offensive, but the rest of his command had been destroyed by the cavalry in six minutes.

The 1st Infantry Division now passed through the 2nd Armored Cavalry Regiment with its cavalry squadron, the 1st Squadron, 4th Cavalry, screening its left flank.

Meanwhile, the 3rd Armored Cavalry Regiment, along with the 24th Infantry Division, had reached the Euphrates River Valley and was slowed by what the troops called "the great dismal bog." The night of 25 February, the cavalry regiment and the 2nd Squadron, 4th Cavalry, of the 24th Division found paths through the bog, which supporting engineers then prepared. The 2nd Squadron, 4th Cavalry, then turned to screening the division west flank.

After accomplishing its initial limited attack, the 1st Cavalry Division rushed to join the offensive effort farther north. Farther east, by the morning of the second day, the 1st Marine Division was already fighting around the Kuwait City International Airport. By the end of the day, they had encircled the city.

By 27 February, the prisoner count was approaching 70,000 and Saddam had ordered his forces to withdraw from Kuwait. The last major escape route, a four-lane highway between Kuwait City and Basrah in Iraq had become an Air Force shooting gallery. By the end of the fourth day, it was all over and a cease fire was declared.

Once again, the cavalry had played a major role in battle, this time as part of an armored team in a classic demonstration of the effectiveness of well-trained, well-equipped ground forces.

TODAY'S MODERN CAVALRY

The modern cavalry of today is much differently organized and equipped than the horse cavalry of the past. However, as changes in weaponry have been made, the cavalry has responded to the demands. Although riding different steeds into battle, both air and ground, the cavalry trooper of today is much like his predecessor. He understands the value of mobility and is always ready to assume the offensive. Cavalry units today retain their historic names, their traditions, and their *esprit*.

Weaponry will continue to change and organizations, tactics, and methods of operation will change. It is doubtful, though, that the time when the missions of cavalry, validated over hundreds, even thousands, of years will go away. So long as there is war, there will be a requirement for the aggressiveness, the flexibility, and the mobility that cavalry brings to the battlefield.

BIBLIOGRAPHY

Skirmish-Red, White and Blue: Korean War 1950-53
Edward L. Daily, author
Turner Publishing Company
copyright 1992

Custer to MacArthur: 7th US Cavalry, 1866-1945
Edward L. Daily, author
Turner Publishing Company
copyright 1995

1st Cavalry Division: Korean War 1950-52
Turner Publishing Company
copyright 1994

1st Cavalry Division: Vietnam War 1965-69
Turner Publishing Company
copyright 1995

National Military Archives
Richard Boylan, Assistant Chief
Military Field Branch
Washington, DC 20409

The History of Cavalry
Z. Grbasic and V. Vuksic, authors
Facts on File, Inc.
460 Park Avenue South
New York, NY 10016

Divided We Fought (Civil War)
David Donald, author
The Macmillan Company
copyright 1953

Army Lineage Series Armor-Cavalry Part I, Regular Army & Army Reserve
Mary Lee Stubbs & Stanley Russell Connor
U.S. Center of Military History
Washington D.C. 1984

Mounted Combat in Vietnam
Donn A. Starry, author
Department of the Army
Washington D.C. 1978

History of the U.S. Cavalry
Swafford Johnson, author
Smithmark Publishers, Inc.
New York. 1985

Order of battle, U.S. Army, World War II
Shelby L. Stanton, author
Presidio Press
Novata, CA, 1984

Tank-vs-Tank Combat in Korea
Vincent V. McRae & Alvin D. Coox, authors
Operations Research Office
John Hopkins University
Chevy Chase, MD, 1954

Certain Victory: the U.S. Army in the Gulf War Center of Military History
Department of the Army
Washington, DC, 1993

The First Cavalry Division in World War II
Major B. C. Wright, compiler
Toppan Printing Company
Tokyo, 1947

MILESTONES IN UNITED STATES CAVALRY HISTORY

1774 Nov 17	Light Horse of the City of Philadelphia organized (later became 1st Troop Philadelphia City Cavalry)
1775 Apr 19	Battle of Lexington (Revolutionary War)
1776 Dec 12	The US Cavalry was established
1777 Sep 11	Battle of Brandywine, PA
1783 Sep 3	Peace Treaty signed, end of Revolutionary War
1788 May 1	1st Company, Governor's Horse Guard, CT Constituted
1789 May 10	Richmond Light Infantry organized (later became 183d Cavalry)
1780 Aug 16	Battle of Camden, SC
1808 Oct	2d Company of the Governor's Horse Guard, CT Organized
1812 Jun 18	Start of the War of 1812
1827 May 8	Fort Leavenworth, KS established
1832 Feb 2	Black Hawk War started
1833 Mar 2	1st Dragoons constituted (later became the 1st Cavalry Regiment)
1833 Mar 4	1st Dragoons organized at Jefferson Barracks, MO
1835 Dec 28	Seminole War begins
1836 Mar 6	Fall of the Alamo
1836 Apr 22	Battle of San Jacinto
1836 May 14	Treaty of Velasco by General de Santa Anna
1836 May 15	1st Dragoon redesignated as 1st Regiment of Dragoons
1836 May 23	2d Regiment of Dragoons constituted (later became the 2d Cavalry)
1836 May 23	2d Regiment of Dragoons organized at Jefferson Barracks, MO
1838 Jun 17	Skirmish at Kenahapa Prairie, FL Territory
1840 Jan 24	Skirmish at Fort Preston, FL Territory
1840 Mar 10	Skirmish at Fort Pearson, IL
1842 Mar 19	Skirmish at Big Hammock, FL Territory
1842 Aug 14	Seminole War ends
1843 Mar 5	2d Dragoons redesignated at 2d Regiment of Riflemen
1846 Mar 28	Fort Brown established
1846 Apr 24	War with Mexico
1846 May 8	Battle of Palo Alto
1846 May 13	Congress declares War on Mexico
1846 May 19	Regiment of Mounted Riflemen constituted (later became the 3d Cavalry Regiment)
1846 May 20	First KY Volunteer Cavalry Constituted (later became 123d Cavalry)
1846 Oct 12	Regiment of Mounted Riflemen organized at Jefferson Barracks, MO
1847 Feb 22	Battle of Buena Vista
1847 Mar 9	Battle of Vera Cruz, NM Territory
1847 Apr 2	Skirmish at Antiqua, Mexico
1847 Jun 20	Skirmish at La Hove, Mexico
1847 Sep 14	US Forces enter Mexico City
1848 Feb 2	Mexican War ended
1850 Jul 30	Skirmish at Canadian River, TX
1851 Jul 27	Fort Union, NM established
1851 Sep 18	Fort Defiance, AZ established
1852 Jun 20	Fort Clark, TX established
1853 Jun 27	Fort Riley, KS established
1854 Mar 8	Fort Bliss, TX established
1855 Mar 3	1st Cavalry Regular Army constituted (later became the 4th Cavalry Regiment)
1855 Mar 3	2d Cavalry Regular Army constituted (later became the 5th Cavalry Regiment)
1855 Mar 26	1st Cavalry Regular Army organized at Jefferson Barracks, MO
1855 May 28	2d Cavalry Regular Army organized at Louisville, KY
1857 Jul 20	Skirmish at Devil's River, TX
1860 Jan 26	Skirmish at Kickapoo Creek, TX Territory
1860 Jan 29	Skirmish at Aqua Frio, TX Territory
1860 Mar 16	Skirmish in La Mesa, Mexico
1860 Aug 11	Skirmish at Blackwater Springs, NE
1861 Feb 8	Battle of Roanoke Island, NC
1861 Apr 12	Fort Summer fired on, start of the War of the Rebellion (Civil)
1861 Apr 19	War of Rebellion
1861 May 4	3d Cavalry Regular Army Regiment constituted (later the 6th Cavalry Regiment)
1861 Jun 8	6th Cavalry Regular Army organized at Pittsburgh, PA
1861 Jul 2	Skirmish at Falling Waters, VA
1861 Jul 8	Skirmish at Bunker Hill, VA
1861 Jul 18	Skirmish at Blackburn's Ford
1861 Jul 21	Battle of Bull Run started, VA
1861 Jul 22	Battle of Bull Run ended, VA
1861 Aug 3	1st Dragoons redesignated as 1st Cavalry Regiment
1861 Aug 3	2d Dragoons (Regiment of Riflemen) redesignated as 2nd Cavalry Regiment
1861 Aug 3	Mounted Riflemen redesignated as 3d Cavalry Regiment
1861 Aug 3	1st Cavalry Regular Army redesignated as 4th Cavalry Regiment
1861 Aug 3	2nd Cavalry Regular Army redesignated as 5th Cavalry Regiment
1861 Aug 3	3rd Cavalry Regular Army redesignated as 6th Cavalry Regiment
1861 Aug 10	Battle of Wilson Creek, MO
1861 Dec 12	Battle of Fredericksburg, VA
1861 Dec 30	Battle of Stone River, TN
1862 Feb 13	Skirmish at Fort Doneleson, TN
1862 Feb 21	Battle of Valverda, NM Territory
1862 Mar 14	Skirmish at Cedar Run, VA
1862 Mar 23	Battle of Winchester, VA
1862 Apr 5	Siege at Yorktown, VA
1862 Apr 6	Battle of Shiloh, TN
1862 May 5	Battle of Williamsburg, VA
1862 May 27	Battle of Hanover Court House, VA
1862 Jun 6	Battle of Memphis, TN
1862 Jun 8	Battle of Cross Keys, VA
1862 Jun 13	Skirmish at Old Church, VA
1862 Jun 27	Battle of Gaines Mills, VA
1862 Jun 30	Battle of Nelson's Farm, VA
1862 Jul 16	Skirmish at St. Mary's, VA
1862 Aug 9	Battle of Cedar Mountain, VA
1862 Aug 29	Battle of Groveton, VA
1862 Aug 30	Second Battle of Bull Run
1862 Sep 19	Battle of Chickamuga, TN
1862 Oct	Fort Wingate, NM established
1862 Oct 3	Battle of Corinth, MS
1862 Oct 4	Battle of Perryville, KY
1863 Mar 17	Skirmish at Kelley's Ford, VA
1863 Apr 29	Raid at Stoneman, VA
1863 Apr 30	Skirmish at Raccoon Ford, VA
1863 May 2	Battle of Chancellorsville, VA begins
1863 May 2	Col Grierson and 1,000 Cavalrymen arrive at Baton Rouge, LA
1863 May 19	Capture of Vicksburg, MS
1863 Jun 9	Skirmish at Beverly Ford, VA
1863 Jun 29	Battle of Gettysburg begins, MD
1863 Jul 3	Battle of Gettysburg ends, MD
1863 Jul 6	Skirmish at Williamsport, MD
1863 Jul 9	Battle of Monocacy, MD
1863 Jul 10	Skirmish at Funkton, MO
1863 Jul 14	Skirmish at Falling Waters, VA
1863 Jul 23	Skirmish at Front Royal, VA
1863 Jul 28	Cavalry Bureau established
1863 Sep 16	Battle of Sharpsburg, MD
1863 Oct 2	Fort Cummings established
1863 Oct 14	Battle of Bristoe Station, VA
1864 Jan 13	Raid at Northern VA
1864 Jan 19	Skirmish at Verde River, AZ Territory
1864 Feb 5	Battle of Dabney's Mill, VA
1864 Feb 29	Skirmish at Charlottesville, VA
1864 Mar 1	Skirmish at Morton's Ford, VA
1864 Mar 13	Skirmish at Raggon Point, VA
1864 Apr 13	Skirmish at Ragged Point, VA
1864 May 7	Battle at Todd's Tavern, VA
1864 May 9	Skirmish at Beaver Dam Station, VA
1864 May 11	Skirmish at Yellow Tavern, VA
1864 May 12	Skirmish at Mechanicsville, VA
1864 May 14	Battle of Resaca, MS
1864 Jun 1	Battle of Cold Harbor, VA
1864 Jun 4	Battle of Petersburg begins, VA
1864 Jun 11	Battle of Trevillian Station, VA
1864 Jun 15	Siege against Richmond, VA
1864 Jun 19	Battle of Peach Tree Creek, GA
1864 Jul 22	Battle of Atlanta, GA
1864 Jul 27	Skirmish at Deep Bottom, VA
1864 Aug 7	Battle of Shenandoah Valley, VA
1864 Aug 18	Battle of Glen Tavern, VA
1864 Aug 24	Battle of Ream's Station, VA
1864 Aug 31	Battle of Jonesborough
1864 Sep 15	Battle of Opequan Creek, VA
1864 Sep 22	Battle of Fisher's Hill, VA
1864 Oct 19	Battle of Cedar Creek, VA
1864 Dec 15	Battle of Nashville, TN
1865 Mar 7	Skirmish at Bent Creek, VA
1865 Mar 8	Battle of Wise's Fork, NC
1865 Mar 12	Skirmish South Anna Bridge, VA
1865 Mar 16	Battle of Avery's Borough, NC
1865 Mar 28	Campaign of Appromattox, VA
1865 Mar 31	Skirmish at Five Forks, VA
1865 Apr 2	End of the Battle of Petersburg
1865 Apr 7	Skirmish at Prince Edwards Court House, VA
1865 Apr 8	Skirmish at Amelia Court House
1865 Apr 9	End of the Battle of Appromattox, VA
1865 May 8	Fort Selden, NM established
1865 Sep 7	Fort McDowell, AZ established
1865 Oct 31	Fort Grant, AZ established
1866 Jan	Fort Lowell and Forte Verde, AZ established

1866 July 28	7th Cavalry constituted		1916 Jun 18	101st Cavalry called into Federal Service (Mexican Border Service)
1866 July 28	8th Cavalry constituted			
1866 July 28	9th Cavalry constituted		1916 Jun 30	101st Squadron A called into Federal Service (Mexican Border Service)
1866 July 28	10th Cavalry constituted			
1866 Aug 21	Fort Bayard, NM established		1916 Jul 1	16th Cavalry constituted and organized at Fort Sam Houston, TX
1866 Sep 21	7th Cavalry organized at Fort Riley, KS		1916 Jul 1	17th Cavalry constituted and organized at Fort Bliss, TX
1866 Sep 21	8th Cavalry organized at Angel Island, CA		1917 Feb 5	11th Cavalry leaves Mexico
1866 Sep 21	9th Cavalry organized at Greenville, LA		1917 Feb 17	End of Punitive Expedition in Mexico
1866 Sep 21	10th Cavalry organized at Fort Leavenworth, KS		1917 Apr 6	Congress declares war on Germany, start of World War I
1866 Sep 29	Battle of Poplar Springs		1917 Apr 16	107th Cavalry constituted Ohio National Guard as 1st Cavalry Ohio NG
1866 Oct 21	8th Cavalry organized at Angel Island, CA			
1867 Jul 28	Battle at Deep Bottom		1917 May 18	13th Cavalry ordered to Fort Riley, KS
1867 Dec 4	Fort Concho established		1917 May 18	301st Cavalry constituted in the National Army
1868 Aug 19	Skirmish at Fort Reno, SD Territory		1917 May 18	302nd Cavalry constituted in the National Army
1869 Jan 8	Fort Sill, OK established		1917 May 18	303rd Cavalry constituted in the National Army
1869 May 16	Skirmish at Spring Creek, NE		1917 May 18	304th Cavalry constituted in the National Army
1869 Jul 5	Skirmish at Sand Hill, CO		1917 May 18	305th Cavalry constituted in the National Army
1870 May 15	Fort Apache, AZ established		1917 May 18	306th Cavalry constituted in the National Army
1872 May 20	Skirmish at Meadwaters Ash Creek, AZ Territory		1917 May 18	307th Cavalry constituted in the National Army
1872 Jul 13	Skirmish at Whetstone Mountains, CO		1917 May 18	308th Cavalry constituted in the National Army
1872 Jul 25	Skirmish at Davidson's Canyon, AZ		1917 May 18	309th Cavalry constituted in the National Army
1872 Aug 4	Skirmish at Prior Fork, MT		1917 May 18	310th Cavalry constituted in the National Army
1873 Jan 2	Skirmish at Clear Creek, AZ Territory		1917 May 18	311th Cavalry constituted in the National Army
1873 Jan 22	Skirmish at Tonto Creek, AZ Territory		1917 May 18	312th Cavalry constituted in the National Army
1873 Mar 25	Skirmish at Verde River, AZ Territory		1917 May 18	313th Cavalry constituted in the National Army
1873 Aug 26	Skirmish at San Carlos Agency, AZ Territory		1917 May 18	314th Cavalry constituted in the National Army
1874 Feb 9	Skirmish at Cottonwood Creek, WY Territory		1917 May 18	315th Cavalry constituted in the National Army
1874 Feb 20	Skirmish at Santa Teresa, NM Territory		1917 May 23	19th Cavalry organized at Fort Ethan Allen, VT
1874 Apr 11	Skirmish at Santa Teresa Mountains, AZ Territory		1917 Jun 1	104th Cavalry reorganized
1874 Apr 28	Skirmish at Arivapa Mountains, AZ Territory		1917 Jun 1	20th Cavalry organized at Fort Riley, KS
1876 Jun 17	Battle of the Rosebud		1917 Jun 1	21st Cavalry organized at Fort Riley, KS
1876 Jun 25	Battle of the Little Big Horn		1917 Jun 5	24th Cavalry organized at Fort D.A. Russell
1876 Jul 17	Skirmish at War Bonnett, WY		1917 Jun 5	25th Cavalry organized at Fort D.A. Russell
1877 Mar 3	Fort Huachuca, AZ established		1917 Jun 13	18th Cavalry organized at Fort Ethan Allen, VT
1877 May 24	Skirmish at Birdwood, NE Territory		1917 Jun 21	17th Cavalry organized at Fort Ethan Allen, VT
1877 Aug 20	Skirmish at Comas Meadows, Iowa Territory		1917 Jun 21	22nd Cavalry organized at Fort Oglethorpe, GA
1879 Aug 14	Skirmish at Popular Creek, MT		1917 Jun 21	23rd Cavalry organized at Fort Oglethorpe, GA
1880 Mar 25	105th Cavalry constituted as Wisconsin's National Guard (as Light Horse Squadron)		1917 Jun 26	146th Cavalry constituted as 1st Separate Squadron MI Cavalry
1888 May 29	115th Cavalry constituted as WY National Guard (as Laramie Grays)		1917 Jul 31	105th Cavalry mustered into Federal Service
1889 Apr 3	101st Cavalry constituted (Troop A Cavalry NY National Guard, later Squadron A)		1917 Oct 23	First American Artillery shot fired in WWI
			1917 Nov 1	18th Cavalry converted (redesignated as 76th Field Artillery)
1890 Jun 3	NJ Essex Troop organized		1917 Nov 1	19th Cavalry converted (redesignated as 77th Field Artillery)
1890 Sep 11	Fort Sam Houston, TX established		1917 Nov 1	21st Cavalry converted (redesignated as 79th Field Artillery)
1890 Dec 29	Battle of Wounded Knee, SD		1917 Nov 1	22nd Cavalry converted (redesignated as 80th Field Artillery)
1892 Aug 5	Fort Ethan Allen, VT established		1917 Nov 1	24th Cavalry converted (redesignated as 82nd Field Artillery)
1895 Feb 9	101st Cavalry expended and redesignated Squadron A		1917 Nov 1	25th Cavalry converted (redesignated as 83d Field Artillery)
1895 Dec 10	101st Cavalry Squadron C organized		1917 Nov 3	23rd Cavalry converted (redesignated as 81st Field Artillery)
1898 Apr 25	US declares war on Spain		1917 Nov 18	20th Cavalry converted (redesignated as 78th Field Artillery)
1898 Jun 22	Battle of Santiago begins		1918 Apr 6	2d Cavalry lands in France
1898 Jul 11	Battle of Santiago ends		1918 Apr 14	U.S. Cavalry engaged Tour Section, France
1898 Dec 10	Spanish-American War ends		1918 Nov 11	Fighting ended in World War I
1899 Feb 4	Start of Philippine Insurrection		1919 Jan 17	94th Cavalry organized in the MN National Guard
1901 Feb 2	11th Cavalry constituted		1919 Feb 2	Treaty of Guadalupe signed
1901 Feb 2	12th Cavalry constituted		1919 May 16	106th Cavalry demobilized at Camp Grant, IL
1901 Feb 2	13th Cavalry constituted		1919 Jun 8	5th Cavalry returns from France
1901 Feb 2	14th Cavalry constituted		1920 Feb 20	112th Cavalry Constituted (as TX National Guard 1st Regiment)
1901 Feb 2	15th Cavalry constituted		1921 Mar 1	117th Cavalry constituted (in the NJ National Guard)
1901 Feb 8	12th Cavalry organized at Fort Sam Houston, TX		1921 May 3	113th Cavalry constituted (Iowa National Guard)
1901 Feb 12	13th Cavalry authorized		1921 Jun 1	104th Cavalry constituted (in Pennsylvania National Guard)
1901 Feb 12	15th Cavalry organized at Presidio, San Francisco, CA		1921 Jun 1	106th Cavalry constituted (in IL & Michigan National Guard)
1901 Feb 19	14th Cavalry organized at Fort Leavenworth, KS		1921 Jun 1	108th Cavalry constituted (to National Guard of GA&LA)
1901 Mar 11	11th Cavalry organized at Fort Myer, VA		1921 Jun 1	109th Cavalry constituted (to National Guard of LA, AL, NC and TN)
1901 May 1	13th Cavalry organized at Fort Meade, SD			
1902 Jul 4	Formal end of the Philippine Insurrection		1921 Jun 1	110th Cavalry constituted (National Guard of MA)
1908 May 11	Fort Reno becomes QM Corps Remount Depot		1921 Jun 1	111th Cavalry constituted (in the NM & CO National Guard)
1910 Feb 14	Skirmish at Tirados Hill, Philippines		1921 Jun 1	114th Cavalry constituted (in the KS National Guard)
1911 Dec 27	101st Squadron A reorganized to include Squadron C		1921 Jun 1	116th Cavalry constituted (in the Idaho and Utah National Guard)
1910 Feb 14	Skirmish at Mount Orut, Philippines		1921 Jun 1	120th Cavalry constituted (allotted to the MA National Guard)
1912 Mar 11	101st Cavalry constituted (as 2d Cavalry NY National Guard)		1921 Apr 29	102d Cavalry constituted and organized at Newark, NJ
1914 Jul 6	103rd Cavalry constituted and organized (as 1st Cavalry PA National Guard)		1921 Aug 17	NJ National Guard 1st Cavalry reorganized as 102d Cavalry
			1921 Sep 26	17th Cavalry inactivated at Presidio, Monterey, CA
1916 Mar 9	Pancho Villa's raid on Columbus, NM		1921 Oct 15	324th Cavalry constituted in Organized Reserves (allotted to the Ninth Corps Area)
1916 Mar 14	Punitive Expedition into Mexico			
1916 Mar 29	Battle of Guereno, Mexico		1921 Oct 15	323rd Cavalry constituted in Organized Reserves (allotted to the Ninth Corps Area)
1916 Jun 3	18th Cavalry constituted			
1916 Jun 3	19th Cavalry constituted		1921 Oct 18	15th Cavalry inactivated at Fort D.A. Russell, WY
1916 Jun 3	20th Cavalry constituted		1921 Oct 15	316th Cavalry constituted in Organized Reserves (allotted to First Corps Area)
1916 Jun 3	21st Cavalry constituted			
1916 Jun 3	22nd Cavalry constituted		1921 Oct 15	317th Cavalry constituted in Organized Reserves (allotted to Sixth Corps Area)
1916 Jun 3	23th Cavalry constituted			
1916 Jun 3	24th Cavalry constituted		1921 Oct 15	318th Cavalry constituted in Organized Reserves (allotted to Sixth Corps Area)
1916 Jun 3	25th Cavalry constituted			

1921 Oct 15	319th Cavalry constituted in Organized Reserves (allotted to Sixth Corps Area)
1921 Oct 15	320th Cavalry constituted in Organized Reserves (allotted to Sixth Corps Area)
1921 Oct 15	321st Cavalry constituted in Organized Reserves (allotted to Seventh Corps Area)
1921 Oct 15	322nd Cavalry constituted in Organized Reserves (allotted to Seventh Corps Area)
1921 Nov 12	16th Cavalry inactivated at Fort Sam Houston, TX
1922 Oct 1	26th Cavalry constituted and organized at Fort Stotsenburg, Philippine Islands
1928 Feb 1	Cavalry MG squad abolished
1928 Mar 22	121st Cavalry organized and federally recognized
1929 Feb 13	122nd Cavalry constituted (allotted to CT and RI National Guard)
1929 Feb 13	124th Cavalry constituted (in the TX National Guard)
1929 Mar 15	126th Cavalry constituted (allotted to the CT & RI National Guard)
1933 Jan 16	1st Cavalry redesignated as 1st Cavalry Mechanized
1936 Sep 26	13th Cavalry reorganized as 13th Cavalry Mechanized
1940 Sep 1	194th Cavalry constituted (in the MN, MO, CA National Guard)
1940 Sep 14	Selective Service and Training Act (Draft) approved
1940 Oct 1	101st Cavalry reorganized as 101st Cavalry Mechanized
1941 Jan 6	102d Cavalry inducted into Federal Service
1941 Jan 13	103d inducted into Federal Service
1941 Jan 27	101st inducted into Federal Service
1941 Feb 17	104th Cavalry inducted into Federal Service
1941 Dec 3	230th Cavalry allotted to TN National Guard
1941 Dec 7	Japanese attack Pearl Harbor, HI
1942 Apr 9	26th Cavalry remnants captured by Japanese
1942 Jul 1	11th Cavalry dismounted at Camp Lockett, CA
1942 Jul 11	11th Cavalry inactivated
1942 Jul 15	2d Cavalry inactivated at Fort Riley, KS
1942 Jul 15	11th Cavalry inactivated at Fort Benning, GA
1942 Jul 15	14th Cavalry inactivated at Fort Riley, KS
1942 Jul 15	14th Cavalry redesignated as 14th Armored
1942 Jul 15	3d Cavalry inactivated at Fort Benning, GA
1942 Jul 21	6th Cavalry redesignated as 6th Cavalry Mechanized
1942 Nov 10	27th Cavalry constituted

1942 Nov 10	28th Cavalry constituted
1942 Dec 19	29th Cavalry constituted
1943 Jan 15	2d Cavalry redesignated as 2d Cavalry Mechanized
1943 Jan 18	3d Cavalry redesignated as 3d Cavalry Mechanized
1943 Feb 23	29th Cavalry activated at Fort Riley, KS
1943 Feb 25	27th Cavalry activated at Fort Clark, TX
1943 Feb 25	28th Cavalry constituted at Camp Lockett, CA
1943 Feb 28	5th Cavalry dismounted at Fort Bliss, TX
1943 Feb 28	7th Cavalry dismounted at Fort Bliss, TX
1943 Feb 28	8th Cavalry dismounted at Fort Bliss, TX
1943 Feb 28	12th Cavalry dismounted at Fort Bliss, TX
1943 Apr 16	Cavalry reorganized as Cavlary Mechanized
1943 Jun 18	Last Element of the 1st Cavalry Division departs Fort Bliss to Australia
1943 Oct 18	317th Cavalry disbanded
1943 Oct 18	311th Cavalry disbanded
1943 Oct 18	315th Cavalry disbanded
1943 Oct 18	313th Cavalry disbanded
1943 Dec 21	4th Cavalry reorganized as 4th Cavalry Mechanized
1944 Jan 2	102d Cavalry becomes mechanized
1944 Jan	9th Cavalry dismounted at Fort Clark, TX
1944 Feb	10th Cavalry dismounted at Camp Lockett, CA
1944 Mar 7	9th Cavalry inactivated in North Afirca
1944 Mar 20	10th Cavalry inactivated in North Africa
1944 Mar 24	28th Cavalry's last review
1944 Mar 27	27th Cavalry inactivated in Oran, Algeria
1944 Mar 31	28th Cavalry inactivated at Oran, Algeria
1944 May 1	29th Cavalry inactivated at Fort Riley, KS
1944 Jun 6	Normandy Invasion, World War II
1944 Jun 12	300th Cavalry constituted in the Army of the United States
1944 Oct 17	Leyte assault, World War II
1944 Dec 15	Luzon assault, World War II
1945 Apr 1	Amphibious assault on Okinawa
1945 May 8	V-E Day officially proclaimed
1945 Sep 1	Japan signed surrender document
1945 Sep 2	V-J Official Declaration Day
1945 Nov 15	104th Cavalry was inactivated at Camp Hood, TX
1945 Dec 10	103rd Cavalry deactivated
1946 Apr 4	Chief of Cavalry abolished
1946 Apr 23	26th Cavalry (less 1st & 2nd Squadrons) disbanded at Ft. Stotsenburg, Philippines
1946 Jun 17	139th Cavalry constituted (allotted to the LA National Guard)
1946 Aug 5	18th Cavalry constituted (allotted to the CA National Guard)
1946 Nov 26	311th Armored Cavalry constituted
1946 Nov 26	314th Armored Cavalry constituted
1948 Nov 26	317th Armored Cavalry constituted
1948 Nov 28	320th Armored Cavalry constituted
1949 Jan 31	238th Cavalry constituted (in the IN National Guard
1949 Mar 15	297th Cavalry constituted (allotted to the AK National Guard)
1949 Sep 15	173rd Cavalry constituted (in the TN National Guard)
1950 Jun 25	North Korea launches full attack on Republic of Korea
1950 Jun 30	Cavalry redesignated as Armor
1951 Jul 30	26th Cavalry, 1st Squadron disbanded
1951 Dec 12	27th Cavalry disbanded
1951 Dec 12	28th Cavalry disbanded
1951 Dec 12	29th Cavalry disbanded
1952 Mar 10	321st Armored Cavalry disbanded
1952 Mar 10	320th Armored Cavalry disbanded
1952 Mar 10	317th Armored Cavalry disbanded
1952 Mar 10	314th Armored Cavalry disbanded
1952 Mar 10	311th Armored Cavalry disbanded
1952 Mar 10	310th Armored Cavalry disbanded
1955 Nov 1	748th Cavalry constituted (allotted to the GA Army National Guard)
1959 Mar 25	82nd Cavalry constituted (allotted to the OR Army National Guard)
1959 May 1	98th Cavalry constituted (allotted to the MS Army National Guard)
1963 Feb 27	26th Cavalry constituted (allotted to the MA Army National Guard)
1963 Mar 7	145th Cavalry constituted (allotted to the OK National Guard)
1964 Feb 5	153rd Cavalry constituted (allotted to the FL National Guard)
1964 Feb 12	163rd Cavalry constituted (allotted to the NE National Guard)
1964 Apr 7	192d Cavalry constituted (allotted to the Puerto Rico Army National Guard)
1965 Mar 15	Vietnam Advisory Campaign
1967 Oct 24	19th Cavalry constituted (allotted to the HI Army National Guard)
1967 Nov 2	151st Cavalry constituted (allotted to the AR National Guard)
1967 Dec 20	140th Cavalry constituted (allotted to the CA National Guard)
1967 Dec 22	43d Cavalry constituted (allotted to the RI Army National Guard)
1972 Mar 30	Start of Cease-Fired Vietnam
1973 Nov 23	348th Cavalry constituted (allotted GA Army National Guard)
1973 Dec 19	713th Cavalry constituted (in the SC Army National Guard)
1975 Mar 31	158th Cavalry constituted (in the MD National Guard)
1977 Apr 29	378th Cavalry constituted (in the TN Army National Guard)
1980 Sep 3	240th Cavalry constituted (allotted to the KY National Guard)
1993 Aug 28	107th Cavalry inactivated

Bill leading the charge. (Courtesy of Jerry Edgin)

CAVALRY AND ARMOR UNITS IN VIETNAM

NOTE: THIS IS NOT A COMPLETE LIST OF UNITS THAT SERVED.

GROUND CAVALRY UNITS

1st Squadron, 1st Cavalry (23rd Infantry Division—Americal)
Troop E, 1st Cavalry, 11th Infantry Brigade (23rd Infantry Division—Americal)
2nd Squadron, 1st Cavalry (4th Infantry Division)
1st Squadron, 4th Cavalry (1st Infantry Division)
3rd Squadron, 4th Cavalry (25th Infantry Division)
3rd Squadron, 5th Cavalry (9th Infantry Division)
1st Squadron, 10th Cavalry (4th Infantry Division)
11th Armored Cavalry (II Field Force, Vietnam)
1st Squadron, 11th Armored Cavalry
2nd Squadron, 11th Armored Cavalry
3rd Squadron, 11th Armored Cavalry
Troop A, 4th Squadron, 12th Cavalry (1st Brigade, 5th Infantry Division—Mechanized)
Troop B, 1st Squadron, 17th Cavalry (82nd Airborne Division)
2nd Squadron, 17th Cavalry (101st Airborne Division)
Troop A, 2nd Squadron, 17th Cavalry (101st Airborne Division)
Troop D, 17th Cavalry (199th Infantry Brigade (Light)
Troop E, 17th Cavalry (173rd Airborne Brigade)
Troop F, 17th Cavalry (196th Infantry Brigade, 23rd Infantry Division—Americal)
Troop H, 17th Cavalry (198th Infantry Brigade, 23rd Infantry Division—Americal)

AIR CAVALRY UNITS

1st Battalion, 5th Cavalry, 1st Cavalry Division
2nd Battalion, 5th Cavalry, 1st Cavalry Division
1st Battalion, 7th Cavalry, 1st Cavalry Division
2nd Battalion, 7th Cavalry, 1st Cavalry Division
5th Battalion, 7th Cavalry, 1st Cavalry Division
1st Battalion, 8th Cavalry, 1st Cavalry Division
2nd Battalion, 8th Cavalry, 1st Cavalry Division
1st Battalion, 12th Cavalry, 1st Cavalry Division
2nd Battalion, 12th Cavalry, 1st Cavalry Division
1st Squadron, 9th Cavalry, 1st Cavalry Division
Troop D, 1st Squadron, 1st Cavalry (101st Airborne Division)
7th Squadron, 1st Cavalry (164th Aviation Group, 1st Aviation Brigade)
Troop F, 4th Cavalry (12th Aviation Group, 1st Aviation Brigade)
Troop F, 8th Cavalry (23rd Infantry Division—Americal)
Troop F, 9th Cavalry (12th Aviation Group, 1st Aviation Brigade)
Troop H, 10th Cavalry (17th Aviation Group, 1st Aviation Brigade)
Troop C, 16th Cavalry (164th Aviation Group, Aviation Brigade)
2nd Squadron, 17th Cavalry (101st Airborne Division, Airmobile)
3rd Squadron, 17th Cavalry (12th Aviation Group, 1st Aviation Brigade)
7th Squadron, 17th Cavalry (17th Aviation Group, 1st Aviation Brigade)
Troop D, 17th Cavalry (11th Aviation Group, 1st Aviation Brigade)
Troop H, 17th Cavalry (17th Aviation Group, 1st Aviation Brigade)

TANK UNITS

Company D, 16th Armor (173rd Airborne Brigade)
2nd Battalion, 34th Armor (25th Infantry Division)
1st Battalion, 69th Armor (4th Infantry Division)
1st Battalion, 77th Armor (1st Brigade, 5th Infantry Division—Mechanized)

SPECIAL ARMORED UNIT

39th Cavalry Platoon (Air Cushion) (9th Infantry Division)

UNITED STATES ARMY CAVALRY UNITS
(REGULAR ARMY REGIMENTS) - 1996

Unit	*Address*
1st Squadron, 1st Cavalry	1st Armored Division APO AE 09076
4th Squadron, 1st Cavalry	USMA West Point, NY (inactive)
2nd Armored Cavalry Regiment	Ft. Polk, LA 71459
1st Squadron, 2nd Armored Cavalry Regiment	Ft. Polk, LA 71459
2nd Squadron, 2nd Armored Cavalry Regiment	Ft. Polk, LA 71459
3rd Squadron, 2nd Armored Cavalry Regiment	Ft. Polk, LA 71459
4th Squadron, 2nd Armored Cavalry Regiment***	Ft. Polk, LA 71459
2nd Squadron, 3rd Armored Cavalry Regiment	Ft. Carson, CO 80913
3rd Squadron, 3rd Armored Cavalry Regiment	Ft. Carson, CO 80913
4th Squadron, 3rd Armored Cavalry Regiment***	Ft. Carson, CO 80913
3rd Squadron, 4th Cavalry	25th Infantry Division, Schofield Barracks HI 96857
1st Squadron, 5th Cavalry**	1st Cavalry Division, Ft. Hood, TX 76546
2nd Squadron, 5th Cavalry**	1st Cavalry Division, Ft. Hood, TX 76546
6th Cavalry (Air Combat)***	III Corps Ft. Hood, TX 76546
1st Squadron, 6th Cavalry (Air Combat)***	III Corps, Ft. Hood, TX 76546
2nd Squadron, 6th Cavalry (Air Combat)***	USAREUR, APO AE
3rd Squadron, 6th Cavalry (Air Combat)***	III Corps, Ft. Hood, TX 76546
6th Squadron, 6th Cavalry (Air Combat)***	USAEUR, APO AE
7th Squadron, 6th Cavalry (Air Combat)*** (USAR)	90th ARCOM
1st Squadron, 7th Cavalry ***	1st Cavalry Division, Ft. Hood, TX 76546
2nd Battalion, 7th Cavalry**	1st Cavalry Division, Ft. Hood, TX 76546
3rd Squadron, 7th Cavalry	3rd Infantry Division, Ft. Stewart, GA 31313
4th Squadron, 7th Cavalry***	2nd Infantry Division, South Korea
1st Squadron, 8th Cavalry*	1st Cavalry Division, Ft. Hood, TX 76546
2nd Squadron, 8th Cavalry*	1st Cavalry Division, Ft. Hood, TX 76546
3rd Squadron, 8th Cavalry*	1st Cavalry Division, Ft. Hood, TX 76546
1st Squadron, 9th Cavalry*	1st Cavalry Division, Ft. Hood, TX 76546
5th Squadron, 9th Cavalry	Schofield Barracks, HI 96857
1st Squadron, 10th Cavalry	4th Infantry Division, Ft. Hood, TX 76546
11th Armored Cavalry Regiment	Ft. Irwin, CA 92311
1st Squadron, 11th Armored Cavalry Regiment*	Ft. Irwin, CA 92311
1st Squadron, 12th Cavalry*	1st Cavalry Division, Ft. Hood, TX 76546
2nd Squadron, 12th Cavalry*	1st Cavalry Division, Ft. Hood, TX 76546
5th Squadron, 15th Cavalry	1st Armor Training Brigade, Ft. Knox, KY 40121
16th Cavalry	US Army Armor School, Ft. Knox, KY 40121
1st Squadron, 16th Cavalry	US Army Armor School, Knox, TX 40121
2nd Squadron, 16th Cavalry	US Army Armor School, Ft. Knox, TX 40121
3rd Squadron, 16th Cavalry	US Army Armor School, Ft. Knox, TX 40121
4th Squadron, 16th Cavalry	US Army Armor School, Ft. Knox, TX 40121
1st Squadron, 17th Cavalry***	82nd Airborne Division, Ft. Bragg, NC 28307
2nd Squadron, 17th Cavalry***	101st Airborne Division, Ft. Campbell, KY 42233
3rd Squadron, 17th Cavalry	10th Infantry Division, Ft. Drum, NY 13602
Troop E, 3rd Squadron	6th Infantry Division
17th Cavalry	Ft. Wainwright, AK 99703-6154

*Tank Battalions
**Mechanized Infantry Battalions
***Aviaion units

UNITED STATES CAVALRY REGIMENTAL INSIGNIA

1st CAVALRY

4th CAVALRY

5th CAVALRY

8th CAVALRY

9th CAVALRY

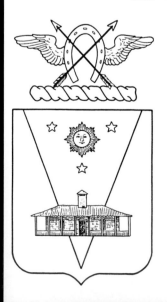

2d ARMORED CAVALRY

TOUJOURS PRET

3d ARMORED CAVALRY

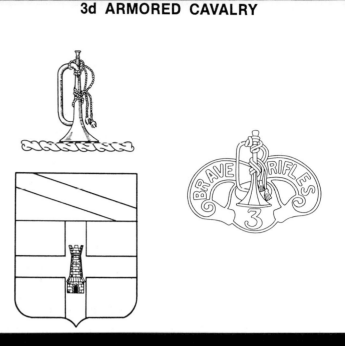

BRAVE RIFLES 3

6th CAVALRY

7th CAVALRY

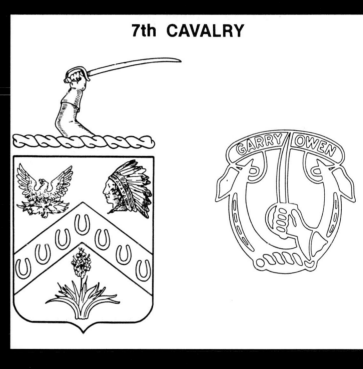

GARRY OWEN

10th CAVALRY

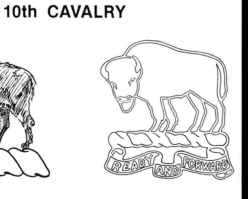

READY AND FORWARD

11th ARMORED CAVALRY

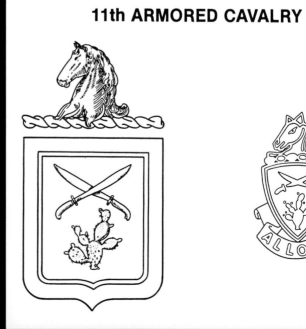

ALLONS

59

12th CAVALRY

13th CAVALRY

16th CAVALRY

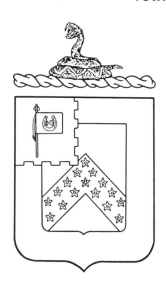

STRIKE HARD

17th CAVALRY

26th CAVALRY

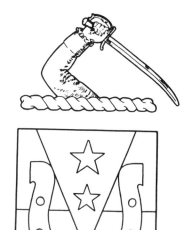

YANKEE EYES

27th CAVALRY

VAMOS

14th ARMORED CAVALRY

15th CAVALRY

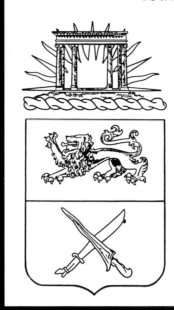

TOUS POUR UN UN POUR TOUS

18th CAVALRY

VELOX ET MORTIFER

26th CAVALRY (PHILIPPINE SCOUTS)

OUR STRENGTH IS IN LOYALTY

82d CAVALRY

TEMERITAS

94th CAVALRY

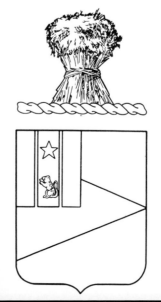

VIKING VANGUARD

101st CAVALRY

102d ARMORED CAVALRY

TO THE UTMOST

FIDE ET FORTITUDINE

105th CAVALRY

OUT IN FRONT

106th CAVALRY

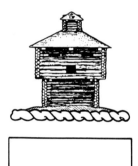

109th CAVALRY

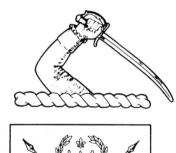

HIT 'EM FIRST

110th CAVALRY

UNION LIBERTY AND THE LAWS

103d CAVALRY

104th CAVALRY

107th ARMORED CAVALRY

FACERE NON DICERE

108th CAVALRY

COME WHAT WILL

111th CAVALRY

PRO CIVITATE ET PATRIA

112th ARMORED CAVALRY

RARIN' TO GO

SCATTER COME TOGETHER

63

113th CAVALRY

WE MAINTAIN

114th CAVALRY

VIA VI

117th CAVALRY

SHOW 'EM THE WAY

121st CAVALRY

124th CAVALRY

GOLPEO RAPIDAMENTE

139th CAVALRY

COME WHAT WILL

115th ARMORED CAVALRY

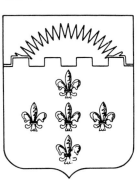

116th ARMORED CAVALRY

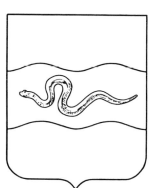

SINE MORA

POWDER RIVER

122d CAVALRY

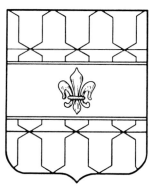

FORWARD WITHOUT FEAR

123d CAVALRY

146th CAVALRY

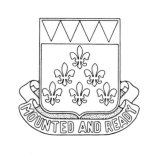

MOUNTED AND READY

150th ARMORED CAVALRY

WE CAN TAKE IT

158th CAVALRY

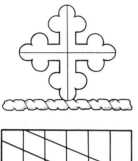

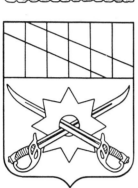

163d ARMORED CAVALRY

196th CAVALRY

223d CAVALRY

238th CAVALRY

240th CAVALRY

173d ARMORED CAVALRY

194th CAVALRY

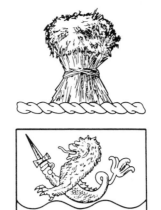

THE ARM OF DECISION

230th CAVALRY

SPEED·STRENGTH·STAMINA

237th CAVALRY

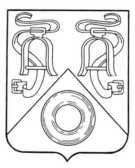

DECISION WITH MIGHT

278th ARMORED CAVALRY

I VOLUNTEER SIR

297th CAVALRY

THUNDERWOLVES

301st CAVALRY

302d CAVALRY

305th CAVALRY

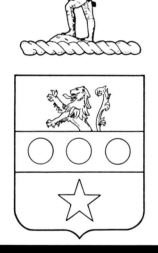

306th ARMORED CAVALRY

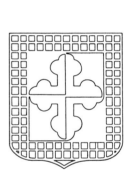

309th CAVALRY

310th CAVALRY

303d ARMORED CAVALRY

304th CAVALRY

307th CAVALRY

308th CAVALRY

311th CAVALRY

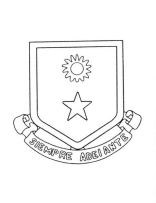

312th CAVALRY

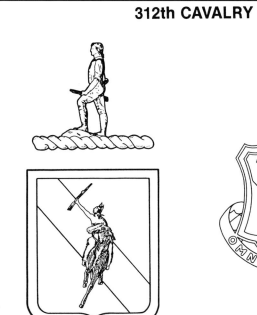

313th CAVALRY

WE ALSO SERVE

314th CAVALRY

UNITY AND SPEED

317th CAVALRY

AUDAX ET VIGILANS

318th CAVALRY

321st CAVALRY

TIENS TA FOI

322d CAVALRY

AUDACTER ET STRENUE

315th CAVALRY

316th CAVALRY

SEE ONLY VICTORY

PATA CONCITA FULMINT NATI

319th CAVALRY

LEAD ME FORWARD

320th CAVALRY

SEMPER PARATUS

323d CAVALRY

PRIMERO

324th CAVALRY

MAH BE-AH

UNITED STATES CAVALRY ASSOCIATION HISTORY

In 1976 a group of ex-cavalrymen met to discuss the plight of the Horse Cavalry. The last of the mounted cavalry units served during the initial stages of World War II, and by 1944 all Horse Cavalry units had been dismounted. (Due to modernization, the cavalry branch of service was eliminated in 1950 and replaced by the armored division.) Since there had been no cavalry units (other than armored cavalry) in over thirty years and no cavalry branch in twenty five years, the major question asked by the group was, what had happened to the uniforms, weapons and equipment of the cavalryman? Also, who had a real interest in preserving the history, traditions and heritage of the cavalry?

In pursuit of the question as to who currently had an interest in the Horse Cavalry, the group found:

1. Since there was no official cavalry branch, the Department of Army had little interest, other than in the history which could provide continuity for the future.

2. The Armor Branch, the successor to the cavalry, placed its primary interest in the development of armor, and justly so. Its museum carried little on the Horse Cavalry.

3. Other military museums had exhibits on cavalry equipment, which normally emphasized the support that it gave to the cavalry.

4. There were a few private and public museums which had some form of cavalry coverage. For the most part, they normally covered a particular unit or a geographical area where the cavalry units served. All were confined to a specific time frame, such as the Indian War or Civil War periods.

5. The US Cavalry Museum at Fort Riley, Kansas, was more of a Fort Riley Museum than a cavalry museum.

6. Many of the old cavalry regiments of the Regular Army and National Guard had unit associations. Most of their members were from the World War II era, and their interest lay in that direction. Since most of the associations also covered current active regiments whose interests were products of the time, there was coverage of the past only to provide continuity for the future.

It was the opinion of the group that no one was really looking out for the interest, the history and heritage of the cavalry. They could find no national organization that had as its primary function the preservation of the history and artifacts of the Horse Cavalry.

Next, the group looked into the status of the uniforms, weapons and equipment of the cavalryman. A search for this equipment proved futile. Most of the major items of equipment had disappeared, and what was left was in the hands of collectors and dealers. It was apparent that this effort was some thirty years too late. It was believed, however, that an effort should be made to initiate a program to save what was left.

Based upon the study of this group, it was decided that a national organization was needed if the history, traditions, heritage and equipment of the cavalry were to be preserved and perpetuated. It was believed that one of its major objectives should be the establishment and operation of a National Horse Cavalry Museum. This would be a museum which would be free of military and political pressures; one in which only the cavalry trooper and his equipment would be featured. The museum would present the history, uniforms, weapons and equipment used by the cavalry from the time of its birth during the Revolutionary War until its end during World War II. Each cavalry regiment, Regular, National Guard and Reserve, would be featured with the history, deeds and exploits told.

The primary purpose of the museum would be to educate the general public on the history of the Horse Cavalry. In addition to cavalry uniforms, weapons and equipment, it would contain a depository of cavalry literature with a research library. It would be financed to insure its perpetuation. An ad-hoc committee was appointed to draft a constitution, which was presented at the first meeting on February 20, 1976. The constitution was approved at that meeting and the US Horse Cavalry Association was officially organized. It was later incorporated under the laws of the state of Texas, and approval was obtained from the Internal Revenue Service as a tax exempt organization. It was established with its initial objectives as follows:

1. To obtain, preserve or reproduce uniforms, weapons and equipment used by the cavalry soldier.

2. To research, record and preserve the history of the cavalry regiments, traditions and customs.

3. To support and coordinate the activities of quasi-military units formed for the purpose of portraying cavalry units of the past.

4. To collect and preserve literature written about the cavalry.

5. To support existing museums that are Horse Cavalry oriented and to finally establish a National Horse Cavalry Museum free of political and military pressures.

6. To establish a comradeship for its members who find the esprit de corps of the cavalry stimulating and rewarding.

The Association was formally organized on February 20, 1976, by the approval of the constitution, by members present at the first meeting at the Del Camino Motel, in El Paso, Texas. Upon approval of the constitution, the following members of the Board of Trustees were elected: Chairman James R. Spurrier, Colonel USA (Ret); Vice Chairman Dean Cole; members: James H. Polk, General USA (Ret); Sherman P. Haight, Jr.; William H. Nutter, Major General USA (Ret); Henry B. Davis; Nester Gonzalez.

Following the organizational meeting, the Board of Trustees met and appointed the following Association Officers: President James R. Spurrier; Vice President Dean Cole; Secretary/Treasurer Levin L. Lee.

The following individuals attended the first meeting of the Association and are considered as the founding fathers of the Association: James R. Spurrier, Charles C. Acuna, Levin L. Lee, Duane H. Baldwin, George B. Hudson, William H. Nutter, Wallace G. Foreman, Frederick G. Lee, Dean Cole, George B. Elms, Sherman P. Haight Jr., Henry B. Davis, W.A. Adams Jr., Ernest W. Nunn, Kenneth A. Tipton, Michael C. Magee, E.V. Higgins, Nestor D. Gonzales, Henry Richie Wilson, Francis Daugherty, James C. Cage, J. Hal Gambrell.

Trooper William H. Nutter became the first official member by being the first to pay the annual dues of $5.00.

The Association spent its first year of existence in studying ways and means to establish a viable organization and in promoting membership. It took steps to obtain legal status for the Association and to obtain tax-free status. It continued its research on the history, traditions, and heritage of the cavalry. It also made its first appeal for the donations of artifacts.

The Association was incorporated under the laws of the state of Texas as of May 22, 1976, and obtained tax-free status as a publicly supported organization under Section 509 (a)(2) of the Internal Revenue Code.

The first member to die was Trooper Percy Haydon.

A limited appeal for members was made, and a total of 104 was obtained by the year's end.

In 1977 the US Horse Cavalry Association's efforts were spent laying the foundation for future developments. Emphasis was placed on obtaining members and in contracting cavalry unit associations. Studies were developed to ascertain the best methods by which the Association could accomplish its objectives.

One of the early considerations was the establishment of a National Horse Cavalry Museum. The Association looked at the US Cavalry Museum, Fort Riley, Kansas, as a possible solution. Henry B. Davis, a member of the Association and recent director of the US Cavalry Museum, believed that the climate was not right for an official contact with the Museum. At the time it did not have a director. Davis further believed that it would be difficult to obtain an agreement with the Museum. This reinforced the Association's thinking on the establishment and operation of a museum that would be free of political and governmental influence.

The Executive Branch completed a study, "A National Horse Cavalry Museum." This study recommended that the Association establish a National Horse Cavalry Museum and that a master plan be developed for its implementation. The Board of Trustees approved the study and directed the Executive Branch to develop the master plan.

In 1978, the Association made inquires into the possibility of working out some form of an agreement with the Cavalry Museum in El Paso, Texas. This Museum had just been established and was operated by the city. The Museum's location and building had an appeal to the Association as a possible site for its National Cavalry Museum. The Association contacted the local authorities; however, it received little encouragement as political factors precluded further efforts.

1978 also produced the first local chapter, "The Paso del Norte Chapter," El Paso, Texas. Colonel A. D. (Patsy) Dugan was elected the first president of the Chapter.

The previous year, the Executive Branch of the Association had completed a study entitled "A National Horse Cavalry Museum." This was a concept study which outlined the requirements necessary for the establishment of a National Horse Cavalry Museum. This study was approved by the Board of Trustees who directed the Executive Branch to prepare a detailed study on the establishment of a museum including cost. A study, "Proposed National Cavalry Museum," was developed by late 1979. This study included the cost of establishing such a museum; it did not cover the cost of a building or grounds. The study contained a detailed breakdown of artifacts, reproductions, display equipment, fixtures and furniture to initially establish the museum. It also included personnel to operate the museum and a proposed annual budget. It was estimated that the initial cost would be approximately $250,000.00 to establish the museum with an annual working budget of $50,000.00, which was considered a conservative estimate.

The study, "Proposal for the National Horse Cavalry Museum," was presented to the Board of Trustees at its February 1980 Meeting. The cost of establishing a National Horse Cavalry Museum would require revenue outside the capabilities of the members of the Association. It would require the financial help in the form of grants from foundations and from other sources. The Board of Trustees approved in principle the study; however, because of the cost of establishing such a museum, the President was instructed to seek alternatives.

A Fund Raising Study was developed during the year and was presented to the Board of Trustees. The Board directed the President to implement as many of the recommendations as possible.

By the summer of 1980, the conditions had changed at Fort Riley, Kansas. A new director had been appointed for the Museum; and a new Commanding General came aboard at Fort Riley, Kansas. It was decided to try and make contact to see if an agreement could be made that would permit the Association to fulfill its objective regarding a museum. Overtures were made to the director, and he thought it was an excellent idea and that a conference should be held to explore the idea. The Chairman of the Board of Trustees contacted the Chief of Military History, Department of the Army, to ascertain the legalities and feasibility of working out some form of agreement. The Chief of Military History saw no major obstacles.

A meeting was held between the Commanding General, Fort Riley, Kansas, Major General E. A. Partain; the Director, US Cavalry Museum, Terry Van Meter; the Chairman, Board of Trustees, Trooper James H. Polk and the President of the Association, Trooper James R. Spurrier. It was a unanimous agreement that such a sponsorship would be of mutual benefit and that the necessary documents should be drawn to create the sponsorship.

The first Association Golf Tournament was held at the Fort Bliss Golf Course during the Annual Meeting.

By early 1981, a draft of a "Memorandum of Understanding," between the US Army and the Association was sent to Fort Riley for approval. By mid 1981, the Commanding General, Fort Riley and the President of the Association, had signed the memorandum. The Chairman, Board of Trustees of the Association, then obtained the signature of the Chief of Military History, Department of the Army, Brigadier General James L. Collins, Jr. By late fall, the sponsorship of the Museum became official.

The "Memorandum of Understanding" stated the following:

1. That the Museum has a permanent home at Fort Riley, Kansas, and that it will be devoted only to the history and traditions of the cavalry branch of the US Army.

2. That the Association and its members shall make cash gifts and loans or donate artifacts (or reproductions thereof) to the Museum to the degree authorized by AR1-100.

3. That in consideration of the financial and other support rendered to the Museum by the Association, the Association shall have the right to make recommendations as to the operation of the Museum.

4. That if the Museum is either terminated or relocated from Fort Riley, Kansas, that the Association be permitted to recover artifacts and memorabilia lent to the Museum, and through the Chief of Military History, Department of the Army, have the first opportunity to acquire such other artifacts and memorabilia as may be desired, providing such acquisition is authorized by law and regulations.

5. That the Museum shall be accountable, but not liable to the Association for damage to or loss of or destruction of any artifacts loaned by the Association to the Museum.

1982 was the first full year of sponsorship of the Museum by the Association and in which the working agreement was implemented. Steps were taken to develop short and long range plans for the Association and to make recommendations for the orderly development of the Museum. The Association submitted a letter to the Director of the Museum, "Future Plans," which outlined the Association's thoughts on the future development of the Museum.

Prior to this time, the administration of the Association had been handled by volunteer help, principally the President and the Secretary, with occasional part time help for major mailings, such as the newsletter and recruiting brochures. The Association had reached the point were it became necessary to obtain paid administrative help. The Association entered into an agreement with a company, "Design Concepts," to handle routine administrative matters on a contract basis.

In 1986, the Association celebrated its 10th Anniversary and recognized that the dreams of the few who met in El Paso in 1976 were being realized. The Association had a broad membership base, was sound financially and was seeing some of its goals being reached.

In December, the Association's Headquarters was moved to Building 612, Fort Bliss, Texas. As of December 31, 1986 the membership was 2,585.

A decision had been made in 1990 to move the Headquarters of the Association from Fort Bliss, Texas to Fort Riley, Kansas, primarily because Fort Riley had been the center for the US Cavalry history and lore since after the Civil War. An added inducement was the presence of the US Cavalry Museum. The Headquarters was to be housed in what was a Cavalry Stable Shack, which Fort Riley had renovated for an office. The move was completed in April 1991.

There were several significant actions taken by the Association in 1993. The first one was the name change of the Association. At the Business Meeting in the fall of 1992, the members approved the name change from the US Horse Cavalry Association to the US Cavalry Association, believing that the elimination of the word "Horse" would make the Association more attractive to other than horse cavalrymen. A special meeting was held on January 5, 1993 in Building Number 283, Fort Riley, Kansas. The members approved the name change as of that date. The Association requested the change of name to the state of Texas, which was approved.

The Chairman of the Board of Trustees touched base with the Chief of Staff, US Army, General Gordon Sullivan and with the Commandant of the Armor Center, Major General Paul Funk. Both expressed their support of the name change.

The next major action was the establishment of the US Cavalry Memorial Foundation. The incorporation of the Foundation was approved by the state of Kansas on January 27, 1993, the Foundation to be the financial tool of the Association.

A major reorganization of the Association was completed in 1995. Committees were reorganized and established to meet the various goals of the Association. Groups of committees were assigned to the appropriate directors for leadership and monitoring. State and area representatives were eliminated with the hope that each of the affected individuals would find rewarding service on a committee.

As of December 31, 1995 there were 2,555 members.

12th Cavalry Regiment, Japan, 1946-47.

USCA MEMBERS

A

MR James S. Abbott, III
MSG Robert E. Abbott USAF (Ret)
MRS Creighton (Julia H.) Abrams
CPT Robert L. Acklen, Jr.
MR John W. Adair
MAJ Junius Millard Adair AUS (Ret)
MR Charles S. Adams
MRS Corlyn Holbrook Adams
MR Wyatt Adams
MR George L. Ahearn
MR Matthew J. Ahearn
LTC Walter A. Ahrens USA (Ret)
COL Bruce Aiken AUS (Ret)
MR Robert W. Ailes
MR James L. Aitken
MAJ Dale S. Albee USA (Ret)
COL Morris E. Albers AUS (Ret)
MR Oliver L. Alcorn
MR Johnnie W. Alcoze
MSG David J. Allen USAF (Ret)
LCDR Duke D. Allen USN (Ret)
MR George K. Allen
MRS George K. (Laura E.) Allen
MRS Jerry Leigh Woodward Allen
COL Marshall B. Allen USA (Ret)
MR Philip W. Allen
MR Robert C. Allen
COL Warren P. Allen USA (Ret)
MR Maynard F. Allington
MR Anthony J. Almo
LTG Elmer H. Almquist USA (Ret)
MR Thomas Amato
MR Glenn G. Ames
MR Walter C. Ames, III
DR Anton F. Anderson DVM
MR Arnold V. Anderson
MR Dale L. Anderson
MR F. Carl Anderson, Jr.
MR Jeffrey L. Anderson
MR John R. Anderson
MR Joseph G. Anderson
MR Lemuel Hooper Anderson
MR LeRoy B. Anderson
MR Robert O. Anderson
COL Dan E. Andrew USA (Ret)
MR Randolph H. Andrews
MSG Warren W. Aney ORARNG
MR Ray C. Apparius
COL Stanley Archenhold AUS (Ret)
MR Henry J. Arledge
MR Jacques Armengol
MAJ John L. Armour USAF (Ret)
MR Harold E. (Steve) Armstrong
MR Richard Roy Arnold
MR James V. Ascenzo
MR Ralph T. Asdel
MR Alfred V. Ashenden
MR Mark C. Atchley
MRS Jane B. (Pidge) Athon
LTC Charles F. Atwell USA (Ret)
MR John F. Aures
MR Harry Leon Austin
MRS Marguerite Spurrier Avant
MR William J. (Bill) Avant
MR Graham J. Avera
MR Karl H. Axelson
MR John V. Aylward
MR Nicholas J. Azzolina

B

MRS C. Stanton (Jadwiga) Babcock
MR Clemente C. Bacani
MR Herbert W. Badgley
MAJ Ralph A. Baer, Sr. USAF (Ret)
LG Robert J. Baer USA (Ret)
MR Charlie C. Baggett
COL Niven J. Baird USA (Ret)
JUDGE Andrew Z. Baker
MR C. Richard (Dick) Baker
MAJ Edward P. (Ed) Baker USAR (Ret)
CPT James L. Baker USA (Ret)

MR Jerry A. Baker
MR Kenneth T. Baker
MR Paul M. Baker
MR Stanley B. Balbach
LTC Charles Woodhull Baldwin USAF (Ret)
MR Edward L. Baldwin, Sr.
LTG John L. Ballantyne, III USA (Ret)
MR Riley Banks, Jr.
MR Richard M. Barber
SGT John G. Barberes (Ret)
MR Mark S. Barfknecht
MR Dean D. Barger, II
MR Dean D. (Chip) Barger, III
MR R.C. (Archie) Barham
MSG Gene F. Barksdale USAF (Ret)
LTC Lucian W. Barnes USA (Ret)
MR Ray F. Barnes
MRS Robert V. (Doris Haffen) Barnes
MR Willar A. Barnes
COL Ralph C. Barnett AUS (Ret)
MRS Ralph C. (Kathleen Armstrong) Barnett
COL Frank H. Barnhart, Jr. (Ret)
MR William M. Barnshaw
COL Andrew Barr USAR (Ret)
COL John Barr USA (Ret)
MAJ Robert John Barren AUS (Ret)
MR Charles G. (Chuck) Barrett, Jr.
LTC James F. Barrett AUS (Ret)
MR John R. Barrett
MR Paul H. Barrett
COL Robert E. Barrett USA (Ret)
JUDGE Robert J. Barrett
COL Gelane M. Barron USAFNC (Ret)
COL Thomas A. Barrow USA (Ret)
MR Daniel S. Barrows
MR Randolph C. Barrows
MR John Carroll Barry
MR William C. Barto
MG J.E. Bastion, Jr. USA (Ret)
MR Douglas F. Batchelar
MR Daniel M. Bates
1LT Quentin W. Battisti PANG
COL Raymond R. Battreall, Jr. USA (Ret)
MRS Michael F. (Nancy J. Owsley) Baty
MR Randy S. Bauer
MR H. Wayne Baughey
MR Paul E. Baum
MRS Claude L. (Wilma) Baumbauer
MR Kirby Lee Bauman
MRS Herbert P. (Alexandra de Vesely) Bearce
MRS W. Conger (Egypt) Beasley
MR Calvin S. Beauregard
MR William Logan Beck
MR Harry R. Becker
MG William A. Becker USA (Ret)
1st LT William G. Becker USAR
CPT John A. Beckham USA (Ret)
LTG Julius W. Becton, Jr. USA (Ret)
MR Theodore W. (Ted) Beeler
MS Patricia A. Beeman
MR Clarence George Beers
MR Roland M. Beetham
MR Raymond Beetz
MR Gesualdo Belfiore
MR Earl C.L. Bell
MR James M. Bell
1LT LeRoy A. Bell AUS (Ret)
LTC Urcel L. (Ding) Bell USA (Ret)
MRS Urcel L. (Peggy Thompson) Bell
LTC William H. (Bill) Bell USAR (Ret)
CPT George Bender USA (Ret)
COL George C. Benjamin USA (Ret)
MR Boyd Benjamin Bennett
MR Milton Benovitz
MR Dexter Lewis Benson
MR Dexter Benson, Jr.
MRS Jacqueline S. Benson
MRS Carol K. Bentley
MAJ Dewey E. Bentley AUS (Ret)
MRS Herbert (Lena E.) Benzel
MR Leonard L. Berce
MR Delbert V. Berg
MR Joseph E. Berg
CPT Eric C. Besch USA

MR Guy F. Bess
MAJ Philip F. Betette AUS (Ret)
MR Steven M. Bettner
LTC Benjamin D. Betts AUS (Ret)
MR James R. Bewley
MR Edwin H. Bidcau, III
MR Paul W. Biehler
MR Alexander M. Bielakowski
MR Edward E. Bigler
DR Harry J. Bingham MD
MR Ray A. Bingham
MR Frank E. Birmingham
COL Gaylord M. Bishop, Sr. AUS (Ret)
MR Fred Bittner
MSG James H. Black USA (Ret)
MR Carroll Blair
COL Robert C. Blair USA (Ret)
MR Gilles Blais
MR Michael H. Blake
MAJ Gordon A. Blaker USA (Ret)
LTC Frank T. Blaskiewicz USAF (Ret)
MR Norman Bleach
MR Clay S. Bleck
MRS Stuart F. (Stephanie H.) Bloch
MR Douglas Blue, Jr.
COL Forrest S. Blunk USAR (Ret)
MR Joseph H. Boatwright
MR Edmond M. Boehlke
MR Ora J. Boelter
MR Herman N. Boiter
MRS James L. (Margaret Eltinge) Bolt
BG Philip L. Bolte USA (Ret)
MRS Philip L. (Lorel Christiansen) Bolte
MR Joseph F. Bonetti
COL Marcello W. (Bluey) Bordley, Jr. USA (Ret)
MR Daine V. Bordner, Jr.
MR Theodore J. Borkowski
MR Joseph C. Bosch, SR.
COL Lyman D. Bothwell USA (Ret)
MR William J. (Bill) Bourke
MR Michael J. Bouzis, II
MR Grayson Hunter Bowers
MR Edward James Bowles
MR Murl W. Boyd
MG Frederic W. Boye, Jr. USA (Ret)
MR Marvin Boyenga
COL Peter E. Boyes USAF (Ret)
MR Andrew J. Boyle, Jr.
MRS Andrew J. (Elaine W.) Boyle
LTG Andrew J. (Jack) Boyle USA (Ret)
LTC William P. Boyle (Ret)
MR John H. Brackbill
CSM Ralph M. (Robin) Brackett
LTC J.W. (Brad) Bradbury USAF (Ret)
MRS J.W. (Roberta J.) Bradbury
DR C. Melvin Bradley PHD
MR Thomas R. Bradley
COL Goerge C. Brady USAF (Ret)
MR Robert F. Brainard
MR Jack G. Branam
MR Joseph L. Brand
MR James Brannick
MR Ralph E. Braunstein
MR Ewart Bray
MR John Bremner
MAJ Frank J. Brennan AUS (Ret)
MR Thomas J. Brennan
MAJ Timothy C. Brennan AUS (Ret)
COL Howard (Bud) Bressler USA (Ret)
MR Donald C. Brett
MR Lyndell Bridgewater
MAJ John Cherry Briggs AUS (Ret)
MRS Patricia (Tricia) Spurrier Bright
SFC David I. Briner USA (Ret)
1LT Paul D. Briscoe USA
LTC Henry J. Brock USA (Ret)
MR Alan C. Brooks
MAJ Gordon B. Brooks, Sr. USA
LTC Thomas M. Brossart USA
MRS Rosanne Sprinkle McQuarrie Broughton
COL Aaron C. (Pete) Brown USA (Ret)
LTC Charles Asa Brown USAR (Ret)
MS Colleen V. Brown
COL Edward D. Brown AUS (Ret)

MR Gordon W. Brown
MR Hubert E. Brown
MR John A. Brown
MRS Marjorie Higley Brown
COL Robert W. (Bob) Brown AUS (Ret)
MR Stephen P. Brown
MR Thomas A. Brown
BG Thomas W. Brown USA (Ret)
1LT Vincent M. Brown
MR Washington H. (Wash) Brown
COL Willard G. Brown, Jr. USAR (Ret)
MR Robert Lee Browning, Jr.
MR Robert Lee (Bob) Browning
MR James M. Bruce
MRS Carl F. (Bernice Garrett) Brugmann
MR Carl F. Brugmann
MR Theodore E. Bruning, Jr.
MR Jobie W. Bryan
MR George W. Bryson, Jr.
LTC John C. Buchanan USAR (Ret)
MR Champlin F. Buck, III
MR James B. Buckley, Jr.
MR Michael R. Budimirovich
MR Thomas R. Buecker
MR Hugo Buerger, III
MR Fred N. Buettner
COL Lanier D. Buford USA (Ret)
MR William Eugene (Gene) Bull
MR Cecil W. Bullard
MR Clophod Frank Bulleigh
MR Hugh Bullock
MR Paul E. Burdett
MR Theodore E. Burgmyer
MR Helmar John Burk
LTC Fred Burke USA (Ret)
MR Timothy J. Burke
MR Vincent P. Burke
CWO Ivan H. Burlingame AUS (Ret)
MAJ Christopher F. Burne USAF
MR Virgil M. Burnett
MR Charles W. Burney
BG John C. Burney, Jr., USA (Ret)
MR Tom Burnham
MR Billy D. Burns
SSG James D. Burt AUS (Ret)
MRS William A. (Helen Audrey) Burt
MG Jonathan R. (Jack) Burton USA (Ret)
LTC Matthew Wales Busey, III USA (Ret)
MR Eugene A. Bush
MR Michael Butler
MR Gardner Butman
MR William N. Byland
MR Daniel A. Byram
MR James F. Byrne
COL William C. Byrns USA (Ret)
MRS William C. (Ellen M.) Byrns
MR William Claude Byrns ESQ.
COL Beverly M. (Bz) Bzdek USA (Ret)

C

MR Charles Cade
MR Charles T. Cadenbach
MR Ralph S. Cadwallader
MR R.B. (Jake) Callaghan
COL John A. Callanan USA (Ret)
MR Kenneth P. Callicott
COL William M. Calnan USA (Ret)
MRS William M. (Marie Baylies) Calnan
MR Arthur H. Cameron, Jr.
MR Robert Camina
MR Ashley Paul Camp
2LT Joseph Wayne Campbell USA
MR Fernando Campos
MR Hoyt E. Cannon, Jr.
MR Ronald W. Caperton
MR Eldridge M. Caple
MR Robert H. Capstick
BG Costas L. (Cary) Caraganis AUS (Ret)
COL Nicholas L. Caraganis AUS (Ret)
COL Christopher V. Cardine USA (Ret)
MAJ William E. Carfield USA (Ret)
MR Ralph A. Carlson
CPT Randall W. Carlson AUS
COL Stan W. Carlson USA (Ret)

LTC George B. Carmack USA (Ret)
MR Arthur R. Carmody, Jr.
CMS Gerald D. Carpenter USAF (Ret)
MAJ John H. Carr USA (Ret)
MR Robert V. Carr
MR Francis X. Carroll
MR James Carroll
MRS Leslie D. (Elizabeth Fleming) Carter, Sr.
MR Lionel Carter
MG George Allen Carver USA (Ret)
COL Scott M. Case USA (Ret)
MR John Gregory (Jack) Cashin
COL Duane S. (Casey) Cason USA (Ret)
MR Richard J. Caspar
MR Custer Cassidy
SGM Ben Castaneda USA (Ret)
MR Ben F. Castaneda
LTC Maynard E. Caster USA (Ret)
MR Dolphus D. Caton
COL Jasper D. Caton USAFR (Ret)
LTC Edwin A. Cavanagh AUS (Ret)
MRS A. Ray (Martha Jo) Cavanna, Jr.
LTC Lee E. Cavey AUS (Ret)
LTC Nicholas E. Cavitt MC USA
MR Bruce W. Chadbourne
DR Richard L. Chamberlain DVM
LTC Jack E. Chambers AUS (Ret)
MR Robert E. Champagne
MSG Rayford E. Chance USA (Ret)
MR T.L. Chandler
COL William E. Chandler USA (Ret)
MS Virginia Chapin
MR I. Lee Chapman III
CPT Robert J. Charles USAR (Ret)
CSM Allen B. Chesser USA (Ret)
LTC Charles E. Childs USAR (Ret)
MR Charles E. Childs
MR Norman R. Childs
MR Edward Chmura
MRS Virgil (Barbara Bullitt) Christian
LTC Gustave R. Christie USNGR (Ret)
MRS Theodore (Cindy Spurrier) Christie
MR Dennis L. Christopher
MR Charles J. Chunko
MR Paul A. Churella
SGT Keith C. Ciancio USA
MS Linda Miller Cibel
COL Donald M. Clark
COL Harry A. (Bud) Clark, Jr. USA (Ret)
MRS Harry A. (Frances Tully) Clark, Jr.
COL Bruce B.G. Clarke USA (Ret)
MR Kenneth Claverie
MR Dewey Clayton
MRS Dewey (Sandy) Clayton
1SG Lawrence L. Clayton USA (Ret)
MR Willard M. Clayton
COL Robert O. Cleary USAR (Ret)
MR Glenn D. Clegg
BG Wallace L. Clement USA (Ret)
MR Samuel Arthur Clements
MR Dean Cleverdon
MR John A. Cline
MR Kenneth D. Close
COL Kelso G. Clow USA (Ret)
COL Arthur F. Cochran USA (Ret)
LTC Raymond D. Coffin USA (Ret)
DR Edward M. Coffman, PhD
MR Stanley S. Cogan
COL Haskell C. Cohen AUS (Ret)
COL Aaron Cohn AUS (Ret)
MR Edward (Ted) Colbridge, Sr.
MR Frederick M. Cole
MR Harold S. Cole
CPT Loren Fletcher Cole USA (Ret)
MR Richard (Dick) Cole
MRS Roy W. (Nancy Ames) Cole
DR Scott W. Cole PhD
MR John F. Coleman
MRS Marlene McCormick Coleman
MR Joseph D. Collea, Jr.
MR Ernest H. Collier
COL John Thornton Collier AUS (Ret)
BG James L. Collins, Jr. USA (Ret)
MR Clyde O. Combs

COL James H. Comings USA (Ret)
LTC Norman F. Comly USAF (Ret)
DR Allan Commander
MR Michael J. Condes
MR Alan F. Cone
MSG Jack W. Connell USA (Ret)
MG John E. Connelly, III USA
COL H.L. Conner USA (Ret)
LTC Pedro J. Contreras AUS (Ret)
LTC Richard A. Cook USA (ret)
MRS Shirley Dockler Cook
MR Thomas P. Cook
MR William R. Cook
MS Deborah Kay Byrns Cooley
MAJ Rodney Dale (Rod) Cooley USA (Ret)
MR Leighton H. Cooncy
COL Harry B. Cooper, Jr. USA (Ret)
MR Jack B. Cooper
MR John L. Cooper
MRS R.E. (Jane Wilson) Cooper
LTC Robert E. (Coop) Cooper USAF (Ret)
MR Robert P. (Bob) Cooper
MR Alan W. Cope
MR Kenneth C. Cope
CHAPLAIN Stan Copeland USA
MAJ Lorelei Wilson Coplen USA
MR Rocco (Rocky) Coppolo
MR M. Wilbur Corpman
MR Harold M. Corray
MR Joseph F. Corrigan
MR Alfred H. Corry
MR Miguel P. (Mike) Cortinas, Jr.
MR John Raborg Cory, Sr.
MSG Robert H. Cosby, Jr. USA (Ret)
MR Henry P. Cosgrove
MR John P. Costin, Jr.
MR Michael A. Coughlin
LTC Paul Kent Coughlin USAR (Ret)
MSG Turl Covington, Jr. USAF (Ret)
COL Richard A. (Rich) Cowell USA
MRS Donald H. (Lois) Cowles
MR Byran L. Cox
MRS Harold L. (Lillian E.) Cox
MR Jesse R. (Ray) Cox
MR Thomas R. (Tommy) Cox
LTC Leo B. Crabbs, Jr. USAR (Ret)
MR John M. Craig
MR Melvin L. Craig
MR Edwin F. Cramer
COL Robert Cranston USA (Ret)
MR Clinton W. Crass
MR Larry R. Craycraft
MRS Robert B. (Lila M.) Crayton
COL Donald P. Creuziger USA (Ret)
LTC Joseph P. Cribbins USA (Ret)
MR Charlie C. Crill
COL Robert R. Crisp, Jr. USA (Ret)
MAJ George C. (Critch) Critchlow AUS (Ret)
MG Willis D. (Crit) Crittenberger, Jr. USA (Ret)
MRS Willis D. (Katharine Clayton) Crittenberger
MR Richard R. Crocker
TSG Edward P. Crook USA (Ret)
MR Benjamin H. Cross
MR Paul S. Crouthamel
MRS Anne Lynch Crusa
LTC Ronald D. Culbertson, Sr. AUS (Ret)
MR T.R. Culler
MR Bertram B. Culver, III
MR Charles R. Cunningham
MR Christopher John Cunningham, Jr.
MR James Ray Cunningham
MSG Albert Curley USA (Ret)
MRS Albert (Consuelo "Connie") Curley
MR Earl P. Curling
MR James C. Curry
MR Leon D. Curry
MRS Eugene R. (Gerry) Curtan
MR Harry Cooke Cushing, IV
LTC James F. Cutter USA (Ret)

D

MR Joseph D'Acunto
MR Jon Dahl
MR Edward L. Daily

COL David L. Dalva, II USA
MRS Virginia Bliss Daly
MR Thomas M. Daniels
MR William B. Daniels
MR E.M. Danemiller, II
LTC Edward McC Dannemiller USA (Ret)
COL Francis (Pancho) Daugherty USA (Ret)
CHAPLAIN Terrence P. Dautel OHNG
MR John C. Dautle
HMCS B.T. Davenport USN (Ret)
CPO Salvatore J. (Jim) Davi USCG (Ret)
COL Walter J. Davies USA (Ret)
MR Abel Davis
MAJ Bruce A. Davis USA (Ret)
MR C.C. Davis
MR Floyd H. Davis
MRS Franklin M. (Erma) Davis, Jr.
COL Harry J. Davis USA (Ret)
MR James R. Davis
MRS Margaret Smith Davis
MR Marvin B. Davis
GEN Michael S. Davison USA (Ret)
MR Mike Dawson
MR Joseph Ed Day
LTC John A. Dean AUS (Ret)
MR Jimmie Clifton Decker
MR James C. Dedman
MR Richard L. DeGowin
MS Gloria de Graffenried
MR Edwin DeGroote
MR Frank Deiman
MR Forrest (Tim) Deitzler
1LT Jose DeJesus USA (Ret)
MR Brian E. Del Vecchio
MR Charles W. Delano, Jr.
MAJ Gordon G. DeLaRonde USAFR (Ret)
MR Juan M. DeLaTorre
MR Carl I. Delau
MR John N. Dellaripa
MR Richard J. DeMasse
COL Robert W. DeMont USA (Ret)
MR John J. Denehy, Jr.
MR Enzo H. DeNino
MRS Enzo H. (Ann L.) DeNino
MR Lorenzo Denson, Sr.
CSM James L. DePriest USA
MR Joseph Derhofer
MR Homer B. Derrick
MR James D. DeValkenaere
MAJ Roger A. DeVall USA (Ret)
MR Frederick L. Devereux, III
MR Robert DeVine
COL Thomas A. Dials USA (Ret)
MR Leonard F. Diana
LTC George F. Diaz USA (Ret)
COL John (Jack) Dibble, Jr. USA (Ret)
CPT Bruce L. Dick USAF
MR James L. Dick
MR Lloyd L. (Bud) Dick
MRS Lloyd L. (Ruth) Dick
LT Earl S. Dickson USN (Ret)
MR Pat R. DiCosmo
MR William A. Dillon
MAJ Louis DiMarco USA
MR James Francis Ditano
MR Arnold W. Doane
BG John W. Dobson USA (Ret)
MRS Charles G. (Patricia C.) Dodge
CWO William C. Dodson AUS (Ret)
SENATOR Robert Dole
LTC Richard E. Donahue, Jr. USA
MR Michael B. Donaldson
MR Joel W. Donnelley
MR Roy G. Doolen
MR Robert A. Dorn
MR Lloyd W. Doty
MR Robert Hughes Doudican
MR Russell D. Doudt
MR Charles N. Doutt
MR Rudy J. Dovale
MR Stanley B. Doyle, Jr.
MR Louis (Lou) Drastal
COL Reno E. Drews USA (Ret)
MR John A. Dreyer

MAJ Heister H. Drum USA (Ret)
MR William E. Dudley
LTC Eugene A. Dueber USMC (Ret)
MR Harold A. Duerring
MR Allen H. Duesing
MS Beth Elaine Dugan
CWO Karl Duggin USMC (Ret)
MR Christopher A. Dugre
COL Ernest F. Dukes, Jr. USAF (Ret)
MR A.E. William Duncan
MR Stephen Dungworth
COL Jack V. Dunham USA (Ret)
MR Frank E. Dunlap USN (Ret)
MG Edward C. Dunn USA (Ret)
MR Edward L. Dunn
TSG Efrain A. Duran USA (Ret)
MR Frederick Dana Durand
RMC Harold L. Durck USN (Ret)
MR John J. Durkin
MR Lester R. Durrett
MR Miles O. Dustin
MAJ F. Sennett Duttenhofer AUS (Ret)
MRS Ruth F. Duvall
LTC John H. Dvergsten USA (Ret)
COL Robert D. (Bob) Dwan USA (Ret)
COL Clarence C. Dye (Ret)
MR Henry A. Dykhuis
MR Henry W. (Hank) Dykstra

E

MR Richard Eagan
MR G. Glenn Eanes
LTC Guy C. Earle USAF (Ret)
MAJ Douglas C. Earley AUS (Ret)
COL Vernon E. Ebert USA (Ret)
CPT Gregory R. Ebner USA
MR A. Ross Eckman
MR Gary Wayne Eddy
MR Jerry A. Edgin
MR Milton B. Edmonson
LTC Lawyn Clayton Edwards USA
MR David C. Edwards
COL Lauris M. Eek, Jr. USA (Ret)
LTC William E. Effinger, Jr. USAF (Ret)
MR Richard Walter (Rich) Einert, Sr.
COL Halvor O. Ekern USA (Ret)
MR Harry B. Elder
MAJ Theodore J. (Ted) Elias AUS (Ret)
MSG Philip S. Ellington USAF (Ret)
MR James R. Ellingwood
CPT Charles B. (Chip) Elliott, IV USA
MRS Charles B. (Polly Shannon) Elliott
MR Tom W. Embleton
MAJ Dretha M. Emo USAR (Ret)
MRS Charles E. (Annie B.) Endsley
WO Charles Ethbert Endsley USMC (Ret)
MR David E. Endsley
MRS Daivd (Betty E.) Endsley
MR James W. Endsley
MG William A. Enemark USA (Ret)
MS Beverly K. Engelbrecht
MR Clarence R. Engh
COL George W. England, Jr. USA (Ret)
MR Harry P. English
MR Richard T. Erb
DR Howard H. Erickson DVM
MR J. Hayward Erickson
CMS Norman C. Erickson USAF (Ret)
MR Vernon A. Erickson
MR Joseph F. Ermer
MRS Elsie W. Ernst
MR Thomas Clifton Etter, Jr.
MR John L. Euart
MR Mark J. Evans
DR William David Evans
MR William Patrick Evans
MR Leroy B. Everett, Jr.
DR Wilson C. Everhart MD
LTC Otto A. Ewaldsen USA (Ret)
MR Walter W. Ey
SMSG Marvin J. Eyer USAF (Ret)

F

MR Allan F. Fabian

MAJ John J. Falbe, Sr. USA (Ret)
MR Dade Farnham
SGM Daniel J. (Dan) Farrell USMC (Ret)
MR Dusan Peter Farrington
MR Michael K. Fausell
MR Michael Edward Fawley
MR Mark Fedorshak
MR Robert H. Feldmann
COL Charles M. Fergusson, Jr. USA (Ret)
MG R.G. Fergusson USA (Ret)
CPT Felipe A. Fernandez USAR (Ret)
MR Ronald Ferraro
COL James P. Ferrey USAF (Ret)
MR William E. Ferris
MR James L. Fieser
COL Gaylord L. Finch, Jr. USA
MR Gaylord L. Finch, Sr.
MR Christopher R. Fischer
MR Kenneth L. Fish
MR Floyd F. Fishell
MR Clarence W. Fisher
DR Edward J. Fitzgerald
MR Charles J. Fitzkee
MR Garfield P. Fiumedoro
CSM Dale M. Flagler USAR
MS Dielle Flesichmann
MRS James P. (Helen K.) Flowers
MR John T. Flowers
MR Robert L. (Bob) Floyd
COL John J. Flynt, Jr. AUS (Ret)
MR Francis Foley
MR John E. Foote
MR David K. Ford
MR John Ford, III
MR John N. (Jack) Ford
MR Roy E. Ford
MR Seabury H. Ford
DR Edward John Forrest DMD
LTG Eugene P. Forrester USA (Ret)
MAJ Horace Waldo Forster, Jr. AUS (Ret)
COL Donald C. Foster USA (Ret)
MRS Donald C. (Joan Thompson) Foster
MR John J. Fortehen
MR Harold C. Fountain, Jr.
MR Chester A. Fowler
MAJ John P. Fowler USA (Ret)
COL Joseph G. Fowler USA (Ret)
LTC John K. Francis USA (Ret)
MR Scott Alan Francis
COL William B. Fraser USA (Ret)
BG Joe N. Frazar, Jr. AUS (Ret)
MR Robert L. (Bob) Frazer
COL Peter A. Fredericksen USA (Ret)
MR Edgar A. Freegard
MRS Edgar A. (Addie) Freegard
MR Frederick R. Freeman
MR Julien W. (Bud) Freeman
MR William J. Freeman, Jr.
LTC Mark R. French USA
MR William H. French
COL Philip S. Freund USA (Ret)
MR Albert R. Frevele
DR Stig E. Friberg
MAJ Charles P. Frinks AUS (Ret)
CPT John H. (Jack) Fritz USAR (Ret)
MR Lloyd W. Frohring
MRS Paul S. (Juanita Irene) Fromer
MR Jon Hemphill (Jack) Frost
LTC Kenneth L. Fry AUS (Ret)
MR Richard M. Fry
MSG Wilbert M. Fry USNG (Ret)
MR Ernest L. Fulford
MR John G. Fuller
MR Robert H. Fuller
MR Robert F. Funkhouser

G

COL Howard M. Gabbert, II USA (Ret)
CWO3 William E. Gage USA (Ret)
LTC Gus Gagel (Ret)
LTC Sidney W. Gaddy USAR (Ret)
MR Timothy P. Gainer
MR Albert T. Gainor

MR John E. Galitz
COL Daniel P. Gallagher USA (Ret)
MR Guy Gallien
MR Dale Gallon
MR Joseph L. Galloway
LTC J. Hal Gambrell USA (Ret)
BG Vincent de P. Gannon USA (Ret)
MR Manuel B. Garcia
MR Adam L. Gardner
MR John J. Garlan
MR James F. Garth
MR William R. Gateley
MR Philip C. Gates, Sr.
MR George W. Gaumond
MR Paul L. Gawlak
MR Peter W. Geery
MR R. Scott Geiger
MRS Marie E. Gfeller
MR H.E. (Bud) Gibson
MR James W. Gibson
MAJ George A. Gilbert, Jr. USAR (Ret)
LTC Thomas H. Gilbert USA (Ret)
MR Paul J. Gilboy
MR Tracy Gilbreth
MR Arthur G. Gilkes
MRS Berkeley S. (Novella L.) Gillespie
MR Mark F. Gillespie
COL Thomas D. Gillis USA (Ret)
COL James W. Gilman AUS (Ret)
MS Sarah Gilmer
CPT Edward N. Giobbe USAR (Ret)
MR Arthur C. Gjertson
MR Lauren E. Gjovig
MR Denis Glaccum
MS Isabel Glasgow-Perkins
LTC Malvin F. Glass USA (Ret)
MR Courtney Glisson, Jr.
SSG Ray E. Glover USA (Ret)
LTC William J. Glynn USA (Ret)
MRS Nancy Hibbard Roberts Godfrey
MSG Ralph E. Godfrey USA (Ret)
LTC Joe Goeppner USA (Ret)
MR Charles M. Goetz
MR David N. Goff
1SG Marshall W. Goff USA (Ret)
MR Alan Gold
MR Wilmer R. Goldsberry
MR Reuben Goldstein
LTC Larry G. Goldston USAR
MR Mark R. Golliher
MR Joseph L. Gomez
MR Cody West Gooch
MRS Joan Henry Gooding
MR John T. Goodwin
MS Marjorie Ann Goodwin
BG Samuel McC Goodwin USA (Ret)
COL Arthur J. Goss AUS (Ret)
MRS Walter J. (Jacqueline L.) Gough
MR Fred F. Gourley
MR Albert A. Grabher
BG Ephraim F. Graham, Jr. USA (Ret)
MR Frank K. Graham
MAJ Ray E. Graham AUS (Ret)
COL Emerson W. Grant USA (Ret)
MR Robin M. Grant
MR W. Ashley Gray, Jr.
COL William H. Greear USA (Ret)
COL Charles H. Greene, II AUS (Ret)
COL James Scott Greene, Jr. USA (Ret)
COL Maurice C. (Cam) Greene (Ret)
BG Michael J.L. Greene USA (Ret)
MRS Michael J.L. (Eileen Conner) Greene
MRS Walter (Mary Logan) Greenwood, Jr.
COL Henry B. Greer USA (Ret)
MR John M. Gribbin
MR Stanley W. Griffith
COL William R. Griffiths USA (Ret)
COL Angelo Grills USA (Ret)
LTC Fred A. Grohgan, Jr.
MR Richard P. Grossenbach
CPT Luke G. Grossman USA
WO Morris J. Grossman AUS (Ret)
LTC Gilbert J. Grout USA (Ret)
DR Michael L. Grozier MD

MSG Lee S. Grubbs USAF (Ret)
MR Edward C. Gruetzemacher, III
MR H. Fuller Grund
MRS Mary M. Schaeufele Guarnieri
MR Louis E. Guerrina
COL A.D. Guffanti USA (Ret)
SMG Leroy Gunn (Ret)
MR Robert F. Gurklies
MR Wayne Gustavus
MR Andreas Gutzeit
MR George S. Guysi

H

MR Harold E. Hackett
LT Robert A. (Bob) Hackett AUS (Ret)
LTC James F. Hackney USAR (Ret)
MR William H. Hackworth USA (Ret)
MR James R. Haga
CSM Roland P. Hahn USA (Ret)
MR Sherman P. Haight, Jr.
GEN Ralph E. Haines, Jr. USA (Ret)
MG Peter C. Hains, III USA (Ret)
MR William G. Haipt
MR John W. Hakola
COL Bunn D. Hale USA (Ret)
MR Donald J. Haley
COL David B. Hall
MR Elmer D. Hall
CPT Gerald D. Hall USA (Ret)
MR Guy P. Hall
COL Howard F. Hall AUS (Ret)
COL James M. Hall USA (Ret)
MRS George W. (Ann Daniels) Hallgren, Sr.
MR Irving M. (Hal) Halpern
MRS Dianne Royder Halpin
COL George F. Hamel USA (Ret)
SFC Joseph L. Hamilton USA (Ret)
COL Norman C. Hammond AUS (Ret)
MR Robert Houston Hamsley
MR John E. Hand, Sr.
MRS John S. (Lois Fleming) Hand
MR Keith Hankins
COL C. Norman Hanson USAF (Ret)
LTC John Andrew Hanson AUS (Ret)
MR Robert Brand Hanson
COL William F. (Bill) Hanson AUS (Ret)
MRS Joan Wilson Hantel
LTC Russell C. Hantke USA (Ret)
MR D. William Hanway
MR Benjamin H. Hardaway, III MFH
MR Lawrence E. Hargrove
MAJ Oscar Harig AUS (Ret)
MR Robert W. Harkins
TSG John C. Harmon USA (Ret)
MR Charles J. Harney
COL Armistead R. (Brick) Harper USA (Ret)
MR Charles E. Harpt
MR M.B. Harrington
COL Tracy B. Harrington USA (Ret)
MR Charles L. Harris
MAJ Nicholas R. Harris
MR Ralph W. Harris
COL Sam Harris USAR (Ret)
MR Shields S. Harris
DR Tom D. Harris, Jr. DVM
COL Eddie E. Harrison AUS (Ret)
MR James R. Harroff
MR Albert Edward Hart, Jr.
MR James W. (Metic) Hart
MR John R. Hart
MR Leo J. Hart
COL James N. Hartford, Jr. USAR (Ret)
MAJ Harvey L. Hartle USA (Ret)
MR John Hartley
SSG Raymond A. Hartley USA (Ret)
MR Ralph E. Hartman
MR Roger W. Harwood
CWO3 Jonathan J. Hasbrouck
COL William L. Hastie USA (Ret)
MRS Sidney S. (Ann M.) Haszard
MR Tyler C. Hathaway
MR Richard (Rick) Hatt
MR Gary P. Hauser
MR Richard Millard Hawk

MR Richard B. Hawkins
MRS James L. (Sugar) Hayden
MR John T. Hayes
MR C.J. Head
MAJ Jerry A. Headley USA (Ret)
MRS G.E. (J.D. Heavey) Heavey
MR Eric D. Hector
TSG Ernest M. Hegeler USAF (Ret)
MR Julius Hegelmann
COL Gerard Heimer USA (Ret)
MR Alfred Hein
MR August (Gus) Heinold
MR Robert Heinz
LTC Richard W. Heldridge AUS (Ret)
BG Jack W. Hemingway USA (Ret)
MR Max C. Hempt
MR Andrew Hughes Henderson
COL Franklin J. Henderson USA (Ret)
MS Gwynn D. Henderson
LTC James R. Henderson, Sr. AUS (Ret)
CSM Joseph P. Henderson USAR (Ret)
COL Lindsey P. Henderson Jr. AUS (Ret)
MS Lorrie Foster Henderson
MR William A. Hendrickson, Jr.
MR Edward M. Henfey
MR Eugene Henrickson
MR Charles A. Hensarling
MR Robert K. Henshillwood
MR R.Y. Henslee
MRS Mary Blunt Henson
MR Stephen E. Henthorne
MR Charles (Chuck) Herbermann
MR Alvin M. Herndon
LTC Patrick R. Heron PAARNG
MR Richard L. Herschede, Sr.
MAJ Edward G. Hertel AUS (Ret)
1SG Warren Hetrick USA (Ret)
COL Albert L. Hettrich USA (Ret)
MR George F. Heuer
MR Brian A. Heuss
DR Lambert R. Hiatt
COL Paul S. Hicks USA (Ret)
MR E.V. (Hig) Higgins
MR Page L. Hiland
MR Harry Gene Hill
MRS Helen C. Hill
MR James J. Hill, III
COL John F.P. Hill USA (Ret)
MR O. Halsey Hill
COL Alvin R. Hillebrand USA (Ret)
SSG Hiram M. Hiller USA (Ret)
MRS Barbara Falck Hillman
COL Cecil Himes USA (Ret)
MR Duane A. Hinshaw
DR William Rex Hinshaw DVM
MRS Malcolm M. (Ardys L.) Hipke
DR Theodore C. (Ted) Hobbs MD
MR Douglas E. Hodakievic
CPT Christopher K. Hoffman
MSG Harry C. Hoffman USAF (Ret)
MG Hugh F.T. Hoffman, Jr. USA (Ret)
MRS Paul K. (Susan Stanley) Hoffman
COL Richard G. Hoffman USA (Ret)
LTC Robert L. Hoffman USAR (Ret)
MR Roger C. Hoffman
MR Jerry Leonard Hogan ESQ
COL Samuel M. Hogan USA (Ret)
COL George F. Hoge USA (Ret)
Miss V. Beverley Hoge
COL William H. Holcombe, Jr.
AMBASSADOR Glen A. Holden
MR Robert Thomas Holden
LG L. Don Holder USA
MR Austin Quinton Hollar
MR Glenn Pierre Hollar
MRS Sarah Mallett Hollar
MR John Hollern
LTG James F. (Holly) Hollingsworth USA (Ret)
LTC L.M. Holman AUS (Ret)
COL Robert Henry Holman AUS (Ret)
MR Harry John Holmes
MR Earle T. Holsapple, Jr.
MR Donald W. Holst
MR Ivers F. Holt

MR Robert A. Holzbacher
MR Edgar M. Hood, III
MR Paul L. Hooper
COL Philip L. Hooper USA (Ret)
COL Ruth Lynn Hooper USA (Ret)
MR Paul J. Hopkins
MR Kenneth P. Hornby
COL Charles J. Hornisher USA (Ret)
MR James B. Horton
MR Mark Davis Horton
COL Richard Hosmer AUS (Ret)
LTC Jacob J. Hotz USAR (Ret)
MR Edward M. House, II
COL Frank W. Houston USA (Ret)
MR George M. Houx
LTC James A. Howden USA (Ret)
MRS James A. (Anita Greeley) Howden
GEN Hamilton H. Howze USA (Ret)
MR William H. Hoyt, Jr.
MR Donald Hubbard
MAJ Robert R. Huber AUS (Ret)
MR Frank A. Hubnik
SFC Russell O. Huck USA (Ret)
SFC James G. Hudson USA (Ret)
COL Raymond G. Hudson AUS (Ret)
COL William E. Hudson USAR (Ret)
DR James M. Huey MD
LTC John S. Huff USA (Ret)
MR Rolland G. Huff
COL Algin James Hughes USA (Ret)
MR Byron Gail Hughes
COL George M. Hughes USA (Ret)
MR Huber C. Hughes, Jr.
MR Hugh R. Hughes
MR Scott G. Hughes
MR Jay Benedict Hughey
MR Robert J. Human
MR Herman J. Humberd
MRS Daphne Griggs Humphrey
MR Joe B. Hunt
MR Arthur B. Hunter, Jr.
CWO George E. Hunter USA (Ret)
MR Emet B. Huntsman
MR Wayne Hurd
MAJ Timothy J. Hurley USAF (Ret)
SGM William J. Hurley, Jr. USNG (Ret)
MR Albert H. Hurst
BG Cary B. Hutchinson, Jr. USA (Ret)
MRS Cary B. (Neppy) Hutchinson, Sr.
MRS Darwin E. (Phyllis K.) Hutzell

I

MR Robert L. Iceman
MR Calvin L. Ifill
MR Lance M. Ililberg
MG Richard L. Irby USA (Ret)
MR John G. Irlam
MRS I.J. (Shirley Valentine) Irvin
MR Ronald P. Irvin
REV/COL Clark O. Irving USA (Ret)
COL Richard R. Irving USA (Ret)
BG Albin F. Irzyk USA (Ret)
MR John T. Ivancic
1LT Eve Iversen USA

J

MR Wallace Jackman
MR Boyd B. Jackson
MR George C. Jackson
MR Michael Jackson
MR Raymond E. Jackson
MG Bruce Jacobs AUS (Ret)
MR John D. Jacobs
MRS Earl Charles (Ellen K.) Jacot
SSG Lewis G. Janack USAF (Ret)
MRS Sally Wilson Janis
MS Cynthia Janiszewski
MR Allan J. Jay
MR Alex H.B. Jeffords, Jr.
MR D.H. Jeffrey
MR Stephen A. (Al) Jelten
LTC Frederick B. Jenkins USAR (Ret)
MSG Hayward A. Jenkins USAF (Ret)
MR Sanford S. (Bud) Jenkins, Jr.

DR Herbert J. Jenne DVM
MAJ Lloyd W. Jennings USAF (Ret)
MR Patrick R. Jennings
COL Raymond Jasper Jennings, Sr. USA (Ret)
MRS Walter S. (Carolyn Hawkins) Jennings
CPT Robert J. Jensen AUS (Ret)
MR Charles M. Jessup
MR Henry L. Johns
MRS Charles L. (Mary Jane Raguse) Johnson
MR Colin Johnson
MRS Donald L. (Betty H.) Johnson
MR Henderson Johnson
MR Jack A. Johnson
MR J.H. Johnson
LTC Joseph M. Johnson AUS (Ret)
MRS Patricia D. Johnson (Howard)
MR Robert D. Johnson
MR Willard L. Johnson, Jr.
MR William E. Johnson
MR William L. Johnson
LTC Charlie P. Jones USA (Ret)
COL Eben R. (Scotch) Jones USA (Ret)
MAJ Everett L. Jones AUS (Ret)
MR Frederick Douglass Jones
MR J. Richard (Dick) Jones
MR James A. Jones
BG John G. Jones
TSG Johnnie A. Jones USAF (Ret)
MR Keith W. Jones
MRS Morton McD (Billie M.) Jones
BG Morton McD (Mac) Jones, Jr. USA (Ret)
MR Ralph C. Jones
MAJ Robert J. Jones USA (Ret)
LTC Roger W. Jones USA
MR Stephen R. Jones
COL Thomas S. Jones USA (Ret)
MR Wayne R. Jones
MAJ William E. (Bill) Jones AUS (Ret)
MAJ William M. (Bill) Jones USMC
MR L.W. Jordan
MR Paul F. Joseph
MR James K. Joyce
MR Lloyd E. Joyce
MR William L. Joyce, Sr.
LTC Richard G. Jung, Sr. USA
MR Alvin A. Junghans
MR Vyrl W. Justice

K

MR Ronald Max Kaim
LTC Matthew P. Kalan USA (Ret)
MR John Kalinowski
CPT Edward F. Kammer AUS
MRS Edward W. (Margaret C.) Kammer
COL Everett H. (Kandy) Kandarian USNG (Ret)
LTC Edmund J. Kane AUS (Ret)
MR Maurice E. Kaplan
MR Glenn L. Kappelman
MAJ Bruce M. Karr AUS (Ret)
MR Arnet G. (Arnie) Kaser
SSG Frederick W. Kassebaum USA (Ret)
SENATOR Nancy Landon Kassebaum
MR Marvin A. Kastenbaum
MAJ Vincent A. Katinas USNG
MR Richard Terry Kauffman
CDT Kevin F. Kaveney
MR John T. Kazmierski
MR Philip J. Kearney, Jr.
MRS Robert (Virginia Lynn White) Keefer
MR Jack Keely
LTC Eugene L. (Larry) Keeth USA (Ret)
MR Richard F. Kehrberg
COL Carl P. Keiser, Jr. USA (Ret)
LTC Russell L. Kelch USNG (Ret)
COL John G. Keliher USA (Ret)
MR Donald Keller
MRS Brodie (Josephine Cross) Kelly
MR S.D. (Jack) Kelsey
CPT O.B. Kemmerer
MR Christopher J. Kemper
MR James M. Kemper, Jr.
COL John J. Kennaley USA (Ret)
MR Burt R. Kennedy
LTC Edwin L. (Ed) Kennedy, Jr. USA

COL William V. Kennedy AUS (Ret)
DR Lawrence Kent PhD
MR Joseph A. Keohan
MR Ray D. Kerns
BG Wayne O. Kester USAF (Ret)
LTC D.M. (Duke) Ketter AUS (Ret)
MAJ Donovan D. Ketzler AUS (Ret)
LTC Lee F. Kichen
LTC W. Wallace Kilbourne USAR (Ret)
MRS Eugene (Sarah Jones) Kilcullen
MR James D. Kimbrough
MR Charles E. Kincaid, Sr.
MR Robert E. Kinckiner
LTC Byron K. King AUS (Ret)
MR George T. King
LTC Harrison Don King USAFR (Ret)
SGT James King USAR
MR John F. King, Jr.
MR Michael P. King
MR Robert P. King
MR Thomas C. Kinnas
MR Lawrence Ray Kipps
MR James Lewis Kirby, Jr.
MRS Philip F. (Sigrid Schjerven) Kirk
MRS Robert P. (Frances McClure) Kirk
CPT Howard I. Kitterman USA (Ret)
CPT John D. Kittrell
MR Charles H. Klein
MR Anthony F. Kleitz, Jr.
MRS Anthony F. (Agnes Rodney) Kleitz
LTC Irving C. Klepper USA (Ret)
MRS Debora Miller Klett
MR Calvin E. Kline
LTC Walter J. Kline AUS (Ret)
CW4 Robert J. Kling NJNG (Ret)
LTC Warren W. Klosterman, Jr. AUS (Ret)
MR George M. Klotz
MR Aloysius (Al) Klugiewicz
REV Max E. Knight
MSG Robert E. Knight USAF (Ret)
MSG Irvin D. Knipp USAF (Ret)
GEN William A. Knowlton USA (Ret)
COL Sidney A. Knutson USA (Ret)
COL Eric Kobbe USA (Ret)
MR Oscar Koberg
MR Philip S. Kobylski, Sr.
MR Henry J. Koenig
CPT William S. Koester AUS (Ret)
MR Karl P. Kohl
MR Wayne Kolstead
MS Sandra M. Kooper
MR Joseph Koppelman
MR Orval A. Korf
LTC Robert J. Kornacki USA
MR Teofil J. Kornacki
MR Edward Dawson (Doss) Kornegay, Jr.
MR John Kottelly
MR Mark R. Kotyuk
MR Emil E. Kovalcik
MR John M. Kowalchik
MR Stanley J. Kozlowski
MR Frank Kozlowsky
MG William R. Kraft, Jr. USA (Ret)
MAJ/DR Richard D. Kramer USAR (Ret)
LTC Robert L. Krasche USAF (Ret)
MR Paul Krauss
MAJ Frank H. Kreger, Jr. AUS (Ret)
CPT Robert L. Kreiling USAR (Ret)
COL John H. Krell AUS (Ret)
MR John P. Kritzer
CPT Darin M. Krueger USNG
MSG Fred F. Krueger USAF (Ret)
MRS Frances Sue Woodward Krukoski
MR Robert C. Krusinger
LTC Don A. Kuebler USAF (Ret)
MR Wallace F. Kuhner
MR Michael D. Kuhns
MRS Margaret Greeley Kurtin
MRS Robert G. (Tish Barnum) Kurtz
MG George Kuttas USA (Ret)
COL Ralph E. Kuzell USA (Ret)
MR James C. (Jim) Kyle
MR Michael Kyle

LTC Donald J. Mehrtens USA (Ret)
MRS Donald J. (Joanie D.) Mehrtens
COL Walter Meigs Meier USA (Ret)
MR James Price Meigs, Jr.
MR Paul Mellon
MR Alfred C. Memole
MR Rocco Memole
MRS Fred (Margie) Mencenberg
MR Robert R. (Red) Mendenhall
SGM Edward B. Menker USA (Ret)
CWO Monroe E. Merritt USA (Ret)
LTC Robert H. Mersbach, Jr. AUS (Ret)
MR Edward C. Merski
MR Leon C. Metz
CW4 Gregory L. Meyer USA (Ret)
MR Jeffrey W. Meyer
MR Louis G. Michael
CPT Wallace D. Michaud CTSM (Ret)
LT William G. Middlemas FLNG
MR Chet Migdalski, Jr.
MR Edward V. Migdalski
DR Scott J. Mighell MD
MG Franklin E. Miles USA (Ret)
CWO4 Robert H. Miles USA (Ret)
COL Alexander M. Miller, III USA (Ret)
MRS Alexander M. Miller, III
MR Ames H. Miller
LTC Clifford L. (Tex) Miller, II USA (Ret)
COL Daniel W. Miller AUS (Ret)
MR Delvin Miller
MR Edgar H. Miller
MR George H. Miller
MR Gregory Kern Miller
MR Harry J. Miller
MR James Alfred Locke Miller, Jr.
MR Mark E. Miller
MR Robert A. Miller
DR Samuel E. Miller MD
LTC Steven Miller USAF (Ret)
MR Walter Miller
MR Richard J. Mills
MAJ John D. Milvo USAR (Ret)
MAJ John Preston Mitcham USAR
MR David Anthony Mitchell
LTC Peronneau Mitchell USA (Ret)
MR John F. Moale, Sr.
MR John E. Mobley
MR David L. Moffat
DR William W. Moir
MRS Cornelius J. (Jean M.) Molloy
MR Daniel J. Monico
MSG Leroy E. Monn USNG(Ret)
LTC Earle S. Montgomery AUS (Ret)
MS Georgiana M. (Gigi) Montgomery
MR John F. Montgomery
MR William S. Montgomery
MR John J. Moon
MR George D. Moor
MR A. Robert Moore
MR James J. Moore
COL Roy Moore, Jr. USA (Ret)
MR Tom Burns Moore
COL Richard C. Moran USA (Ret)
MRS Richard C. (Virginia Baylies) Moran
MR Wilson Morehead
MR Lawrence A. Morgan
MR Leonard B. Morgan, Jr.
COL Thomas L. Morgan USA (Ret)
MR Hobart P. Morris
MAJ Douglas J. Morrison USA
COL James L. Morrison, Jr. USA (Ret)
MRS James V. (Mary E.) Morrison
DR Robert K. Morrison DVM
MRS Henry P. (Louise D.) Morse
MR Henry T. Mortimer
MR LaVerne W. Morton
MR Philip M. Morton
MR Bruce M. Moseley
MR George C. Moseley
LTC Zackur Moser AUS (Ret)
SFC William Mosezar NJARNG
DR Richard H. Mosier
MR Charles E. Mosse
MR Carl Hook Mote, Jr.

CWO4 William H. Mott USA (Ret)
LTC W. Jeremiah Moulton USAF (Ret)
MAJ Kenneth B. Mountz AUS (Ret)
HON Bertrand D. Mouron, Jr.
MR James M. Moyer
MR Mario F. Mucci
MR George Muck
MR J. Herbert Muller
MAJ John Francis Mullery (Ret)
MAJ Paul E. Mulrenin USAF (Ret)
CPT Jay Albert Munn AUS (Ret)
LTC Richard A. Munn, Jr. USA (Ret)
MG F.J. Murdoch, Jr. USA (Ret)
MR James L. (Jim) Murdock, Sr.
MAJ Harry D. Murphy AUS (Ret)
MR James P. Murphy
MR John V. Murphy
MR Leon B. Musser
MR Benjamin N. Myers
MR Milton W. Myers
COL Samuel L. Myers, Jr. USA (Ret)
MRS Samuel L. (Frances F.) Myers
MRS Robert E. (Faye Sargent) Mytinger

N

MR George Naas
MR Joe L. Nabor
MR Robert D. Nailor
CPT Peter F. Najera USA
MR Joe L. Nanny
MR Fank Narducci, Jr.
MR Andrew J. Narel
MR Arthur A. Naulin
COL Leo J. Nawn USA (Ret)
MR J.E. Neeley, Jr.
CPT Albert A. Nelson USA (Ret)
MR John Thomas Nelson, Jr.
COL Hugh J. Nevins USAF (Ret)
COL Robert H. Nevins, Jr. USA (Ret)
MR Peter B. Newkirk
CPT John E. Newlin, Jr. AUS (Ret)
MR Charles W. Newport, Jr.
MR James D. Newton
MRS Thomas J. (Clarice) Newton
LTC Fred A. Nichols USA (Ret)
SHERIFF John F. Nichols
COL Wallace J. Nichols USA (Ret)
LT Frederick John Nicoll USNR (Ret)
COL Jack W. Nielsen USA (Ret)
MR Lawrence P. Nielsen
MR Edmund F. Nighan
COL Hugh W. Nixon USNG (Ret)
MR C. Louis (Chuck) Noeding
MR John R. Nolan
MR Francis A. Norman
LTC Richard B. Noonan USA (Ret)
MR Robert D. Norris, Jr.
MR Jimmy H. Northcutt
MR Philip S. Notestine
LTC Lawrence D. Nuckles AUS (Ret)
MR George T. Nuoffer

O

MR Hugh O'Brian
COL Robert E. O'Brien USA (Ret)
DR Gary E. O'Connor PhD
MR Roderic S. O'Connor
LTC Padraig M. O'Dea AUS (Ret)
MR Gregory R. O'Linc
GEN Andrew P. O'Meara USA (Ret)
MR James S. O'Neal
MR Bob F. O'Neill, Jr.
MR Edward R. O'Neill
MR Raymond F. O'Pray
GEN Curtis H. O'Sullivan USNG (Ret)
MR Richard T. Oakes
MG John Oblinger USA (Ret)
MG Delk M. Oden USA (Ret)
CPT Lee G. Offen USA
WO1 William B. Oglesby AUS (Ret)
MR Robert K. Ogren
MR Leonard R. Olavessen
MR Charles B. Oliver, Jr.
MR Edward James (Ed) Oliver/Bohld

MSG Merle Olmsted USAF (Ret)
MRS Roger J. (Nancy Wilson) Olson
LTC Peter W.J. Onoszko USA
MR Michael E. Opalak
LTC Myron W. Opfermann USAR
MR Fred B. Orange
MR Jack L. Orman
SFC Robert W. Orr USA (Ret)
MR Lewis W. Osborn
MR Norman R. Osterby
DR Roger A. Ott, Sr. MD
MR James A. Ottevaere
MR Edward L. Otto
1LT Emil H. Otto USNG (Ret)
MAJ Benjamin P. Owen USA (Ret)
MR Louie Michael Oxford
MR John T. Oxley
MR J. Wayne Oxtoby

P

MR Steven F. Pach
MR Michael Padar
MR Harry S. Padgett, Jr.
MRS Harry S. (Rita) Padgett
MR Albert F. Padley, Jr.
MR L.H. Page, Jr.
MR Sam Roy Paken
GEN Bruce Palmer, Jr. USA (Ret)
MR Sam D. Palmer
MR Solon M. Palmer
MR William Jack Palmer, Jr.
MR Angelo Palmeri
LTC Joseph R. Paluh (Ret)
MR William Harold Parady
MR Menandro B. (Mendy) Parazo
MR Lewis Howell Parham
MR Mark A. Parish
REV Alvin H. Parker
MRS Betty Augur Parker
MR Gary Parker
COL Van R. Parker USAF (Ret)
CSM Gary L. Parkey USA
MR James Parkey
COL Gordon M. Parks USA (Ret)
COL Charles J. (Chuck) Parsons, Jr. USA (Ret)
MR Robert L. (Bob) Parsons, III
MR Ignacio Passos
MR John T. Patela
COL Edward H. Patterson USAF (Ret)
MR Lou Patterson
MR John Patterson
MR William R. Patterson
MRS William R. (Oralee Bliss) Patterson
BG Hal C. Pattison USA (Ret)
MG George S. Patton USA (Ret)
MR Rodney A. Paulsen
MR James R. Pawlowski
MR James H. Paxson
MR Timothy H. Paxson
MG George O. Pearson USNG (Ret)
MRS Charels M. (Kathleen O'Donnell) Peeke
MRS Elizabeth Caw Peele
LTC Alan R. Pehrson USA (Ret)
MSG Everett R. Pemberton USA (Ret)
MR Francis L. Peniston
MR Howard L. Penley
MR Arnold L. Penney
MAJ Howard B. Pennington USNG (Ret)
LTC Robert J. Percy AUS (Ret)
MR Bruce M. Peret
MRS Alfred L. (Dorothy J.) Perkins
MR Gilbert G. Perret
MR Robert G. (Bud) Perry, Sr.
COL John W. Pershing
MR Robert B. Persinger
LTC Charles E. Peters AUS (Ret)
MR Paul R. Peterson
MR Robet C. Peterson
MR Edward J. Petrie
MR Michael Petrillo
MR Gerard S. Petrucci
MR Edward D. Pettit
LTC Harry P. Pfeiffer AUS (Ret)
CPT Arthur L. Phillps, Jr.

BG Eugene Phillips USA (Ret)
MR Glenn H. Phillips
COL James H. (Jim) Phillips USA (Ret)
SGM Joe W. Phillips USA (Ret)
MRS Louella Avant Spurrier Phillips
MAJ Austin W. Piccolo (Ret)
MG George B. Pickett, Jr. USA (Ret)
COL Thomas C. Piddington USA (Ret)
CPT Duncan B. Pierce USNG
MSG Robert Felton Pipes USAF (Ret)
COL George T. Pitts USA (Ret)
MR Willis L. Platt
MR Stephen K. Plume, Jr.
COL Walter W. Plummer USA (Ret)
COL Robert (Bob) Poland USAR
MR James H. Polk, III
MRS James H. (Joey) Polk
MR Acton V. Pomante
COL William M. Pond USAF (Ret)
MRS Glenn A. (Ina Culver) Poole
MR Thomas M. Pope
LTC Stanley E. Porche AUS (Ret)
GEN Robert W. Porter, Jr. USA (Ret)
LTC Clifford E. Porterfield USAF (Ret)
MR Gregory A. Posta
LTC Joseph D. Posz USA (Ret)
MR David R. Powell
MR Merritt Harber Powell
MR Gregory Michael (Greg) Powers
LTC Vernon L. Poynter AUS (Ret)
MR Isaac L. Prentice
MR Larry A. Preuss
MRS Howard C. (Amy Allen) Price, Jr.
MR Thomas F. Price, Sr.
MR Charles M. Pride
MRS Jane A. Priester
MR Jefferson P. Pringle
LTC Charles H. Pritchard USAF (Ret)
MAJ Rowland Pritchard AUS (Ret)
MR A. Douglas Proctor
MSG John Prokopchak USA (Ret)
SGT Joseph Przutula AUS (Ret)
MR John R. Puffer
MR Michael B. Putnam
LTC John W. Putt AUS (Ret)
MR John R. Puffer
MR Michael B. Putnam
LTC John W. Putt AUS (Ret)

Q
MR Thomas M. Quek
MRS James B. (Louise E.) Quill
COL Robert J. Quinn, Jr. USAF (Ret)
MR Richard C. Quint

R
MRS Thomas H. (Opal S.) Raab
PFC Clarence L. Rach USA (Ret)
LTC Jack M. Radkey USAR (Ret)
LT Bryan P. Radliff USA
MR Thomas M. Raftery
CPT W.D. (Bill) Raftery USA (Ret)
MR Lee F. Ragland
MR Thomas L. Raines
MAJ James B. Rainey USA
MR James F. Ralstin
MR J. Grier Ralston, Jr.
MR Norman F. Ralston
COL Stanley M. Ramey USA (Ret)
MR Stanley Wheeler Ramey
LTC Edwin Price Ramsey, Sr. AUS (Ret)
DR Raquel R. Ramsey PHD
DR Harvey H. Randolph, Jr.
COL Thomspon L. (Tom) Raney USA (Ret)
MR James H. (Jim) Ranke
COL Alexander J. Rankin USA (Ret)
MR Andy Ransom
COL Thomas A. Ratliff, Jr. AUS (Ret)
MR Hubbard M. (Tod) Rattle
MR Edward H. Rautenkranz
MS Beverly T. Rawson
MR James M. Ray
MR William R. Ray
MR Gilbert Rayburn

MR Robert A. Read
President Ronald Wilson Reagan
MR James M. Reb
MR Chris Redmon
MS Nancy B. Reed
MR Philip T. Reed
MAJ Stanley Reed USA (Ret)
COL William S. Reeder, Jr. USA (Ret)
1SG George A. Reeve AUS (Ret)
MRS Kathryn (Kate) Randall Reeves
MR Laurence E. Reeves, III
MR Edward P. Regan
MR Robert C. Rego
MR Hugh D. Reich
MRS William F. (Anna Marie) Reich
MR John A. Reichley
MAJ Thomas J. Reilly, Jr. AUS (Ret)
MSG Z.V. (Zeb) Reinhardt USA (Ret)
CPT Spencer Reitz USN (Ret)
MR Don J. Renaud
COL George A. Rentschler USAR (Ret)
MR Ignatius J. (Iggy) Repp
LTC Robert Bruce Reppa MD USA (Ret)
COL Robert M. Reuter USA (Ret)
MR Charles Rew
CPT Richard M. (Rick) Reyno USA
MR Jack M. Reynolds
LTC Reginald (Reg) Reynolds USAR (Ret)
BG Royal Reynolds, Jr. USA (Ret)
COL Edwin M. (Rocky) Rhoads USA (Ret)
MR Charles A. Rhodes
MR William E. Rice
MR E.K. Richards
MR George B. Richards
CWO4 Howard C. Richards USAF (Ret)
COL Ira B. Richards, Jr. USA (Ret)
MAJ William A. Richardson AUS (Ret)
MR Dale G. Rickards
MR Maynard G.A. Riddle
MR Arnold B. Rifkin
MR Robert J. Rigacci
LTC Loehr M. Rigby USA (Ret)
COL Cecil H. Rigsby USAF (Ret)
MR Claude R. Rigsby
MR Gerald F. (Jerry) Riley
MR R.R. Ripley
COL Richard M. Ripley USA (Ret)
MR Robert H. Robar
MR Richard W. (Dick) Robbins, Jr.
CWO2 Harry E. Roberson USA (Ret)
MR Albert L. Roberts
MR Darrell S. Roberts
LTC James R. Roberts USA (Ret)
CHAP/COL Malcolm Roberts, III USA
LTC Malcolm (Mal) Roberts, Jr. USA (Ret)
MRS Malcolm (Nancy) Roberts, Jr.
MR George W. Robertson
MR H. (Robbie) Robertson
MAJ Alfred G. Robinson USA (Ret)
MR Charles Robinson
MR Robert E. Robinson
MR James Robison
MR Charles W. Rodda
MAJ George H. Rodgers AUS (Ret)
MR Herbert C. Rodgers
CSM Stephen C. Rodina KSARNG
LTC Christopher H. Roe USAR
LTC Howard R. Roe USAR (Ret)
BG Frederick C. Roecker, Jr. USA (Ret)
MR W.H. (Moe) Roettger
MR Charles W. Rogers, Jr.
COL Ralph M. Rogers USA (Ret)
MR William L. Rohde
MR Weldon A. Rolfe
MRS Gordon D. (Dorothy P.) Rood
MAJ Robert L. Rooker USA (Ret)
MR Leonard Rose
MR Neil M. Rose
COL Robert M. Rose USA (Ret)
MR Max J. Rosenbaum
COL David G.Ross AUS (Ret)
MR David M. Ross
MRS Jane Franklin Rossell
MR Richard A. (Rik) Rossetti

MS Pauline S. Roth
MR Robert E. Rouch
MR Harold M. Roum
LTC Kenneth C. (Ken) Rowe
MR Michael J. (Mike) Rowe
SFC Rowland M. Royer USA (Ret)
MR Ranson C. (Rozy) Rozelle
COL Harry Rubin USA (Ret)
DR Albert H. Rudner DDS
COL Roy H. Rudolph AUS (Ret)
COL Ronald W. Ruff USAR
MG George Ruhlen USA (Ret)
MR Stanley M. Rumbough, Jr.
MR John P. Rumin
MR George A. Rummel, Jr.
MR George A. Rummel, III
MAJ James J. Rumpler AUS (Ret)
1SG Jim Ruotsala AUS (Ret)
COL Robert O. Rupp USA (Ret)
MR Clifford A. Russell
LTC James G. Russell USA (Ret)
MSG Carl L. Rutherford USAF (Ret)
MRS Harriet Irvin Rutland
MR Michael Ryan
MR Richard A.P. Ryan
COL Glenn O. Ryburn, Jr. USA (Ret)

S
MR John Sagan
MR John Raymond Sagner
LTC Joseph R. Sain USAR (Ret)
COL A. John Sajo USA (Ret)
MRS Stanley (Freda M.) Sala
MR Fred H. Salter
COL Harold J. Samsel AUS (Ret)
MS Kristen Sanders
CW4 Michael B. Sandler USNG
MR Kenneth L. (Ken) Santoyo
LTC George E. Sapora AUS (Ret)
MRS George E. (Margaret K.) Sapora
MR Wayne M. Sarf
MR Malcolm L. Sarna
MSG William J. Sasek USA (Ret)
MR Richard Sassone
MR S. Sandy Satullo
MR Stuart J. Satullo
MR George S. Saunders, Sr.
CPT George J. Sawyer, IV USA
1LT Gerald A. Scaglione AUS (Ret)
LTC John J. Scanlan USAR
COL Norman E. Schaefer USAF (Ret)
MR Gilbert P. Schafer
MR Gary Schaub
MR Gary L. Scheel
MR John H. Scheidegger
MG Edward C.D. (Pony) Scherrer USA (Ret)
MG Larry L. Scheuchzer USAR
MAJ Adam Edward (Ed) Schlanser, Jr. USAF (Ret)
MG Lawrence E. (Bud) Schlanser USA (Ret)
MR Norbert F. Schlosser
MR Harry F. Schlueter
COL Joseph L. (Joe) Schmalzel USA (Ret)
MR Henry F. Schmidigal
MR Harry L. Schmidt, Jr.
MR Louis G. Schmidt
MR Roger M.L. Schmitt
MR Mark F. Schneider
LT Robert Schneider AUS (Ret)
MSG John Schock USA (Ret)
MR Edwin H. (Ed) Schoenbeck
MR Bernard Schoichet
MR George F. Scholl
MR Paul H. Scholtz
MR Toby Schoyer
MR Charles Elwood Schrader
MG Henry C. Schrader USA (Ret)
MR M.D. Schram
MS Deborah Schroeder
LTC Howard R. Schroeder USAF (Ret)
SGT Eugene Schuly USNG
MR John R. Schwartz
MRS Jonathan D. (Jody Polk) Schwartz
MR Walter J. Schweitzer
MR George G. Sciacqua

MR David R. Scott
JUDGE George F. Scott
MR Stephen Searles USAR (Ret)
LTC William H. Searles USAF (Ret)
DR Edwin H. Season, Jr.
LTC Frederick G. Seavers USA (Ret)
MR John A. Seay
MR William E. Sebastian
MR John P. Seburn
CPT Ernest C. (Ernie) Seibel AUS (Ret)
LTG George M. Seignious, II USA (Ret)
MRS J.A. (Dorothy E.) Seitz
COL John A. Seitz, III USA (Ret)
LTG Richard J. Seitz USA (Ret)
MR Larry Selman
SFC John T. Semich USNG (Ret)
MR Frank J. Sepanek
COL Russell K. Sesto USA (Ret)
MSG Mike Sewick USA (Ret)
MR Mike Tyrone Sewick
MS Debbie Seybold
MR Paul A. Seymour Jr.
MRS Paul A. (Dorothea Wofford) Seymour, Jr.
MR Harry S. Shannon
MR Howard E. Shapiro
LTC Irwin T. (Tom) Shaw USA (Ret)
MAJ John T. Shaw USAF (Ret)
MR Samuel L. Sheffler
MR Russell N. Shefrin
LTC Alfred H. Shehab USA (Ret)
MSG Delbert E. (Del) Shell USA (Ret)
1LT Orville E. Shelton AUS (Ret)
MR Charles Shenloogian
1LT Robert R. Shenton NJARNG
MR Peter Sherayko
MG Stan R. Sheridan USA (Ret)
MR Joseph H. Shields
MR Ernest W. (Ernie) Shillak, Jr.
MR Winsotn H. Shillito
MR Timmy Shipley
LTC Frederick L. Shope AUS (Ret)
COL Moyers S. Shore USA (Ret)
LTC Harold A. Short USA (Ret)
MR Joseph Allen Short
MRS W.E. (Lucile Hanford) Showalter
MR Al R. Shrawder
LTC John L. Shriner AUS (Ret)
LTC James L. Shroyer USA (Ret)
MR Alex Sidelnik
COL L. Gene Sidwell USAF (Ret)
MR Edward G. Siebert
MR Harry J. Siebert
COL Robert H. Siegrist USA (Ret)
MR John M. Siekierka
MR Robin Siems
MS Sandra A. Silva
MR Sam Silverman
SGM Harold Simkin USA (Ret)
SGM Janet Miller Simkins USA (Ret)
MR Jeffrey D. Simmons
DR Jerry L. Simmons DVM
MR Glenn W. Simpson
MR James Sinkay, Jr.
MRS James (Barbara E. Bruce) Sinkay
MR Eugene Sipin
MR Tom Sitter
MR Charles L. Skaggs
LTC Bernard H. Skold USA (Ret)
COL Stephen M. Slattery USA (Ret)
MSG William M. Slayton USA (Ret)
MR John C. Sloan
MR Louis Joseph Slobinsky
MR John D. Smarsh
MR Donald N. (Jack) Smeltz
MR William H. Smiley
MR Alen Smith
MR Buell B. Smith
CHAP (MAJ) Emmet C. Smith USAR (Ret)
LTC George Robert Smith AUS (Ret)
MR Jack Martin Smith
MG James C. Smith USA (Ret)
LTG Jeffrey G. Smith USA (Ret)
1LT John A. Smith USAR (Ret)
MR John W. Smith

MR Martin A. Smith
MRS McCain (Helen) Smith
LTC Millard Fillmore Smith USAF (Ret)
COL Norman Smith USNG (Ret)
MRS Peggie Smith (Walter)
SGT Raymond G. Smith USA (Ret)
MR Richard S. Smith
MR Rick Smith
MSG Robert Joseph Smith USAF (Ret)
MR Robert T. (Smitty) Smith
MR Roy L. Smith
MS Sherrie L. Smith
MR W. David Smith
MRS Walter S. (Peggy Smythe) Smith
2LT William Charles Smith USAR
LTC William H. H. Smith USAF (Ret)
MAJ Wilson G. Smith AUS (Ret)
MR Marion H. Smoak
MR Robert C. Smykal
MR Kerry L. Smythe
MR Donald C. Snedeker
COL James W. Snee USA (Ret)
MRS Olive H. Snow
COL James M. Snyder USA (Ret)
MR Charles H. Sodeman
MR Wendell Sollis
MR Chris R. Sorensen
MR Stephen J. Sosinski
MR Morton I. Sosland
MAJ Robert L. South USAR (Ret)
MR Bernard B. Spalding
MR Phil Spangenberger
MSG Kenneth T. Sparks USA (Ret)
MRS Richard E. (Nancy K.) Sparks
MR Robert C. Sparks
MR George W. Sparrow, Jr.
MR Paul A. Speck
MS Ashley Danielle Spencer
MRS Dorothy Steffen Spencer
MS Jessilyn June Spencer
CPT Richard W. Spiegel USA
MR Gerald Spiro
MR Carlton B. Sprague, Sr.
COL James R. Spurrier USA (Ret)
MRS James R. (Lucile Lafferty)Spurrier
COL R. F. St. Germain AUS (Ret)
MG Adrian St. John USA (Ret)
MS Madeline F. Staggers
MS Anna Staib
CPT J. D. Stallings USNG (Ret)
MR Frank Stanecki
MR Walter J. Stanecki
SGT Arthur J. Stanley, Jr. AUS (Ret)
MR Lacey Gardner Stanley
MR John Patrick Starrs
GEN Donn A. Starry USA (Ret)
MRS Donn A. (Letty G.) Starry
MR Carl A. Stefan
MR Paul S. Stefurak
MR Robert J. Stefurak
MR William F. Stefurak
MAJ Robert C. Steiger USAR
MRS W. C. (Norma Curtis) Steiger, Jr.
LTC Wallace C. Steiger, Jr. USA (Ret)
MR William C. Steinkraus
MR Christian L. Stenberg
MR Richard K. Stenberg
MR David L. Stephens
MG Elmer Lewis Stephens USNG (Ret)
LTC James Darwin Stephens USA (Ret)
CSM Robert E. Stephens USA (Ret)
MR Gary E. Stevens
COL Hugh W. Stevenson USA (Ret)
LTC Hal D. Stewart USA (Ret)
MR Charles S. Stewart
MR Donald G. Stewart
DR Franz H. Stewart MD
MR Lawrence Fricks Stewart
MR Thomas Melville Stewart
MRS Thomas (Sallie Spurrier) Stewart
SGT Adam K. Stickney USNG
MR Alwyn B. Stiles, Sr.
1SG Raymond Still USA (Ret)
MR Morton C. Stivison

MR Dudley W. Stoddard
MR Jere Stone
MR Leon C. Stone
MR John C. Strader
COL Wilbur C. Strand USAF (Ret)
DR John J. Stransky
MR James H. Stricklan
LTC Oscar H. Stroh USAR (Ret)
CW3 Thomas P. Strom USA (Ret)
MR Carsten Stroud
SSG Patrick R. Stroud USNG
MR Ervin T. Struck
COL Alex J. Stuart, Jr. USA (Ret)
MRS Alex J. (Teeny Wilson Powers) Stuart, Jr.
MAJ Alfred E. Stuckert AUS (Ret)
MR Daryl C. Stuhr
MR Vallie Henry Stump
LTC Edwin W. Sullivan AUS (Ret)
MR Louis J. (Lou) Sullivan
MR Stanley A. Sullivan
MR William A. Sussmann
MR James Robert Swallows
MR James Allen Swan
MAJ William H. Swan AUS (Ret)
COL Robert L. Sweeney, Jr. USA (Ret)
MR Mitchell S. (Mitch) Swieca
MR Lee Wilson Swift, Jr.
MR Robert F. Swift
MR James T. Swindle
MS Daphne S. Swint

T

MR Joseph F. Tabor
MR Donald V. Tadiello
MG Thomas H. Tait USA (Ret)
TSG Mickey H. (Mike) Tamsett USAF (Ret)
MR Elbert Leo Tanner, Jr.
MR J. (Traveling J) Tanner
MR Salvatore F. Tarantino
MR John R. Tarver
MR Alfred Taylor, Jr.
COL Dale W. Taylor USA (Ret)
CPT Emmett P. Taylor, III
MR Frank H. Taylor
MR John M. Taylor
MS Kathleen Taylor
MR Myron D. (Mike) Taylor
MAJ Richard P. Taylor AUS (Ret)
MR Robert M. Taylor
MR Robert P. Taylor
CPT Vincent J. Tedesco, III
MR James D. Teel, II
MR Louis W. Teissler
LTC Howard W. Tejan USAF (Ret)
MR Frank A. (Frank) Templeman
MR Ellis Fuller Temples
MR Robert L. Templeton
MR Albert C. Tercero, Jr.
MRS Linda D. Terrell
MR Warren C. Terrell
MSG William M. (Bill) Tevington USA (Ret)
MRS Donald W. (Virginia) Thackeray
COL Benjamin E. Thomas AUS (Ret)
COL Gordon F. Thomas USA (Ret)
MR Ray Thomas
MR Ray M. Thomas
DR Frederick E. Thompson MD
COL John G. Thompson USA (Ret)
MRS Earl F. (Lorraine C.)Thomson
LTC Willis M. Thomson USAF (Ret)
COL Francis H. (Cappy) Thrush USA (Ret)
MR Kenneth W. Tieman
LTC Phillip W. Tiemann, Jr. AUS (Ret)
MR Edward C. Tietig
MRS Sharon Mullins Tigue
MR Charles M. Tillinghast
MG John C. F. Tillson, III USA (Ret)
MR Charles O. Tilson
MAJ A. J. Timpano AUS (Ret)
LTC Edgar J. Tingle USNG (Ret)
MR William E. Tirk
MR John C. Tirrell
CPL James Titus NJARNG
LTC Richard W. Titus AUS (Ret)

MG W. Russell Todd USA (Ret)
LTC William N. Todd,III USA (Ret)
MR Harold H. (Hal) Tollefson
MR George M. Tomlinson
MR Orford W. (Tommy) Tomlinson,Jr.
LTC Ira G. Tompkins
MR Ellis J. Tonik
COL Allan C. Torgerson USA (Ret)
MR Roy M. Towers
MRS Charles (Lois) Towns
COL W. B. Townsend USA (Ret)
LTG T. J. H. Trapnell USA (Ret)
SPC Charles L. Tremel, Jr. USNG
BG Anthony C. Trifiletti USA (Ret)
MR Roger S. Tripp
MAJ Arthur A. Tritsch USA (Ret)
MRS Phyllis G. Tritsch (Arthur A.)
MR Donald F. Trout, Jr.
MR John (Jack) Tuberty
MAJ Ernest R. Tucker AUS (Ret)
LTC William D. Tucker
MR Owen D. Turner
MAJ Robert N. Turner, Jr. USNG (Ret)
MR Vern M. Turner
MR Lawrence W. Turnquist
MAJ Joseph G. Twombly USA (Ret)

U

LTC Robert W. Ulmschneider AUS (Ret)
MR A. Preston Utterback

V

COL William H. Vail USA (Ret)
SGM Leon Van Autreve USA
MR Virgil T. Van Dyck
MAJ Joseph B. Van Horn AUS (Ret)
MR William C. Van Horn
COL R. Thomas Van Kleeck AUS (Ret)
LTC Marinus Van Kleef, Jr. AUS (Ret)
MR Terry Van Meter
MRS Elizabeth C. Van Norden
MR Harold Francis Van Wie
CPT Craig T. Vanderhoef USN
COL Dean T. Vanderhoef USA (Ret)
MRS Dean T. (Jeanne Lambert) Vanderhoef
MS Lee S. Vanderhoef
DR Leonard Vanderveld, Jr.
MS Phyllis M. Vanhecke
COL Frank E. Varljen USA (Ret)
MR Jack B. Vaughn
MR Gary C. Vennes
MR Daniel E. Verniero, Jr.
MR Malcolm B. Vilas, Jr.
MR Richard A. Villarreal
MR Charles A. Vincent
COL Albert E. (Dutch) Voelkel USAR (Ret)
MS Carolyn R. (Molly) Vogel
MR Frederick Herman Voigt
MR Joseph Les Volkmer
MR Peter Von Gontard
COL Benjamin F. M. Vonstahl USA (Ret)
MR David Schuyler Vroom
LTC Peter D. Vroom USAF

W

TSG Edward A. Wade USAF (Ret)
COL William Franklin Wadsworth, Jr. USA (Ret)
MR Frank Hall Wagner
GEN Louis C. Wagner USA (Ret)
MRS Melvin J. (Esther E.) Waite
MR Bruce A. Wales
MR Donald F. Walker
MR Joseph Carl Walker
MR Jack Wall
MR Eugene S. Wallace
LTC Jerry G. Wallace USA (Ret)
LTC John F. Wallace USAR

COL Marshall Wallach USA (Ret)
LTC Richard L. Walther AUS (Ret)
MR Wayne W. Waltman
MR Bennie E. Walton
MR Don H. Walton
DR Robert G. Walton MD
MR Bryan L. Waltz
SGT Wade A. Wantoch USA
MR Robert E. Warburton, Sr.
MR Robert G. Ward
MR Roger M. Ward
MG William F. Ward USA (Ret)
MR Don L. Warlick
MR W. Montgomery Warman
MR Donald G. Warner
LTC Edmund G. Warner USA (Ret)
MR Jared Warner, Sr.
MR Donald S. Warnock
MR Gary R. Warren
1LT Morrill Warren USA (Ret)
LTC William H. Warren USAF (Ret)
BG Huba Wass De Czege USA (Ret)
MR Michael F. Waters
MR Frank F. Watkins
MRS Barbara Batchelor Watrous
COL John R. Watson USA (Ret)
LTC Maurice F. Watson, Jr. NYNG (Ret)
MR Victor W. Watson, Jr.
BG Robert H. Wedinger AUS (Ret)
SFC Houston D. Wedlock USA (Ret)
DR Philip T. Weisbach MD
MR L. H. (Pete) Welch
CPT Shawn A. Welch
MR Thomas J. Welle
MR Frank H. Wellerding
MR F. Richard Wemmers, Jr.
MR John P. Wenner
1LT Merrill H. Werts AUS (Ret)
MR Richard B. Wessel
MR G. A. Wessels
MR Tom H. Wessels
MR Addison I. West
MR Alan Prescott West
DR Doral N. West
COL John L (Jack) West, Jr. USA (Ret)
MR Gerald C. Westfall
MR Leslie M. Westfall, Sr.
MR Henry P. Whaley
MR Jeffrey O. Whamond
BG Sherburne (Sim) Whipple, Jr. USA (Ret)
MAJ Alfred K. White, Jr. USAR (Ret)
SGT Bryan C. White USA
CPT Clifford T. White USA
MR Donald C. White, Jr.
LTC Jack C. White USA (Ret)
MRS Jane Brite White
MR Jeffrey M. White
COL Joel C. White, Jr. AUS (Ret)
LTC Stramer F. White USAF (Ret)
MR Timothy P. White
MR William E. White
MRS Wyndham K. (Connie) White
MR Terry B. Whitenight
MR Kenneth W. Whiting
MR Ellis Whitley
COL Nelson L. Whitmire USA (Ret)
MR Robert U. Whitney, Jr.
MR Lawrence R. Whitson
MR Robert B. Wick
MR Harold H. Widmann
MAJ Henry Wider AUS (Ret)
MR Joseph J. (Joe) Wieland
MR Mark H. Wikane
MR Charles L. Wilbur
SGT Keith L. Wilden USA (Ret)
MAJ Thomas P. Wilder AUS (Ret)
MR Clifton Wilderspin

MR Frank S. Wilk
MR Robert S. Wilkerson
MS Wallis Wakefield Wilkinson
DR Horace R. Willard DVM
MRS Adriel (Mary Daly) Williams
MR Ben Williams
MRS E. W. (Patricia Henry) Williams
COL Frank A. Williams USA (Ret)
MR Frederick Howard Williams
MR John E. M. Williams
MR John T. Williams
MRS Katherine T. (Hamby) Williams
MR Robert J. Williams
MR James L. Willows
COL Donald H. Wills AUS (Ret)
MR Jeffrey L. Wilmer
COL Arthur Philip (Phil) Wilson, Jr. AUS (Ret)
COL Robert (Bob) Wilson USA
MR Steve Wilson
MRS Velma Stepp Wilson
COL Paul M. Wimert, Jr. USA (Ret)
COL Albert G. Wing, Jr. USA (Ret)
MR Franklin F. Wing, III
MR George Winkelman
MR John K. Winkler
MAJ/REV William C. Winlock USA (Ret)
MR Lewis H. Winne
LTC Frank A. Wiswall USAF (Ret)
MR Raymond S. Witkowski
COL Carl G. Witte USA (Ret)
MSG Lester H. Witter USA (Ret)
MR Phelps Witter, Jr.
MR James C. Wofford
MR Warren William Wofford
MR Charles E. Wolf
MR Robert H. Wolfe
MR Delbert F. Wombacher
MRS Irene Kelly Wood
MR James P. Wood
MAJ William A. Wood AUS (Ret)
MR John F. Woodhull
COL Owen E. Woodruff, Jr. USA (Ret)
LTC W. B. Woodruff, Jr. AUS (Ret)
MR Robert L. Woodward
MR Roy Francis Woodward
COL William D. Wooldridge USA (Ret)
MRS William D. (Kip Valentine) Wooldridge
MR Robert B. Wofford
COL Robert A. Wright, Jr. USA (Ret)
LTG William H. S. (Sterling) Wright USA (Ret)
MR Willie D. Wright

Y

COL Wesley W. Yale USA (Ret)
COL William Glenn Yarborough USA (Ret)
MR James K. Yarbrough
MR William B. Yarbrough
MR Gerald T. Yaxley
MS Mary O. Yearwood
DR Harry C. Yeatman MD
LTC Clifford L. Yinger USAF (Ret)
LTC John S. Ylinen USA (Ret)
MR Michael Yocina
MR William James Yoss
MAJ Charles H. Young USAR (Ret)
CPT Hollis H. Young AUS (Ret)
CPT Frederick B. Youngblood AUS (Ret)
MR Jack F. Yule

Z

BG Phillip J. Zeller, Jr. AUS (Ret)
MS Bert E. Zellner
MG Alfred R. Zent AUS (Ret)
MR Ronald Zerges
MR L. J. Zielinski
COL William D. Ziler USA (Ret)
MR Peter P. Zillick
MR William P. Zirkel

Oat Land Plantation, VA. July 10-11, 1993, Battle of Brandy Station. Cpl. Jack A. Johnson, guidon from 1st N. J. M Co. re-enactor and movie star Sam Elliott. (Courtesy of Jack A. Johnson)

UNITED STATES CAVALRY
SPECIAL STORIES

WITH THE MULES IN BURMA

by W. B. Woodruff and John J. Scanlan

Baptised at Mindanao
Beside the Sulu Sea
With a tow and a tow
And a tow row row row
From the Mountain Battery.

This verse from *The Mountain Battery*, along with *The Red Guidon*, *O'Reilly's Gone to Hell*, and other pieces of music from the early days of the field artillery was composed by Colonel Gerald E. Griffin and depicts the proud heritage of the mountain or pack artillery. Most of this music dates from the Cuban Army of Pacification (1906-1909) where a US force of infantry, cavalry, and jackass artillery was posted at Camp Columbia, 10 miles outside Havana. As *The Mountain Battery* recognizes, the modern day mountain artillery traces its heritage and first blood to the Phillipines during and after the Spanish War.[1]

Colonel Alonzo Gray, serving with Captain John J. Pershing in 1903 noted in his memoirs, "In all these Moro expeditions, Gatley's Battery of Mountain Artillery played an important part. His organization was superb and always ready."[2] In 1941, the US Army pack artillery was represented by the 23rd FA Philippine Scouts armed with the WWI-era Vickers-Maxim 2.95 inch mountain gun and one battalion of the 13th FA in Hawaii armed with the newest and last 75mm mountain howitzer in the inventory, the Model 1925. Additionally, at Ft. Clayton, Canal Zone lived the 2nd FA and at Ft. Bragg the 4th FA. Service in these units took a special, tough individual and all recruit training included the memorization of *The Mountain Battery* and pertinent regimental facts which usually included significant events and famous marches...with embellishments.

In 1923, Battery A, 2nd FA, recently "reflagged" from the 4th FA, with three officers, 100 men, and 90 mules with four howitzers and supplies, "confounded the experts" by blazing a trail across the Isthmus of Panama west to east. This feat was repeated in 1939 going in the opposite direction.

In 1912, the 4th FA made its famous "thousand-mile march" out of Ft. Warren, WY, to include a service practice at Argentine Pass, elevation 13,000 feet, in the Rocky Mountains. In 1914, the 4th FA, during the Vera Cruz expedition, marched from Houston to Texas City in two days noting in its log"...outmarching the cavalry by 20 minutes". Again in 1916, the 4th FA participated in the chase of Pancho Villa and marched six days in northern Mexico, averaging 26.6 miles per day.[3] The 4th FA made its last march in 1955 when it marched from Ft. Carson to Cheyenne, WY for daily demonstrations of pack artillery at the rodeo before inactivating in 1956.

THE MULE

Poems, statutes, paintings, and ballads pay tribute to the horse, but his half brother, the mule, is a noble beast without whom history would be quite different. Instead of singing praises of the sturdy hybrid, those who know him best devote their talents to framing new jokes about him.

Most gibes directed at the mule focus on one of three matters: 1) he is sterile - quite incapable of propagating his kind, 2) he is the offspring of a jackass, and 3) in season or out, he kicks with great skill and every evidence of malice aforethought.

Perhaps the ancient herdsman who saw the world's first mule blinked his eyes and concluded that nature had played a joke, for even the most ardent admirer of the animal never entered him in a beauty contest. He looks just like what he is: a cross between a donkey and a horse. What he loses in looks, he gains in fortitude. From his mother, the mare, he derives strength and courage. From his father, the jack, he inherits patience, sobriety, and surefootedness. His skin is harder and less sensitive than that of the horse. He is less impatient under heavy loads, more cautious in places of danger, and less susceptible to disease. Like his father, the mule thrives on a diet so coarse that it would make a horse ill. He has the donkey's indifference to heat, the horse's capacity to pack heavy loads, and as a work animal in hot regions, he is magnificent.

Mules were still comparatively rare when David became King of Israel some 3,000 years ago. His sons, the princes, were proud to have them for their personal mounts. Solomon even rode a mule when he was proclaimed King, and the high value that was placed on them is indicated by the fact that they were among the yearly presents given him during his long reign. Old Testament references indicate the mule was used as a beast of burden and a baggage animal of war. He was harnessed to litters as well as ridden. The Romans, who became masters of the known world, had a high opinion of the mule.

Detailed knowledge of genetics is still lacking. Hybrids seem to get the size and body of the mother, whereas the feet, head, and tail appear to be most affected by the father. So a horse father and a donkey mother produce a creature that most people consider all but useless, the little hinny, while a donkey father and a horse mother produce the sturdy, sure-footed mule.

Some argue, in fact, that the derogatory views of the mule may stem, at least in part, from centuries of strife between horse breeding Christians and mule breeding Moslems. Christopher Columbus in 1505 asked for a special license that would permit him to ride mule back instead of horseback. Her Majesty graciously granted it to the old explorer by virtue of his age and infirmities, but she made it clear that this Moorish practice was not for everyone.

It was the mule who proved hardy enough to survive the rigors of swamps, deserts, and mountains. Cowboy movies to the contrary, the mule played a more significant role in development of our West than did the more glamorous horse. Mules survived heat and poor food that no horse could endure. They reached a peak of usefulness on the Santa Fe Trail where Mexican muleskinners packed animals with loads of up to 300 pounds.

Camp Hale Company.

Camp Hale Company.

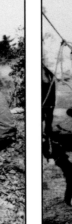

Burma 1944-45.

During the second half of the last century, mules literally built empires. They hauled supplies and equipment for work camps along railroad lines, worked mines with some spending most of their lives underground. They pulled barges through canals, streetcars in growing cities, and lumber wagons in forests. By 1875 the mule's prestige had become so great that some of the animals were exhibited at the famous Crystal Palace show.

The mule is the most successful hybrid that man ever developed. Bred one generation at a time for more than 3,000 years, his patient labor was essential to the mechanized culture that has made him obsolete.

During WWII an additional sixteen battalions of pack artillery were organized.[4] Before the war ended, most of these units had given up the mules and Pack 75s for other missions. Although the consensus of the general officers supported larger caliber weapons, the theaters where it was employed effectively - Europe to Burma and the Aleutians to Guadalcanal, the Pack Artillery proved that mobility and flexibility in many cases is superior to speed and mass. Even the powerful logistic argument of maintaining animals in distant theaters was moot when domestic forage and grain could be substituted.

The contribution of the pack artillery man to the overall war effort added many new chapters to an already proud tradition. The 601st and 602nd FA BNs(Pk) earned amphibious honors in the Aleutians and airborne honors in southern France. As part of the 1st Allied Airborne Task Force, the 602nd landed men and guns via glider and mules by landing craft. The Pack 75 howitzer as well as her cannoneers found a natural home in the Airborne with the first experiments being conducted by the 98th FA Bn(Pk) "Led the Way" in New Guinea. Other pack artillery men "Led the Way" in Ranger operations. Colonel William O. Darby, the senior Ranger commander in Europe, began the war with the 99th FA Bn(Pk). The 98th FA(Pk) contributed a key contingent of volunteers to Merrills Marauders and was subsequently re-designated the 6th Ranger Battalion. Colonel Arthur D. "Bull" Simon progressed from battery commander of Battery C, 98th FA(Pk) to Ranger company commander. The Cabanatuan raid in 1945 foreshadowed his later efforts at Son Tay and Tehran.[5]

The 97th and 603rd FA BNs(Pk) worked the steamy jungles of Guadalcanal, the later attached to the 1st Marine Division. The 604th, 605th, and 616th FA BNs(Pk) wrote new chapters on high mountain operations with the 10th Mountain Division among the plateaus and snow-capped peaks of northern Italy.[6]

THE CBI THEATER

By far the longest, heaviest, most sustained, and most instructive employment of mules in war, of all time, was in the China-Burma-India Theater of WWII. This effort was in many respects pioneered by the British General Orde Wingate and his successors, perfectors of the long-range penetration force. His Chindits were well known for their effective and efficient use of pack animals - elephants, camels, native mules, and Australian pack horses. The full capability of the mule was not realized by them, however, until they acquired the larger, more durable, American mule. Much experimentation was done including air dropping equipment and mules. Although much of the equipment including the Pack 75 howitzer adapted well to air-drop, the mortality rate of mules by this means of delivery was unacceptable. However, in the second Chindit campaign, a brigade-size force including mules was air landed by glider successfully.[7]

As the CBI theater matured, an American unit code-named Galahad began making its mark on the war. Initially, the 5307th Composite Regiment later the 5307th Composite Unit (Provisional), was commonly known by its GI moniker, "5307th CUP". It is said that when the going got a little rough its members would utter a common cry, "Where in hell are the other five thousand three hundred and six CUPS?" One soldier received a letter from his girlfriend who said that his unit designation sounded like a Quartermaster outfit and that she was relieved that he would not be in the fighting. When some enterprising reporter, out of ignorance or otherwise, began calling the unit Merrills Marauders, the name stuck and the girlfriend got worried.

The British objective of this entire effort was to drive the Japanese from those colonies that rightfully belonged to the Crown. American organization and operations in this theater were typically American: a mix of incredible tactical and logistical achievement pursuing strategically worthless objectives at maximum cost via a nightmarish mix of amateur improvisation on our part and devious skullduggery on the part of several of our allies. Even among Americans there was no general consensus as to purpose or method. Hugely complicating this picture was the 18th Japanese Division, the highly capable combat force defending North Burma, headquartered at Myitkyina; another sleepy provincial town thrust suddenly into tactical center stage. General Stilwell's mouth watered for a solid American military force to lead his drive on Myitkyina, the key to a secure land-based line of communication to China. Up to that time he had to make due with Chinese troops, supposedly under

his command but in fact operating according to their own inscrutable agenda. General Wingate, on the other hand, anxious to recover colonial real estate having value and prestige, could not have cared less about the capture of Myitkyina and re-opening communication lines with China. Into this interesting mix blundered Galahad, originally planned as a reinforcement to Wingate - out from under whom the rug was deftly jerked by Stilwell. When the dust settled with Galahad firmly under Stilwell's control, the leader and the led simply merged — in that magical and fortuitous way that sometimes happens if both parties are very lucky. Galahad consisted of about 3000 men, who were all volunteers, and several hundred assorted pack animals who were not. It had no artillery.

These pack animals were organized into Quartermaster Pack Troops -the equivalent of a modern Truck Company. Each maneuver battalion was assigned one QM Pack Troop with the 1st and 2nd Battalions of Galahad arriving with their own Pack Troops from the states. The 3rd Battalion had been raised from volunteers already in theater and needed a Pack Troop. No matter, General Walter Krueger secured 119 volunteers from the 98th FA Bn(Pk) on New Guinea and 3rd Battalion had its allocation of mulepackers.[8]

This Redleg contingent proved fortunate. At about Easter-time 1944, Galahad found big trouble at a place called Nhpum-ga. Sergeant John "Red" Acker, formerly of the 98th, suggested he could organize gun crews from his ex-artillery men if howitzers could be found and air-dropped to them. They were and he did. Galahad now had organic field artillery, increased its two-gun battery to four guns, and rushed off a requisition to Washington for Field Artillery Officers. Once again, one might say, the Queen of Battle found the going rocky until joined by her natural consort.

At about the time Galahad got to India to prepare for the First Burma Campaign to secure Myitkyina, there began to take shape the units which would fight the Second Burma Campaign to linkup with the old Burma Road at the Burma-China frontier. On orders from the Pentagon, a sizable number of young draftees, just completing field artillery basic training at Ft. Bragg, received a special and peculiar physical examination. Of particular interest was height (needed to be six feet or more) and soundness of back and joints. Those who "passed" were culled out and put aboard troop trains bound for Camp Gruber, OK. Gone for these stout-hearted souls were all hopes of zipping across flat country at high speed towing big guns behind motorized prime movers. Their fate as they later learned, would be to move afoot, at 4 miles per hour, dragging behind them their mules (MULES?), loaded down with component parts of the little, short-tubed 75 mm pack howitzer.

Off to nearby El Reno Remount Station went a requisition for mules. Off to nearby Ft. Sill went a requisition for trained for trained mule packers. Off to Ft. Sill went selected men for training as saddlers, pack masters, and farriers. Down from Camp Carson, Colorado came an officer and non-commissioned officer cadre with prior experience in pack artillery.[9] Shortly there opened for business four new pack artillery battalions - the 610th, 611th, 612th and 613th. It was December, 1943. At Ft. Sill, Batteries C and E, 26th Battalion, 100 newly trained men each to the 612th and 613th Battalions(Pk). All units moved to Camp Carson, Colorado for advanced training until summer.

In May 1944, many men of the 612th and 613th received unexpected furloughs. Upon return to Carson they learned the reason—overseas movement was imminent.[10] Activity intensified. These preparations were aided by a number of senior NCOs who already had oversea experience. Typically, the First Sergeant and one or two others in each battery had returned from the South Pacific, most from the 97th and 603rd FA BNs(Pk). Many of these had served together before the war, especially in the old 4th FA at Ft. Bragg, and had been sent back to the states expressly to cadre some of the new pack units.[11]

The 612th moved first in June, 1944, and the 613th moved about one month later. To insure confusion, both to the troops and the Japanese, Batteries A and C, 612th moved by rail to California and completed the journey to Bombay, India via Australia one month later by Navy transport. Batteries B and Headquarters/Service moved by rail to New Orleans via Denver and St. Louis. The mules moved to New Orleans via Amarillo, Dallas, and Shreveport. Men and mules linked up at Camp Plauche.

According to Francis, the 1100-pound Missouri Mule of Hollywood fame, his deployment to Burma began at a mule's principal point of embarkation at Camp Plauche, Louisiana near New Orleans. During the war, this vast facility held and shipped over 8000 mules via a large wharf near Westwego where they were loaded aboard Liberty ships fitted with stalls for 320 mules and accommodations for 60 army personnel.[12] Each ship was manned by Merchant Marine crews and fitted with a 3-inch gun (for-

ward) and a 5-inch naval gun (aft) manned by Navy personnel. Francis was assigned to the S. S. Henry Dearborn, the first of three ships in this merry flotilla. The entire experience was so romantic that Francis' faithful driver(H/S Battery, 612th FA Bn(Pk)) was moved to poetry,

"But on that day, that sunny day, the Dearborn put to sea. There'll never be another boat like the S. S. Henry D. For crew she had a mixture of scholars, thieves, and fools, And the cargo that she carried was 320 mules.

We fed them oats and linseed meal, we fed them bran and hay, We swept and washed and scrubbed and groomed and watered 'em twice a day. But the choicest job of all I'd say, if I may make so bold, Was standing at the hatch to pull manure up from the hold."

After sundry delays and mishaps all three ships

arrived in Calcutta in late September; the Dearborn's voyage lasting 73 days. Boarding a train on the Indian Railway System, the mule packers arrived at its terminus at the town of Ledo on the western frontier of Burma. At this point they disembarked, packed their mules and walked for four weeks along the track of the "Ledo Road", still under construction. The S. S. Dearborn element having departed New Orleans on July 15, 1944, led its mules into the corrals at Camp Landis on the Irrawaddy River above Myitkyina at 0200 hours on November 2, 1944. Three mules were lost enroute.[13]

Twelve days later the MARS Task Force began offensive action to clear the land route to China. Officially designated the 5332nd Brigade (Provisional), it consisted of the 475th Infantry Regimental Combat Team (612th FA attached) and the 124th Cavalry Regimental Combat Team (613th FA at-

December 9, 1995 L toR: Bredenburgh (C1612FA), Eddy (C1612FA), Carr (C1613FA), Neinast (C1613FA), Scanlan (D13-83FA), Laahs (B1612FA), Colvin (C1613FA), Woodruff (H-S1612FA), and Church (A1612FA).

tached).[14] The campaign ended in April, 1945, at the central Burma town of Lashio, nestled in the foothills of the Himalayas near the Chinese border, was the point where the Burman road and rail system met the old Burma Road, constructed by the Chinese early in WWII when Japan closed all China ports. It extended from Kunming, China, over continuous mountain terrain almost 1000 miles to Lashio.[15] This route, used by mountain tribesmen for uncounted centuries, crossed several of the world's major rivers and deepest valleys and is still known locally as "the old Marco Polo Trail".

Along this same route, beginning in May, 1945, the final saga of the 612th and 613th FA Battalions(Pk) story took place. In three march serials, 240 men and 900 mules moved up the Burma Road to Kunming, China from Myitkyina, Burma— a distance of 750 miles.[16] These mules ended up in Chinese units or contracted disease and had to be destroyed. In Korea in 1951, one of these U. S. Army mules, Preston Brand 08K0, was recaptured by the 1st Cavalry Division from the Red Chinese Army and "re enlisted" for U. S. Army pack service.

These mules were essentially the same herd brought by the three-ship flotilla from New Orleans the previous summer. It is apparent that out of 960 mules, animal losses amounted to 60 head after 6 months of campaigning halfway around the world. Earlier in the war, at least two transports of mules bound for the Marauders were sunk by Japanese submarines.

Although the high-level detractors of mule pack artillery were little impressed by the feats of these battalions in all major theaters of World War II, the men who served with them or who benefited from their support are convinced that the job would not have been done without them. Plainly said, the alternative to pack artillery in Burma and several other combat zones, was NO artillery! Both the 612th and 613th FA Battalions(Pk) amassed similar statistics during the Second Burma Campaign. As the log of the 612th indicates, they moved 412 miles during 152 days in combat missions, expended 12,000 rounds of 75mm howitzer ammunition, and sustained 53 casualties in support of the MARS Task Force defeat of elements of the Japanese 2nd, 18th, and 56th Divisions.

Epilogue: The Mountain Artillery Association of the MARS Task Force, made up of veterans of the 612th and 613th FA (Pk), along with members of other pack artillery units comprise the last of the mule packers. On December 9, 1995, 8 members of this association met at Camp Shelby, Mississippi to pack and move a howitzer muleback one more time. Although only two loads out of six were successfully packed and moved, the enthusiasm of the participants and interest shown by the witnesses to this re-enactment were encouraging. We are all indebted for the proud traditions that this breed of Redleg has brought to the King of Battle.

FOOTNOTES:

1. The first use of mountain artillery by the U. S. Army involved the 12-pounder mountain howitzer, Model 1841. It could be towed by one mule or packed on three mules. During the Mexican War, Lt. U. S. Grant directed the disassembly and emplacement of a howitzer on a rooftop of an adobe house and placed effective fire on advancing Mexican troops.

2. Quoted in March 1993 issue of *Crossed Sabers* bulletin of US Cavalry Association.

3. Quoted form unpublished manuscript, "History of the 4th Field Artillery", compiled by 4th FA Assn., Fayetteville, NC.

4. The added battalions consisted of the 97th; 98th; 99th;(1st Cavalry Div.); 601st; 602nd; 603rd; the 604th, 605th, and 616th(all assigned to 71st

Infantry Div.); 610th; 611th; the 612th and 613th(both assigned to Mars TF). It is commonly believed that the activation of the 616th rather than the 606th was due to typographical error at the War Department.

5. Detailed coverage of these three operations can be found, respectively in *Cabanatuan: Japanese Death Camp*, by Vince Taylor, Texan Press, Waco, 1987; *The Raid*, by Benjamin F. Schemmer, Avon Books, New York, 1976; and *On Wings of Eagles*, by Ken Follett, Wm. Morrow & Co., New York, 1983.

6. See *The King of Battle-A History of the 616th FA Bn (Pk) and More*, by Charles W. Webb, an unfinished manuscript to be published in 1996. Major (Ret) Webb enlisted in 2nd FA in 1941, ended WWII as CSM of 616th FA Bn (Pk) before commissioning.

7. In 5 days, 9000 troops and 1100 animals were landed by glider and aircraft; see General the Viscount Slim, *Defeat Into Victory*, David McKay & Co., New York, 1961.

8. Correspondence in author's files from Edward A. Wade, one of the 119 volunteers from the 98th FA Bn(Pk). Wade states that General Krueger personally explained the "dangerous and hazardous mission" before asking for 110 privates, 6 corporals, and 3 sergeants.

9. Most of these came from the 71st Light Division, chiefly the 607th, 608th, and 609th FA BNs(Pk). Many had prior service in other pack outfits. Camp Carson(Camp Hale Mountain Warfare School) was commanded by General David Ruffner, an old pack artillery veteran who was to the Pack Artillery what Patton was to Armor.

10. When the 612th and 613th were alerted for oversea movement, they were brought to TOE strength by members of the 610th(inactivated) and 611th which was moved to Ft. Riley in reduced configuration as school troops for the Cavalry School.

11. A gun section in pre-war pack units consisted of 22 troops and 18 mules. The new pack units were refined with some organic motor transport for ammunition and supplies modifying a gun section to 17 troops and 10 mules.

12. Statistics on mule movement from Dr. Andy Crawford, *Mules Go to War*, published privately by author, 1979. Crawford served as Port Veterinarian at New Orleans. Memories of Liberty ship configuration, by W.B. Woodruff, Jr. Animals were kept in five "holds", one on weather deck and four below decks. Each stall held one mule and feed trough. Water provided in buckets. Manure removed daily and piled on weather deck until nightfall(a submarine countermeasure) and pitched over the side. A small veterinary detachment accompanied each ship.

13. Memory of author. One mule died of an unknown illness and was buried at sea. Another "escaped" from its car on the Indian Railway and was last seen prancing off into the jungle — no doubt later making a fine meal for a hungry tiger. A recollection of the third mule's demise is lost to the ages.

14. The composition of the 5332nd Brigade (Provisional) was: 475th Inf. RCT -475th Inf. Regt; 612th FA Bn(Pk); 31st, 33rd, 35th QM Pack Trps.;44th Portable Surgical Hospital
124th Cav RCT - 124th Cav (dismounted); 613th FA Bn (Pk); 37th, 252nd, 253rd QM Pack Trps; 49th Portable Surgical Hospital

15. Closing the "original" Burma Road was a major objective of the Japanese in their 1942 invasion. Until the Ledo-Burma Road was completed and cleared of enemy in the spring of 1945, the only means of re supply to the Chinese was by air over "the Hump" from India.

16. This data is taken from an article in the April 1981 issue of "EX-CBI ROUNDUP", entitled *Mules for China*, by John A. Rand, highly respected commander of Battery C, 613th FA Bn (Pk) and the OIC of the mule march to China.

HOOPER THE DUCK

by Lionel Carter

Our story begins as all stories do at the beginning but with an unusual happening: Cpls. Bill Hillson and Harvey Thompson had returned from a visit to Noumea on the island of New Caledonia with two Muscovy ducklings. However, if one considers the condition in which they usually returned to camp, it wouldn't have been surprising if they had come back with two elephants. But two baby ducklings! Especially when they paid a dollar each for them which would have bought a few more beers in that war year of 1942. The two ducklings became two new members of G Troop, 112th (horse) cavalry who had landed on the island on August 11th.

GIs were great at coming up with names for people, places, and animals, and some wiseacre in G Troop proved equal to the task in this case. One duckling had a tuft of feathers on the top of his head and he was promptly named "Mosshead" after our regimental commander, Col. Julian Cunningham whose sole hair adornment was a few wispy white hairs. Since the second duck followed Mosshead around like Captain Phillip Hooper, the colonel's aide-de-camp, followed the colonel, it only followed that the second duckling should be called "Hooper".

Now for our city-raised readers it might be well to point out that a Muscovy duck is all white with orange feet and bill as when you mention "duck" most people envisage a wild Mallard, a gray duck with a green head and a narrow white ring around the neck.

With a bit of bran from the stable shack and lots of puddles to wade in (we had little showers every day in New Caledonia to say nothing of the rainy season when that is all it did for forty days), the ducklings had settled down to a hum-drum existence and a steady area abounded with huge rats, and one of these monsters apparently made off with Mosshead one night. No trace of him was ever found. Hooper was despondent and moved into our tent for safety and companionship. Perhaps our proximity to the kitchen and mess hall accounted for Hooper's choice of a home, as he seemed to show no preference for any individual, but he quickly learned that one of the cooks beating on a pot lid and yelling, "Chow!" meant food. Then it was a race between Elmer Krebs, Hippo Paulsen, Jake Zaboudil, Fatty Lewis and Hooper to see who would be first in line. After nearly being stepped on at the end of the mess line by troopers trying to balance half a peach or pear on the flat lid of their mess kit, Hooper learned to stand at the entrance to the mess hall and fix every trooper with a beady, one-eyed stare. It was only the "chow-hounds" and stone-hearted troopers who could then refuse a small piece of bread for him.

Hooper quickly learned that there were better things in life than bread, as he developed a fondness for peanuts. He hammer on a jar of peanuts until given some, and he thought every candy bar had peanuts, and the rustle of the wrapper would bring him on the run much as my dog, Bubbles, used to come. If ignored, he'd grab my pants leg in his bill and yank on it until given a few peanuts.

A great affinity developed between Hooper and I, and I was pleased when he would come down to the corral to meet me when we returned from a morning's ride, much like a dog would do. After getting his attention with a call of "Peep, peep! Peep, peep!", I'd reward him if he came over to me by giving him a few peanuts. Soon I could call him from F Troop (was it Kenneth Stokes of Rockford who was a good friend of Howie Kush?) and said, "Hey, Carter, I hear you have a pet duck!" I said, "Yes, if you want to see him?" So I did just that, going to the door of the tent, I yelled, "Peep, peep!

Peep, peep!" Hooper was out of sight and several tents away, but suddenly around one of the tents came a mass of white feathers with wings flapping and orange feet churning the ground and quacking as loud as a duck could quack. I'd seen this apparition too many times to be surprised, so I looked at the F Trooper instead. He was rooted to the ground in amazement, his mouth hanging open. Hooper dashed up to me, pulled on my pants leg with his bill, and I gave him a small helping of peanuts. The F Trooper shook his head in astonishment and left without another word.

Of course, Harvey Thompson accused me of "stealing" his duck, and I guess I did. But then no one seemed to care more about Hooper than I did. Even part of the one bottle a month beer issue we received went to Hooper. Give him some bran and add a little beer to his water, and he'd sleep most of the afternoon with his head tucked under his wing.

One of the funniest experiences in my life with Hooper came early in the spring of 1943. We were awaiting a visit from the Inspector General, and everything was in spotless order. Lt. McInyre was making his last minute rounds when he came into our tent. "Clean up those feathers and get that damn duck out of here," he roared. I grabbed Hooper and carried him down to the hay shack where I left him with an ample supply of bran and water, while Cpl. Thompson saw to it that Pvts. Fell, Snell, Krebs and Harbiezwski removed the last traces of said duck. Came the big inspection with Capt. Hooper accompanying the Inspector General. Our tent and equipment were spotless as we snapped to attention, and everything seemed to proceed nicely until the General reached Cappy Fell. "What's your name, soldier," asked the General not unkindly, "Joe Penner?" Lt. McIntyre froze as he looked under Cappy's cot, but Hooper (the duck, not the man) seemed unconcerned as he slept with his head under his wing. But the General only grinned. "What's the duck's name?" he asked. But before anyone could answer "Hooper" (assuming anyone would, with Capt. Hooper standing there), Lt. McIntyre blurted out: "Donald, sir."

On April 15th I reached up to take my saddle down and dislocated my right knee (I had dislocated my left knee in 1942 and one knee or the other had slipped in and out of joint five times since then. Lt. McInyre gave me a stick to bite on while two men pulled the upper part while the lieutenant tried to push the knee back into its joint. The pain was excruciating. Twice they tried and failed, but on the third attempt succeeded. Two days before a trooper had accidentally stepped on Hooper's leg in the chow line, so now we became very close friends with me on the cot and Hooper under it. I'd hobble up every day and bring back food for both of us. During the day I'd talk to him and pet him, so he became even more like a dog than a duck.

On May 14th as we prepared to leave New Caledonia, I looked everywhere for Hooper but he was not to be found. No rushing duck in answer to "Peep, peep!" and I wondered what had happened to him. Some of fellows in second squadron headquarters who were being left behind had offered to look after him when we left, but I didn't like the hungry look in their eyes. Perhaps they had gotten him! Once more I looked around the troop area. No Hooper. With heavy heart I climbed into the truck with the rest of the first platoon, but I soon joined in the laughter of the rest of platoon at the efforts of the quartermaster squad to round up the two hundred horses of G Troop. The lieutenant didn't think it was so funny. "Who turned those horses loose?" demanded Lt. McIntyre, but no one answered. On a dare, Zeno Periman, Harbiezwski and I had gotten up in the early morning darkness and opened the corral gates.

A few miles down the road Periman nudged me and pointed to a very oddly shaped barracks bag. The bag was square like a big box, and with good reason: inside the bag was a box and inside the box was Hooper!

And so later that day Hooper shipped out with us aboard the "Sands", a WWI destroyer. And what a seasick trip he had! If duck feathers could change color, Hooper's would have been green! For five days that old destroyer bucked the waves, and Hooper got sicker and sicker. Then came the really bad news. The captain of the ship said that no fowls or animals could be taken into Australia (and we had been told that we were headed for, which would be a staging area for a surprise night landing on Woodlark Island), and during that final night at sea, Hooper disappeared. Rumors were rife that he had been killed by the ship's cook and would be served to the officers that day. For once the rumors proved correct, but when Hooper appeared on a serving tray in the officers' mess, Harbiezwski filched my poor web footed friend and took him to our quarters below deck. Summoned to the area, I was offered a juicy drumstick, but how could I eat my old friend? As I look back on that scene today and remember how the Japanese had called the 112th Cavalry murderers for taking no prisoners, I know they were wrong. They weren't murderers, they were cannibals!

SHOWDOWN AT PLATTE BRIDGE

by Benjamen Barrett

About 2 o'clock a. m. on the 26th of July, Lt. Bretney with ten men arrived at the post (Platte Bridge) from Sweetwater Station (Company "G" headquarters, 52 miles west of Platte Bridge station) en route to Ft. Laramie to draw pay for his company. He had passed a train in the night camped at Willow Springs 25 miles west of P.B. He tried to induce them to come onto P.B., but Sergeant Custard said the stock was too fatigued.

When Captain Bretney arrived at P.B., he went directly to Mayor Anderson, Eleventh Kansas Cavalry, Post Commander, and urge him to send a rescue party to Willow Springs to bring the train in safely. Mayor Anderson thought he was unduly alarmed and went back to sleep. Next morning, Mayor Anderson was unable to find officers available for duty, so he ordered Lt. Caspar Collins, who was not under his command, only casually passing through, to take 20 men and go to the rescue of the Custard train.

Against strong urging from Captain Bretney and John Howard a telegraph operator, not to go, he would not disobey orders. Unseen by Lt. Collins, the hills were swarming with Indians and after Lt. Collins had proceeded about 1/2 mile, they came out of hiding and attempted to surround him and cut off any retreat to the fort.

It was then that Captain Bretney, seeing the danger, also with Captain Lybe and his ten men, charged across the bridge, dismounted and set up a firing line to the cover retreat of Lt. Collins and his men, for by this time Lt. Collins saw that several of his men had been killed and half of his men, including himself, had been wounded, so he gave the command to return to the bridge. In stopping to rescue a wounded soldier Adam Culp, his big gray horse, because of two riders, became unmanageable and whirled and headed straight into the Indians and horrible death for them both.

"The troupers returning to the bridge were protected by the fire of the dismounted men under the command of Bretney and Lybe until they got safely to the bridge, then Captain Bretney, with his ten men, came down from the hill with all possible speed; he gave the order to run for the bridge, and the soldiers then returned to the fort just in time to keep from being cut off by the Indians."

U-105 RECOMMEND, A TRUE LADY

by R. C. Rozelle

We met while I was in basic training with "A" Troop, 3rd. Cavalry. I had been assigned as "stable police," we had just finished the morning clean up when a load of about twenty horses pulled up and we were ordered to help with the unload. We had tied several on the picket line when a pretty, but a bit smaller horse was giving the men in the trailer a hard time, kicking, biting, and just being hard to live with. She was tied on the line with the others and started picking on the horses next to her. The sergeant told me to tie her to the ring in the wall of the stable away from the other horses. I did, then started to talk to her a bit, she calmed down some and let me rub her mane and neck. She seemed to like it, but as I turned she reached out and bit me. I slapped her nose, she looked at me and then seemed to say I'm sorry.

The next morning we were assigned to the stable sergeant to help the vets inspect the new mounts. Somehow "Recommend" (U-105) and I ended up together. She sure was a pretty "little lady," that's what I started to call her. We were told to check the hoofs, what a job that turned out to be, she did not want to lift her legs. The sergeant and I both tried, finally the sergeant took hold of her nose and ear I reached and managed to lift the right front hoof. Then we went to the rear hoof, again a struggle, she would try to squeeze us in the stall, or kick us after a bit we did get to inspect all four hoofs. A lieutenant came by as I was brushing her down (Lady seemed to like the brushing) and said "throw my saddle on her, lets see how she behaves." I took her outside and put a blanket on her, she flinched a bit, but when she seen the saddle coming, she just wanted to argue about it. After several moments we had her saddled. Lady and the lieutenant took off faster than he expected, he almost ended up on the concrete, Lady slipped a bit, both ended up coming to a sudden stop and reassessing each other.

Thirty of forty moments later they came back, the lieutenant shoved the reins in my hand and said "take care of her." After removing the gear I took a bit of old blanket and rubbed her down real good, then curried and brushed her, boy did she shine. I think I fell for her charms right then. Whenever I could I'd go by the stables and talk to her, brush her, some times take her a lump of sugar or an apple. It wasn't long before I felt that she recognized me, even looked for me when we were saddling up. Most of the time an officer or non com rode her. No one really got along well with her. She was transferred to HQ Troop because an officer thought she would make a polo pony. I was transferred to HQ Troop soon after my basic training with "A" Troop.

Once again "Lady" did not like the polo nor did she get on well with people or horses. The word was, she was soon to be transferred. I had ridden her several times on weekends and whenever I could during drills. She never did give me much trouble except when she was squeezed while performing with other horses, then she would kick or rear up.

With the pay, I think it was like $27.00 or $28.00 per month, by the time my allotment and PX coupons plus a few bucks for pressing uniforms was taken out, I did not have the dough to go to town much. My time was spent on the post, part of that with "Lady", we got to be good friends, she would follow me around like a puppy. I rode her a lot in a woodsy area that bordered the post. It had a name, but I don't recall what it was. It was easy to teach her most anything. We did pretty good in the bridleless ride routine after just a few sessions. I did end up on the grass some, but Lady never left me. She seemed to have a smile on her face whenever we parted and I hit the ground. She would just stand there and wait for me to climb back on. We would start with full gear and remove saddle first, then blanket, then bridle which left us riding without any gear. With only a nudge of my knees or legs she would turn first one way then another, then the cross court, guess the years have dimmed the exact maneuver of the ride.

Lady and I became real good friends and as fate would have it, our platoon leader decided to assign Lady to me for most of our mounted activities. We became a team she was a real friend, I shared many of my problems and happenings with her. She always had time to listen and rub her soft nose against me, look at me with her big brown eyes and seemed to say "I'm here whenever you need me. I was given a thirty day furlough. When I returned the stable sergeant told me she had been off her feed some and had to be treated by the vets. She had bitten another horse on the picket line and had thrown a trooper during a mounted review. I went back to her stall to talk to her, she looked sad and not as shinny as she did before my furlough. Guess she was mad at me too, because she tried to squeeze me in the stall, she bit my behind when I tried to check her hoofs. Not sure she meant to, but she did step on my foot and I had a black sore toe for awhile. A week or so after my return she began to settle down and we renewed our friendship. We rode in a show or two in the Riding Hall, several reviews on the parade grounds, and all mounted exercises during the months that followed.

A leathery looking old buck sergeant, Sgt. Davis, some 25 or 30 years in, don't think he weighed more than 125 or 130 pounds, had helped me many times with advise about the cavalry and training, often went riding with me and would point out how to keep Lady happy and well behaved. Qualifying for mounted pistol was coming up soon so he started showing us what was expected. The slow steady canter around the figure eight track. The firing of our 45 targets placed at various places on the track and most important how to hit the target, Sgt. Davis was good at it and was very good showing how to qualify. Lady and I made countless trips around the course, she settled in and just loped along smooth as silk, steady pace and soon got accustom to the piece of wood I used to simulate the pistol, flashing first one side then the other of her head. Finally the day for our first of three practice rounds, Sgt. Davis had Lady and me stand by for a number of trips by other troopers. It took a long time before Lady calmed down, the shots made her nervous and real jumpy. I kept talking to her, rubbing her nose and neck. Our turn came, I mounted up rode to the start and off we went, not the slow steady lope we had practiced, but a jerky rough gate. My first shot went wild as did all, but one of the others. Lady was nervous and I wasn't much better. The 45 seemed real heavy and the recoil rough. Our second and third try did not improve much, Sgt. Davis advised that I ride another mount for my qualifying ride, after talking to Lady and telling her what was expected of her, I decided to ride her. The start was as bad as any of the practice rounds and we missed the first target. Lady seemed to get the idea and settled down and we loped around the target range and I ended up with only two misses. On the ride back to the stables I swear Lady had her chest stuck out and was saying "see, we done it real good."

While on Tennessee maneuvers, we had been on a march for many many hours, cold wet tired and generally miserable well after dark when we made bivouac. We had somehow gotten lost and it took much longer than planned to reach our designated area. Many a trooper had dosed off in the saddle, me no exception. The walk ten, trot ten, ride ten was not always followed. The rain was steady and cold, real cold. We unsaddled, tied up on the picket line and preceded to wipe down the horses. A nearby stream provided water for the mounts, and we each had grain in our saddle roll. After seeing to the horses we looked for a place to grab a few winks, I had made a bedroll out of my shelter half and blanket, the saddle blanket provided additional cover and a spot under a tree and on a bit of higher ground was my beddown area. I had just dropped off to sleep when all heck broke loose. Somehow, the picket line had come loose and the horses were all over the place. As you know Lady was anti-social and had been tied to a small tree near me. When I woke up she was standing over me ears back head stuck out teeth showing daring any horse to come close. After rounding up the mounts I managed to come up with a few more oats that I had squirreled away to be sure Lady was well fed on our adventure. She had proved once more to be a true friend.

PARTING COMPANY

Orders came down transferring the whole Third Cavalry to Fort Oglethorpe, Georgia. It was tough leaving the brick barracks of Fort Meyer, the good food our mess sergeant put out while on Garrison Rations; were going to be a thing of the past. The pleasant surroundings of the historic post and Arlington Cemetery, the beauty of Washington where one could walk and look at government buildings and monuments was to be a thing of the past. National Airport was under construction as was The Jefferson Memorial, the war was causing many changes and we were part of the change.

Loading the box cars with our horses was a real challenge. One trooper would push the head an another the rump, forcing the horses to stand parallel and tight to the previously loaded mount. They were loaded from head to tail and each end simultaneously. Squeezing the last two horses in was tough. They were not happy about the situation and gave us a rough time. Lady was loaded in another car and I did not see her loaded. In fact, we did not get together until we reached Georgia. When I first saw her she was looking tough and not the least bit happy. She had skinned her rear legs and scratched her nose. We spent most of the day unloading, cleaning up the mounts, walking them around trying to settle them down. The next day we cleaned our wooden barracks and went through some drills. The horses seemed to brighten up some once they were back doing what they were used to.

Chickamauga Park bordered the post and was a wonderful place to ride. Many historical monuments of the Civil War, nice trails to follow, lots of trees and fields. Lady and I enjoyed the little time we had here. Someone promoted a "Fox Hunt" on a weekend, don't remember who or why, but officers, enlisted men all in uniform took part. The hunt started and off they went at a full gallop. Lady had her own ideas and shortly after the start we headed to a more open field and were soon passing others that had been ahead of us. It was great having the wind in our face charging to some unknown place, we were free. She started to slow down and stopped dead still and just stood there, I spoke to her, she just put her ears back and starred into the wooded area along side of us. I dismounted and went to check the area and she followed along. At first I did not see anything then I heard a rustling sound and looked closer, it was a mother cat and three kittens. They were in a clump of bushes covered with leaves. Mother did not like us getting too close and told us so. Lady and I returned to the stables and called the Fox Hunt a success. We talked as I brushed her down and tried to come to grips with a rumor that the horses were going to leave soon. Seems the war did not have a place for Horse Cavalry. Word had it some horses would go to a post in Georgia for use by officers, others would be sent other places to be disposed of. The historic Horse Cavalry traditions were going to be just memories, what a shame. In the short time I had been involved, I had developed a huge hunk of pride about being in the Third Cavalry.

The day came to load the horses, what a sad time it was. Even our First Sergeant Evans, a tough, long-time trooper was seen shedding a tear. I shed more than one, I was loosing my buddy and confidant. I loaded Lady, this time she went along without any of her usual objections to doing something

11th Cavalry leaving Camp Lockett to form the 11th Tank Division, 10th Armored. 1943. (Courtesy of Sam Silverman)

she was not used to. She seemed to know we were about to part company for good. She just seemed to be really down, her usual high spirit crushed and had decided to let nature take its course, for better or worse. I'm not sure where she ended up and have always wondered how she made out. Now, as I recall these events a tear seems to be forming in my eyes.

I can't guarantee the story as told here is 100% fact, it is the best a seventy nine year old can recall after some fifty years. I guess every trooper has memories that have also varied over the years, it sure had added pride to my memories of the 1941-1945 time period of my life. I'm sorry it took so long to learn about The United States Cavalry Association.

THE LOST PATROL

by PFC Lionel Carter (Ret)

The date was July 8, 1944. The place was Afua, New Guinea on the west bank of the Driniumor River, where the 112th Cavalry Regiment had been attached to the 32nd Infantry Division to repel an attack by the Japanese 18th Army pushing down through a trackless jungle after being cut off at Wewak by American landings at Aitape and Hollandia. But where were they? Headquarters was getting restless; patrols would have to be sent out. One was the first platoon of G Troop under Lt. Raymond Czerniejewski accompanied by a machine gun squad, an artillery lieutenant, two radiomen and a medic with orders to scout to the Harech River, a five day patrol.

Our trail was a well marked native trail that followed a high ridge through the jungle. We could look down upon the jungle on both sides yet a canopy of jungle growth hid us from the spotter plane, a reassuring sight circling overhead to pick up our radio signal... but the second day out, the radio went dead!

I had done a very stupid thing for a foot soldier who had to depend on the condition of his feet; I had put on a new pair of unwashed socks and helped along with the sand that had gotten into my shoes when we waded across the Driniumor, my feet were rubbed raw by the end of the second day. I had ignored the pain as the usual pain of walking

all day but when I removed my shoes and socks I found by feet in such terrible shape that I begged off a small patrol that went down to the Harech River and found no sign of the Japanese. Patrols move fast on the homeward journey, and we could have reached the Driniumor but decided not to risk crossing it in the gathering darkness and be mistaken for Japanese. We had seen no one and heard nothing.

The next morning we stuffed ourselves with our remaining food and as we waded across the Driniumor, I waved at an Australian bomber that passed overhead, and several others followed suit. Everything seemed quiet, too quiet. When we reached the G Troop area we discovered why, no one was there! What little shelter we had from the weather was ripped and torn apart, ammunition had been dumped into the river. Worse yet, I found Japanese footprints and Japanese cigarette butts which told us that the Japanese had broken through and we were now behind Japanese lines!

Lt. Czerniejewski decided to go south toward the Torricelli Mountains and around the Japanese line. I didn't think we could do this without food and with maps of that area marked "unexplored". (We would later cross three rivers where the map showed only two!). An attack by Australian bombers—a pilot had reported seeing a patrol of Japanese soldiers dressed in American uniforms who even had the audacity to wave to him—sent us hurry on our way, and for the rest of that afternoon, the planes bombed and strafed us, but always behind the ridge of the area we had just vacated. For once darkness was welcomed as it halted the attacks.

Our squad took stock of our food supply and found we had one bouillon cube (our breakfast with two swallows per trooper), one small tin of meat (supper that night) and one fruit bar for the next day. The second day of our trek, our squad was leading when we came upon a native garden, but our dream of an abundance of food was quickly dispelled when all we found was a green pineapple about the size of a baseball which was cut into six small portions which were quickly devoured. The second squad following us, picked the discarded rinds out of the dirt and ate them. Now that's hunger. Luckily, water was no problem as we'd dip our steel helmets into every stream we crossed and drank our fill of water.

By this time my feet were so sore and so swol-

len I knew better than to take by shoes off as I'd never get them on again, so I staggered along behind the rest of the patrol, sometimes so far behind that when the patrol changed directions, Tony Frangella would wait until I came into view so he could point the way for me. Sometimes I would catch up with the patrol when they stopped for a ten minute break only to see them get to their feet and start off again.

The third day of our hike we entered a swamp of gooey mud which made walking difficult. We walked all day but failed to get out of the swamp before nightfall, so we had to spread our ponchos in the slimy, stinking mud. It rained most of that night and we awoke to find two inches of water had covered not only the swamp but our ponchos as well. Worse, huge leeches had latched onto everyone and we were soon pulling these horrible blood suckers from our bodies. Two I had ripped off my leg in my sleep left scars that are visible to this day. But I was lucky. Others had leeches in their mouths and up their noses. A lighted cigarette made most of them drop off, but I don't know how the fellows got them out of their noses.

The ninth day of our patrol and the eighth day since we had been reported missing in action, we staggered into headquarters of the 112th Cavalry! At last I could remove my shoes and socks; tears of relief rolled down my cheeks, but I had lost all the skin off my feet from the ankles down to the soles. When Lt. Czerniejewski saw the condition of my feet he paid me the finest compliment I have ever had: "I wondered what was wrong with you. Always before, the tougher things got, the funnier you got!" Our platoon became known as "The Lost Patrol".

RUSSIAN ENCOUNTER

by Charles G. Barrett Jr.

The 2nd CGB Platoon under Lt. Murphy was in the lead of C Troop with the 3rd Platoon in reserve position in the rear. When we entered the dorf of Apollensdorf, the German citizens did warn of the Russians down the road and a German citizen, after the 2nd CGB Platoon fired our flares and no response from the Russians, went down and tried to inform them of the US Army trying to make contact. The response he got was, "Get out of here or we will kill you." At this time, Platoon Sgt. Howard Rouse volunteered to try and contact them. Now I must digress a moment. On the morning of April 30th, Corporal Spatea was standing outside the door of the house in which I was billeted and looked like he had not slept much that night. To my question as to "what is the matter, Spat?", his response was, "nothing," and after a little pause, said "can I ride up front with my jeep in second place?" "What for?" "Oh, just want to ride up front." (He normally was in the third section of the 3rd platoon and oftentimes missed the initial action.) My reply was to see Sgt. Gard and if it was all right with him, OK! Now hold on to your thought process here. Originally Sgt. Rouse, whom we had given up to the 2nd platoon for platoon sergeant, had been the 3rd platoon point sergeant and Vernon Bozman had been the point Jeep driver. We had appointed Woodrow Wean to Sgt. Rouse's position, but had loaned him and Bozman to 83rd Inf. Div., I believe, for a little detached service for some reason which escapes me now.

So on the morning of April 30th, the 3rd platoon was in the rear with Staff Sgt. Raymond Gard riding the point jeep with Ray Lombardi driving and Ralph Cabana as rifleman. Following was Cpl. Spatea in the 2nd jeep with Lujohn, who had a nickname I cannot remember, as driver, and Bernard McCaulley (I believe it was McCaulley rather than McCallum) as rifleman. McCaulley was a recent

From the steps of the former hospital at Fort Statensburg, Clark Field, Luzon, P.I., General MacArthur and members of his staff watch American Artillery pound Jap position in the nearby hills. Jan. 31, 1945.

replacement and one I had not gotten to know very well, except that I had noticed that he, up until this day, had seemed rather depressed. But on this day, I had noticed that he was in good spirits and joking and laughing with the men. Cpl. Spatea was riding in the front of the jeep on the right side and McCaulley was riding right behind him. The 3rd vehicle was an armored car with Nickos the driver, Charles Overstreet, radio operator, D. Dunlay, gunner, and Lt. Barrett, car commander and 3rd platoon leader. Following were two more sections and the armored half-track. Now for the action. Our platoon was not aware of the communications going on with our headquarters. At this time, Capt. Ploehn, Commanding Officer of C Troop, came back and told the 3rd platoon to take a road down along the Elbe River that ran between the river and the town, and try and contact the Russians. Sgt. Gard put a white flag on the wire catcher of the front jeep and we proceeded ahead. It seems that we went through a wooded area for a little ways then we came out into an open area above the river and a short distance from the outskirts of the town. A Russian tank was situated alongside a house on our left and some warning shots, small arms, were fired over our heads. We halted the platoon and surveyed the situation. We could see some activity straight ahead with a house to the right of the road. (See map insert.) After waiting a while longer and conferring with Sgt. Gard via radio, he suddenly announced, "I'm going to make a run for it," (exact words). I said, "You be careful because you don't know what's up there." However, he was in a better position to see than I was. So he took off. He made it and the Russians came out of hiding to receive them, I guess. The 2nd jeep then made a run for it and hit one of the mines that the 1st jeep had straddled. To this day, I do not know whether the Russians made any attempt to warn the 2nd jeep of the mines or not. Anyway, when the 2nd jeep hit the mine, the driver Lujohn was evidently thrown out to his left, while the main force of the explosion was on the right side. It was so terrific that the jeep seemed to go about 60 feet in the air and the bodies of Spatea and McCaulley went several hundred feet, Spatea to the left of the house in the orchard, and McCaulley to the right of the house down in a gully. I had dismounted and ran as fast as I could up there. Lujohn was alive but in much pain. We called for the Medics. Cpl. Spatea was lying on his back on the grass among some fruit trees, with a most peaceful look on his face. One of the men got a blanket from the Russians and covered him. Then I said, "Where is McCaulley?" I think the Russians found him first, but when I got there, he was expiring, both hands and feet were blown off. A Russian medic gave him a shot, I presume of Morphine, but it was useless. By this time, I asked the Russian lieutenant in charge to take me to his headquarters, which he did. He led the way and I followed and a Russian soldier followed me with a .45 Cal. Sub-Thompson machine gun on me. I was somewhat comforted when I looked over my shoulder and saw one of our men, T/5 Maine, who was across the street and slightly in the rear, with his Tommy gun at the ready. After showing my identification to two Russian majors and one colonel, they agreed to accompany me back to the scene of the crime for which only ignorance and suspicion could have been responsible. When we got back to the scene, Capt. Ploehn, Lt. Col. Kleitz and Col. Biddle were there. Someone, I do not remember who, took a picture (enclosed) of the three Russian officers, myself right behind, a Russian soldier and behind and to the right in the picture is t/5, Maine. To the far right at the border of the picture under a flowering tree lies the body of Cpl. Domonic Spatea under a blanket. In the forefront, mounted on two wheels and also under a blanket, is a Russian machine gun. Charles Overstreet

Sam Silverman, 11th Cavalry. 1941.

remained on the radio and finally got the Medics for Lujohn who miraculously was not injured badly. The graves registration got the bodies of the two men. It was the end of the war. I was shocked; I was depressed; I was disgusted, I was perplexed; I was angry; I was mad. The utter senselessness, the stupidity, the callousness, the disregard for human life! In the next few days when they picked the 3rd platoon to the honor guard for the General to make the meeting official, I refused to go, but told Sgt. Gard to take it. I heard later that the Russians offered to shoot fourteen of their men for the loss of our two, which proved two opinions I had already formulated. First, they had a terrific inferiority complex and the second, utter disregard for human life.

In which, I believe, was a sincere effort to relieve my pain, I was given a ten day leave to Cannes, France on the Riviera, so I escaped the withdrawal of our troops to the other side of the Elbe and the rape, looting and plundering of the civilian population by the Russian "Conquerors" of a territory that we had already possessed.

Now if Sgt. Gard were alive and we could locate Lombardi, Cabana and Lujohn, if they are still living, they might be able to give us additional information on the first immediate contact before the disaster, but I'm convinced that it would not be contradictory to the narrative of an also eyewitness. I only have myself to blame for not keeping in touch with the outfit, so I blame no one for the story as it was given to you.

Now about meeting the Russians as I remember it. As you remember, we started from Barby, Germany, and crossed the Elbe River. I do not remember where or what kind of a bridge we crossed. We started out looking for the Russians where we were told to expect them, kept going and running into Germans who were still fighting the war, and had several engagements, one in which Lt. O'Donnell (the Lt. who had come all the way and had such a good record-medals, etc.) was killed. We got artillery fire for almost a day as we were advancing down the highway. We called back to headquarters and they told us no American artillery was firing. They later told us it was coming from the Russian area, as we were sure by then that it was. I do not remember how many days we were on this mission, but it seemed to me about three days, and we finally came to the town of Apollensdorf. The Germans told us the Russians were there, and they

were. The Russians were either under orders to hold the town, or did not know who we were, what our flag or military symbols or vehicles were, or were distrustful of everyone. I never knew why they kept firing on us until our "C" Troop 3rd Platoon found that side road around the edge of town and our 3rd platoon rushed them, waving flags, etc. I remember that Cpl. Spatea's jeep was in front of our M8 armored car, and he was standing up reaching out his hand to shake hands with them to show that we were not their enemies when his jeep hit that mine. I was looking down at the radio and trying to call headquarters and tell them that we were making contact with the Russians. (If I remember right, they had quit firing at us then.) When the mine blew them out of sight, all I could see was what was left of the jeep. I looked to my left and was looking into the barrel of a large gun on a Russian tank. If they had fired that gun, our M8 would have been about like the jeep. Lots of confusion then, for as we were making that run up the road, our troop headquarters had received orders to break off contact with the Russians and move back until further orders, but we had already made contact.

I began calling for medics and stretchers but Troop Headquarters would only say to "stand by". By that time, Spatea and one of the others in the jeep had been found and we were all upset and everyone wanting the medics. I guess I got rather rough on my request for medics and told Headquarters that "if they could find time, we had dead and wounded up here, and could sure use some stretchers and medics" real fast. About that time, I looked back behind the M8 and saw Capt. Ploehn coming as fast as he could run, them long legs taking several feet at a step, and holding a stretcher in one hand that was about sticking straight out behind him.

When the dead and wounded were taken back, the Russians were all over the place, passing out drinks and shaking hands, and taking pictures, etc. They seemed a lot happier than we were.

The next worse part was we were told to move back and let the Russians take over. The Russians followed us back, and it looked to the Germans that we were retreating from the Russians. They were really worried and frightened. I was sure they had good reason to feel that way.

Write back and tell me your version of this, as I was on the radio all the time and could not get around to see much.

RELIEF OF BASTOGNE

by Colonel Thomas D. Gillis, USA Ret.

It was December 18, 1944, the third day of the German drive into the Ardennes. General Eisenhower had summoned his senior commanders to the 12th Army Group's rear headquarters in Verdun. After a discussion of several plans of attack, the decision was made and Eisenhower asked Patton when he could start. Patton said that he could attack the morning of December 21st with three divisions. This in spite of the fact that Third Army was engaged 150 miles to the southeast. Patton, upon given the go-ahead for the 22nd, reached for the field telephone, cranked the handle, and was connected with Lucky Forward. When one of his staff officers answered all Patton said was, "Put Plan A into effect!" Within the hour the Reserve Command (CC-R) of the 4th Armored Division was on the road northward.

The march of the 4th Armored Division of 151 miles, starting in the southeast from Fenetrange in French Lorraine to Vaux-les-Rosieres in Belgium was made in 19 hours and was the longest made by a division. Third Army moved its front 90 degrees with a speed that astonished the Germans. I was then a LTC, the deputy commander of the CC-R (the reserve command). Efforts of CC-R to contact the 101st Airborne Division by radio had been fruitless, so on December 20 volunteered to drive into Bastogne to determine the situation first hand and learn what supplies the 101st needed most. Arriving at the C.P. of the 101st I reported in to BG Anthony C. McAuliffe, Asst. Div. Comdr., who was acting commander, and LTC (later Lt. General) Harry W. O. Kinnard, the G-3 of the Division. I also had a reunion with LTC Hank Cherry, C.O. of the 3rd Tk. B., 9th Armd. Div., a West Point (1935) classmate of mine. Having determined that the 101st was in dire need of medical supplies and ammunition primarily, I was about to take my leave. I told Gen. McAuliffe that I had to get back to appraise my people of the problems.

In response I was told, "How are you going to do that? We are surrounded!"

I replied, "The same way I got in here. I am going to drive back! As we left the perimeter defenses, I told my jeep driver, Harry Moritz, a gung-ho lad from Chicago, to put the pedal to the metal and not to stop for anything. With my carbine cradled in my arms and our backs bent low in the jeep, the forest was a blur of green as we sped southward. No one fired at us, although I saw some figures vaguely in the background. Apparently the Germans figured we were the point of a larger force and planned on ambushing the main body. They waited for a better target. We later learned that we had gone through the lines of the German 5th Parachute Division. As soon as my report reached 4th Armd. Division headquarters that the 101st had lost its collecting station, along with most of its surgeons and medics, and that it was in dire need of ammunition, the division G-4, LTC Bernie Knestrick, started planning the composition of the relief column for the 101st Abn. Div. At 0600 hours on December 22nd, CC-A and CC-B started the drive to Bastogne, pushing to Burnon and Martelange respectively. It was that day the General Patton issued his Christmas prayer. Miraculously, starting on December 23, and continuing to the 27th, there was a break in the weather. Christmas Eve 1944 was bitterly cold, as the thermometer plunged below zero. The gently rolling hills and snow covered patches of pine woods just south of Bastogne glistened under a brilliant full moon, and one could imagine the Star of Bethlehem among the myriad's of stars gleaming in a cloudless sky. The Reserve Command was ordered at two o'clock Christmas morning to pull out of the line on the east flank of the Fourth Armored

A machine gunner and pack horse traversing a hill.

Division and march from Bigonville around the division's rear to its west flank at Bereheaux, preparatory to launching a surprise attack north to relieve the beleaguered 101st Airborne Division surrounded in Bastogne. In spite of the beauty of the night and the brilliance of the moon, the 30 miles were torture for the G.I.'s who were poorly equipped for such biting cold. Even though I wore mittens sewn from three thicknesses of G. I. blanket and fleece lined boots, I could feel my hands and feet getting frostbitten. Every time the column stopped momentarily we would all dismount from our vehicles and double time in place trying to restore circulation in our feet. But in spite of this, many of us had our hands and feet frostbitten.

At a sudden stop in the column, Col. Wendell Blanchard, the CO of CC-R was projected through the windshield of his jeep just in front of me. With great difficulty because of my stiff fingers, I was able to remove his helmet and work his head back between the shards of glass without his suffering any more cuts. He refused medical attention until 0600 that morning when the command surgeon sewed up his neck and forehead at our new C.P. at Bercheaux, while he issued his verbal attack order up the Bastogne corridor. The last 16 miles into Bastogne were the toughest the 4th A.D. ever fought.

The exploits of LTC Creighton Abrams and his 37th Tank Bn., and his side-kick, LTC "Jigger" Jaques, C.O. of the 53rd Anti Tank Bn., in blasting their way into Batogne are well documented by historians. In succession, the Reserve Command captured Vaux-les-Rosieres, Nives, and Remoiville. Chaumont changed hands three times. Remichampagne was cleared by noon. They charged Assennois with all guns firing, and the tankers moved in under the barrage of four friendly artillery battalions. The final attack jumped off early the next morning as tanks and half-tracks charged into Clochimont. Our tanks then burst through the outer defenses of the 101st Airborne before the Germans could react. The road was open at 1645 hours December 26th.

At 0200 hours the next morning I led the relief column of doctors, nurses, and some 200 ambulances and trucks into Bastogne. Mission accomplished, the three days and nights without sleep took their toll, and I collapsed in my sleeping bag. When I awoke that afternoon and glanced out of the window and saw that the large building across the street had been reduced to a pile of rubble while I slept soundly. Harry Kinnard and I were boyhood playmates at

the Presidio of Monterey. He wrote to me later, "I was worried as hell about you would fare dodging krauts on the way back to Arlon. But our needs were so desperate that I wouldn't have tried to dissuade you even if I could. I only wish I had seen you to thank you when you arrived with the manna from heaven. But if late is better than never, let me say all these years later-from the bottom of my heart-THANKS FOR YOUR SUPERB DELIVERING OF THE LIFESAVING GOODS! WELL DONE!"

LTC Creighton Abrahams, who later became a four star general, commanding the 37th Tank Battalion, of the CC-R, followed through with the initial break through. Major General Maxwell D. Taylor, who also later became a four star general, commanding the 101st Airborne, didn't get back until the whole thing was over.

OLD BILL

The Horse I Rode Overseas in WWII

by Lionel Carter

On August 11, 1942, the 112th Cavalry landed on the strategically located island of New Caledonia, between Australia and New Zealand and the next objective of the Japanese. Rather mountainous with few highways, horses were needed to reach any part of the island upon which the Japanese might land; the horse, after all is but a form of transportation and not for cavalry charges as dramatized in movies and TV.

Shortly after we arrived, we were informed that the first boatload of horses shipped from Australia had been sunk by a Japanese submarine, which left us with the easy life of an infantryman; after all, we had the same equipment and were expected to march as far as an infantryman plus about 150 horses per troop, and horses have to be fed, watered, groomed and cleaned up after whereas machine guns and rifles don't.

This life of ease came to an end with the arrival of a second shipment of wild horses from Australia, supposedly broken for riding, but so many troopers were hospitalized with broken bones and cracked heads as to draw a complaint from Col. Cunningham. My inferiority complex as always caused me to under estimate my ability be it high school basketball or in the bank after the war where I refused a promotion to be in charge of over half of the employees in the bank until rebuked by the chairman of the board with: "Do you want to move up to management or be an employee all your life?" Nor do I mean to imply that I was a rider equal to those Texas cowboys, but my trepidation was such that I might end up with a horse I couldn't ride. The cries of derision on being thrown always bothered me more than the bumps and bruises I sustained. So I selected a runt of horse who was so sickly he could hardly hold his head up, who couldn't keep up at a walk so I was always forced to make him trot and couldn't keep up at a trot, so I would have to make him gallop, a very tiring experience for both of us on a long ride. Looking at the more elegant looking horses ridden by the other troopers made my regret my choice even more.

When I joined the 112th I began telling them amusing and highly fictional stories about my home town, Colfax, Illinois, so that when I began playing outfield on the baseball team, my personal cheering section would chant "Colfax! Colfax!" instead of "Carter". Some troopers even greeted me as "Colfax". One night when Lt. McIntyre was recording names of our horses for the official army records, he would yell a trooper's name and the trooper would yell back the name of his horse. When he yelled, "Carter," such a roar came from the tents around me for "Colfax! Colfax!" that I have in and told him: "Colfax". "That's a hell of a name for horse!" he said. I didn't think it was that bad; several months later I discovered he had written down: "Cold Facts"! At a movie one night Cary Grant and Ginger Rogers (I think) danced to the tune of "Drum Boogie". The tune kept spinning around in my head, and I began calling my horse "Drum Boogie", then finally just "Boogie"; the name by which he became known.

Meanwhile a horse known as "Old Bill" went unridden. Oliver Lovelady, a Texas cowboy, had selected him, but one day when Lovelady tried to make him do something he didn't want to do, he showed his displeasure by rearing up on his hind legs and falling directly backwards on his back. Luckily, Lovelady was not pinned between the pommel of the saddle and the horse or his chest could have been crushed and Lovelady killed. Lovelady would never ride him again and his prediction that: "That horse will kill somebody!" gave everyone else second thoughts. Finally, he had to be sent back to "remounts" to be broken for riding, since no one had ridden him for so long. When he was returned to G Troop, Cpl. Harvey Thompson suggested that I ride him. I didn't think much of the idea. Harvey said, "I'll ride him for awhile, and you can see how nice he handles!" A choice between a "dead head" and a horse that might like to see me dead!

In January, 1943 we received a group of replacements, and Tony Frangella from Chicago, who had never ridden a horse was assigned to our squad. He needed a gentle horse to take to a school on horsemanship, and I suggested giving him "Boogie" and I would ride "Old Bill". Tony returned from riding class livid with rage and spoiling for a fight. (I've always thought he wanted to fight me, but he claims it was Cpl. Thompson). He said that Boogie bucked. I said, "He can't get two feet off the ground at the same time!" After supper, I took Tony down to the corral where I took a short run, placed my hands on Boogie's rump and vaulted onto his back. "Does that look like a mean horse to you?" I asked. He had to admit that it did not. Then I said, "Let me give you some good advice. Keep that temper under control. Some of these Texans might start calling you "Dago", if they do, ignore it and keep your mouth shut. If you fight one of them, you're going to have to fight them all. Ignore it and survive!" Tony did and he did!

Old Bill proved more of a problem than I had expected. When I returned from riding him that first day and led him to the picket line to tie him up with the other horses, Lt. McIntyre yelled, "Don't tie that horse to the picket line! Tie him to a tree!" Seems in one of his moments of anger, Old Bill had reared up and fallen backward on his back and brought the whole picket line down with him, badly frightening the horses. Mornings I had to walk around the empty corral with him with a saddle blanket in one hand and try to get it on his back without him throwing it off, then repeat the same process with the saddle, hoping he hadn't thrown off the blanket in the meantime. I was always concerned that I wouldn't get him saddled before the troop rode out! One day as I was trying to saddle him, 1st Sgt. Currier walked by and said, "Stay with him, Carter!" which coming from the top kick gave my morale quite a boost.

However, having to tie him to a tree and not on the picket line removed from close supervision and I could groom him as leisurely as I wanted. Removing the saddle and saddle blanket, I'd always talk to him in a low voice and stroke his neck, being careful to move leisurely and with no sudden movements. He began to relax more and more, and a bit of a friendship began to develop between us. One day as I finished brushing one side, I noticed a small group of onlookers watching me, and to show off, I did a rather dangerous thing: Instead of walking around to the other side, I stooped down and went under his belly. The startled gasps of the onlookers was clearly audible. If Old Bill had been frightened and had reared up on his hind legs, I could have been one dead trooper. As he was undisturbed by my unorthodox method of getting to the other side, I would do it whenever I had an audience, never failing to bring gasps from them. However, one day Lt. McIntyre saw me doing my fearless act, "Carter," he yelled "Get that horse over here and tie him to the picket line!" My days of leisurely grooming were over!

Riding Old Bill became a dream; a slight nudge of my heels and he'd pick up the gait, a slight tug on the reins, and he'd drop from a gallop to a trot or a trot to a walk. However, one Monday when I was recovering from a trip into Noumea with too much booze and too little sleep, we were riding in formation when Lt. McIntyre gave the order to trot; I was in a mental fog and forgot who I was riding and gave Old Bill both spurs. Hard. He threw me not only out of the saddle but also slightly forward, so that when he took off at a gallop, he ran under me, so that I fell sickeningly back into the saddle on the two most tender parts of man's body. I was nauseated and wishing he had thrown me off on the ground as without stirrups, I struggled to tighten the reins. With Old Bill in a headlong gallop we quickly passed the entire column including Lt. McIntyre who yelled, "Where in the hell are you going?" And I yelled back "How in the hell would I know? Ask him" Seesawing on the reins, I brought Old Bill under control and rode back to the platoon.

Returning one day from an all day ride, I was joined by "Colonel" Webb, a private but a leader of a motley crew of alcoholics, a thief, a bully and other misfits (all proved worthless in combat) who flourished under our cowardly lieutenant as their "General". Webb was my worst heckler and whenever I'd make an observation, he'd sneer and say, "I suppose you read that in the Reader's Digest!" He once put me down with the statement: "I've been in more jails than you've been in towns!" A retort I put to good usage on our long train ride from Ft. Clark, Texas to San Francisco. Every little town we passed through, I'd call out, "Hey, Webb, have you been in jail here?" After the third town, he threatened to come up and punch me in the mouth, so I couldn't wait for the next town so I could test his threat. He ignored my question, also at the following town, and the next and the next, until it was no longer fun. Now we rode along without speaking until he saw who I was riding and a startled look spread over his face. "Is that Old Bill you're riding?" he asked. When I replied in the affirmative, he reined in his horse and dropped back about three horse lengths. "I'm not riding next to him!" he said. Made me feel really, really good!

Old Bill came to an untimely end. Taken to the blacksmiths to be reshoed, he was so frightened by the fire, the noise, the rough handling that they were unable to control him. In anger and frustration, one of the blacksmiths hit him in the head with an iron rod, and he had to be destroyed.

It has been said that humans can learn from animals and birds. What did I learn from Old Bill? I learned that a little kindness can change the worst of us, be he man or beast!

THE ROUGH RIDERS

by Dr. Cyla Allison

The Nassau-Suffolk Horsemen's Association is a charitable organization dedicated to promoting humane equine practices and to providing educational services to the equestrian community and the public. The NSHA began 30 years ago, growing from a local riding club to become the largest regional organization of its kind in New York.

The NSHA Rough Riders appear mounted in parades and at equine exhibitions, uniformed and equipped to commemorate the hisotry and service of horse cavalry in the United States from Revolutionary War times through the early 20th Century. The troop has been designated an official "Cavalry Memorial Unit" buy the U.S. Cavalry Association at Fort Riley, KS, providing horses and color guards for veteran memorial services and events. The ROUGH RIDERS also ride at public festivals and celebrations to "Keep the Guidons Flying."

MEMORIES OF A VMI HORSE CAVALRY TROOP

As a "city-slicker" from New Jersey, I realized my desire to ride for the first time as a "Rat" (freshman) at the Virginia Military Institute (VMI) in September 1946 under the instruction of Colonel John M. Fray, VMI '08. The Department of the Army still supported horses at VMI until June 1948, at which time horses were replaced with M-24 "Chaffee" light tanks which I learned to drive as a cadet. One of the tests of a cadet's horsemanship training was to surmount a series of one foot jumps spaced several yards apart without stirrups or reins and blindfolded. Balance, of course, was the point of the exercise. However, by the fourth blindfolded jump, I began to slip from the saddle until I fell from my mount on the sixth jump. My horse galloped off into the distance while Colonel Fray bellowed at me to retrieve my horse and immediately repeat the exercise. I did. Not wanting to incur the wrath of Colonel Fray again, I made the rerun successfully by gripping the horse so tightly with my legs that I limped around the VMI post for a week recovering.

That same year of 1946, I passed in review with the cadet horse cavalry troop on Founder's Day, November 11, before the VMI Board of Visitor's in which General of the Army George C. Marshall, VMI '01 was a member. Instead of Polo Pony #33 that I had been customarily riding, I drew from the VMI stables an unruly horse artillery mount. On the second pass in review before the VMI Board of Visitors, this time at a trot, my horse broke out into a gallop and I lost control. He charged forward from my position in the 2d Platoon (rank) of horses and plunged through the 1st Platoon (rank) and almost ahead of the troop commander and guidon bearer before regaining control, but not before I discarded my red and white pennant lance on the parade ground. The episode proved embarrassing to me in more ways than one.

8TH CA

LRY BACHELORS

936

1ST LT WYATT ADAMS was born July 14, 1916, in Chicago, IL; and received his BS degree in insurance from the University of Illinois. Joined the service on Feb. 11, 1942, and was stationed with the Mec Cavalry. His stations were in Italy, France, Rhineland Central Europe. He served with the 102nd Cav. MEZ REGT and 117th Cav. MECH SQDN.

He received discharge in February 1945, with the rank of 1st lieutenant. Awards include four Battle Stars and one Bronze Arrowhead.

Memorable experiences include the time their unit moved 1,000 miles across North Africa in 40 hours; landing in Southern France on Aug. 15, 1944, with full mechanized equipment on D-Day H-Hour; and the Battle of Bitch, which began on Dec. 31, 1944, midnight, Alscace Lorraine.

Married Theresa L. Adams and has three children. He worked as an insurance agent in Indiana until Sept. 1, 1986, and then as a residential appraiser for the Veterans Administration. He now works for HUD.

T/5 GLENN G. AMES was born Sept. 26, 1926, Leapwood, MO; and completed the seventh grade of school. Joined the service on Jan. 22, 1941, and was assigned to the 9th Armored F Troop, 2nd Cav. and served with F Troop, 2nd Cav.

He was discharged on Oct. 18, 1945. Awards include the Purple Heart and Good Conduct Medal.

Memorable experience was being with the 9th Armored Div., A Company.

Married Dev and has six children, six grandchildren and two great-grandchildren. He worked for the Charleston Army Ammo Plant and retired in October 1982.

LT COL AUS (RET) JOHN R. ANDERSON was born Jan. 6, 1918, La Grange, IL and received his BA degree from the University of Chicago. Joined the US Army in October 1940 and received assignment to the cavalry. Participated in WWII, ETO, Normandy, Northern France, Ardennes and Germany; and served with the 106th Cav., 5th AD, 707th Troop Battalion.

Retired in October 1968. Awards include Battle Stars and Theater Ribbons.

Memorable experiences include entering the service in the Horse Sqdn., 106th Cav. Regt.; platoon leader, Recon Company, 34th AR, 5th AD; commanding officer of the LT Troop Company, 707th Troop Battalion; executive officer and commanding officer, 9/34 Troop Battalion and 6/5 Cav. Recon Sqdn.; USAR, Boston, MA, Asst. 62, 33rd Infantry Div., ILNG.

Married Marilyn Menagh on Sept. 9, 1946, and has three children and 10 grandchildren. Marilyn passed away in 1994. He worked for Swift and Co. as a plant manager and Midwest Jobbers as a manager. He retired in 1980.

2ND LT WALTER D. ARMER SR. was born Feb. 11, 1916, Globe, AZ; and received his BS degree from the University of Arizona. Received commission as 2nd lieutenant from the University of Arizona ROTC in June 1939 and called to one year active duty on Jan. 20, 1941. Received assignment to Troop A, 1st Horse Sqdn., CRTC, Ft. Riley, KS. Dec. 7, 1941, put a stop to any thought of one year duty.

Attended the Cavalry School from July 2, 1942, to Sept. 26, 1942; and was promoted to captain Oct. 12, 1942. In December 1942, he received assignment as commanding officer of the Recon Troop, 28th Infantry Div. in Louisiana. They moved to Camp Gordon Johnson, FL for amphibious training in preparation for overseas duty. He wound up on limited duty for about a year after he was accidentally shot on April 13, 1943. After getting out of Lawson General Hospital in Atlanta, GA, he returned to Ft. Riley.

Receiving a transfer in May 1944 to the QMC, he finally arrived in England in December 1944 and then went on to France. Upon returning to the United States in December 1945, he finished his year of active duty on March 26, 1946.

After returning to Arizona he went back to ranching and ranch related activities where he still rides and supports a few cattle.

Married Virginia Little in June 1941 and has two children, four grandchildren and one great-grandchild. He recently married Ina Culver Poole and now has four children, six grandchildren and two great-grandchildren.

MAJ LAYMON L. ARMSTRONG was born March 12, 1916, Oliver Springs, TN, and graduated from Crofton, KY High School. He did his pre-dental work at Western Kentucky University, graduated from the University of Louisville Dental School, took the Kentucky State Board and received orders to active duty, all in March 1943. Enlisted and served as private 123 with the Cavalry Machine Gun Troop and the KYNG from 1932-35, before enlisting in CCC. Received assignment as 1st lieutenant dental officer in the medical department of the 237th Engineer Combat Battalion. Received training in North Africa and England and participated in the landing of Normandy and the Battle of the Bulge.

Upon returning home after VE-Day, he received assignment to the Veteran Administration Brown Hospital, Dayton, OH. He then transferred to Wadsworth Hospital, VA Center, Los Angeles, CA and then as a dental officer at Camp White Medford, OR.

Retired in March 1974 with the rank of major. Awards include an ETO Ribbon w/5 Campaign Stars and Bronze Arrowhead.

Married Marie Sexton on Dec. 23, 1939, and has one daughter, Connie Lyn Horn, and two grandchildren. He passed away on March 5, 1995.
Submitted by LTC Lucian W. Barne

CHARLES F. ATWELL was born March 7, 1916, Topeka, KS. Graduated Topeka High School and attended Washburn College for one year before dropping out to go to work. Joined the KSNG on June 10, 1934, with HQ Troop, 114th Cav. They were only 62 miles

from Ft. Riley and Ft. Leavenworth, with many of their facilities available for their use. Their troop was very active training wise, so horsemanship and marksmanship on all weapons available at that time were the highlights of their training.

Attended the NG non-commissioned officer's class 1939-40 at Ft. Riley, KS, and was commissioned a 2nd lieutenant cavalry shortly after graduation. Transferred to the US Army and served with the Horse Cavalry, field artillery, tank destroyer battalions and ordnance corps.

In 1941 the 114th Cav. Regt. was redesignated the 127th FA, and all their commissions were changed to field artillery. The tank destroyer battalions were formed in 1941 and many of them were reassigned. Those were sad days for many former cavalrymen as they had to part with their mounts and their spurs.

Attended the officers classes at the tank destroyer school, Field Artillery School and the natural resources conference conducted by the industrial college of the armed forces in Detroit, MI. In September 1945 he was shipped overseas to the Far East command and joined the 158th Regt. Combat Team at Leyte, PI. In December 1945 they moved to Yokahoma, Japan and joined the 11th Army Corps as ordnance officer. Then he was reassigned to HQ 8th Army as assistant ordnance supply officer. Returned to Conus and assigned to Benicia Arsenal, CA, where he served as chief of stock control and chief of storage; then to Ft. Leavenworth, Riley and Sheridan and back to AFFE HQS, ordnance supply and maintenance thence to Korea. Returned to Conus and assigned to Detroit Arsena, MI; on to Camp Stanley, TX as post commander; then Sierra Ordnance Depot as post commander.

Retired as deputy post commander on June 30, 1960. It was a terrific 26 years from private to lieutenant colonel. He would do it again.

Married Clarice Alyce Stewart, who passed away on June 2, 1981. They have five children, 18 grandchildren and six great-grandchildren. Married Henrietta Bernice Johnson on July 28, 1982, and has one child, two grandchildren and one great-grandchild. Spent five years with Areojet Corporation; five years in real estate sales; and 10 years in sales with Capp Homes. His final retirement was in June 1981.

T/5 REYNALDO G. BACA was born Dec. 8, 1916, Radium Springs, NM. Enlisted in regular Army on Jan. 20, 1942, in El Paso, TX. Was assigned to the 11th US Horse Cav., 1942-43, and the 10th Armored Div.

Memorable experience was being the cowboy that he was; he and a buddy, on a three day pass, went to a Salinas, CA Rodeo and were entering a bucking horse contest when a MP tapped him on the shoulder and said, "Come with me." This ended his rodeo participation and he got three days of KP duty.

Apparently they were not supposed to ride bucking horses in uniform in a public rodeo at that time. To help feed the Army, he was released from service early in order to get back in the beef producing business of ranching in New Mexico. After horses were about phased out in the Army, he saw an officer about getting back in the horse cavalry. The officer told him, "About Face," then got him a discharge.

Discharged on June 19, 1943, 10th Armored Div., Ft. Benning, GA.

Baca was popular among ranchers and was sought out often to help sick or injured livestock, or to "float" some horses teeth. He seemed to have considerable ability to heal livestock and castrate ornery tom cats. He worked at one time for the famous "Drag A" Ranch at Datil, NM.

Married Mary Magdalene Davila and had five children: Regina, Gilbert, Evelyn, Edwin and Lola. He passed away on July 14, 1993, in Socorro, NM. *Submitted by: J.C. Briggs, Ret.*

MAJ EDWARD P. BAKER was born Aug. 15, 1916, Richmond, VA. Enlisted in the US Army, Richmond, VA, 3rd Cav. Regt. on Sept. 14, 1940, and served in three horse cavalry regiments from 1940-44: the 3rd, Ft. Myer, VA; the 5th, Ft. Bliss, TX; and the 27th, Ft. Clark, TX. Commissioned AUS upon graduation from the 29th class, OCS, Ft. Riley, KS, April 22, 1943. Cavalry assignments were Troop F, 3rd Cav. Regt., Sept. 14, 1940, until June 1941; Troop F, 5th Cav. Regt., 1942 until February 1943; Troop G, 27th Cav. Regt., April 1943 to December 1943; OCS, 29th OCS Class, Horse Class, February 1943 until April 22, 1943; and MECZ, 45th Infantry Recon Troop, WWII, 1944-45.

Sent to Tunisia, Africa with a provisional horse cavalry squadron in January 1944 and was disbanded after arrival. Assigned to the 45th Cav. Recon Troop, May 1944 at breakout from Anzio. Celebrated birthday landing with the 45th Infantry Div. during the invasion of Southern France. Served with the 45th until near end of hostilities.

Accepted USAR commission on his return to the States. He was recalled to active duty during the Korean War. Retired from the USAR, April 24, 1964. Awards include the Army of Occupation Medal, ETO Ribbon w/ 4 Battle Stars and one Invasion Arrow and WWII Victory Medal.

Married Ruth M. Loving in 1943 and has two sons, David and Stephen; one daughter, Deborah, and four grandchildren. He is a life member of the US Cavalry Association.

2ND LT CHARLES WOODHULL BALDWIN (WOODIE) was born Aug. 23, 1910, Coxsackie, Greene County, NY. Attended Irving School for Boys, Ridgefield Prep, Trinity College and received the college equivalency in the service. Enlisted in 1936 with Sqdn. A, Manhattan Units 101st Cav. NYNG and entered active duty as 2nd lieutenant with the cavalry on Jan. 27, 1941.

Memorable experiences were working with the Lease Lend Organization as aide to Russian representative in Ohio and helping establish the Lease Lend Depot in Florida. Also memorable was being assigned to the Pentagon at the time of the establishment of the USAF as a separate service. He wore the first USAF "silvertan" uniform in the Pentagon. He also worked closely with the Arabs and ARAMCO at the airbase at Dhahran, Saudi Arabia.

Married Mary J. Snyder, an industrial engineer with ARAMCO, on Oct. 17, 1952 at the RAF Chapel,

Bahrein, PG. They have one daughter, Helen, born at West Point Army Hospital in 1962. He put her on a horse as soon as she was old enough.

S/SGT RILEY BANKS was born Aug. 27, 1921, Boley, OK; moved to Newton, KS at the age of one; to Wichita, KS, age nine, where he attended grade and high school to the 11th grade; attended two years of college, 1948-49; and worked five years with a refrigeration service engineer society. He joined the CCC and became an excellent cook and baker and served one and one-half years before coming out in November 1940.

Enlisted in the US Army on April 29, 1941, being assigned to the 9th Cav.; and was stationed at Ft. Riley, Camp Rucker, Ft. Knox and Ft. Ord. He made the Arkansas Louisiana maneuver, on to the cadre to Army Air Corps then to the Quarter Masters Trucking Company. After training at Ft. Ord, he left for Port Moresby to Kweka, New Guinea to Lingoyen Gulf to Manila, PI. He had 85 points and was able to return to the States.

Memorable experiences include their 3477 AM touch unit hauling special supplies to Gen. MacArthur's headquarters in downtown Manila, PI; and his greatest achievement was to be a part of the mounting of the buffalo movement with Gen. Colleir at Ft. Leavenworth, KS.

Discharged on Nov. 3, 1945. Awards include the Good Conduct Medal, American Defense Service Medal, American Campaign Medal, Asiatic Pacific Campaign Medal, WWII Victory Medal, Philippine Liberation Ribbon and the Republic of the Presidential Unit Citation Badge.

Married Melinda Banks, Aug. 31, 1950. Owned his own air conditioner refrigeration business until he retired. Worked as a machinist for A.T. & S.F.R.R.Y Company for 35 years. He retired on Aug. 31, 1981. Melinda is now deceased.

TSG R.C. BARHAM (BILL) was born Jan. 28, 1923, Riverside, CA; and attended high school. Enlisted on Feb. 4, 1943, with the US Horse Cav., 124th Cav., with stations in Myitkyina, Sen Wi Valley, Hosei Valley and Burma. He served with the Mars Task Force.

Memorable experiences include horsemanship and pack training, Ft. Riley, KS; being in the last mounted cavalry unit, Horse Trooper, 124th Cav., Ft. Brown, TX; 31 day boat ride from San Pedro, CA to Bombay, India; combat in Burma, Burma Road; leading a mule pack 300 miles into combat; and eight months in Kunming, China.

Discharged in January 1946. Awards include the Good Conduct Medal, China Combat, Purple Heart and Expert Pistol, mounted and dismounted.

Married Irene Martin, April 5, 1947, and has three

children and three grandchildren. He still helps his son with the ranch work in South Central New Mexico, raising limousin cattle and registered quarter horses.

LTC LUCIAN W. BARNES was born June 15, 1926, Haley's Mill, Christian County, KY. Graduated Crofton High School, 1935, and attended the University of Kentucky. Enlisted on May 30, 1933, in the 123rd Cav. Horse Machine Gun Troop, KYNG. Enrolled in CCC, 1935, and entered the University of Kentucky in 1936, receiving his BS degree.

Commissioned 2nd lieutenant on May 20, 1942. Arrived at Camp Kilmer, NJ, and departed on Dec. 12, 1942, NYPE; OGA-241 on SSHF *Alexander*, arriving at Mer-el-Kebir, Algeria on Dec. 26, 1942. He was assigned to the 1st Replacement Depot at Canastel and was then assigned to the 246th QM Depot Supply Company, a veteran of Northern Ireland. They operated in Oran and bone.

Departed with one-half the company from Bizerta, Tunisia on Oct. 27, 1943, via LST for Cagliari, Sardenia. Attached to the 12th Air Force, 42nd Wing furnishing depot personnel to operate various service depots. Departed Allied Garrison of Sardenia on Oct. 25, 1944, via Naples for Bari, Italy, joining parent unit attached to the 15th Air Force flying from Foggia.

Departed Bari on June 8, 1945, for Pisa, Italy, staging for duty in the South Pacific. Departed Leghorn, Italy, July 18, 1945, on *Gen. R.M. Blanchford* with a refueling stop in Panama. He was aboard ship for 49 days during two atomic bomb drops and two days for a refueling stop in Hollandia, New Guinea. Arrived at Langaga Gulf, San Franino on Aug. 30, 1945, and Manila a day later. Disembarked on Sept. 5, 1945, for Batangus, Luzon. A week later he returned for depot operation in the Camp Murphy area. Departed the Philippines on Nov. 10, 1945, aboard the SS *Adm. Sims*, arriving in San Francisco and Camp Stoneman on Nov. 25, 1945.

Departed Camp Stoneman via rail and spent five days on a troop train to Ft. Knox, KY for briefing and separation. Relieved from service on March 21, 1946, with assignment as commanding officer of a parachute maintenance company, 100th Air Borne Div. In 1952 he was assigned to S-2 Section 2085th, and then attended USAR School. Retired on July 10, 1964, with the rank of lieutenant colonel.

Married Lucille and has three lovely children: Mitchell, his partner in the truck parts warehouse, has a BS degree in business; Harry, who served as 1st lieutenant in the Infantry Vietnam, having BA and MA degrees in education and taught in the Dayton, OH school system; and Karen Jo, who has BS, MA and MD degrees, taught at Northern Illinois University at De Kalb and the University of Illinois at Champaign-Urbana prior to attending Medical School. All are alumni of the University of Kentucky.

He thanks God for His watchfulness and guidance in his life at all times and especially during this world conflict. He was allowed to visit many places including Si-di-bel-Abbe; Tunis; Ole' Carthage; Ajaccio, Corsica; Athens, Greece; Florence, Genoa, Milan, Rome, Venice, Italy; with the points in between.

MSG RAY F. BARNES SR. was born Nov. 16, 1922, Lewisville, TX; attended high school; and two years of college, studying real estate and appraising. Enlisted in the US Army on Aug. 19, 1940. He served with Troop E, 5th US Cav., 1st Cav. Div. and participated in the Admiralty, Leyte and Luzon campaigns as a platoon sergeant and acting platoon leader. He was with the 2nd Sqdn., 5th Cav. when the "first team" entered Manila and the Gate of Santo Tomas POW Camp in Manila.

Considers the dash to Manila as being the most important phase of his war experiences with the famous "first team," and considers this maneuver to be one of the most brilliant phases of the war in the Pacific as to planning and execution. It was a thrilling experience to be one of the first troopers to enter the compound of Santo Tomas after the barrier was broken by a tank.

Discharged with the rank of staff sergeant. Awards include the Bronze Star, Purple Heart and numerous campaign ribbons and decorations while a member of the 1st Cavalry.

His stories of being a member of the 5th US Cav. have been told many times over, as he considers the experience of being a horse soldier very unique and one that some citizens of today have a hard time believing.

On Feb. 8, 1947, he joined the USAF and served in the States, Japan and Hawaii. Discharged in 1961 with the rank of senior master sergeant.

Married Vondean Arnold, Jan. 26, 1946. They have one son, Ray F. Barnes Jr. (married to Vicki), a captain in the USAF, C130 pilot, Vietnam era, and is now a captain for Delta Airlines. They also have two grandsons, Stephen C., a geology senior at the University of Colorado, and Brandon T., who is a pre-med sophomore at Vanderbilt University. Barnes was employed by the civil service as a real estate officer and appraiser. He retired on Jan. 3, 1986.

CPT ROBERT VERTREESE BARNES was born Nov. 5, 1921, Plainview, TX; graduated high school in 1940. Joined the US Army on Nov. 18, 1940, and was assigned to Special Weapons Troop, 112th Cav. at Ft. Bliss, TX. Shipped to New Caledonia and returned to Officers Training School at Ft. Riley, KS in July 1943, graduating in August. Graduated Officers Motor School in November 1943. Then was assigned to Troop A, 18th Cav. Recon, Camp White, OR. Transferred to Camp Maxey, TX, May 1944; and was shipped to ETO, August 1944.

Captured during the Battle of the Bulge at Roth, Germany, and was sent to Stalag 13D on Dec. 27, 1944. Transferred to Olflag 13B, Jan. 13, 1945, and was freed by the 4th Armored Div. in March 1945. He was recaptured five days later. He escaped again on April 22, proceeded to Wartenburg, and was given a ride to Freising

by the 86th Div., from there to LeHarve and the States in May 1945.

Assigned to Ft. Riley, KS, from July to December 1945. Discharged Feb. 7, 1946, with the rank of captain. Awards include the EAME w/4 stars, Asiatic Pacific, WWII Victory Medal and Good Conduct Medal.

Returned to Dallas, TX, and served as company commander of the NG unit until 1950. Retired from Gifford-Hill Company in February 1983, as executive vice president.

Married Doris Haffen, June 4, 1944, and has four children: Robert, Marsha, John and Maria; nine grandchildren; and one great-grandchild. Barnes passed away on Aug. 24, 1993.

COL JOHN BARR was born Sept. 12, 1913, and graduated from the University of Indiana College of Law in 1937. In September 1940 he enlisted in the 106th Cav. NG that was called into national service in November and sent to Camp Livingston, LA. After attending the first OCS class of cavalry at Ft. Riley, KS, he was assigned to the 12th Cav. Regt., 1st Cav. Div., Ft. Bliss, TX, with which he served throughout WWII and in command of Service Troop when they landed in Japan on Sept. 2, 1945. With orders to the JAG School, then to Ann Arbor, MI, he was the first member of the division to leave Tokyo on September 14.

Following school, he was assigned to the office of the JAG in Washington, DC. With temporary orders to Bad Nauheim, Germany, he defended four of the accused in the Litchfield trials. Integrated in the regular Army in February 1947, from 1948-52 he was in the JAG office of the Army HQs, Canal Zone, and returned to the States to the JAG office, Ft. Leavenworth, KS, before attending the Command and General Staff School, graduating in 1955.

After assignments at the 5th Army HQ, Chicago, IL, and Ft. Sheridan, IL, he was sent to Korea where he rejoined the 1st Cav. Div. as division staff JA. For 10 years he was assigned to the US Army Judiciary and served as a law officer (judge) in both the States and Europe and as chairman of board of Review No. 4 prior to retirement October 1968.

Citations received include Combat Infantryman Badge, Bronze Star, Distinguished Unit Badge and Legion of Merit. From 1968 to 1978 he taught in a police science program at a vocational technical college in Kenosha, WI.

Married Elinor Newell Coble in the 1st Brigade Chapel, Ft. Bliss, in December 1941; they now live in Lake Bluff, IL. They have three sons, one of whom is deceased.

PVT BENJAMIN BARRETT was born March 2, 1843, Winchester, VA. On July 29, 1863, he mustered in at Camp Dennison, OH, at the age of 20, with the US Army. He was stationed with the 11th Ohio Cav., Volunteers, Ft. Laramie, Dakota Territory, and served with Company G.

Participated in the Battle of Platte River Bridge, Ft Caspar, Dakota Territory, where Lt. Casper Collins, of Company G, was massacred by Indians while trying to rescue a supply train of three wagons and 24 men on July 26, 1865.

Discharged on July 21, 1866, at Ft. Laramie, Dakota Territory. His awards are unknown.

Married Hulda Jean Porter, Aug. 17, 1871, and had seven children and 18 grandchildren. Hulda passed away on Oct. 20, 1918. He was a homestead farmer. He passed away on March 6, 1923, in Smith Center, KS.

1LT CHARLES GUY BARRETT JR. was born Oct. 7, 1916, Smith Center, KS. He completed four years of high school, two years of college and one year at the university. He enlisted in the US Army on Sept. 30, 1941, attending basic training in antiaircraft. He was commissioned 2nd lieutenant, Horse Cav., on Dec. 17, 1942.

Served overseas from June 6, 1944 until November 1945, during the European Theater of Operations. Served with the 28th Cav., CTR 125th Cav. Recon Sqdn.

Memorable experiences were of being the platoon leader of the 3rd Platoon, CTR 125th Cav. Recon Sqdn. Mech.; making the first contact for the 9th Army, with the Russian Army on April 30, 1945, at Apollensdorf, Germany; and night patrol across Rhine River.

Discharged Jan. 6, 1946, with the rank of 1st lieutenant. Awards include the Bronze Star.

Married Ruthelma Daugherty, March 11, 1944, at Ft. Riley, KS. They have seven children, 12 grandchildren and five great-grandchildren. He was employed as a procurement and service officer for the state of California. Retired on Dec. 29, 1979.

LTC JAMES F. BARRETT was born July 27, 1920, Grosse Pointe, MI. Enlisted as a private in the cavalry at Ft. Riley, KS on June 22, 1942. Completed basic training at Ft. Riley's Cavalry Replacement Training Center in the last remaining horse training troop; was retained at CRTC as training NCO; and was later sent to attend the last horse class (29th) at the Cavalry OCS. Was commissioned 2nd lieutenant and assigned to the last Horse Cavalry Division's 9th Cav. Regt. at Ft. Clark, TX, in April 1943. In February 1944 the division was dismounted and shipped to North Africa. They were loaded on trains at Casablanca and assembled near Oran, Algeria. The division was deactivated and became service troops. He requested a combat assignment and was sent to the 45th Div. at Anzio Beachhead.

Stations included Rome-Arno, Southern France, Rhineland, Central Europe and Korea. Became platoon leader with the 45th Cav. Recon during the drive on Rome and the August landing on the coast of Southern France. Was transferred to the 36th Div. Cav. Recon Troop in Southern France and through the war across Alsace, Bavaria and into Austria. In 1947 he served in the US Constabulary opposite Russian troops during the German occupation. Later his squadron became part of a newly organized 14th Armored Cav. Regt. during the Cold War.

In 1950 he returned to the States to the 82nd Abn. Div., 44th Heavy Tk. Bn.; then to Armor Officers' School at Ft. Knox; and cadre training officer at the newly opened Camp Erwin, CA, tank training center. He requested overseas assignment and was sent to the 3rd Div., 64th Tank Battalion along the Imjin River in Korea in March 1952 as company commander. Served a year in Japan with 24th Div., 6th Tank Battalion as operations officer and was then returned to the States to assist in opening a new tank firing center at Ft. Steward, GA. In 1957 he was sent to Ft. Hood, TX to join the 4th Armored Div., 37th Tank Battalion as the division prepared to gyroscope with another division in Germany. He then served three years as operations officer with the 37th and combat command B Headquarters.

Discharged in June 1963 with the rank of lieutenant colonel. Awards include the Silver Star, Bronze Star w/ OLC, Purple Heart, Invasion D-Day Arrowhead and Army Commendation Medal.

Memorable experiences include leading a task force south from Bad Tolz, Germany, along a lakeside road curving around hills at the approach to Tegernsee, a resort town where Himmler and Goering both maintained summer homes near the Bavarian Alps, in May 1945. Rounding a bend, they were met by very heavy machine gun, small arms, and panzerfaust fire. Pinned between lake and hills, they were unable to back up as mortar shells began to zero in on their light vehicles. With his armored car burning, they bailed out. Later, their infantry cleared the hills above them as darkness fell. The next morning, unbeknown to him, his troop commander sent out his section sergeant with a small patrol to reconnoiter the road ahead. He was busy with some task and did not see his sergeant return to their lines with a few prisoners. Later that morning, he was told that as they passed across the road from where he was visible, that one prisoner, a German lieutenant, had pointed toward him and told his sergeant, "I saw that officer yesterday firing his machine gun when we stopped you!" His sergeant replied in the negative when asked, "Did you shoot him?"

Married on May 16, 1965, and has one daughter. He worked as a public high school teacher before retiring on March 1, 1989.

WILLIAM WILLET BARTO was born Oct. 27, 1893, Bay Shore, NY. Enlisted on May 1, 1917, with Troop H, 19th Cav., Ft. Ethan Allen, VT. Cavalry assignments were Troop H, 19th Cav., May 1, 1917, until Sept. 25, 1917; and Troop G, 16th Cav., Dec. 15, 1917, until March 20, 1919.

Discharged on March 20, 1919, Ft. Brown, TX. Awards include the Mexican Border Service and WWI Victory Medal.

Memorable experiences were being a part of the United States and Mexico border service; international bridge at Brownsville, TX; patrolling the Rio Grande; and chasing Mexican bandits.

Married Agnes Borowski and has one son, William Chester.

COL RAYMOND R. BATTREALL was born Sept. 19, 1926, St. Joseph, MO, and graduated from Central High School, Omaha, NE in 1944. Enlisting in the USAAC, he served at Sheppard Field, TX, before attending the US Military Academy at West Point, where he graduated in 1949 with a bachelor's degree and a commission as 2nd lieutenant, cavalry. He received his

master's degree from the University of Pennsylvania in 1956 and graduated from the Army War College in 1971.

Claims to be the last person to put Chief, the last cavalry horse, over a jump during the last Cavalry School Horse Show, Ft. Riley, 1949. He commanded units from platoon through squadron in the 14th, 11th, and 3rd Armored Cav. Regt. in Germany and the CONUS; served as a staff officer with the 1st Cav. Div. in Korea; fought for three and one-half years as senior advisor to the Republic of Vietnam Armor Force; served as secretary of the joint staff of US Southern Comman; and completed 16 1/2 years of overseas service as deputy chief of the military mission to Saudi Arabia. In between, he returned twice to West Point: once, as an English teacher and second as a regimental level tactical officer. His final assignment was as director of armor doctrine at Ft. Knox where he helped develop the combined arms doctrine used in Operation Desert Storm before retiring in 1979 as a colonel with almost 36 years total service.

Married the former Ann Clark Hannigan and between them they have eight grown children by former marriages and 11 grandchildren. Having held the barbarians at bay on the borders of the Empire for 36 years, he now does what he can to keep Nero from fiddling in Phoenix and Washington by being active in the Arizona Republican Party. His decorations include four Legions of Merit, three Bronze Star Medals, Purple Heart, three Meritorious Service Medals, Air Medal, Army Commendation Medal and Combat Infantry Badge. Vietnamese decorations include two Distinguished Service Gallantry Cross w/Silver Star, Honor Medal w/1st Clasp and RVNAF Armor Badge.

PVT HAROLD WAYNE BAUGHEY was born June 22, 1919, Adrian, MI, and attended three years of college. Enlisted at Ft. Hayes, Columbus, OH, in 1938 with the 11th Cav. He was sent to Brooklyn Army Base; then to Panama aboard the USS *Republic Army Transport*; on to Monterey, CA. After the cavalry went to the 126th Infantry then to the USAAC as a flying sergeant. Graduated as a flight officer.

Memorable experience was the last peace time cavalry charge of a whole battalion at Ft. Ord, CA.

Discharged in 1939 with the rank of private. After WWII he enlisted in the USN.

Married and has two children and two grandchildren. Worked as a fireman and deputy sheriff before retiring in 1975.

MGEN WILLIAM A. BECKER was born April 2, 1919, Kaufman County, TX. Received his BA degree from Texas A&M University; attended USA Command and General Staff College; and Army War College.

Enlisted in June 1941 with the field artillery. Was assigned to the Southwest Pacific Theater during WWII, 1943-45; the Occupation of Japan, 1945-46; and Vietnam, 1965-67. Served with the 61st Field Artillery Battalion, 1st Cav. Div., Horse (later dismounted); 2nd Infantry Div. Artillery; 9th Field Artillery Missile Gp.; 1st Field Artillery Brigade; and 1st Cav. Div., Airmobile.

Transferred to the retired list on Jan. 1, 1971, with the rank of major general. Awards include the Distinguished Service Medal w/OLC, Legion of Merit w/3 OLCs, Bronze Star w/OLC, Air Medal w/10 OLCs.

Married Frances Carlyle in 1949, and has four children and six children. Has worked in ranching and real estate brokerage since 1971.

LTC URCEL L. BELL was born Sept. 30, 1912, Traverse City, MI. He attended the University of Michigan for two years and Michigan State University for three years. Enlisted in March 1937 with the cavalry. Was commissioned 2nd lieutenant in March 1938. Stations included New Guinea, Bismarck, Leyte and Luzon. Served with the F and E Troops, 2nd and 7th.

Retired Sept. 30, 1964, with the rank of lieutenant colonel. Awards include the Silver Star and Purple Heart w/cluster.

Memorable experience was the flag raising in Tokyo, Japan.

Married Margaret Thompson and has two children and one grandchild.

COL GEORGE C. BENJAMIN was born Sept. 2, 1916, Pittsfield, MA. Attended Lee schools and graduated from Massachusetts State College, 1939. Entered the US Army under Thomason Act, assigned to the 3rd Horse Cav. Regt., Ft. Ethan Allen and commissioned regular army in 1940. During 30 years of service, 13 years were in command assignments at all levels from platoon leader to regimental and combat command commander. Included were cavalry, armored infantry, reconnaissance, constabulary, tank and armor units, nine months of which was in active combat in Europe. Staff assignments included: department director, Command and General Staff College; chief of staff, Armor Training Center, Ft. Knox; chief of staff, 4th Armored Div. in Germany; deputy for operations and training, 6th Army Headquarters; president, US Army maintenance board, Ft. Knox; deputy chief of staff, I Corps (group) Korea; and acting chief of maintenance, Army material command.

During WWII he served with the 5th Armored Div., commanding the 85th Cav. Recon Sqdn. and fought in five campaigns, including the Battle of the Bulge.

During the Korean conflict, he served in GHQ and on joint staff in the United Nations, Far East command.

Decorations include the Legion of Merit w/OLC, Bronze Star Medal w/2 OLCs, Joint Service Commendation Medal, Purple Heart, French Croix de Guerre w/ Gold Star, Combat Infantryman's Badge and five Campaign Stars.

Selected for assignments of special nature including special aide to the White House; escort to the wife of the president, Eleanor Roosevelt; escort to the assistant Secretary of Defense for Manpower and Personnel; aide to General Mark Clark; aide to LTG Joseph Swing; 6th Army coordinator for Desert Rock atomic explosion training and testing operation; team chief of logistics experts for on site evaluation and recommended redesign of the supply and maintenance organization of the kingdom of Saudi Arabia's Army. Upon retirement from active duty, was appointed GS-15 consultant to commanding general, Army material command, as team chief of logistics group in Taiwan for seven months in support of Vietnam War.

Retired to the country living in Maine with his wife, Ruth Sylvester, where they are involved in civic and social activities, a tree farm and organic gardening. Their children, Peter and Virginia (Miller) live on the west coast.

1LT DEXTER L. BENSON was born Oct. 2, 1922, Buffalo, NY. Graduated New Trier High School; received AD degree from New York A&T Institute; and BS degree from Kansas State University. Joined the service in December 1942 with the US Cavalry. Stations included Ft. Bragg; Cavalry School, Ft. Riley; 124th at Ft. Brown; Ft. Riley; and Cav. Det., Ft. Myer. While at the Cavalry School, he graduated in the last horse class as 2nd lieutenant in January 1944.

Was assigned to the 124th, Ft. Brown, TX. Returned to Ft. Riley to train horse and mule packers bound for CBI theater. Ordered to Ft. Myer, VA in July 1945, where later as 1st lieutenant he assumed command of the station complement cavalry detachment. Included in this command were the horses used for caisson duty, presidential parades, the White House horses and those of the general staff.

Married Jacqueline Staley in 1945 and has two sons and four grandchildren. Worked for Castleberry's Food Company as the northeast regional marketing manager, retiring in December 1990. Jacqueline is a retired deputy superintendent of Fairfax County School.

MSG LEONARD LORAIN BERCE was born March 8, 1920, Berthold, ND. Started his military career in 1938 as a member of the 164th Infantry, NDNG. After a three year enlistment, he transferred to the regular Army. Attended Cavalry School, Ft. Riley, KS, and was assigned to Troop A, 8th Cav. Regt., 1st Cav. Div., Ft. Bliss, TX, June 8, 1942.

Dismounted on April 3, 1943, and cleared Ft. Bliss, June 18, 1943. Staged through Camp Stoneman, CA, departed from the States on July 3, closing at Strathpine, Queensland, Australia, July 26, 1943. Next he went to Oro Bay, New Guinea. Participated in the Admiralty Campaign and the Invasion of the Philippines near Tacloban, Leyte, Oct. 20, 1944, Evacuated in late November 1944, classified totally disabled. Returned to the States in December 1944, after a lengthy hospitalization.

He waived total disability and rejoined the 164th Infantry, Co. E, NDNG, Williston, ND in 1947. Discharged in 1950 as master sergeant.

Worked for Great Northern Railway in Williston until 1953. Married Dorothy Monson and worked for oil service companies until his retirement in 1986. They have four children and seven grandchildren.

COL LOGAN C. BERRY was born May 8, 1901, Starke, FL. He attended Staunton Military Academy and USMA, class of 1924. Joined the service in 1924 serving with the cavalry and armor.

Participated in the WWII battles of France D+17, commander, 6th T.D. Gp.; commander, 15th Cav. Gp.; staff, 3rd Army until May 1945. Stations were Cavalry School, CSGC, 1939-40; Ft. Riley, Cavalry School Institute; Ft. Oglethorpe, 6th Cav.; Ft. Hood, TD School staff; Washington DC; commander, AGF and Army Nar College; Ft. McNair; Ft. Monroe, HQ Combat AGF; Heidelberg, Germany, chief opot, European Campaign; Ft. Knox, staff and Faculty, Armor School; and Mexico, military attache, 1952-54.

Retired in October 1954, with the rank of colonel. Awards include two Bronze Stars and the Mexican Government Medal.

Married Betty B. of Jacksonville, FL, in 1932. They have one daughter, Carroll; two grandchildren; and three great-grandchildren. He worked for the civil defenses, state of Oregon, 1955-63. Retired in October 1963.

PFC GUY F. BESS was born July 20, 1923, Holcomb, WV; and attended high school in Richwood, WV. Joined the US Army in September 1943. Stations were Admiralty Islands and Philippine Islands of Leyte and Luzon. Served with C Troop, 7th Cav., 1st Cav. Div.

Memorable experiences include joining the 1st Cav. Div. in 1943; Admiralty Islands; making both landings at Leyte and Luzon; helping form the 1st Cav. Div. Association in the Admiralty Islands in 1943; and being shot in both legs south of Manila in September 1945.

Discharged in September 1945 with the rank of private first class. Awards include the Good Conduct Medal, Pacific Campaign w/3 Battle Stars, Purple Heart, Bronze Star, Philippine Liberation Ribbon w/2 Battle Stars and Combat Infantry Badge.

Married Vivian Adams in 1949 and has four children and five granddaughters. Served with the International Brotherhood of Boilermakers Local 193, Balto, MD, as secretary treasurer for 17 years. Retired in August 1984.

MAJ PHILIP F. BETETTE was born Oct. 10, 1913, Rochester, NY. Attended McKechney/Lunger School of Commerce, Rochester, NY; University of Rochester Extension; Fordham University, New York; Harvard University, Cambridge; Institute Francois, University of Geneva, Switzerland. His education could be considered that of a dilettante, but somehow, it worked—especially without a student loan. He was commissioned in 1932 in the cavalry. Stations were Arno River, Apennines; Ft. Benning; Camp Polk; Ft. Myer; Presidio; United Kingdom; Camp Ethan Allen; and served with the 2nd Armored, 19th Corps, 3rd Armored Corp.

Memorable experience includes the surrender of

the Germany army in Italy by Gen. Pemsel to Gen. Willis D. Crittenberger.

Discharged in November 1945 with the rank of major. Awards include two Army Commendation Medals w/OLC and he is an Honorary Colonel in the Yellow Legs Regt.

He is a widower and has three children and six grandchildren. Began training at Standard Statistics, now Standard and Poor and later entered the wine and spirits business and 22 years later the tobacco business. Belongs to the Military Order of Foreign Wars. He attended the 1995 annual Bivouac, US Cavalry Association. Retired from the Reserves in 1975.

SP/4 GILLES BLAIS (DOBIE GILLIS) was born Aug. 11, 1940, Noranda, Quebec, Canada. Attended Daytona Beach Jr. College, receiving an AA degree; the University of Florida, BAE degree; BA degree from Florida Technological University; and MS in criminal justice from Rollins College. Joined the US Army Feb. 26, 1962, participated in the Cold War and served with the 3rd Armd. Div., 1st Bde.

Discharged on Feb. 11, 1965, with the rank of SP4 E-4. Awards include the Good Conduct Medal, National Defense Service Medal and Infantry Badge.

Memorable experiences include the conversation and training with the members of 2nd and 13th Cav., 2MTB 32nd Armor, especially the reserve officers (pre WWII Horse Soldiers); and working up on the weapons platoon from the lowest position to fire direction control. Was carried in an E-5 for 16 months and moved up to Brigade to be the 6 TANGO. Trooper #85-0827 (Kraft Jr., MGEN William R. USA Ret) was the brigade commander. According to his notes every day was memorable. From the Fulda area to Graf. was a challenge. The Hawk (winter) in the field was worst. Couldn't tie his boots, but thanked the Lord for tanker's boots and dry socks. His pride and joy was a 1961 military sedan belonging to Gen. Creighton W. Abrams in the days he was the division commander. In 1964 it was passed on to the brigade and it became the top sedan in the division at the end of 1964. The day the brigade commanding officer pinned his EIB on his shirt was such an event that he blanked it out. The biggest surprise of those days was the day he was awarded the proficiency rating 131.10. He was carried in that slot and made the grade, but no M60 tank. So, thank you, you old horse soldiers who came across his path, he was one of those studs (young) that had a short-timer stick longer than the post flag pole.

Married Freda L. Blais and has four step-children and six grandchildren. Spent 21 years in time in grade as a sergeant; tried two years teaching science on the secondary level during the Vietnam War years. He is the local commander of the local veterans council. Being the senior sergeant training comes under his realm. Risk reduction liability is the coin word. The men on the horse lives on; look at the local officer.

BG PHILIP L. BOLTE

BG PHILIP L. BOLTE was born March 24, 1928, Ft. Benning, GA. Graduated from USMA in 1950, commissioned in cavalry; the last class to have that distinction. After brief service in the 3rd Armored Cav. Regt. at Ft. Meade, MD, he joined Co. I, 7th Cav. in Korea, serving from October 1950 until wounded in February 1951. Subsequent troop assignments included platoon leader, 11th Abn. Recon Co.; Ft. Campbell, KY; executive officer and commander, Co. H, 3rd Bn., 14th Armd. Cav. Regt., Germany; company commander, 1st Tng. Regt, Ft. Knox; commander, 1st Sqdn., 1st Cav., Vietnam; and commander, 1st Armor Tng. Bde., Ft. Knox. Other assignments included various staff positions; Armor Board; Staff and Faculty, Army War College; Test and Evaluation Command; assistant project manager, Abrams tank; and program manager, Bradley fighting vehicles. His decorations include the Distinguished Service Medal, Silver Star w/OLC, Purple Heart w/OLC and two awards of the Combat Infantry Badges.

Since retiring in 1980 as a brigadier general, he has worked as a consultant and freelance magazine writer. He married Lorel Christiansen in 1953, a marriage that produced four sons. They have four grandchildren.

EDWARD JAMES BOWLES was born Sept. 12, 1912, Temple, TX; and attended Southern Methodist University receiving a BS degree. Joined the US Army in the Spring of 1930, participating in the lynching riot at Siterman, TX, in 1930; and the oil pro ration in 1931. He served with Troop B, 112th Cav. Discharged in 1933.

Married Pannie Land and has two children, six grandchildren and three great-grandchildren. Served as president of Bowles and Edens and retired in September 1977. Also served as a charter and life member of the US Horse Cavalry Association.

PFC MARVIN W. BOYENGA was born in Jan. 5, 1926, on a farm near Hampton, IA. Went eight years to a county school, then to high school at Hampton, IA. Drafted in the US Army in March 1944, he was sent to Camp Hood, TX, to train as a truck driver. Was transferred to the US Horse Cavalry at Ft. Riley, KS, to train to ride horses and pack mules.

Sent overseas in October 1944, to Burma to join the Mars Task Force at Myithyino, Burma, where he served with the 475th Infantry, 3rd Battalion, Company L. Their job was to re-open the Burma road into China. Was wounded in a battle near the village of Namhpakka on the Burma road. Sent back to the States in April 1945.

Discharged in February 1946. Awards include the Combat Infantry Badge, Bronze Star, Purple Heart, Asiatic Pacific Theater w/2 Bronze Battle Stars, WWII Victory Medal and American Theater Medal.

Married Ruth Thomsen in February 1951 and has four children and seven grandchildren. He owned a new car dealership in Mason City for 22 years. Sold out in January 1977 and retired to trading the stock market. He enjoys tennis, golf, skiing, swimming and bike riding.

CPT LYNDELL BRIDGEWATER was born Aug. 6, 1920, Walkerville, IL; and received his BS degree from CPCU. Was commissioned in the ROTC in June 1942 with the cavalry. Stations include Admiralty and Leyte, PI. Served with Troop A, 8th Cav. Discharged in February 1946 with the rank of captain.

Married Ellanore M. Fackler in August 1945 and has one child. Worked for Allstate Insurance Company as a claims representative. He retired in January 1989.

MAJ JOHN CHERRY BRIGGS was born Nov. 15, 1917, in a log teacherage in Colquitt, GA. Served in ORNG, Machine Gun Company, 11th US Horse Cav., 7th US Horse Cav., 36th Cav. Recon Sqdn., MECH, 124th Cav., Burma, 88th Div., Cav. Recon Troop, 1st Guided Missile Regt. and 495th Missile Battalion. Retired in June 1960 at Ft. Richardson, AK.

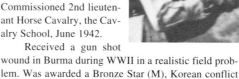

Enlisted in regular Army, 11th Cav. in 1940. Commissioned 2nd lieutenant Horse Cavalry, the Cavalry School, June 1942.

Received a gun shot wound in Burma during WWII in a realistic field problem. Was awarded a Bronze Star (M), Korean conflict when with the 2nd Infantry Div., under Gen. James Fry. Memorable service was under Gen. Earl Heathcote AAARTC, Ft. Bliss, TX.

Served with PIO Alaska Department of Health and Welfare for two years. Homesteaded and hunted in Alaska in the 1960s. Received BA degree at the University of the Americas, Mexico City after retirement.

Briggs and wife, Carol, live in a log home he built in a small 160 acre horse pasture with their horses, at 7,000 feet altitude in western New Mexico on the edge of the Apache National Forest with about 3,000,000 acres of semi wild country to roam. He has two sons from a previous marriage, Garry Owen and T. Allen, and one grandson, Karl Hilario of McMinnville, OR.

LTC THOMAS M. BROSSART was born Dec. 17, 1955, Cincinnati, OH. Attended the University of Cincinnati and received his BA degree; and the University of Missouri, receiving his MPA. Joined the US Army on Dec. 18, 1978, and held stations at Bambery, FRG; Ft. Carson; Ft. Bliss; and Cairo, Egypt. Served with the 2/2 Cav., 1/10 Cav. and 3ACR.

Was commissioned as a distinguished military graduate in armor from the University of Cincinnati in 1978. Attended the cavalry officers basic course and was assigned to the 2nd Sqdn., 2nd Armd. Cav. Regt. in Bamberg, Federal Republic of Germany. Served as a platoon leader in G Tp. for 18 months, as a border camp OIC and as border sector commander. He was then assigned as executive officer of H (Hawk) Co. for eight months. He was then selected to be the squadron S-3 Air. Then due to a shortage of majors in the regiment he was selected to be the S-3 for the 2nd Sqdn.

Attended the infantry advance course, the junior officer maintenance course and the joint fire power command and control course at Hurlbert Field. He was then assigned to the 1st Sqdn., 10th Cav., 4th Inf. Div., at Ft. Carson, CO. He was then selected to command B Tp. Was assigned to the 2nd ROTC Region as an assistant professor of military science (APMS). After 18 months as an APMS he was selected to be the senior APMS and OIC of the ROTC extension center at Northern Kentucky University. He was then nominated by Armor Branch for duty with the UN Truce Supervision Organization assigned to the Middle East.

He was initially assigned as a military observer with duty in Cairo, Egypt, he stood OP tours in the Sinai. He was nominated by the United States and selected by the UN to be the adjutant to the station chief in Cairo. He was then selected to attend the Command and General Staff College at Ft. Leavenworth, KS. Upon graduation from CGSC he was selected for the Army's co-op program and attended the University of Missouri. Upon graduation he was assigned to the 1st Sqdn., 3rd Armd. Cav. Regt. as the squadron S-3. He was the S-3 for NTC rotation 93-12. In November 1993 he was selected to be the regimental S-3. He was by name selected by the 3rd Corp. to be part of the crisis planning team sent to the Far East in June 1994. He returned in August 1994 and was assigned as the executive officer of 2nd Sqdn., 3rd ACR. He completed his tour with the 3rd ACR in May 1995. Presently he is serving as the US exchange officer with The Royal Armored Corp. at the Armored Tactics and Reconnaissance Div., Combines Arms Training Center, Warminster, United Kingdom.

Discharged with rank of lieutenant colonel. He is still on current active duty. Awards include three Meritorious Service Medals and three Army Commendation Medals.

Married Kathleen Susan Newton of Cold Spring, KY. They have two children, Alexander and Jonathon.

LTC CHARLES ASA BROWN was born Oct. 17, 1912, Woodsfield, Monroe County, OH. He has received his BAVM and JD degrees. Joined the horse cavalry in June 1935, and was stationed in the ETO. He served with the 3rd Cav., 1st Cav., 2nd Cav. Regt. and the 2nd Armd Regt, 9th Div. Discharged in January 1946 with the rank of captain. Awards include the American Defense, Bronze Star w/OLC, Purple Heart, WWII Victory Medal, Reserve Medals, Caribbean Defense, Germany Occupation Medal and a medal for readiness on D-Day.

Memorable experience includes the coined phrase, "bastardes of Bastogne."

Brown is happily divorced and has two children and three grandchildren. He is an attorney at law, the only member in the firm.

SGT JOSEPH R. BROWN enlisted at Philadelphia at the age of 15, arriving in 1820 at what now is called Ft. Snelling, territory of Minnesota. Discharged in 1828 with the rank of sergeant.

After the service he became a fur trader was important in the development of the territory and was appointed a major general in the Militia of the new state of Minnesota in 1858.

Several days after the onset of the Dakota conflict in August 1862, he was with a burial detail ambushed at Birch Coulee. A breastwork of 87 horses and 23 soldiers killed in the fight, gave protection until relief came after 48 hours.

Following expulsion of Indians from their Minnesota reservations, he was placed in charge of an unique and successful military experiment. Friendly Dakota who did not participate in the warfare were enrolled as scouts, staffing a line of camps providing mounted surveillance patrols between Indian territory and Minnesota settlements. Brown's son Samuel, followed him as scout commander in 1865. *Submitted by Sibley County Historical Society*

ROBERT W. BROWN was born Dec. 1, 1908, Hncon, Panama Canal Zone, and attended Temple University. Joined the USAR on April 23, 1930, with the 305th Cav. Regt. Was stationed with the 21st Tank Battalion, 10th Armored Div., during the European Theater operation; the 3rd Cav. Horse; 3rd Cav. Armor; and 6th Cav. Constabulary.

Retired July 31, 1960. Awards include the Silver Star, Purple Heart and Bronze Star w/V device.

He is a widower and has two children and five grandchildren.

SAMUEL J. BROWN, the son of Joseph R. and Susan Brown, was born in 1845 at Cica Hollow, near Sisseton, SD, at his father's trading post. He was fluent in the Sisseton-Wahpeton Dakota language learned from his mother and her family. He was held captive with relatives during the early weeks of the Sioux uprising which began Aug. 18, 1862, in Minnesota.

Was chosen by his father and uncle Gabriel Renville to serve the US Army as one of the "friendly" Dakota scouts protecting the Minnesota border against the return of the hostile Indians. He became inspector of scouts in 1865 when his father resigned his commission.

In 1866, during his Army service, he rode 150 miles through a blizzard to warn scout outposts of a threatened Indian uprising. His heroic effort left him crippled for life. He passed away in 1925. His pension papers indicate he received $72 per month.

Submitted by Sibley County Historical Society

LTC WASHINGTON H. BROWN was born March 19, 1907, Wyandotte County, KS. He attended Kansas City School of Law and Cavalry School. Joined the US Army and was ordered to active duty in May 1941. He served with the 2nd Cav.

Resigned from the regular Army and then went back to the Reserves, where he retired in 1967.

He is a widower and has two children and six grandchildren. Worked as an attorney at law in a private practice. He retired in April 1967.

SSG CARL F. BRUGMANN was born Jan. 16, 1918, Lexington, KY; and attended high school. Joined the service on Jan. 2, 1936, and served with the 12th Cav. Weapons Troop. During his first hitch from 1936-39, much of the time was spent in training, and there wasn't any of the patrolling along the border that would come

later for some of the horse soldiers stationed at posts along the Rio Grande.

Was recalled on Feb. 10, 1941, and was assigned to a machine gun troop. After mopping up south of Manila, they were preparing to go into Tokyo when the atomic bomb was dropped on Japan. When he was given a choice to return to the 12th Cav. in 1941, they had moved from Brownsville to El Paso. It was there they trained for overseas after giving up their horses.

In the summer of 1942, he was at Ft. Bliss when his unit, the 12th Cav. Regt., 1st Cav. Div., turned in its horses and saddles. The 12th Regt. became foot soldiers after that. Left Ft. Bliss in 1943 and went to Brisbane, Australia, for amphibious and jungle training, then to New Guinea, and from there to Admiralty Islands where they first saw combat against the Japanese. After retaking the islands, they re-equipped and moved to recapture the Philippines. They went in at Lady Island and moved to Luzon and Manila. They landed at the same place where the Japanese had landed; and three days later they were in Manila, 135 miles; most of that was by foot. They were the first outfit to hit Manila, and that is when business picked up. They came in on the south and the 77th Infantry came in on the other end; they met at the Walled City.

Discharged on Sept. 12, 1945, with the rank of staff sergeant.

Married Bernice Garrett and has one son, Lester. Worked for Victoria Machine Works as a foreman. He retired in 1983. He is an active charter life member and Gulf Coast representative for the US Horse Cavalry Association, and his wife, Bernice is state delegate.

SGT MICHAEL BUDIMIROVICH was born July 2, 1918, Lackawanna, NY. Attended Canisius College, 1946-47, receiving a BS degree; and 1947-48, MA degree in secondary education. Joined the US Army on Oct. 9, 1942, with the cavalry. Stations were Normandy, Brittany, Rhineland and Central Europe. Served with the 15th Cav. Gp., 17th Cav. Sqdn. and the 644th TD Battalion Recon. He held the rank of RCN-NCO-SGT with the first, third and ninth armies.

Discharged on Dec. 13, 1945, with the rank of sergeant. Awards include four Battle Stars, Purple Heart w/cluster, American Campaign, American Defense, Bronze Star, WWII Victory Medal, Army of Occupation, Good Conduct and Gold Star Medal. He was named Distinguished member of the 15th Cav. Regt. by order of the Secretary of the Army, Thomas Foley, major general, US Army, chief of armor.

Memorable experiences were seeing his sister, a nurse of the 96th Evac Hospital, prior to June 6, D-Day; and the 15th Cav. Groups (9th Army) making contact with the 1st Army at Lippstadt, which was called the greatest encirclement in military history.

Married Florence and worked as a history teacher and then a supervisor at Bethlehem Steel. Retired in October 1977. At the 50th anniversary, the council appointed him a member of the 50th anniversary council for the Battle of Normandy. He is a member of the VFW, Col. Weber Post 898; life member of DAV, Chapter 135; American Legion. M. Glab Post; US Cavalry Association; Department of the Army; US Army Military History, Carlisle, PA.

PLT/SGT WILLIAM E. BULL was born Feb. 21, 1920, Seattle, WA. Received his BA in business administration, USMC basic course and primary course, MCS; and numerous computer and systems courses.

Joined the USMC June 19, 1939, until Aug. 10, 1945. Was assigned to the Recruit Depot, San Diego, Sea School, until Sept. 9, 1939; transferred to Marine Det., USS *Pennsylvania*, fleet flagship, Sept. 9, 1939, to Sept.

19, 1941. Went to Marine Corps Schools, Quantico, VA as an instructor, Sept. 19, 1941; to the 5th Mar. Div., Camp Pendleton, CA, Jan. 5, 1944; 28th Mar. Regt., H Co., 3rd Bn. He was transported aboard the USAT Etolin to Hilo; USS *Lubbock* to Saipan, Marianas Islands; to landing in Iwo Jima on Feb. 19, 1945. Evacuated via

the USS *Hocking* to Fleet Hospital #111, Guam; USNH #10, Oahu; SS *Lurline* to San Francisco, CA, April 15, 1945; and Newport, RI, Aug. 10, 1945. Retired with rank of major general.

Enlisted in the US Army and served with HQ CO, 159th Inf., CANG, Army Reserve, Oakland, CA, Feb. 10, 1936, to Aug. 19, 1936; Machine Gun Tp., 11th Cav., Monterey, CA, Aug. 20, 1936, to May 10, 1937; and HQ Btry., 6th Coast Arty., Ft. Winfield Scott, San Francisco, CA, May 10, 1937, to Oct. 18, 1938. Received honorable purchase discharge.

Memorable experiences include being with the Machine Gun Tp., 11th Cav, Monterey; the theft of his saddles; the mess sergeant selling their eggs and butter to the Del Monte Hotel; and passing out while galloping in the rain.

Married the first time to Regina Jane Murphy and the second time to Geraldine I. Campbell. He has two children, seven grandchildren and four great-grandchildren. Worked for the IRS, Federal Government, USN, USAF, aerospace and private practice. Retired May 30, 1970.

MSG CHARLES WESLEY BURNEY was born Aug. 31, 1919, Montgomery County, Clarksville, TN. Attended two years college, 1940, and two years, 1947, on the GI Bill, and received his BS degree. Enlisted Sept. 19, 1937, in F Tp., 109th Cav. Regt., TNANG. Participated in battle campaigns at Hollandia and Biak, New Guinea; Leyte and Luzon, Philippine Islands. Stations were in Camp Forrest, TN; Arkansas and Louisiana maneuvers; and Camp Roberts, CA.

Summer encampments were Camp Peay, TN; Ft. Oglethorpe, GA; maneuvers in Mississippi; Camp Polk, LA; Ft. Campbell, KY; Ft. Knox, KY for four months; Ft. McClellan, AL; Ft. Jackson, SC; Ft. Steward, GA; and Camp Drum, NY. Served with F and K Troops, 109th Cav. Regt.; 181st FA Regt.; 947th FA BN; attached to the 41st Inf. Div., 1st Cav. Div., 30th Armd. Div.

Discharged from the US Army on June 30, 1965; and TNNG on Aug. 31, 1979. Awards include the Bronze Star for heroism near Manila, Philippine Islands.

Memorable experiences are of traveling in a cattle car from home station in Tennessee to Camp Polk, LA, with 24 horses and making the return trip; flying column to Manila, attached to the 1st Cav. Div.; and front row seat to dog fight on Biak Island.

Married Katherine Trice on July 18, 1947, and has three sons: Charles Dennes, Robert Wesley and Philip Lynn; and seven grandchildren. Worked for eight years as an administrative assistant for the TNANG unit; 28 years for the Clarksville Housing Authority, with 10 years as urban renewal projects manager and 18 years as project manager for public housing units. Retired on

March 31, 1984, from the Clarksville Housing Authority.

MAJ EUGENE A. BUSH was born July 17, 1920, Newark, NJ. Attended the University of Arizona and completed his degree. Joined the service on Sept. 1, 1941, with the armor and was stationed in France and Germany. He served with the 4th Armored Div., 102nd Cav.

Discharged in April 1945 with the rank of major. Awards include the Bronze Star, Silver Star and three Purple Hearts.

Married and has one son. Worked as a small businessman until retirement in 1982.

COL WILLIAM CLOYCE BYRNS was born Nov. 25, 1919, North Little Rock, AR. Attended the University of California, Institute of Radio Broadcasting and Command and General Staff School. Enlisted in the US Army in September 1940. Stations were North Africa, Italy, Korea, Vietnam, Philippines, Japan and Germany. Served with the 124th Cav., 9th Cav., 91st Div., 2nd Armored, V Corps, 1st, 6th and 8th Armies.

Retired on April 1, 1969, with the rank of colonel. Awards include the Distinguished Service Cross, Silver Star, Legion of Merit, Bronze Stars, Joint Services Commendation Medal, Army Commendation Medal, Combat Infantry Badge and Purple Hearts.

Memorable experiences include being promoted to corporal which was recommended by Gen. George Patton; being a pioneer in the Armed Forces Radio and television service; tech advisor to the motion picture and television industry; combat, The Green Berets, Patton.

Married Ellen Marie Wilson and has two children, Deborah Kay and William Claude; three grandchildren: Chin and Marissa Byrns and Michael Driskill. Worked as a manager of a radio station, and as a consultant to the motion picture and television industry. He retired in November 1978.

1ST LT KENNETH P. CALLICOTT was born Oct. 7, 1923, Harrison, AR. He attended two years at Harding College. Joined the 1st Cav., 12th Regt., in October 1945 and was stationed at Camp McGill and Japan. Served with Regimental HQ, 12th Cav. Regt.

Discharged on Oct. 31, 1946, with the rank of 1st lieutenant. Awards include the Army Occupation Medal (Japan), Asiatic-Pacific Service Medal, American Campaign Medal and WWII Victory Medal.

Memorable experiences included being platoon leader, I&R Plt., 12th Cav.; and serving one year in the Army of Occupation.

Married Mary Carolyn Landree and has three chil-

dren and six grandchildren. Worked as a purchasing manager for FMC Corp. and then as a real estate broker. He retired on Jan. 1, 1985.

PFC GEORGE LIONEL CARTER was born Jan. 28, 1918, in Colfax, IL, and graduated from high school there. Drafted June 25, 1941, attended basic training at Ft. Riley, KS; assigned to the 112th Cav. Regt. at Ft. Clark, TX; served overseas mounted on New Caledonia; and dismounted with landings on Woodlark Island and Arawe, New Britain, in the Driniumor River, New Guinea Campaign. Returned to the States and was assigned to the 129th Horse Cav. Tng. Sqdn., then the Animal Pool. Discharged June 22, 1945.

Awards include the Asiatic-Pacific w/three Battle Stars and a Bronze Arrowhead, WWII Victory, American Defense Service Medal, American Campaign Medal, Good Conduct Medal, Texas Service and the Combat Infantry Badge.

He was employed at the North Shore National Bank of Chicago for 37 years, where he met his wife, Irma Matthes, and retired as auditor and security director on Jan. 28, 1983.

COL DUANE S. CASON was born April 5, 1920, Dallas, TX. Attended the University of Maryland and received his BSM degree. Joined the cavalry/armor on July 29, 1938. Stations included Presidio of Monterey, CA, 1938-41; California-Mexican Border, Camp Lockett, 1941; Ft. MacArthur, CA, three months, 1941; Ft. Riley, KS, 1941-42; Ft. Jackson, SC, 1942; Eastern Defense Command, 1943-44; China Theater, 1944-46; Naval War College, Newport, RI, 1946-47; Armored School, advanced course, Ft. Knox, KY, 1947-48; Heidelberg, Germany, 1948-1952; Camp Irwin, CA, 1952-53; Ft. Leavenworth, KS, student, CGSC, 1953-54, and faculty, 1954-57; Air War College, Maxwell AFB, AL, 1957-58; The Pentagon, 1958-60; Paris, France, 1960-63; 1st Armored Div., Ft. Hood, TX, 1963-64; State Department, Washington, DC, 1964-66; Vietnam, 1966-67; The Pentagon, 1967-69.

Served with the 11th Horse Cav., Cavalry Replacement Training Center (horsemanship department); The Cavalry School; 2nd Cav. MECH; 27th Cav. Recon Sqdn.; 36th Cav. Recon Sqdn; HQS, US Army Europe; HQS, US European Command; Supreme HQ Allied Powers Europe (Live Oak); 1st Armored Div.; Arms Control and Disarmament Agency (Joint); and HQS, US Army Vietnam.

Retired on Aug. 31, 1969, with the rank of colonel. Awards include the Legion of Merit w/OLC, Bronze Star w/Valor and OLC, Joint Service Commendation Medal w/OLC, Army Commendation Medal w/2 OLCs, Republic of China Special Breast Order of Clouds and

Banners; Hwa-Tsou Medal of Honor, Republic of Vietnam, Gallantry Medal in 1965, and Combat Infantry Badge.

Married and has two children and one grandson. Employed as a management consultant for Sea Pines Plantation Company until retirement.

SGT MAJ BEN CASTANEDA was born Oct. 23, 1917; attended high school in Mercedes, TX, public schools. Joined the US Army on Jan. 9, 1936. Participated in four campaigns with the 1st Cav. Div., WWII, Admiralty Islands and Philippine Islands; and five campaigns with the 1st Cav. Div., Korea.

Retired on Aug. 1, 1964, with the rank of sergeant major, E-9. Awards include the Bronze Star w/2nd Award, Commendation Medal w/2nd Award, Good Conduct Medal w/6 Loops, American Defense Medal, American Campaign Medal, Asiatic-Pacific Campaign Medal w/4 stars and one Arrowhead, WWII Victory Medal, Occupation Medal w/Japan Bar, National Defense Medal, Korean Service Medal w/5 stars, Philippines Presidential Citation Ribbon, South Korean Presidential Citation Ribbon and Combat Infantryman's Badge w/star and 2nd Award.

Memorable experience was being proud to have served with the 1st Cav. Div. under the command of some of the best leaders of that era.

Married Avelina Galvan-Castaneda, Jan. 5, 1941, and has five children, 10 grandchildren and six great-grandchildren. Worked for the New Mexico State Highway Department, 1964-79, as a supply supervisor in the general office laboratory. Retired on Oct. 23, 1979.

SGT RAYFORD EARL CHANCE was born Aug. 22, 1924, Sevierville, TN; and attended 12 years of high school. Joined the US Army on Jan. 30, 1943, and participated in campaigns at Admiralty Islands, Leyte Samar and Luzon; and served with G Troop, 12th, Cav.

Saw combat in Korea, 1950-51; and Vietnam, 1965-66 in the US Cavalry.

Retired on Jan. 6, 1946, after 30 years of service, with the rank of command sergeant major. Awards include the Combat Infantry Badge, two Bronze Stars, 10 other medals and 15 service ribbons..

Memorable experiences include being one of the first troopers in the city of Manila, Philippine Islands and Tokyo, Japan.

Married Mary E. Halstead, and has two sons, James and Robert; and one grandson, Jake. Worked for the State of Colorado as a public safety sergeant. He retired on Aug. 1, 1986.

CHARLES E. CHILDS was born Aug. 8, 1919,

Stockman, TX. Enrolled at the University of Arizona in 1938. Cavalry ROTC was required of all students for the first two years. Approximately 40 students were accepted for advanced ROTC, which began in the fall of 1941. Joined the US Army on April 1, 1943; and graduated in June 1943 with a BS degree in agriculture, and orders to Ft. Riley, KS, to attend Cavalry OCS. OCS was at that time mechanized training. Upon completion he was commissioned as 2nd lieutenant in the cavalry with orders to officers communication class at Ft. Riley. He spent the next year as a platoon leader in the Horse Cavalry Replacement Training Center before overseas orders arrived.

During the 21 day cruise to the Philippine Islands, the war in Europe ended; and he was assigned to the 5th Replacement Depot in Manila. In July 1946 he returned to the States and signed with the active USAR. The next four years were in Pulman, WA attending the College of Veterinary Medicine. In July 1951 he again received orders to the 1st Armd. Div., Ft. Hood, TX. He served as battalion supply officer until reporting for overseas duty in Korea. Upon arriving in Korea he was assigned to the 40th Inf. Div., 140th Tank Bn., assigned as S-2 intelligence officer, where he served until reassigned to the UN Civil Assistance Command in Pusan, Korea as a veterinarian. He was released from active duty in October 1952.

Remained in the active Reserves, completing his last assignment to the Command and General Staff College (Reserve), Ft. Levenworth, KS, in the summer of 1967. He then took a mandatory retirement and completed his Army duty at that time. Retired in 1967 with the rank of lieutenant colonel.

Married Carol J. Childs and has three children and seven grandchildren. Was self-employed as a veterinarian until retirement in 1984.

CLARK-GIDDENS FAMILY totals 3 ancestors who gave their lives in the Civil War on the Union side. The Clark brothers, Reuben, Ransome and Levi, enlisted in the Union Army in Rolla, MO. Reuben served ten months and 9 days. He enlisted Aug. 20, 1864 and was discharged June 29, 1865. Levi enlisted at the same time but was killed in a shoot-out and charged as deserting in Nov. 1864. Ransome became ill with pneumonia and died Jan. 5, 1865.

Samuel F. Giddens enlisted in the Union Army as a wagon boss in Rolla, MO. He died of pneumonia on Dec. 20, 1862. His sons, John and Brad, evaded capture by the Confederate Army, traveling at night en route to Rolla and ultimately enlisting in the 16th US Cavalry Volunteers. Both served until peace was made and were honorably discharged.

COL PHILIP C. CLAYTON was born on Dec. 19, 1891, in Annapolis, MD. He attended the Annapolis High School and St. John's College of Annapolis, MD.

In 1916, while in South Carolina, he enlisted in the Machine Gun Co. of the 1st South Carolina Inf. and appointed a sergeant. Upon receiving his commission as 2nd lieutenant of cavalry, Clayton joined the 23rd Cav. at Ft. Oglethorpe, GA. He served in France, the Transcausas and in Germany before returning to the States and joining the 1st Cav. at Douglas, AZ.

He attended the Cavalry School at Ft. Riley, KS and reported to the 6th Cav. at Ft. Oglethorpe, GA, where he served as troop commander, regiment S3 and post judge advocate. From Oklahoma he went to the 12th Cav. serving with that regiment at Brownsville, TX; served with the 26th Cav. at Ft. Stotsonburg, Philippines; and served with the 4th Cav. as regimental executive at Ft. Meade, SD, and later commanded the 605th Tk. Dest. Bn. at Ft. Custer, MI, and Camp Hood, TX.

Landing in Normandy in July 1944, he served for a short time with the 6th Armd. Div. and then was assigned to HQs 3rd Army. He served as post executive officer for over two years and later as chief of staff of Ft. Jackson and the 8th Inf. Div. and retired there on Dec. 31, 1951.

His service ribbons consist of the following: Mexican Border, WWI Victory Medal, Occupation of Germany Medal, American Defense Medal, American Theater Award, European Theater w/6 Campaign Stars, WWII Victory Medal and a second Occupation of Germany Ribbon.

His decorations include the Legion of Merit, Bronze Star w/OLC, Army Commendation Medal, French Croix de Guerre w/Gold Star, Luxembourg Croix de Guerre and the Luxembourg Couronne de Chone.

Col. Clayton passed away on Dec. 30, 1962. He was buried with full military honors in Arlington on Jan. 3, 1963.

Colonel and Mrs. Clayton had three children; Carol, the wife of Col. Francis S. Conaty, US Army retired; Katharine, the wife of Maj. Gen. W.D. Crittenberger, Jr., US Army retired; and Philip Coleman, Jr., who served as a Marine officer before becoming a professional in the Internal Revenue Service.

Mrs. Clayton passed away on July 17, 1982, and is buried with her husband in Arlington National Cemetery.

CAPT LOREN F. COLE was born April 30, 1909, Washington, DC. Received his BS degree from USMA in 1931. Joined the cavalry in 1931 and was stationed at Ft. Myer, VA, 1931-35, auxiliary duty with Civilian Conservation Corp, Military Aide at the White House. Graduated from the US Cavalry School, Ft. Riley, KS, 1936; served with the 13th Cav. Mech., Ft. Knox, KY, 1937-38; Ft. Myer, VA, 1938-40, auxiliary duty, White House Military Aide, part-time supervisor of Mrs. Franklin Roosevelt's horses and riding companion to her; and Recon Bn., 4th Div. Motorized, Ft. Benning, GA.

Retired in 1942 for physical disability, with the rank of captain.

Memorable experiences include the fall of 1933 when the Regt. HQ and 2nd Sqdn., 3rd Cav. were ordered to Yorktown, VA, to participate in the sesquicentennial re-enactment of Lord Cornwallis's surrender to Gen. Washington, commander in chief of the revolutionary Army. This was an exciting event since some of them wore British uniforms and others wore American uniforms in portraying the events. They freshened their historical knowledge and met a number of interesting people connected with the project. An amusing aspect of the train trip down was that the officers sat-up straight in coach cars and complained of being uncomfortable. Finally one decided to make an inspection of the train and found that the enlisted men had taken the backs off

the seats and filled in the spaces between the seats to make two long bunks and were sleeping soundly. The officers copied this maneuver and got several hours sleep before arriving.

Married Anne Marshall Magruder in 1946 and has three children and three grandchildren. Worked as an attorney, 1949-89; and as a real estate broker, 1959-89. He retired in 1989.

ERNEST H. COLLIER was born April 1, 1922, in Ft. Stotsenberg, Philippine Islands. Joined the US Army, 9th Cav. Regt. in 1942. Trained at Ft. Riley, KS, and Ft. Clark, TX, for mounted combat duty. Reassigned to the 5th Army, serving in Africa and Europe assigned to the 92nd Div. and the Italian campaign. After WWII he was reassigned to occupational duty in Japan and served with the US Army Engineers. At the outbreak of the Korean War, reassigned to the 24th Inf. Regt., 25th Div., 8th Army.

Severely wounded during the battle of Puson and sent to Letterman Army Hospital in San Francisco for treatment. While there, awarded the Purple Heart Medal by Gen. Mark Clark. Honorably discharged from the Army in 1952.

Decorations include American Defense Service Medal, EAME Service Medal, Combat Infantry Badge, Korean Victory Medal, and Good Conduct Medal.

Employed with the Federal Civil Service. Retired after 20 years at North Island Naval Air Station. Life member of MOPH #49; DAV #2; a member of the American Legion, all of San Diego, CA; member of VFW; US Horse Cavalry Assn.; 9th and 10th Cavalry Association; 1402nd Army Engineers; and the 24th Inf. Assn.

Married to Juanita M. Collier, past national president of the ladies auxiliary to the MOPH. They have four children.

JOHN T. COLLIER, a Tennessee native, received cavalry ROTC training at the University of Illinois. During five reserve training tours he was a cavalry CMTC platoon leader. In the 2nd Cavalry (1940-42) he served as a troop officer and regimental S2, continuing such assignments after conversion to Armor (1942). As S3 and later executive officer, 776th Amphibious Tank Bn., he led 7th Div. assault units in seizing Leyte and Okinawa beachheads. He was executive officer of the task force that "swam" amphibious tanks 125 miles through enemy held areas to attack the enemy rear. In the Camotes Islands (1944) he assumed temporary command when the acting commander was killed. He was executive officer throughout the Okinawa campaign and finally commander during mop-up and demobilization.

During postwar tours he was assistant chief, Armd.

Cav. Bn., Army Field Forces; and associate editor, *Army Digest*. Before retiring as a Reserve colonel, he made the armor evaluation, operation big lift (Germany, 1963) and the environmental evaluation, Ft. Campbell reservation, 1965. He is a graduate of the Cavalry, Armor, Command and General Staff, Strategic Intelligence and Electronic Warfare Schools. Awards include the Silver Star, Bronze Star Medal and commendation from Gen. Jacob L. Devers, Chief, Army Field Forces. Also, his unit received a Presidential Unit Citation.

COL JAMES H. COMINGS was born Sept. 18, 1909, Eau Claire, WI. Attended the University of Maryland, receiving a BS degree. Joined the US Army on March 18, 1931, and served in Europe from 1944-45, with the 95th Inf. Div.

Retired on Jan. 31, 1957, with the rank of colonel. Received the Bronze Star.

Married Doris M. and has four children and five grandchildren. Served AARP as chapter president and district director. He retired on Jan. 31, 1957.

MICHAEL J. CONDES was born June 25, 1919, Sunbury, PA. Received his BS degree from Rolling College; graduate studies, FIT, Foreign Service Institute, Department of the State, Spanish and Latin American studies. Joined the services through the CMTC in 1937, Ft. Meyers, in the cavalry. Stations were the 9th AF, WWII, England, France, Germany and Berlin. Participated in the air lift as logistics advisor to the Greek air force, 1950-53; logistics advisor to the Salvadorian air force, 1955-58; F-104 weapons manager, Tyndal AFB, ADC; logistics advisor to Colombian AF, Bogota, Columbia, 1961-64.

Retired on Aug. 1, 1964. Worked as a logistics engineer with Boeing on the Apollo Saturn program and 14 years as a high school teacher, 1969-83.

Married Ethel M. Condes of St. Petersburg, FL, and has one daughter. He is currently involved in equine activities and a freelance writer for equine magazines.

1SG HAROLD L. COX was born Sept. 23, 1918, Hazelton, IA. Attended high school through the 10th grade and Louisville, KY Radio School, and the Kentucky Radio School, Louisville, 1947. Enlisted in the US Army, Troop E, 14th Cav., Ft. Riley, KS, private first class, July 17, 1937. Attended Saddlery School and qualified as marksman. Participated at Ryukyus Islands; Leyte; Philippine Islands; Hawaii; Mandated Islands; Guam; and Ie Shima, Okinawa; serving with Co. C., 706th Bn. Was honorably discharged by reason of expiration of service on July 26, 1940.

Re-enlisted at Ft. Riley on July 27, 1940, as private for Combat Car Sqdn. and transferred to Ft. Knox, KY. Received training in chemical warfare agents and fire fighting. Was tank commander and driver, artillery mechanic and maintenance instructor of basic training and small arms. Received promotions from private through 1st sergeant. Was sent to Pine Camp, NY for destination

S.W. Pacific. Departed March 28, 1944, to serve as driver and tank commander in Co. C., 706th Bn.

Received honorable discharge on Nov. 16, 1945, Camp Atterbury, IN, Wakeman Convalescent Hospital, with the rank of 1st sergeant. Awards include the Bronze Star Medal, Purple Heart, American Defense Medal, Philippine Liberation Ribbon w/star, Good Conduct Ribbon and Asiatic-Pacific Ribbon w/3 stars.

Memorable experiences include being wounded n the left arm on Okinawa, May 17, 1945; and returning to the States Aug. 1, 1945.

Married Lillian E. Watkins, Oct. 1, 1959. Worked as a ratio operator and technician for WLKY in 1947 and WHAS in 1950. Retired from WHAS radio and television in Louisville, KY, on Oct. 1, 1978. He passed away on Sept. 17, 1988.

Submitted by Lillian E. Cox

MAJ GEORGE C. CRITCHLOW was born May 2, 1910, Butler, PA; and attended four years of college. Joined the cavalry in January 1932, as a 2nd lieutenant, 323rd Cav. Res., CA. Stations were Korea Tank Bn., 1950-51; supply officer, 27th Inf.; combat liaison officer; and commanding general, 25th Div.

Served with CMTC Cavalry, 1927-29, and 1931, with the 11th Cav., Presidio of Monterey; CANG, staff sergeant, 1930-31; 323rd Cav. Reserve, southern California area, 2nd lieutenant, January 1932; 63rd Coast Arty. Band, sergeant (musician), 1935-38; CCC, 2nd lieutenant, 1939; 2nd Cav. Regt, 2nd lieutenant, Ft. Riley, 1940-41; Cavalry School, advanced officer course (horse), 1941; Cavalry School Staff and Faculty, detachment adjutant and equitation, 1st lieutenant, 1942-43; 4th Cav. Bde., Commandant Special Training School, captain, 1943; 28th Cav. Svc. Tp., commanding officer, captain, 1943-44, Camp Lockett, CA; 6467th QM Truck Co., commanding officer, captain, 1944, Italy; 6742nd QM Remount Depot (horse) S-3, captain, 1944-45, northern Italy; 579th Air Corps Band, March Air Force Base, 1946-48, staff sergeant musician; 22nd Inf. Div., Ft. Ord, battalion adjutant, captain, 1948-50; 27th Inf. Regt., 25th Div., Korea, 1950, Tank Bn., supply officer, captain, 1950; 25th Inf. Div., combat liaison officer for commanding general forward HQ, 1950-51, Korea; 13th Tank Bn., Ft. Hood, adjutant, major, 1952-53; HQ Area Command, Germany, judge advocate sec., legal officer, major, 1953-56; and 2nd Armd. Cav. Regt., 3rd Bn., S-3, Ft. George Meade, major, 1957.

Retired June 30, 1957, with the rank of major.

Memorable experiences include September to November 1945. He attended a three month course at the University of Florence, Italy. This was given especially for American military personnel, now that the war was over. The professors were world renown, English speak-

ing in any college subject the American personnel wished to take. Also, other officers seeing him in boots and breaches said they wanted to ride. He learned from an Italian co-ed, who three years later became his wife, that the Flormtine Cit Park had empt stables and requisitioned them. He found 16 of them and then called LTC K.F. Lafayette, Cavalry, his commanding officer of the 10th Mountain Div. Remount Depot, and asked for 16 high trained German horses (captured in the Po Valley) to occupy the 16 empty stables. Three days later they arrived complete with bridles, English saddles and Italian grooms, also all the hay and grain necessary. At 3:00 p.m. every day and on weekends for a number of hours, he and 15 student officers would board a streetcar to the city park for a one and one-half hour equitation class. The horses would be all saddled and really ready to go. At the end of three months, they had some very fine horsemen; and he had the most wonderful future wife in the world.

Married Nicoletta Tesi of Florence, Italy, 1948, whom he met at the University of Florence in 1945. They have three children and two grandchildren. Worked as a grocer, orange grower, symphonic musician and administrative officer, State of California, 1958-72. Retired in August 1972 from the State of California.

WILLIS DALE CRITTENBERGER was born Dec. 2, 1890, in Anderson, IN, the son of Dale Jackson and Effie Alice (Daniels) Crittenberger. After completing his early education at Anderson High School in 1907 and attending the Braden Preparatory School, Highland Falls, on the Hudson, NY, for a year, he graduated in 1913 at the US Military Academy. Commissioned a 2nd lieutenant of cavalry in the US Army in 1913, he was promoted to lieutenant general in 1945, the rank he held when he retired in 1952. His first assignment after graduating at the Military Academy was with the 3rd Cav. in Texas. In 1916 he became aide-de-camp to Gen. James Parker, who was then commanding all cavalry units along the Mexican border.

Returning to Ft. Knox in 1940, he became chief of staff of the newly organized 1st Armd. Div. In 1941-42 he commanded the 2nd Armd. Bde., 2nd Armd. Div., and later in the latter year he was commanding general for several months of the division at Ft. Benning, GA, and for one month of the II Armd. Corps.

During its sweep through Italy the IV US Army Corps liberated over 600 cities and towns and captured the remnants of some 23 German divisions. After the war ended, he served as commanding general of the Caribbean Defense Command and the Panama Canal Department from 1945-47 and in the following year was commander in chief of all US forces in that command area, including Army, Navy and Air Force units. In 1948 he returned to this country and was assignment to the office of the joint chiefs of staff, Washington, DC, as US Army member of the military staff committee of the United Nations (UN), serving simultaneously as chairman of the US Army delegation to the Inter-American Defense Board. A few months later he took over the chairmanship of the US delegation to the United Nations Military Staff Committee, with headquarters in New York City. He was next detailed as this country's deputy representative on the military committee of the North Atlantic Treaty Organization (NATO) and was named acting chairman of the committee's Standing Group, with permanent headquarters in Washington, DC. In 1950, retaining his UN duties, he became commanding general of the First Army on Governors Island in New York City, in which post he served until his retirement from active service at the end of 1952.

Gen. Crittenberger has served as president of the US Assn. of Cav. and Armd. and is a director of the Assn. of Graduates of the US Military Academy. A horseman, he often rode in exhibitions during the early years of his army career. He was married in San Antonio, TX, June 23, 1918, to Josephine Frost, daughter of Mr. and Mrs. Jesiah Townsend Woodhull of San Antonio, TX a banking family; and had three sons: Willis Dale, a major general, US Army retired; a second son, Townsend Woodhull, was killed in action in a tank in the Remagen Bridgehead area, Germany, in March 1945; and a third son, Col. Dale Jackson Crittenberger, was killed in action in a helicopter in Vietnam in September 1969.

MGEN WILLIS D. CRITTENBERGER JR.

was born on Jan. 10, 1919, Baltimore, MD. He was commissioned a 2nd lieutenant of artillery on May 29, 1942, from USMA, West Point, NY. He attended the battery officers course at the Field Artillery School, the Command and General Staff College, the Armed Froces Staff College, the National War College and the Advanced Management Program at Harvard.

Was appointed 1st lieutenant, October 1942; captain, May 1943; major, November 1943; lieutenant colonel, February 1945; colonel, July 1955; brigadier general, March 1966; and major general, August 1969.

He has served overseas in Europe three times and one tour each in Korea, Japan and South Vietnam. Duty assignments started at the basic officer's course at Ft. Sill, OK. Following graduation he joined the 10th Armd. Div.; here he was battery executive, assistant S-3, battalion S-3, battalion executive and commanding officer of the 420th Armd. FA BN, 10th Armd. Div., in the States and Europe.

Following the war, he was in G-3 section of Patton's 3rd Army. Upon return to the States in 1947, he joined the general staff, US Army, Washington and concurrently served as an aide at the White House. He was next the military aide to the Secretary of the Army. Moved to West Point in 1949, where he was an instructor in tactics and company commander of a company of cadets. After the Command and General Staff College, he went to Korea in 1953 as G-3, 2nd Inf. Div., and later executive officer, 2nd Div. Arty. Later he was ordered to Japan for duty in J-3, HQ, Far East and United Nations Command. Returned to the Armed Forces Staff College, Norfolk, VA, and to Washington again on the Army Staff in DCSOPS and later in the office of the Army chief of staff. After graduation from the National War College in 1960, he became the executive officer, 4th Armd. Div. Arty., USAREUR. From here, he was ordered to the 7th Army as the deputy G-3 in August 1961. In June 1962 he reported to HQs Central Army Group, NATO, as the G-3, until his return to Washington in July 1964.

In Washington he was chief of the War Plans Division, ODCSOPS; in June 1965, the assistant and then the deputy director of the strategic plans and policy directorate, ODCSOPS. In February 1966 he was assigned to the US Army Vietnam as commander, II Field Force Arty., in the general Saigon area.

In September 1966 he joined the US Embassy in

Saigon as the military assistant to the deputy ambassador in the pacification effort. In January 1967 he returned to II FFORCEV Arty., where he remained as commander until May 1967, when he was assigned assistant division commander, 2nd Armd. Div., Ft. Hood, TX. In March 1969 he returned to Germany as the deputy chief of staff operations, US Army Europe and 7th Army. He served in that position until June 1971. In August 1971 he reported to the joint staff in Washington as deputy director (international negotiations), J-5. in August 1972, he became deputy directory (regional), J-5, and in March 1973, vice director, J-5. In September 1973, he was named the JCS representative on the US Delegation for the Mutual Balanced Force Reduction (MBFR) talks. On Feb. 1, 1975, he was reassigned to the defense intelligence agency as the director for the defense attache system. On Sept. 1, 1977, in addition, he became chief of staff, DIA.

After retiring in April 1978, he became the executive director for the Association of Military Colleges and schools of the United States and National Defense Advisor to the NSDAR. Awards include the Distinguished Service Medal, Legion of Merit w/4 OLCs, Bronze Star Medal w/2 OLCs and V, Air Medal w/3 OLCs, JCSM, Army Commendation Medal, Croix de Guerre w/Gold Star (France), Croix de Guerre w/Palm (Belgium), Vietnamese Armed Forces Honor Medal, Cross of Gallantry w/Palm, Civil Actions Medal w/1st Clasp, US Distinguished Unit Badge, Republic of Korea Presidential Unit Citation, Chungmu (Korea) Distinguished Military Service Medal and US Meritorious Unit Badge.

Married Katharine Coleman Clayton, July 19, 1948, Ft. Jackson, SC, and has three children: Kathy, Ginger and Jacquie.

TSG EDWARD P. CROOK (CHICKEN) was

born Oct. 14, 1921, Lorena, TX. Received his GED in 1946 and attended Texas State Tech in 1972, and studied animal husbandry. Joined A Troop, 5th Cav., in 1939. Stations included Ft. Clark, TX; Ft. DA Russel; Ft. Bliss; Strathpine, Australia; Orel Bay; New Guinea; Battle of Admiralty Islands; Invasion of Leyte clear to Omar Valley, Philippine Islands.

Discharged on Aug. 21, 1945, with the rank of technical sergeant. Awards include six Battle Stars, Combat Infantry Badge w/OLC, two Presidential Silver Stars, Purple Heart, Good Conduct Medal, Philippine Liberation Medal and Asiatic-Pacific Ribbons.

Married Frances Cunnick Romer in November 1954, and has five children, seven grandchildren and one great-grandchild. Retired in 1959 at the Veteran's Administration Hospital, Waco, TX.

MAJ CHARLES RAYBURN CUNNINGHAM

was born July 26, 1921, Buckholts, TX; and earned a BBS and LLB degree. Joined the USAAF, 124th Cavalry in November 1940. Stations were combat tour, pilot, USAAC and Italy, January to July 1944. Served with the 124th Cav, 460th BG.

Discharged from the cavalry in 1942 and the USAFR in 1953, with the rank of major. Awards include the Distinguished Flying Cross and Air Medals.

Memorable experiences include 1941 Louisiana maneuvers and combat tour as aircraft commander (pilot) of the 460th BG, 761st Sqdn, January to July 1944.

Married Juanita (Sammy) and has one child and four grandchildren. He is an active lawyer.

CPL CHRISTOPHER J. CUNNINGHAM JR.

was born Sept. 25, 1927, Albany, NY; and attended three and one-half years of high school. Joined the US Army on Oct. 2, 1944, and was stationed at Ft. Bragg; Ft. Riley; Ft. Dix; Ft. Benning; LeHarve France; Freising, Munich, Stuttgart, Heidelberg and Bad Reichenhall Laufen; Reit im Winkle, Germany; and Yokohama, Japan. Served with the 2nd Cav., 2nd Constabulary, 7766th Horse Tp., attached to HQ US Constabulary, 7th Base PO Yokohama, Japan.

Discharged in September 1948, with the rank of corporal. He was recalled in 1953 for the Korean conflict and discharged in May 1954. Awards include the WWII Victory Medal, Army of Occupation Medal, Korean Service Medal, UN Service Medal and the National Defense Service Medal.

Memorable experiences include the friendships formed in the horse platoon in Germany that still endure to this day.

Was married to the most wonderful lady in the world for 42 years, who passed away on March 14, 1992. They have four children, eight grandchildren and one great-grandson. Worked for a newspaper as national adv. manager and retired on Jan. 8, 1993.

TSG JAMES RAY CUNNINGHAM was born

Sept. 3, 1925, Clay County, AR; and attended three years of college. Joined the US Army Nov. 25, 1942, at Jefferson Barracks, MO. Stations included Ft. Riley, KS, and Camp Van Dorn, MS. Served with the Mort. Plt., I Troop, 29th Cav.

Discharged July 27, 1947, with the rank of technical sergeant.

Memorable experience was going on night compass exercise on a black, cold, rainy night in late 1943, or early 1944, with Col. Roland Delmar.

Married Yvonne Y. Toyoda, Dec. 14, 1958, and has one child and two grandchildren. Worked for the federal civil service, GS-11 and retired May 31, 1983, Ft. Carson, CO.

PFC JON WESTON DAHL was born June 20,

1924, Chicago, IL. He attended the University of Illinois and Columbia School of radio. Joined the cavalry on Dec. 7, 1942, Ft. Riley, KS. Served during the Italian Campaign with the 124th Horse Cav., Ft. Brown, TX; 755th Tk. Bn., Italy; *Star and Stripes* Newspaper, Mediterranean Ediiton, artist and correspondent.

Discharged Dec. 31, 1945, with the rank of private first class. Awards include one Service Stripe, four Overseas Service Bars, EAME Theater Ribbon w/3

Bronze Battle Stars, Good Conduct Medal; Bronze Arrowhead Medal, Croix de Guerre w/Vermillion Star and WWII Victory Medal.

Married Margaret A. Marinelli, Nov. 22, 1952, and has two daughters and two grandchildren. Civilian employment included announcer WDMJ, Marquette, MI, 1947-51; state representative for National Foundation March of Dimes of Michigan, 1951-61; executive director, Phoenix March of Dimes, 1961-63; and West Coast director of Cystic Fibrosis Foundation, 1963-65. Retired in 1988.

EDWARD L. DAILY enlisted directly into the 1st Cav. Div. in 1948. After completing armored-infantry basic training at Fort Knox, KY, he was sent immediately to the Far East Cmd. in Japan. Arriving in Tokyo, Japan, in February 1949, he was assigned to Co. H, 2nd Bn., 7th Cav. Regt.

He soon found himself learning his new trade as a machine gunner in the 1st Plt., but at that particular time, most of their training consisted of occupation duty that existed within the 8th Army. A major influence soon appeared in his life and military career, which came from his company commander, Capt. Melbourne C. Chandler. Chandler attempted to instill in every trooper a dedicated effort to become a better soldier and he further emphasized the strict guidelines of the heritage and tradition of the famous Garry Owen Regt.

When the Korean War started, the 7th Cav. Regt. departed from Japan in July 1950 to fight against communist aggression from the North Korean army. Fighting a savage enemy, the 2nd Bn. experienced many battle casualties during the early stages of combat. This created a very serious condition because there was a shortage of replacements and, in some instances, there were none at all! Because of this desperate situation, promotions within the ranks came to those capable survivors. From the recommendations of Lt. Robert M. Carroll, Capt. Mel Chandler and Maj. Omar Hitchner, commander, 2nd Bn., he received a battlefield commission to temporary 2nd lieutenant Aug. 10, 1950.

Assuming leadership of the same 1st Plt., it was a very proud time in his life and military career. However, two days later, on Aug. 12, 1950, during a vicious battle on the Naktong River, the forward elements of his platoon were overrun and he could not evade capture.

With the grace of God, he managed to escape from the enemy on Sept. 12, 1950, and was held captive only 32 days. Receiving the appropriate medical treatment, he volunteered to return to his previous unit and active duty Sept. 23, 1950. This time conditions had changed greatly in favor of the UN Forces, because the US Marines and the 7th Inf. Div. previously had made an amphibious landing at Inchon, South Korea, thus cutting off the entire supply line of the North Korean Army. Nonetheless, he would face many struggles and hardships as he remained in combat with the 7th Cav. Regt. On May 10, 1951, he returned to the States and was honorably discharged from the Army May 27, 1952.

Among the medals awarded him are the Distinguished Service Cross, Silver Star Medal, Bronze Star Medal (V), Purple Heart w/2 OLCs, Army Commendation Medal, Korean Campaign Medal w/5 Bronze Battle Stars, South Korean Presidential Unit Citation, Combat Infantry badge and the Army Parachutist Badge. In June 1988 he was awarded the American Ex-Prisoner of War Medal by the Department of Defense.

He is a life member of the 1st Cav. Div. Assoc. and the 7th US Cav. Assoc. and over the years he has remained loyal and dedicated to both organizations. Currently, he is a member of the Board of Governors of the 1st Cav. Div. Assoc. The 1st Cav. Div. is stationed at Ft. Hood, TX. He is past-president of the 7th US Cav. Assoc. and the Korean War Veterans Chapter, 7th US Cav. Assoc.

COL WALTER J. DAVIES was born Jan. 15, 1919. He was awarded a BS degree from Michigan State University in 1945. He joined the 9th US Cav. Regt. as a cavalry 2nd lieutenant in July 1940. He later served as a company grade officer in various armored cavalry units.

Primary assignments included commander, 143rd Cav. Recon. Tp. (Sep); intelligence staff officer, GHQ Far East Command; assistant PMS and T for armor, University of Georgia; commander, 826th Tk. Bn., USAREUR; staff officer, office of the deputy chief of staff for personnel, Department of the Army; Div. G-2, 7th Inf. Div., Korea; unit chief, US Army Armor Human Research Unit; deputy commander of the Edgewood Arsenal Maryland Complex which included Rocky Mountain Arsenal, CO; and Pine Bluff Arsenal, AK; and DPCA US Army Flight Training Center, Ft. Stewart, GA.

Military schools include the Cavalry School, Armor School, Command and General Staff College, Army Management School and Senior Officers Chemical Course. He retired in February 1972.

Married Barbara C. Gribler in 1940, has a son and daughter, four grandchildren and one great-grandchild.

MAJ BRUCE A. DAVIS was born May 16, 1921, Las Cruces, Dona Ana Co, NM. Attended Long Beach, CA City College and the University of Georgia Columbus Center.

Joined the cavalry and armor on Oct. 16, 1939. Served only in the 1st Sqdn., 8th Cav. Regt., mostly in C Tp., from Oct. 16, 1939, to Nov. 8, 1945. His basic training was on a horse; fired a pistol both mounted and dismounted as expert; transferred from Ft. Bliss, TX, to Australia, then to New Guinea; and first combat was in the Admiralty Islands.

In January 1945 he received a field promotion to 2nd lieutenant platoon leader. Promoted to 1st lieutenant in May 1945. As enemy opposition ended, they prepared for the invasion of Japan. Landed on Oct. 2, 1945, at Yokohama and participated in the surrender of Japan. Returned to the States and released from active duty at Ft. MacArthur, CA, Nov. 8, 1945.

In February 1948 he re-enlisted as a technical sergeant in the 1st Cav. Div. Upon arrival at Camp Drake, in Asaka, Japan, he was assigned as the chief clerk of the Div. AG Sec. Promoted to permanent master sergeant on board ship on the way to an amphibious landing at Pohang dong, Korea in July 1950. In Pusan Perimeter, then in the breakout and to the North Korean Capital city of Pyongyang and the port city of Nampo.

After the Chinese communists intervention CCI, pushed back below Taegu. Reassigned to the ZI in 1951 as sergeant major of Ft. MacArthur, San Pedro, CA. Shortly thereafter recalled to active duty as 1st lieutenant, armor and assigned to 11th AC, Ft. Carson, CO, as a platoon leader. Later assigned as post information officer to command general staff. Attended armor basic officer course, Ft. Knox, KY. In February 1954 he was assigned as PIO, to Berlin Command in Europe. Visited East Berlin via Check Point Charlie. Requested reassignment to armor unit. Approved for the 322nd Tk. Bn. (120 mm gun), Camp Denny T. Clarke, Hammelburg, Germany as platoon leader. Named changed to 826th Tk. Bn. (120 mm gun). Was captain S-2, then commanding officer, HQ, HQ and Svc. Co. and finally adjutant. Name changed to 3/66 Armor and moved to Conn Barracks, Schweinfurt, Germany. This tank battalion gyroscoped to Ft. Benning, GA, early 1957 to support the Infantry School. He was battalion adjutant during this time. Participated as battalion representative in the atomic blast in Nevada. The battalion was deactivated and he was reassigned as adjutant then as commander, B Co., 2/69 Armor, 2nd Inf. Div., Ft. Benning, GA. Later promoted to major ad reassigned to Bn. S3. Retired from active duty on May 31, 1962.

Served with A, B and C Troops, 1st Sqdn. 8th Cav. Regt., 1st Cav. Div.; Div. HQ&HQ Tp., 1st Cav. Div.; Post HQ, Ft. MacArthur, CA; 11th A/C Regt., and HQ, Ft. Carson, CO; Berlin Command, Germany; 322nd Tk. Bn. and 3/66 Armor (all the same unit with name changes.; Camp Denny T. Clark, Hammelburg, Germany and Conn Barracks, Schweinfurt, Germany, then via gyroscope of the 3/66 Tk. Bn. to Ft. Benning, GA; 2/69 Armor, 2nd Inf. Div., Ft. Benning, GA.

Awards include the Bronze Star w/OLC, Army Commendation Medal w/OLC and Purple Heart (wounded three times).

Married Rosa Lee Hadsall on May 18, 1946. They have seven children, nine grandchildren and one great-grandchild.

He worked for 20 years and one day for the IRS as revenue officer and group manager in Los Angeles area and Bakersfield, CA. He retired in 1982.

MAJ GORDON G. DE LARONDE was born June 26, 1916, Rockford, IL. Received a BS degree in industrial education and MS degree in education administration. Joined the US Horse Cavalry in 1938. Applied for active duty in August 1941 and was assigned to the USAF. He served with the 4th Air Base Sqdn., Selfridge Field, MI, August 1941 until October 1943; 70th Replacement Depot, 8th Air Force, October 1943 until December 1945; took leave from December 1945 to March 1946; 437th Troop Carrier Wing, inactive Reserve, April 1946 to August 1950; and active duty August 10 until August 30.

In August 1950 he transferred to honorary Reserve and retired due to hearing loss acquired during WWII duty. Awards include the Meritorious Service Unit Insignia, American Defense Service Medal, American Theater, WWII Victory Medal, four Overseas Service Bars and National Defense Service Medal.

Married Ann M. Winter and has three children and two grandchildren. Worked as a high school teacher in industrial education, head of the department. Retired in June 1975.

CPL JUAN M. DE LA TORRE was born Sept. 27, 1922, San Antonio, TX. Attended high school, Phoenix Technical School and two semesters at Compton Junior College. Joined the 1st Cav. on Aug. 7, 1940, and was stationed in New Guinea, Admiralty Islands and Leyte Island, Philippines. Served with the 12th Cav., G Tp.

Discharged May 19, 1945, with the rank of corporal. He was awarded the Good Conduct Ribbon, Purple Heart, Asiatic-Pacific Theater Ribbon, American Defense Service Ribbon and Combat Infantry Badge.

Memorable experiences consist of being wounded in action on Leyte Island, Philippines, Oct. 22, 1944.

Married Mary Louise Morales on Nov. 26, 1942, and has five children and 11 grandchildren. He worked for the Bureau of reclamation and opened his own business, Precision Auto Parts, in 1954. It is still going stronger than ever. Three of his children run the business.

THOMAS A. J. DENHAM joined for duty and enrolled on Aug. 20, 1862, in Edmonson County, KY, and mustered out on Aug. 23, 1865. As with so many of the Civil War soldiers, he acquired many of the diseases of the men around him. He entered the service as a strong, healthy man and came out "broken down in health," "poor and emaciated." His testators said that the flesh on his right leg and breast had gradually shrunken, "he had a very bad cough with hemorrhage of the lungs," and was unable  to do his normal work. This sounds like polio, tuberculosis, pneumonia, or malaria, and possibly a staph infection also. His hospital diagnosis in 1863 recorded that he had measles at that time. At the end of his three year term, he applied for and was granted a pension.

He was born in Tennessee in 1837. He married Sarah Jane Sanders on Jan. 16, 1865, while he was still in the cavalry. His bride was the daughter of his long time friend, Samuel B. Sanders, with whom he served in the war. He and Sarah Jane had four children who survived to adulthood; Edward, Rosa Bell, Clarence and Samuel. In 1876 he and Sarah Jane, along with her parents Samuel and Ellenore Sanders and several of her brothers and sisters migrated to Chanute, Neosho County, KS.

Tom survived until 1879, when the ravages of all his war acquired diseases overwhelmed his weakened body and he died. He is buried in old Greenwood Cemetery, three miles east of Chanute, beside his war partner and father-in-law Samuel Sanders. In 1889 his widow and their four children moved to Idaho where she took out a homestead. Sarah Jane and the three sons all remained in Idaho and are buried there. Rosa Bell and her husband homesteaded in Oklahoma where they are buried.

CSM JAMES L. DEPRIEST was born in Oak Ridge, TN. He entered the Army in August 1973. He attended Basic Combat Training at Ft. Jackson, SC and Advanced Individual Training at Ft. Knox, KY, where he received training as an armor crewman.

His military education includes the First Armored Div. Noncommissioned Officer Academy, Basic Noncommissioned Officer Course, Advanced Noncommissioined officer course, first sergeant course, US Army Sergeants Major Academy (Class 36) and M1 Abrams Master Gunner Course.

His assignments include 2nd Bn., 69th Armor, Ft. Benning, GA, as a driver for a target tank; various duties in G3, 1st Armored Div., Ansbach, Germany; tank commander, 2nd Bn., 1st AIT/OSUT Brigade, (Armor) Ft. Knox, KY; tank commander and assistant operations sergeant, 1st Bn., 68th Armor, Wildflecken, Germany; and platoon sergeant, operations sergeant, and first sergeant, 2nd Bn., 5th Cavalry, 1st Cavalry Div., Ft. Hood, TX. His unit became COHORT and rotated to Kirchgoens, Germany, and was redesignated as 4th Bn., 32nd Armor, where he continued as 1st sergeant and then became operations sergeant again. He served as the Division Master Gunner, 5th Inf. Div. (Mechanized) and g-3 sergeant major, 5th Inf. Div. Mech. and 2nd Armored Division. His next assignment was squadron sergeant major for the 1st Sqdn., 7th Cav., 1st Cav. Div. He was then assigned as command sergeant major, 1st Bde., 2nd Inf. Div. He is currently assigned as command sergeant major 1st Bde., 1st Cav. Div.

Among his awards and decorations are the Meritorious Service Medal w/4 OLCs, the Army Commendation Medal w/OLC, the Army Achievement Medal w/ OLC, the Good Conduct Medal w/7th Award, the Driver Badge (Wheel), and an Overseas Ribbon w/4th Award.

He graduated from the University of the State of New York with a BS in liberal arts in 1996.

He has one daughter, Mrs. Neenah Miller, and two grandsons, James and Geoffrey, who live on Lookout Mountain, in Georgia.

He is currently CSM of the 3rd Bn., 66th Armor (FORCE XXI), 4th Inf. Div., Ft. Hood, TX.

COL JOHN DIBBLE JR. was born Nov. 6, 1917, Ft. Bliss, TX, while his father, an Army surgeon, was supporting Gen. Pershing's punitive expedition against Pancho Villa. Attended high school outside Ft. Sheridan, IL, where he was active in polo and jumping and received BA degree from West Point in 1940. Influenced by the presence of Col. Harry D. Chamberlain, he moved to Carlisle Barracks, PA, and enlisted in the 104th Cav. prior to entering the class of 1940 at West Point. He played polo until injured during a game and rode on the Modern Pentathlon Team. Upon graduation he was assigned to the 18th Field Artillery's horse drawn battalion, riding on the 18th FA Horse Show Team, polo team and riding steeplechase. Graduated from the advanced horsemanship course, and on outbreak of the WWII he was assigned to the 7th Tank Destroyer Gp., later commanding the 705th Tank Destroyer Bn. during, and following, the Battle of the Bulge.

Qualifying as an Army aviator, he developed sky car equipment and tactics. He served in Vietnam as deputy commanding general of the 1st Aviation Bde. Participated at Normandy, Brittany, Bulge, Germany and Austria, serving with C Btry, 18th FA, 705th TD Bn., 1st Armd. Bde.

Discharged in July 1970 with the rank of colonel. Awards include the Silver Star, Distinguished Flying Cross, Legion of Merit w/cluster, Air Medal w/6 clusters, Bronze Star w/cluster and Purple Heart.

Memorable experiences include WWII, the Normandy breakout, siege of Brest, and supporting the 101st Abn. in Bastogne siege.

Married and has three children and four grandchildren. Worked for Grumman Aircraft, 1970-71; professor, FIT, 1983.

SSG LLOYD L. DICK was born Aug. 15, 1916, Brooklyn, NY; and attended two years of college. Joined the cavalry and entered active duty on Jan. 27, 1941. Participated in Central Europe and Rhineland, serving with Troop A, 116th Cav. Recon.

As sergeant of the 3rd Plt., Troop A, 116th Cav. Recon. Sqdn. Mech., he made the first complete penetration of the Siegfried Line in the 7th Army sector and captured the town of St. Ingbert, March 15, 1945.

Discharged Oct. 23, 1945, with the rank of staff sergeant. Awards include the Cavalry Medal, American Defense Medal, European Theater Ribbon and Bronze Star. The Cavalry Medal was awarded on Sept. 24, 1994, at the annual meeting of the US Horse Cavalry Association, held at Ft. Huachuca, Sierra Vista, AZ.

Married Ruth W. Baecker, June 29, 1940, and has two children and four grandchildren. Worked for Continental Insurance Co., 1937-81 as an office boy, payroll audit reviewer and superintendent retrospection. Retired Feb. 1, 1981.

LTC JOHN B. DONNELL was born Oct. 23, 1914, Los Angeles, CA. He received a BA degree from the University of Arizona. Joined the cavalry in June 1940, and was stationed at Ft. Bliss, Ft. Riley, North Africa and San Francisco Port. He served with the 7th Cav.

Saw combat in 1943 with the 91st Recon Sqdn., which was attached to the 1st Armd. Corps. In North Africa they were the connecting link between two infantry divisions. They were headed for Mateur and Bizerte, through the Sedjenane Valley. The 91st Recon Sqdn. was among the first troops to reach Bizerte. Although an armored unit, they were on the ground most of the time, because the terrain was too steep for trucks and armored cars.

He was a major and training officer for the squadron. As they advanced one day, they came in contact with the enemy and had a good fire fight. Since the men all had rifles or tommy guns, he took over a light machine gun. They beat them back, but in the fight he got hit in the shoulder by machine gun fire. It knocked out some of his collar bone and put him out of action.

Two men picked him up in a jeep to look for an aid station. Since it was dark by then they could not find it, so they camped out on the ground for the night. The next day they found an aid station in the outfit next to them. The medic gave him a big shot of whisky, and he realized that things were going to be OK. He went through the evacuation system, ending in Bou Hanifia where the US Army had set up a hospital. Later on he was sent to Oran to get a hospital ship for the States. He then spent six months in the US Army hospitals. On release from Winter Hospital in Topeka, KS. He was assigned to teach at the Cavalry School at Ft. Riley.

Discharged March 1946 with the rank of lieutenant colonel. Awards include the Silver Star and Purple Heart.

Married Suzanne and has three children and five grandchildren. Worked as a manufacturers representative of engineering products and retired in 1982.

SSG RUDOLPH J. DOVALE was born Nov. 22, 1921, in Brooklyn, NY, of parents emigrating from the Netherlands Antilles. He graduated Metropolitan Vocational High School with vocational and college preparatory diplomas. He served three years in the 13th Inf. Regt. of the NY State Guard from 1940 to 1942, before entering the US Army at Camp Kilmer, NJ, Dec. 18, 1942.

January 1943 saw him at Ft. Oglethorpe, GA, in B Troop of the newly reactivated 16th Cav. Regt. His basic training took place at Oglethorpe and Camp Forrest followed by the 1943 Tennessee maneuvers as a recon. corporal.

In November 1943 the regiment was moved to Ft. Devens, MS, and was reorganized as the 16th and 19th Cav. Sqdns. Transferred to the 3rd Corps, Eastern Defense Command as the 16th Cav. Gp., they actively patrolled the coastline from Canada to New Bedford, RI, earning the American Theater Campaign Medal. May saw the Troops in Camp Picket, VA, and A.P. HJill preparing for Shanks, NY. Out of camp they boarded the *Queen Elizabeth* and sailed for Grennock, Scotland on November 21.

With Dovale as a buck sergeant leading a B Troop Recon Section, the squadrons joined Patton's 3rd Army in February. Early in March they were attached to Col. Jim Polk's 3rd Cav., in the Siegfried Line serving as Gen. Walton Walker's XX Corps Cav. A short period of patrolling East of Trier was followed by the breakthrough to the Rhine.

Leading his men in a dismounted attack on the town of Waldrach on the Rower River, one of the final strongholds West of the Rhine, he was wounded by machine gun fire. He remained on the field throughout the day assisting his wounded comrades and evacuating them until dusk, when he then went back through the lines to the Troops CP. He returning with stretcher bearers who helped him get out all the rest of his wounded men and he was awarded the Bronze Star in this action.

He was jeeped to the 104th Field Hospital in Trier, then flown to Hospital Lariboisiere in Paris. He returned to his troop in early May, having been "checked out" of hte hospital by several buddies. Promoted ot staff, he was a platoon leader in the Army of Occupation.

In July, the 16th and 19th Squadrons left for Arles, France, where they sweltered in heat and choked in dust until August 14 when they boarded Troop Ships on the to the Philippines. The Japanese war ended on the 15th, and the SS *Breckinridge* "swapped courses in mid stream" and went to New York Harber instead of the Panama Canal.

After three months of furlough, he returned to Ft. Dix, receiving his honorable discharge and $300.00. He enlisted in the USAR and in the 13th Inf. of the New York State Guard where he served for three more years as a platoon sergeant, before moving to Curacao in the Netherlands Antilles. In Curacao he established a home, family and a business career which carried him for 45 days.

He now serves as vice president of the 16th Cav. Assn. He has been a commander in the American Legion, president of rotary, president of the International Advartising Assn., and presiden of Skall. He has been knighted by her Majest, Queen Beatirx of the Netherlands for service to the crown. He has five children by his previous marriage to Helen Sargent. His present wife Jacquelin is a driving force in all his endowers.

COL RENO E. DREWS was born Oct. 27, 1912, in Winneconne, WI. Joined 32nd Div., NG in 1934. Mobilized with unit for active duty in October 1940 and sailed to Australia in April 1942. Received a direct commission as 2nd lieutenant, infantry, Sept. 15, 1942. Participated in Papua, New Guinea, Philippine Islands and Luzon Campaigns.

Awards include the Silver Star, Bronze Star w/ cluster, Combat Infantry Badge, Purple Heart, Legion of Merit, Army Commendation Medal, Presidential Unit Citation w/cluster, Philippine Presidential Unit Citation, Armed Forces Reserve Medal, American Campaign Medal, National Defense Service Medal, Asiatic-Pacific w/4 Clusters, Army of Occupation-Germany, WWII Victory Medal and Philippine Liberation Medals. Was integrated into regular Army in cavalry as 1st lieutenant, permanent rank July 7, 1947.

Served as commanding officer, 2nd Bn., 6th Armd. Cav. from October 1952 to October 1953. Was commanding officer of 4th Armd. Div. Trains, July 1960 to July 1961, and commanding officer, Combat Command C, July 1961 to July 1962. Retired with permanent rank of colonel, Feb. 1, 1968.

MAJ HEISTER H. DRUM was born Dec. 21, 1914, Mifflinville, PA. Graduated from USMA, 1941 and New Mexico School of Law in 1953. Joined the US Cavalry, June 11, 1941. Participated in Normandy, North France, Ardennes and Rhineland, serving with the 14th and 12th Cav.

Departed the States on April 6, 1944, for the European Theater Operation. He was wounded on March 2, 1945, in Germany and returned to the States on July 13, 1945.

Retired Jan. 14, 1947, with the rank of major. Awards include the Silver Star, Bronze Star Medal, American Campaign Medal, American Defense Service Medal, WWII Victory Medal, Croix de Guerre w/Silver Gilt Star, Purple Heart, EAME Campaign Medal w/4 Bronze Battle Stars.

Married Mary Ruth Reynolds, Aug. 17, 1942, and has one child and two grandchildren. Worked as a lawyer in a private practice. Retired from the US Army on March 31, 1947, and retired again on Jan. 1, 1987, from being a lawyer.

1LT CHRISTOPHER DUGRE was born June 12, 1969, Stoughton, MA. Received BA degree in English and master's degree in education in 1996. Joined the US Army on May 3, 1991, with the armor. Served with the D & A Troop, 1-110th Cav. MAARNG.

Memorable experience was his scout platoon leaders course, Ft. Knox, February 1993.

He is currently in active guard with the rank of 1st lieutenant.

TSG EFRAIN A. DURAN was born March 24, 1920, Starr County, TX. Attended high school and some college. Joined the infantry and cavalry on Nov. 1, 1939, and participated in the EAME serving with Troop G, 12th Cav., Co. B, 363rd Inf. Regt.

Discharged July 10, 1945, with the rank of technical sergeant. Awards include the EAME Theater Award w/3 Battle Stars, Bronze Star w/cluster, Purple Heart w/ cluster, Good Conduct Medal, WWII Victory Medal and Medal of Occupation.

Memorable experiences include the break through at Apennines; Battle of Monticello, Gothic Line, Italy; and training in North Africa.

Married Dina P. and has seven children and 18 grandchildren. Worked as a county tax collector, county commissioner, school board president and is at the present manager, Star County Water District.

HAROLD L. DURCK was born Aug. 9, 1920, in Louisville, KY. Enlisted in the US Army Oct. 24, 1936, at age 16. Stationed two years, Schofield Barracks, C Btry. 11th FA; one year Presidio of Monterey, CA. E Btry., 76th FA (horse drawn artillery).

Enlisted US Navy May 28, 1940, covered entire Pacific war beginning with Pearl Harbor, Coral Sea, Midway, invasion of Guadalcanal where his ship the USS *Astoria*, (CA-34) was sunk in a surface engagement on his 22nd birthday.

Served in the Flag of Adm. Halsey, Commander Third Fleet, was on the USS *Missouri* (BB-63) when the Japanese signed the surrender documents.

Received the Navy Commendation Ribbon, Good Conduct Medal w/2 stars, the Asiatic-Pacific w/10 stars among the eight ribbons received during his career.

Transferred to the Fleet Reserve after 20 years as a chief radioman.

Married Sylvia, a former sergeant in the RAF WWII on Oct. 19, 1951. They have two children, Craig who is a doctor in the Army serving at Ft. Hood, TX; and Teri, who is a school teacher. Also has an older son, Gregory. They have six grandchildren: Brianna, Sean, Shannon, Christian, Josh and Ashley.

CPT CHARLES LOVELL DUSTIN was born in 1835, Nashua, CT. The family settled in or near Red Oak, IA. He enlisted in the 1st Cav. Regt. on Aug. 22, 1855. One of the many Indian campaigns during his enlistment was the 1857 Cheyenne Expedition during which the 1st Cav. under Col. E.V. Sumner, was in the field for four months pursuing and fighting the Cheyenne on the banks of the Solomon River in Kansas. Also participated in the Civil War, 1861-66.

Discharged in 1860 with the rank of colonel.

Memorable experiences were the Cheyenne Expedition, 1857; Civil War; Battle Prairie capture of Van Buren; capture of Little Rock; and the scrimmages with Gen. Price and Gen. Forrest.

Married Margaret Morris, Sept. 13, 1882, Durango, CO, and has four children and an unknown number of grandchildren. He worked as a farmer.

MAJ FRANCIS S. DUTTENHOFER was born July 8, 1916, Cincinnati, OH. Attended Cincinnati Country Day School; Culver Military Academy, Black Horse Troop, varsity rifle squad, varsity polo team, graduating in 1935; Duke University; and the University of Cincinnati.

Joined the I Troop, 107th Cav., ONG, in order to continue polo in 1937. Inducted as 2nd lieutenant with Troop B, 107th Cav. (horse-Mech.), March 5, 1941. Served with the XII Army Corp, Louisiana Maneuvers followed by completion of horse and mechanized course at Cavalry School, Ft. Riley, KS, Dec. 23, 1941.

Rejoined the regiment at Ft. Ord, CA, and requested a transfer to the 11th Horse Cav. Regt. stationed at Camp Lockett, CA. Assigned duty with A Troop under Capt. Thomas Chamberlain. Was promoted to 1st lieutenant on June 19, 1942, SO #127, 11th Cav., relieved by the 4th Cav. Bde., and ordered to proceed to Ft. Benning to cadre the 11th Armd. Regt., 10th Armd. Div. Completed fourth tactical course, Armored School, Ft. Knox, KY, Oct. 14, 1942. Promoted to captain, Feb. 19, 1943, and commanded Co. A, 11th Armd. Regt.

Was injured during the Tennessee Maneuvers on July 12, 1943. Upon release from Lawson General Hospital he was ordered to ARTC, Ft. Knox, KY. Transferred to the 21st Tank Bn., 10th Armd. Div., Camp Gordon, GA. Assigned temporary duty at HQ XII (G-3 section), Ft. Jackson, SC, relieving TD and was then reassigned S-2, 11th Tank Bn., Jan. 28, 1944. Promoted to major, Aug. 10, 1944, S-3, 11th Tank Bn.

Received head wounds and lost his right eye in action at Laumsfeldt, Nov. 16, 1944. Evacuated to the 117th General Hospital, Swindon, UK for treatment. Released from Wakeman General Hospital, May 21, 1945, and returned to limited service duty as assistant S-3, Armd. RTC, Ft. Knox, KY.

Retired with permanent physical disability on April 30, 1946, Ft. Knox Regional Hospital. Awards include the Bronze Star, March 15, 1945; and Purple Heart, Jan. 7, 1945. Returned to Miami, FL, and organized public workshop.

Married Ann Louise Dom (Woody), Aug. 22, 1938, and has two sons, Dale Sennett and Eric Dom. Associated with R.B. Grove, Inc. in 1953 and retired as president in 1975. Other activities include board of trustees, Ransom School; commodore, Biscayne Bay Yacht Club, 1965; and rear commodore, Florida Station, Cruising Club of America, 1985.

LTC JOHN DVERGSTEN was born Jan. 4, 1916, Watson, MN; and attended college. Joined the US Army March 25, 1941, and participated in the European campaign. Served with the 4th Cav. and 240th QM Depot Supply. Discharged in 1968 with the rank of lieutenant colonel.

Memorable experiences include April 7, 1942, riding with the 4th Cav. Regt. in Omaha during a bond drive parade; April 9, 1942, riding in a review marking the turn in of 4th Cav. horses at Ft. Robinson, NE; Sept. 9, 1988, riding with seasoned troopers of the 4th Cav. in Omaha in a parade celebrating, "The 4th Cav. Rides Again" reunion. He is proud of his more than half century association with the great 4th Cav. troopers.

Married, has two children and five grandchildren. Owned a small chain of retail ladies stores and retired in 1984.

MAJ DOUGLAS C. EARLEY was born Aug. 2, 1918, Olean, NY. Attended Texas A&M University, receiving his BS degree. Joined the cavalry June 3, 1941, and was stationed at Ft. Bliss, El Paso, TX, and Ft. McIntosh, Laredo, TX. Served with the 1st Horse Cav. Div., 56th Cav. Bde., Supreme HQ, Allied Expeditionary Force HQ, London, England.

Discharged Oct. 4, 1945, with the rank of major. Awards include the European Theater and Bronze Star.

Married Ann Tandy and has three children and four grandchildren. Worked for FMC Corp, agricultural chemicals, technical service division. He retired in 1975.

E-4 JERRY ALLEN EDGIN attended Libby Elementary, 1963; Gage Park High School, 1966; GED, US Army, 1967, and R.J. Daley College, AAS with honors, 1979. Joined the US Army on Oct. 3, 1966, and was transferred to Baumhaolder, Germany in February 1967. He redeployed with the 3rd Armd. Cav in June 1968 to Ft. Lewis, WA.

Upon completing tank qualifying in Grafinvear, Germany, in the fall of 1967, their tank qualified second in the entire squadron. They all received a promotion.

Discharged Aug. 20, 1969, with the rank of E-4/SP-4. He received the Expert Marksman, M14, .45 caliber handgun, machine gun and tank weapons.

Memorable experiences include waiting to make reveille one morning, and hearing two soldiers who had just rotated in talking about music and their guitars. Soon a third soldier stated that he played drums. The first guy said, "All we need now is a lead singer and bass guitar player, and we have a band." Edgin jumped around and said, "Ta-Da." Within three weeks there was a talent show at the Cascade Service Club on post. They entered and won the contest as the opening act in front of 1,100 service men and women and their families. They were asked to play weekly for the USO Club in Tacoma, WA, where they performed until two of the guys, Frank Marion (Warwick, RI on drums) and Gary McPhill (San Luis Obispho, CA on rhythm guitar) were rotate home. He has lost touch with Frank and Gary, but he and Myron (Tiko) Kaeo (Honolulu, HI on lead guitar) still keep in touch after 28 years.

Married Cynthia S. Martinek-Edgin, March 7, 1970, and has two children, Patrick Michael and Jennifer Lynn. Worked for the US Postal service for 20 years as an EPA compliance coordinator.

MILTON B. EDMONSON was born Oct. 13, 1918, in Kansas City, MO, where he attended Park College. Received his selective service card Oct. 16, 1940, and was inducted into the 2nd US Cavalry March 21, 1941, taking part in the Louisiana Maneuvers that summer.

On Dec. 8, 1941, with the 2nd, was sent to US border at Yuma, taking part in border patrol; one high point was the location of a biplane under camouflage loaded with explosives, obviously meant to damage one of the dams on the Colorado and possibly flood the area around Baja.

When 2nd Cav. deactivated in fall of 1942, he was reassigned and accompanied the 13th Armd. Div. to Europe, December 1944, participating in the liberation of Dachau. Was discharged in December 1945.

After law school at University of Kansas City, has practiced law, and for 20 years, served as Municipal Judge in Greenwood, MO. Presently engaged in the practice of law.

LTC LAWYN CLAYTON EDWARDS was born Aug. 7, 1953, at Camp Gordon, GA. His parents were stationed there in the US Army, his father a 2nd lieutenant in the military police who later became an army chaplain and completed a thirty year career in 1977. He spent his young life stationed around the world with his father, always returning to the family home in north central Florida when his father was on unaccompanied tours, including three wars. He graduated from Smithsburg High School, Smithsburg, MD in 1971 and, two weeks later, was admitted to the US Military Academy at West Point, NY. He received a Regular Army commission as a 2nd lieutenant of Armor upon graduation on June 4, 1975. He was concurrently awarded a BS degree with concentrations in civil engineering and French. He also holds a master of science degree in aeronautical engineering from the Air Force Institute of Technology, Wright-Patterson Air Force Base, OH (1987), and a MMAS degree in history from the command and general staff College at Ft. Leavenworth, KS (1990). His military education includes completion of the Armor Officer's Basic and Advanced Courses, the Aviation Officer's Advanced Course, the US Army and US Marine Corps Command and General Staff Officer's Courses, and the Army War College.

Key assignments include; 4th Sqdn., 7th Cav., 2nd Inf. Div., Korea, 1976-77; 4th Sqdn., 9th Cav., 6th Cav. Bde., Ft. Hood, TX, 1978-79; 7th Sqdn., 17th Cav., 6th Cav. Bde., Ft. Hood, TX, 1979-80; 3rd Aviation Bn., 3rd Inf. Div., US Army Europe, Germany, 1981-85; Air Force Institute of Technology, Wright Patterson Air Force Base, OH, 1985-87; US Army Safety Center, Ft. Rucker, AL, 1987-89; 2nd Sqdn., 4th Cav., 24th Inf. Div., Ft. Stewart, GA, USA, and Southwest Asia, 1990-92; US Army Training Doctrine Command Aviation Liaison Officer to French Army Aviation, Le Cannet-des-Maures, France, 1992-95; present US Army Combat Aviation Training Bde., Ft. Hood, TX, USA Deputy Commander.

Awards include the Bronze Star Medal, the Air Medal, the Meritorious Service Medal w/2 OLCs, the Army Commendation Medal w/OLC, the Army Achievement Medal w/OLC.

Married Deborah Lou Jones and has three children: a set of twins, Darby Lea and Nathan, and Caitlyn.

JEROME BONEPARTE EFNER enrolled Sept. 9, 1861, at Livingston, Polk County, TX, by Capt. James M. Crosson, mustered into service Sept. 25, 1861, at Camp Sibley near San Antonio, TX, by E.R. Lane. His horse was valued at $120.00 and equipment's at $30.00. On Feb. 21, 1862, his horse was killed in battle at Valverde.

He was wounded and taken a rebel prisoner to St. Louis, US Hospital at New Orleans, admitted June 30, 1863. He suffered a shell wound in his left foot and was amputated at the thigh. He died July 18, 1863.

LTC DAVID HUGH ELDER JR was born July 16, 1944, in Wilkinsburg, PA. In high school he was in the USNR, but upon graduation in 1962 joined the US Army. After training at Ft. Jackson and Ft. Knox, he was assigned to the 1st Cav. Div., Korea, 3/40 Armor, later redesignated the 2/15 Cav. In 1964-65 he served with the 3/68th Armor in Germany, was discharged and lived in Germany for a short period, but re-enlisted to become a topographic computer. After completing Infantry Officer Candidate School at Ft. Benning, GA, he was assigned to the US Army John F. Kennedy Center for Special Warfare (Airborne).

He was then assigned to the 815th Engineer Bn., Pleiku, Vietnam. While in RVN he also earned the Red Beret of the 2nd ARVN Ranger Group and the Black Beret of the RVN Armor Command, and a promotion to captain. After an extended Vietnam tour, he served with the US Army Computer Systems Command, Ft. Belvior, VA; completed the Industrial College of the Armed Forces/Management in the Department of Defense Course, then the Adjutant General Advanced Officer Course and Manpower Control Officer Course in Indianapolis, IN; and his undergraduate degree in English and psychology at the University of Nebraska at Omaha.

After tours in Cincinnati and Washington, DC, he returned to Korea and served in Teagu, attaining a black belt in Tae Kwon Do. He left active service to attend South Texas College of Law, Houston, TX, where he received his Doctorate in Law in 1979. While on active duty tour as a market analyst for N. W. Ayer, the Army's advertising agency at the time, he was promoted to major. After teaching at the University of Houston and practicing law in Houston, in 1981 he returned to active military duty as the Army Reserve advisor to the commandant, Academy of Health Sciences, Ft. Sam Houston, San Antonio, TX. His next assignment took him to the 124th Army Reserve Command, Seattle, WA, as the Medical Education and Training Officer, and a promotion to lieutenant colonel. He was reassigned to New York, first to station hospital, then to the 74th Field Hospital, which during his tenure was recognized as the "most improved unit" in the command, and was selected to be the first Field Hospital, active or reserve, to be trained on the new Deployable Medical System (DEPMEDS).

Retired from active service to Lake Tahoe in 1989, but was offered a number of high school ROTC assignments, and moved to Galveston, TX, where he is the Director of Army Instruction at Ball High School.

While establishing a mounted cavalry unit for the school, he determined that the best way to learn horse cavalry was to live it, and so began reenacting Civil War Cavalry, enlisting as a trooper. Little more than a year later, he was promoted to Executive Officer, 3rd Texas Cav. Regt. (Ross Brigade) and 6th US Cav. (the unit "galvanizes" to even the sides up at various events).

Married Alejandra and has four children: David H., Joseph Edward, Ryan Isaac and Scott David.

MAJ THEODORE JOSEPH ELIAS was born June 13, 1914, Des Moines, IA. Attended Iowa State University, receiving a BS degree in chemical engineering in June 1942. Joined the IANG, 113th Cav., 1932-36; Horse Drawn FA, Iowa State University, ROTC, 1938-42; commissioned 2nd lieutenant, field artillery, but due to chemical degree he was transferred to chemical warfare service.

Transferred to England in September 1942 and was assigned to the 82nd Abn. TC as CWS officer. Stationed at Folkingham, England, Bapaume and Rheims, France and Germany; and was strafed at Wessel, Germany by jet, heard but not seen.

Discharged Jan. 19, 1946, with the rank of major. Awards include the American Theater, EAME Theater Medals, Purple Heart and Bronze Star.

Worked as a chief engineer for Chem Equipment Co., Los Angeles, CA, 1945-48; chief chemical laboratory, Technicolor Film Corp., 1948-58; Division of Occupational Health, Los Angeles County, 1958-60 and 1965-77; senior engineer, State of California Air Pollution Control, 1960-65; and retired on March 1, 1977.

Has been married more than 49 years and has four children: T.J. Jr., Woodrow, Amy and Donna; and three grandchildren: Corey, Christopher and Catherine.

MAJ TOM W. EMBLETON was born Jan. 3, 1918, in Guthrie, OK. Started schooling in Tucson, AZ. Graduated from University of Arizona in 1941 with a BS degree in horticulture and a ROTC commission as 2nd lieutenant. Ordered to active duty January 1942, CRTC, Ft. Riley, KS. Jan. 22, 1943, married and transferred to the cadre to reactivate the 2nd Cav., Ft. Jackson, SC. While there attended the Advanced Cavalry School at Ft. Riley. Early in 1944 ordered to port of embarkation, went to England and landed on Cherbourg Peninsula on D+40. Became part of the 3rd Army. His Troop F (light tanks) 42nd Sqdn. ended the war in Planice, Czechoslovakia.

Served five campaigns in Europe and was awarded the Purple Heart and Bronze Star. Separated November 1946. Major in Reserves.

Received his Ph.D. (Pomology), Cornell University, 1949. After a brief employment at Prosser, WA, as an assistant horticulturist. Retired December 1986 as professor of horticultural sciences and horticulturist, University of California, Riverside. Currently professor of horticultural sciences, Emeritus.

He feels fortunate that he could participate in such a crucial period of our country and world. He feels lucky

to be a very small member of a team that made it possible for him to assist during the period that he developed a family of four living sons and nineteen grandchildren, and he praises all of them.

J.H. FANNING was born at Camp Halleck, NE, where his father, Thomas J., was a sergeant in Tp. K of the old 1st Dragoons, forerunner of the famous "fighting 1st" Cav. Div. He was riding horses with the troops from Walla Walla, WA, to Lewiston, ID, where the Nez Perce Indian battles occurred, at the age of 10.

Enlisted at the age of 16 in Tp. C, 1st Cav. as a trumpeter. During the following 10 years, he took part in many campaigns against the Sioux Indians. He was a noncommissioned officer in the Apache wars in Arizona. In the Boxer Rebellion, he was a 1st sergeant of Tp. G, 12th Cav., and led the point of attack on the Sacred City of Peking, China.

Re-enlisted in the cavalry when the Spanish-American War began. He was known for his horsemanship, and was selected as a fancy rider in fund-raising shows to provide the Army with its first cots. He was also an expert broadswordsman and marksman and held gold medals for pistol and rifle shooting.

Retired in 1913 but was recalled for WWI service. As a captain in the 26th Yankee Div., he was on the general staff of the American Expeditionary Force in France. He was an Army Reserve major 16 years.

After WWI he was a partner in a bottling works. Later, he was an Army civil service employee at the old Rockwell Field on North Island.

He was a member of John Wesley Green Camp, United Indian War Veterans; San Diego Camp, United Spanish War Veterans; Dawson Post, VFW; Cabrillo Council, Knights of Columbus and the 3rd Order of St. Francis. Served as past national commander of the United Indian War veterans. He retired as an Army captain in 1922 after 35 years of active service, including the Spanish American War, the Boxer Rebellion, the Philippine Insurrection and WWI.

Married Genevieve and has a son, Thomas J.; four grandchildren and a great-grandchild. He passed away in 1965.

COL CHARLES FERGUSSON was born and raised in Texas. While attending the University of Texas and serving in the National Guard, he was Congressman Lyndon Johnson's first appointee to West Point. After graduation, he served with the 11th, 14th, and 16th Cavalry groups. He participated in the Polar Bear Expedition in Canada and served with the 1st Cav. Div. in the Philippines and Japan.

He is a graduate of the Cavalry School, Armor School, CGSC, AWC, Princeton (MPA), and Texas (Ph.D.). He taught at West Point and the AWC. He commanded the 2nd Sqdn., 10th Cav. in Korea and the 14th Cav. at Fulda, Germany. He served in Turkey (HALFSEE), in Belgium (SHAPE) and in OSD. His decorations include the Legion of Merit w/2 OLCs.

In Tokyo he married Peggy Almond. They have three children; Col. Tom Fergusson, Ned Fergusson and Sarah Royal. They reside in retirement at "Fiddlers' Green," a ranch in the Texas hill country.

MGEN ROBERT G. FERGUSSON was born May 20, 1911, in Chicago, IL and spent his early years in Forest Park and Maywood. He entered Beloit College in 1929, joined the Wisconsin National Guard and in the spring of 1932 won an appointment to the US Military Academy at West Point by competitive examination.

Graduated from West Point in 1936 with a commission of 2nd lieutenant of cavalry and was assigned to the 11th Cav. Regt. (horse) at the Presidio of Monterey, CA.

In September of 1936 he joined F Troop at the Presidio, where he met and later married Miss Charlotte Lawrence, the daughter of Col. and Mrs. Charles Gest Lawrence of nearby Carmel. Col. Lawrence had served in the 6th Cavalry Regt.

He and Charlotte lived at the Presidio where he was a troop officer and on the polo and horse show teams. Next they moved to Ft. Winfield Scott in San Francisco where he was aide to Maj. Gen. Henry T. Burgin.

In 1941 they moved with the Burgins to Hawaii. Three months after the Japanese attack at Pearl Harbor they returned to California where as a Major he commanded the 7th Recon. Sqdn. (armored cavalry) attached to the 7th Motorized Div. at San Luis Obispo, CA.

After several months training on the California Desert, the 7th Div. was demotorized and began amphibious training before the Aleutian Campaign. The 7th Recon. Sqdn. was detached; and he was appointed G-2 for the Attu, Kwajalein and Leyte Campaigns. While in the Aleutians their son, Robert C.L., was born.

When the war ended, he had achieved the rank of colonel and was on the staff of the Pacific Command. Then followed routine assignments until the Korean War when he was assigned to the 8th Army in Taiga as deputy G-2 and chief of combat Intelligence. After one year he was ordered to the Army War College as a student and later to command the 14th Inf. Regt. in Hawaii. Following that he was assigned to the staff of the Naval War College.

He was promoted to brigadier general and became assistant division commander of the 24th Inf. Div. in Augsburg, Germany. After one year, promotion to major general followed and duty as chief of staff, Central Army Group (NATO) in Heidelberg. In 1965 he became commander of Ft. Ord and in 1967 the US commandant and the commander of US forces in Berlin. While in Berlin their son, Robert C.L. Fergusson of the 101st Abn. Div., died of wounds received in Vietnam and was given, among other medals, the Distinguished Service Cross for Valor and Leadership. He retired from the Army in 1970.

Awards include Legion of Merit w/OLC, Bronze Star w/3 OLCs, Distinguished Service Medal for Berlin Service in 1970, Knight Commander's Cross w/ Badge and Star, Federal Republic of Germany in 1965, Legion of Honor (Officer) Republic of France in 1973.

CPT FELIPE A. FERNANDEZ was born Aug. 13, 1916, in San Nicolas Pangasinan, Philippines. Graduated from the Pangasinan Academic High School in 1935. He enlisted in Tp. E, 26th Cav. (PS) on Dec. 23, 1936, promoted to corporal in 1939 and to sergeant on Dec. 21, 1941. He was commissioned 2nd lieutenant in the Army Reserves and was called to active duty on Aug.

13, 1946. He was promoted to 1st lieutenant in 1947, relieved from active duty in 1949 and immediately reenlisted as master sergeant.

Was again called to active duty as 1st lieutenant in 1951, promoted to captain in 1953 then relieved from active duty in 1954 and once again re-enlisted as master sergeant. When the super enlisted grades were created, he was promoted to master sergeant (E-8) in 1959 and finally promoted to sergeant major (E-9) in 1965 to become the first sergeant major of the 171st Support Bn. in Ft. Wainright, AK. He held this grade until he completed more than 30 years of active military service when he retired and advanced to the rank of captain on July 1, 1967.

He was then a sergeant and participated in all of the battles that the 26th Cav. fought from Damortis to Bataan. One of those was a river defense in Tayug Pangasinan on Dec. 24, 1941, where he was awarded the Silver Star Medal.

The night before Bataan surrendered he was able to withdraw his platoon to Marevelis, and together with an Antiaircraft Battery, boarded a barge and escaped to Corregidor where he was attached to the 4th Inf. Mar. His platoon was the only combat unit of the 26th Cav. to fight in the last stand to defend the Philippines at Hooker point where he was wounded on the neck and was evacuated to the hospital and taken prisoner with the other patients.

In 1952 when he was called to active duty as 1st lieutenant, he was sent to Korea to join the 21st Inf. Regt. (Gimlets) 24th Inf. Div. He served with the 17th Inf. (Buffalo) of the 7th Inf. Div. and also with the 160th Inf. (Doughboy) of the 40th Inf. Div. when he injured his back during his last combat patrol.

Besides the usual decorations which were authorized for just being present in the theater, he was awarded the Silver Star Medal, two commendation medals (one of which had a v device which was awarded to him for saving a drowning boy in Alaska), the Combat Infantry Badge and the Prisoner of War and Good Conduct Medals.

After his retirement from the Army, he went back to school and earned his bachelor's degree in management at the Golden Gate University of San Francisco. He then worked for the Federal Civil Service for another 20 years enabling him to finance the college education of his five children, one of whom earned a Doctorate degree in philosophy at Vanderbilt University in Tennessee. He and Emilia, his wife for 52 years, are now busy attending fraternal reunions and visiting their children and seven grandchildren.

JAMES L. FIESER was born April 9, 1936, Washington, DC. Attended the University of Georgia, receiving a BA degree. He was in the US Army ROTC at the university.

Worked in commercial real estate sales, leasing and asset management in Maryland, Virginia and Washington, DC area. He has represented such firms at Boston Chicken and Goodyear Aerospace in their business locations. Prior to this period he was in aerospace with Fairchild Industries for 10 years and SAIC International for eight years.

His interest in the US military history goes back to his teenage years when he was very much interested in the US Cavalry history. This interest of several decades

has brought him into many facets of collecting and living history. He currently has one of the largest collections of vintage US Cavalry horse and personnel equipment spanning over a century including over 45 complete and original saddles and all accessories for each item plus 60 bridles and numerous uniforms and weapons from the 1830s to the 1940s.

He is currently a member of the 5th US Cavalry Memorial Regiment located in the Maryland, Pennsylvania area. Through this organization and others, he has participated in national Park Service living history events and displays plus selected reenactments in the Maryland, Virginia, and Pennsylvania area. He has two horses, one having been used by actor Sam Elliott during the three day 130th Brandy Station event in Virginia in July 1993. He is widowed and has no children.

HENRY OSSIAN FLIPPER was born a slave, March 21, 1856, Thomasville, GA. Attended West Point Military Academy, class of 1877, and was the first black graduate. He was commissioned lieutenant in 1877, and assigned to Tp. A, 10th Cav. Regt. Military stations included Ft. Leavenworth, KS, Ft. Sill, OK, and Ft. Davis, TX.

Cashiered on Dec. 8, 1881. He was honorably discharged.

Wrote the book, *The Colored Cadet at West Point*. The Henry Flipper Award is given at West Point and the Henry Flipper Statue can be seen there.

He passed away April 26, 1940, and is buried in the Thomasville Old Magnolia Cemetery, Atlanta, GA.

Submitted by James Alfred Locke Miller Jr.

CAPT EDWIN S. FRANKS was born Nov. 7, 1915, Chicago, IL. Attended Northwestern University and received his BA degree. Joined the US Army in March 1941, 122nd FA, 1932-35. He was stationed in Normandy during the ETO and participated in the Battle of the Bulge. Served with the 62nd QM, 60th Div., in Ardennes, Rhineland, Central Europe.

Discharged in May 1959, with the rank of captain. Awards include the American Theater Ribbon w/4 Battle Clusters, Germany Occupation Medal and WWII Victory Medal (Normandy).

Married Lois V. Franks and has two children and two grandchildren. Worked for Lockheed as a manufacturing engineer and retired on Dec. 30, 1978.

COL WILLIAM B. FRASER was born April 25, 1910, Port Arthur, TX. Graduated high school, Oklahoma, 1928; voted "outstanding member of the class"; received BS degree, West Point, 1932, and ranked first in mechanical engineering and horsemanship; MSME, MIT, 1935, thesis "The Use of X-Ray Diffraction Spectra in Determination of Solid Non-Metallic Inclusions in Centrifugal Castings."

Assumed command in 1932 of marines on the battleship *Wyoming* immediately after graduation from West Point. Assigned to the 8th Cav., 1932-34. He was the first and only winner of the 1st Cav. Div. Hunt Bowl in a two and one-half mile steeplechase. The race was never again contested because the course as prescribed by the then Secretary of State, Henry L. Stimson, was judged unduly hazardous. Assigned 2nd Cav. in 1935; graduated troop officers course, Cavalry School, 1936;

and member of Cavalry School Steeplechase Team, 1936. Assigned to the 13th Cav. (Mechanized), 1936-39; redesigned the cavalry light tank, 1938; and designed and manufactured mobile kitchens for armored cavalry. Graduated School of Advanced Equitation, Ft. Riley, 1940; assigned to the 6th Horse Cav. Mech. (experimental), 1940, and modified motorcycles for military uses; chief, motors department, Cavalry School, 1940-41, and technical advisor, The Cavalry Board; delivered keynote address to the Society of Automotive Engineers (SAE), 1940; commanding officer, 1941-42, Troop A, USMA Cav. Sqdn. and senior instructor in horsemanship, West Point; executive officer, tank regiment (44th AR), 1942-44; deputy G-2, 9th army, 1944-45; chief, intelligence and counter-intelligence, German State of Bavaria, 1947; chief, armor, armament and gun fire control, The Armored Board, (AFFB#2), 1948-51.

Turned down an assignment as special assistant in Armored Warfare to President Harry S. Truman to accept command of the Arctic Research and Test Agency (ATB) in Alaska, 1951-53.

Retired in 1959, 40% disabled, with the rank of colonel.

Married in 1938 and has two children and four grandchildren. As a hobby he designs transistor/electronic circuits. Several of these have been published nationally in *Audio Engineering* or *Audio*.

COL PHILIP S. FREUND was born June 5, 1931, Munich, Germany. Attended the University of Milwaukee, BA degree; and Marquette University, MED. Joined the US Army on March 19, 1951, as a private E-1. Military stations were numerous; served with the HQS INSCOM.

Retired in 1991, with the rank of colonel (O-6). He received the Meritorious Service Medal.

Married Belle Ann and has four children and five grandchildren. Worked as a guidance counselor and teacher until retiring in 1991.

MAJ ALBERT R. FREVELE was born Nov. 19, 1913, in St. Paul, KS, where he graduated high school. Enlisted in the 13th Cav., Ft. Riley, KS on April 30, 1931; honorably discharged April 29, 1934, (ETS); re-enlisted in same organization, September 1934; was transferred from 13th Cav. to 2nd Cav. in 1936 when the 13th was redesignated the 13th Armd. Cav. and the regiment assigned to Ft. Knox, KY. Honorably discharged from 2nd Cav. in 1937; voluntarily transferred to 11th Cav., Presidio of Monterey, CA, April 1938; honorably discharged September 1940, (ETS); re-enlisted in 11th Cav. September 1940; obtained a Reserve commission, second lieutenant, cavalry through the 10-series, Army extension course; discharged Dec. 5, 1941, for convenience of government, to accept extended active duty on Dec. 6, 1941, for a period of one year; on Dec. 10, 1941 service was extended for the duration of the war plus six months.

Upon entering active duty as a commissioned office, he was assigned to the 115th Cav. (H-MECH), at Ft. Lewis, WA. During his assignment to the 115th, attended the advanced officers course at the Cavalry School, Ft. Riley, KS. Upon completion of the course at Ft. Riley, returned to assignment with the 115th Cav. During assignment with the 115th, was promoted to 1st lieutenant in July 1942 and to captain in February 1943.

Duties included assistant supply officer, and later to regimental personnel officer. In October 1943 he was hospitalized at Ft. Lewis and diagnosed as having an ulcer. He was subsequently sent to Harmon General Hospital, Longview, TX, for reevaluation and was found physically unfit for military service and was recommended for relief from active duty.

Upon relief from active duty in June 1945, he subsequently re-enlisted in the Army and was assigned to headquarters, the Cavalry School for duty in the personnel section of the school.

In 1948 was assigned to headquarters US constabulary in Germany. His assignment was chief clerk with the secretary to the general staff. Remained with that assignment through the conversion from constabulary to 7th Army. He was reassigned to the armored center under the command of MG I.D. White in May 1951. Retired for physical disability effective May 31, 1953, with rank of major. Awarded service ribbons for duty.

Memorable experience in the military was the year 1932 when he was assigned to the 13th Cav., at Ft. Riley, KS. All mounted units at the post were ordered on a forced march of 100 miles in 24 hours. There were two regiments of cavalry, 2nd and 13th, plus the headquarters and special troops; one battalion of field artillery, plus contingents from the quartermaster, engineers, signal corps, and veterinary detachment. Our casualties were very low because of the intense training they underwent in preparation for the march. They completed the march in good time, within the hour designated.

Married Carola Ruf on Dec. 17, 1951, and they have three children and five grandchildren. Was an automotive accountant from 1953 to 1981 when he became fully retired.

CHARLES OLIVER FRINKS was born Oct. 26, 1904, in Alexandria, VA. Following his schooling he went to work with the Richmond, Fredricksburg and Potomac Railway at their major facility, Potomac Yards. After several years "riding the cars" as brakeman, he entered apprentice training as a machinist at Fruit Growers Express company's overhaul and repair shops located at Alexandria's Seminary Station.

In 1940 he relocated with his family to Philadelphia to work in the US Navy Yard where he was employed as a machinist turning ship's propellers. Upon America's entry into the war he enlisted in the Regular Army, received basic training at Ft. Leonard Wood and was subsequently assigned to the 8th Recon. Tp., (later squadron), 8th Inf. Div. during its formative and initial training period. In 1943 the squadron was transferred to the 11th Cav. group and redesignated, 44th Cav. mechanized reconnaissance squadron. He was assigned to C Tp., of the 44th and remained there until his death.

The 11th Cav. Gp. was employed during its stay in CONUS guarding strategic fixed facilities and asset on the east coast and undergoing desert training in California and Arizona. The group deployed to England in late

summer 1944, thence onward to the continent later in the year to join 9th Army's XIIIth Corp. The group remained with the XIIIth, performing with distinction for the duration of the war. He was killed in action on April 17, 1945 at Salzwedel, Germany. He now rests in Plot E, Row two, grave 14 in the US Military Cemetery, Margraten, Holland. *Submitted by Charles Purvis Frinks*

MAJ CHARLES PURVIS FRINKS, son of Charles Oliver Frinks, born Sept. 8, 1928, in Alexandria, VA. He attended Hargrave Military Academy, University of Maryland and earned an arts degree from the State University of New York. He enlisted in the Regular Army in 1945, received a direct commission as a 2nd lieutenant armor in 1952, entered the Army Aviation program in 1955 and retired in 1966.

During his years of active duty he served as a mounted rifleman, squad leader, tank commander, platoon leader, troop company, commander, several staff assignments and finished as the Director of Methods of Instruction at the US Army Primary Helicopter School. Ft. Wolters, TX. Units served in: F Trp., 15th Cav. Recon. Sqdn.; Horse Platoon, 15th Constabulary Regt.; 73rd Hvy. Tk. Bn.; 1st Medium Tk. Bn.; 6th Arm. Cav. Regt.; 504th Avn. Co.; 3rd Sqdn. 7th Cav.; 22nd Special Warfare Avn. Det.; 52nd Avn. Bn.; Avn. Co., 6th Special Forces Gp.

While in these various positions and units he served three tours in Germany, one in Korea (1950-51), two in Vietnam (1962-63-64), and briefly in the Dominican Republic (1965). Stateside assignments included tours at Forts Knox, Benning, Bragg and Hood.

Upon retirement from active duty, he joined a defense industry firm and was again subject to overseas tours in Korea (1967-68), Vietnam (1969-70), the Mideast (1974-78) and was present in Saudi Arabia and Kuwait during Desert Storm and Shield and the cleanup period (1990-92). His last overseas assignment was as project manager for a civilian firm that had a contractual requirement to assume responsibility for the accountability, care, storage and maintenance of all US Army equipment left in Kuwait, maintaining it in a ready for issue status for troops deploying to Kuwait for contingency or training purposes.

He now devotes his time to technical writing involving proposals, manuals and procedures.

LTC KENNETH L. FRY was born June 4, 1911, Carlisle, PA. Attended grade school through the eighth grade and received his high school GED. Enlisted in the PANG Jan. 14, 1929, as a private (bugler). Received appointment at 2nd lieutenant, PANGR in June 1939. Accepted appointment to active PANG with Tp. E ad later with Tp. C, 104th Cav. until mobilized for active duty on Feb. 17, 1941, at IGMR.

In May 1941 they were deployed to Co. K, 112th Inf. Regt., 28th Div. In May 1944 he was transferred to HQ, 3rd US Army, G3 section (air liaison) and duty with the 354th Fighter Bomber Gp., USAAF, Maidstone, England.

Attended Ground Liaison Officers School in Meridian, MS for future deployment in the South Pacific Theater. In November 1946 he received orders (RIF) for termination of service in December 1946. In May 1948 he received orders to active duty with the 2nd Armd. Div., Camp Hood, TX. He had various assignments until July 1950. He was then ordered to Camp Pendleton, CA for shipment to Japan and Korea with the 17th Inf. Regt., 7th Div. In Japan he joined the 17th Regt. as battalion executive, 3rd Bn., with LTC Jones form TIS, Ft. Benning, GA.

In July 1951 he received orders to return to the States for duty with AFSA in Washington, DC. He was assigned to S-3 section as liaison officer in joint chief of staff area at the Pentagon. In August 1954 he was transferred to Ft. Devon, MA to attend advanced officer class ASATC. He completed the course ad graduated in April 1955. He was then deployed to ASAEUR for duty with the 6th USASA Field Station at Herzo Base, Bavaria, Germany. In 1957 he was transferred to Ft. Hamilton, NY for termination of active duty.

Re-enlisted in December 1957 in the Regular Army with the grade of sergeant first class (E6), 2nd Army HQs, Ft. Meade, MD. In May 1960 received orders for PCS to USAEUR for assignment to the 14th Armd. Cav. Regt.

In January 1962 he applied for retirement and it was issued stating that April 1, 1962, would be the first day of retirement with the rank of lieutenant colonel. Awards include the Distinguished Unit Citation, French Croix de Guerre w/Palm, American Theater Medal, American Defense Medal, EAME Award, Bronze Stars for Air Defense Europe, Normandy, Northern France, Ardennes and Rhineland, WWII Victory Ribbon, Combat Infantry Badge, ROK Presidential Unit Citation, Korean Service Medal, UN Service Medal, Armed Forces Reserve Medal, four Overseas Bars, National Defense Service Medal and Good Conduct Medal w/Bronze Clasp w/1 Loop.

Married Isabel M., of Shippensburg, PA, Dec. 7, 1930, and had three children and 15 grandchildren. He worked as a machine operator from 1931-41, and retired on April 1, 1962. Isabel passed away Feb. 3, 1967.

CMD SGT LEONARD GADOMSKI was born
July 3, 1919, Cleveland, OH. Attended one year of college, military communication CW and 9th Armored. Joined the Horse Cavalry on June 21, 1941, and was stationed on the Mexican border on patrol and in Central Europe during WWII. Served with the 2nd Cav., 9th Armd.

Discharged Dec. 24, 1945, with the rank of commanding sergeant. He received 12 awards.

Memorable experiences include the 18 months he patrolled the Mexican border with the 2nd Cav, Ft. Riley, KS; and the 18 months in France and Germany with the 9th Armd. Div. During peace time his communication unit also served, breaking the wild horses which came off the plains to the cavalry by Army buyers. As horses were scarce during WWII, the ranchers sold to the Army the wild horses they rounded up, free off the ranges, unbro-

ken. They were shown to the Army buyers with a saddle on and tied to a fence corral as tame and saddle broke. They had surprises.

Worked as a horse breeder and construction contractor until retiring in 1972.

JOSEPH L. GALLOWAY was born Nov. 13, 1941,
in Bryan, TX. He was a war correspondent and author. Assigned to South Vietnam by United Press International 1965-66, 1971, 1973 and 1975. Volunteer rifleman with the 1st Battalion 7th US Cav. at landing zone X-Ray, the Ia Drang Valley, Nov. 14-16, 1965.

In 1990 and 1991, he, then a senior writer with US News and World Report magazine, returned to duty as a war correspondent in the Persian Gulf. Covered 1st Cav. Div. in Operation Desert Shield. In January 1991, was sent by Gen. H. Norman Schwarzkopf to the 24th Inf. Div. (Mech). He accompanied the 24th Mech on its 250 mile attack into the Euphrates River Valley during Operation Desert Storm.

Co-author, with Lt. Gen. Harold G. Moore, (Ret.), of the best selling history, *We Were Soldiers Once....And Young*, a detailed account of the 7th Cav. in the Ia Drang Campaign of 1965, and is co-author of *Triumph Without Victory: The History of the Persian Gulf War*.

He is the only civilian life member of both the 1st Cav. Div. Association and the 7th Cav. Association, and is a member of the Board of Advisers of the 1st Cav. Assn.

Married Theresa M. Null in 1966 and has two sons, Lee, age 17 and Joshua, age 15.

LTC JAMES HALBERT GAMBRELL JR. was
born Feb. 2, 1920, El Paso, TX, where he grew up and was educated until his senior year in high school. He transferred to New Mexico Military Institute, graduated in 1937 and from college in 1939, receiving his certificate of capacity as a 2nd lieutenant in the cavalry. Returned to New Mexico as an instructor of military science and tactics, 1939-40; Texas A&M, 1940 to January 1942. Enlisted on May 19, 1941, and was called to active duty at Ft. Riley and assigned to the 10th Cav., 2nd Cav. Div.

When the division went to North Africa and was deactivated, he was officially the last member of the 10th Cav. He was later assigned to the 1st Armd. Div., 1st Recon Bn. in Italy and on the divisions reorganization to triangle. The division transferred to the 3rd Inf. Div. and went onto Southern France where he acquired three Purple Hearts and a trip to the Leyte Islands for some two years of hospitalization. He later served with the 11th Armd. Cav. and wound up in Army Security Intelligence, from which he retired in 1966 as a lieutenant colonel.

Memorable experience was being coordinator for all intelligence and guerrilla (partisan) activities in the Yellow Sea area of Korea.

Married Edwina, who is now deceased, then married Byrdie Hart. He has three children and three grand-

children. Worked for Americraft, Inc. as president, until retiring in July 1982. Served as vice president of the US Cavalry Assn., 1989-91; past president, El Paso Kiwanis; past lieutenant governor, southwest district Kiwanis; past president, Chavis County, NM sheriff's posse; and past president, El Paso County, TX sheriff's posse.

COL THOMAS D. GILLIS, the son of an Army
officer, was born Oct. 29, 1912, at the Presidio of San Francisco. Following his boyhood in Monterey, he attended West Point and graduated in 1935. After four years of the peacetime Army in the horse cavalry at the Presidio of Monterey, he saw the handwriting on the wall and transferred to armor in 1942. He was ordered to Pine Camp, NY, when the 4th Armd. Div. was activated.

Fought in WWII with the 4th Armd. Div., and in Korea with I Corps and the 25th Inf. Div. Combat assignments; WWI, Asst. G-3, 4th AD and XO, Reserve Command (CC-R), 4th AD Korea-Armor Officer & G-3 Air, HQ, I Corps; XO, 7th Cav. Regt.; deputy assistant division commander, 25th Inf. Div.; commanding officer 24th Inf. Regt.; chief, field training command, KMAG.

Awards include the Silver Star w/OLC, Legion of Merit w/OLC, Bronze Star, Air Medal w/2 OLCs, American Campaign Ribbon, Purple Heart, Distinguished Unit Citation, Republic of Korea Presidential Unit Citation, Croix de Guerre w/2 Palmes, GSC identification badge, Distinguished Marksman Badge, five Overseas Bars. Also eight service medals with numerous battle stars.

Retired in 1965, he served as an officer in Crocker Bank in San Francisco for five years. Since then he has devoted himself to community service, serving in such capacities as director of the local taxpayer's group, founding president of the Revere Chapter, Sons of the American Revolution; president of the California Society, SAR; secretary, Golden Gate Chapter, Veterans of the Battle of the Bulge; and director of the local genealogical society. In addition, he is editor of four newsletters for various groups.

On three separate occasions in combat, he found himself deep behind the enemy lines; shot at but only wounded once, and never captured. As he says, "I led a charmed life. But, more to the point, the last 54 years have been charming...with Billie."

Lives in Greenbrae, CA, with his wife of 54 years, Billie, a native of Ann Arbor, MI. They have two children, Leah and George, and two grandsons.

BG SAMUEL McC. GOODWIN was born Dec. 3,
1916, in New York City, NY, NMMI Ex-37, West Point, 1940, served with the 6th Armd. Cav. 1940-45, rising from junior lieutenant to commander during WWII. This encompassed five major campaigns: Normandy breakout, across France into the Saarland, Ardennes, across the Rhine, pursuit into Czechoslovakia. 1946-47 he activated and commanded the 16th Constabulary Sqdn. in Berlin. He completed all Army schools including The Army and National War Colleges, instructing at The Armor School. He served three tours on Army and Joint Staffs in Washington. In Korea he was G-4 and Chief of Staff 24th Inf. Div.; commanded CCB, 4th Armd. Div. in Germany. As Brigadier General 1965-70 he served as G-1, Army Pacific; senior advisor to CG 1st ROK Army, Korea; CG US Army Berlin Brigade; Dep. CG and Chief of Staff, III US Corps, retiring in 1970.

Awards include; Distinguished Service Medal, Silver Star, Legion of Merit w/2 palms, Bronze Star, Commendation Medal, Distinguished Unit Citation plus numerous service medals.

Married Kiki and has three children and four grandchildren.

CPT JOHN GROETCH was a German immigrant. At the age of 26, in March 1862, he enlisted in Co. D, 10th Minnesota Volunteers. He and his company left Ft. Snelling for Ft. Abercrombie, Dakota territory to relieve the unit there for Civil War service. He was in command on September 3rd, when Dakota warriors began a series of unsuccessful attacks.

After discharge in 1863, he settled in Kelso Township, Sibley County, MN. As developer of New Rome, he was hotel keeper and postmaster. He organized the New Rome Cavalry which thankfully was called to duty only on ceremonial occasions, such as the Centennial celebration of the United States of America on July 4, 1876. *Submitted by Sibley County Historical Society*

SSG ROBERT F. GURKLIES was born Dec. 8, 1925, Covington, OH and attended high school. Joined the 1st Cav. Div. Aug. 15, 1944, and was stationed in the Philippines during the Asiatic-Pacific Theater. Served with the 12th Regt., D Troop.

Discharged Aug. 29, 1946, with the rank of staff sergeant. Awards include the Asiatic-Pacific Theater Ribbon w/2 Bronze Battle Stars, Philippine Defense Ribbon w/Bronze Battle Star, WWII Victory Medal, Good Conduct Medal, and Army of Occupation Medal (Japan).

Married and has four children and three grandchildren. Worked as a postal carrier for 31 years, retiring on Sept. 2, 1983.

WALTER TRUNBULL HALL served in WWI in the 356th Field Remount Sqdn. at Camp Joseph E. Johnston, FL. He considered himself a horse cavalryman, although armistice was declared before a horse was issued to him, which was the day before he was to have sailed for Europe.

He came to New Mexico in 1926 and homesteaded in 1927 with a bushel of chickens and a bushel of pigs. Married Myrtle Campbell and built a log house one mile east of Torrerro, NM.

Memorable experience was walking guard in Florida and the end of the post was the point of a peninsula with a stump at the edge of the water. He figured the stump was a good place to rest and the sergeant of the guard, nor the corporal of the guard, nor the officer of the guard could catch him resting there in the dark, and because anyone approaching would have to

come down that narrow peninsula, unless they came by water. So he modified the general order to "walk my post in a military manner" by resting awhile and by "sitting his post" on the stump by the water's edge. The solitude was ruptured suddenly by the bellow of a bull alligator in the water behind the stump on which he was sitting. He exploded off that stump and immediately began to "walk his post in a military manner."

He passed away Feb. 26, 1994.

MGEN PETER CONOVER HAINS III was born May 11, 1901, Boston, MA. Commissioned on June 12, 1924, USMA, West Point, NY, as 2nd lieutenant. Assignments were Troop A, 7th Cav., 1924-27; and 1st Armd. Regt., July 1942 to July 1943.

Discharged on June 1, 1961, Ft. Meade, MD, with the rank of major general. Awards include the Distinguished Service Medal, Silver Star, Legion of Merit, Legion-Air w/2 OLCs, Bronze Star Medal w/OLC, Purple Heart, American Defense Service Medal, American Campaign Medal, Asiatic-Pacific Campaign Medal, EAME Campaign Medal, WWII Victory Medal, National Defense Service Medal, Order of SUVOROV USSR, Order of Military Merit Mexico, War Cross w/Palm (France, Croix de Guerre), Order of the Oak Crown Officer; Luxembourg (Order de La Couronne de Chene) and general staff and department to defense identification badges.

Memorable experiences were of the US Olympic Teams, 1928-32; North Africa, May 30, 1942; Normandy of VE-Day, 1944-45; and the Philippines to V-J Day.

Married Bernard Montgomery (Ada) and has four children: Peter, Ada Louise, Joan and Frederick.

JOSEPH L. HAMILTON was born Feb. 13, 1930, Los Angeles, CA. He received his high school GED in the US Army after enlisting on May 7, 1946, at 16 years of age. As sergeant first class he spent 20 years in the Arm of which 12 years were overseas in such places as Germany, Africa, Korea, Japan and Vietnam.

While in the service he participated in six major campaigns, three in Korea and three in Vietnam. Among his 13 decorations are the Air Medal, Bravery Gold Medal of Greece, Parachute and Glider Badge.

Served with a number of airborne, cavalry, armored and other ground units which included the 7766th Horse Tp., US Constabulary, 1948-49, until the mission of patrolling the east German and Czechoslovakian border.

Upon retirement from the Army in 1966 he spent 23 years with the US Post Office, retiring Nov. 30, 1989. He has been married to Ingrid for over 36 years and has three children and three grandchildren.

TSGT JOHN C. HARMON was born May 8, 1922, Altus, OK. He has a BS, MS and Ph.D. degree. Joined the US Army Cavalry on Aug. 4, 1940. Stations included New Guinea, Bismarck, Archipelago, south Philippines and Luzon, serving with the 8th Cav.

Discharged Aug. 19, 1945, with the rank of technical sergeant. Awards include the Bronze Star w/OLC, Combat Infantry Badge, Philippine Liberation Medal w/ 2 Bronze Stars, Good Conduct Medal, Southwest Pacific Campaign Ribbon w/4 Bronze Stars and American Defense Service Ribbon.

Memorable experiences were of being in the first

wave of every landing in the southwest Pacific as a platoon leader of the 604th.

Married and has two children and five grandchildren. Worked as an associate professor of biology, Oklahoma Higher Education Division. Retired in June 1986.

CAPT CHARLES J. HARNEY was born Aug. 26, 1922, Brooklyn, NY. He attended three and one-fourth years of college. Joined the cavalry in September 1940. Stations included Mars Task Force; Central Burma Campaign; Ft. Riley, KS; Ft. Brown, TX. Served with the Cavalry School 44th; Horse Officer Class; 124th Cav. Regt.; Mars Task Force; and China Liaison.

Discharged in February 1948 with the rank of captain. Awards include the Combat Infantry Badge and Purple Heart w/cluster.

Memorable experiences include the march through Central Burma; interaction with the Vietnamese and Japanese at the conclusion of the war.

Married Anna Lou Taylor over 50 years ago, and has six children and 13 grandchildren. Worked in sales for The Bonden County Sales, Medical Reference books, W.B. Saunders. He retired in 1984.

JOHN R. HART was born June 14, 1917, Westbrook, TX. Was inducted Feb. 19, 1941, Lubbock, TX, and assigned to the 1st Cav. Div. Participated in Luzon, New Guinea, Bismarck Archipelago and the Southern Philippines.

Was sent overseas July 3, 1943, to Australia. Returned to the States Sept. 23, 1945.

Discharged Sept. 29, 1945, with the rank of sergeant. Awards include the Good Conduct Medal, Asiatic-Pacific Service Medal, American Defense Service Medal and Philippine Liberation Medal.

COL WILLIAM LANGHORNE HASTIE was born June 18, 1921, in Monrovia, CA, and raised in nearby Glendora. Since his enlistment in the Regular Army in August 1941, he has served in the Cavalry

(CRTC and in the 10th Cav.), Infantry, QMC and Military Intelligence.

In addition to being stationed at many US posts during his career, Hastie has served in Morocco, Algeria, Italy, Korea, Japan and Thailand. He put in four years on the faculty of the Army Intelligence School and seven years as a Professor or Assistant Professor of Military Science at two civilian universities. Another nine years were spent on the staffs of joint commands (i.e., four years with the defense atomic support agency and three years on the staff of CINCPAC).

College degrees earned were; an AA from Citrus College, BA from Stanford and a master of liberal arts from John Hopkins. His military education includes his graduation from Army Command and General Staff College, Armed Forces Staff College and the Industrial College of the Armed Forces. Some of his decorations are; the Legion of Merit, Bronze Star ("v") w/cluster, Purple Heart, Army Meritorious Service Medal, Joint Service Commendation Medal and the Combat Infantryman's Badge.

He retired in 1972 in the grade of colonel, Regular Army, after completing over 30 years of service. He then worked as a staff employee of the University of Southern California for 14 years. He is now a volunteer with a charity which feeds the needy, and is located near his home in Pismo Beach, CA.

Married Gail Peirce in 1948 and their son, Scott, was born in 1956. He is a member of the 9th and 10th (Horse) Cavalry Association and a charter member of the US Cavalry Association in which he served on the Board of Directors for a four year period.

SP/4 RICHARD HAWK was born July 31, 1947, Washburn, IL; moved to Sisseton, SD, 1950, where he was raised on a farm. Graduated high school at Sisseton, SD in 1965. He was drafted into the US Army on Oct. 27, 1966, and attended basic and AIT at Ft. Riley, KS, and held the MOS of armor.

Was sent to Troop A, 3rd Sqdn, 4th Cav. at Cu Chi, South Vietnam on July 31, 1967. Served on personal carriers the first six months and then the last six months on A27 tanks in Saigon, Hoc Mor, Tap Ninh Hobo Wood, Ben-Suc, Bo Loi, Godau Ha, Michelin Plantation, Dau Tieng, Trang Bang, Cho Lon.

Discharge July 26, 1968, in California with the rank of SP4. Awards include the National Defense Service Medal, Vietnam Campaign Medal, Vietnam Service Medal and Army Commendation Medal w/V Device.

LINDSEY P. HENDERSON JR. was born July 14, 1922. The Hussars were the traditional Henderson family guard unit which was organized by Gen. James Edward Oglethorpe, Feb. 13, 1736, and continues existence today as a hereditary organization. His great-grandfather, Charles B. Patterson, fought with Co. B of the Hussars under Gen. Joe Wheeler in the Army of Tennessee during the war between the states.

His great-granduncle, Lt. John Ash, fought with Co. A in the Jeff Davis Legion, Army of Northern Virginia under Gen. J.E.B. Stuart. His uncle, BG A. Lester Henderson, was captain of the Hussars ad his father, Lindsey P. Henderson Sr. was also a member. He was the last member of the family to be in the troop and as squadron bugler, he blew taps the night before the horses were taken away. His son, Charles W. Henderson, was the last member of the family in the troop, then a battery of field artillery.

He enlisted in Tp. A, 108th Cav., GANG in May 1940. He was working on an appointment, through the guard, to the US Military Academy at West Point, NY. Called to service in February 1941, and his unit was the first American battalion to go into action against the Japanese in the Southwest Pacific area in Papua, New Guinea in May 1942.

During WWII he received a battlefield appointment as a 2nd lieutenant, was wounded and could not pass the physical. He was later disabled out of service.

Just before graduation from the University of Virginia, he passed a physical and received his commission. He was called to active duty in the Pentagon in January 1949 and worked under Gen. Omar Bradley. He was the first "editor of the officers' call" and the only 2nd lieutenant on active duty in the Pentagon.

Transferred to Ft. Benning, to Infantry School and the 30th Inf. Regt. From there to Japan and the 31st Inf. Regt. When the Korean War conflict broke out, he immediately volunteered and was transferred to the 21st Inf. Regt., 24th Inf. Div., which was fighting desperately to stem the North Korean advance. He was assigned to Co. L, a truly great, hard fighting unit. He was wounded and evacuated to Japan and the States.

After hospitalization, he was assigned to a special operations unit as he excelled in Unconventional Warfare. Then on to Taiwan, Matsu and Quemoy, Indo China, Vietnam, Cambodia and Laos. After all that, a return to mundane duties as a sub-sector commander to the USAR, in his hometown of Savannah, GA. There he trained infantry, transportation and medical units. He recruited, organized and trained a fine USAR Special Forces Detachment.

He was then assigned to the 513th Military Intelligence Group at Camp King and then on to Berlin to command the 513th Military Intelligence Unit there. After a year he was returned to Camp King as deputy group commander. On his return to the States, he was hospitalized and retired on the disability list.

A Combat Infantryman and Paratrooper, his decorations include the Silver Star w/3 OLCs, the Bronze Star w/V device and OLC, the Army Commendation w/OLC, Purple Heart w/3 OLCs, Presidential Unit Badge WWII and OLC (Korea), Combat Stars for WWII, Korea and Vietnam. He also received the Freedom's Foundation of Valley Forge, PA George Washington Patriots award in 1966. He received additional Freedom Foundation Awards in 1972 and 1978. He received the top "Commendation" from the American Assn. of State and Local History and is a Fellow and governor of the Company of Military Historians. He has written for the Combat Forces Journal *Company L's Four Days* and *My ROKS Were Good.*

He is married to the former Eve Whitfield of Savannah and they have four children: Lindsey P. III, Charles W., Susannah H. Fawcett and Eve Elizabeth; and five grandchildren. He is a member of many civic and patriotic organizations.

CAPT WILLIAM A. HENDRICKSON JR. was born Jan. 18, 1919, Boston, MA. Attended Massachusetts State College receiving a BS degree. Joined the cavalry in June 1941. Stations included Europe; Ft. Myers; Ft. Benning; Ft. Riley; Ft. Gordon; Ft. Oglethorpe; and Ft. Knox. Served with the 3rd Cav., 10th AD, 777th Tank Bn. Discharged in 1945 with the rank of captain.

Memorable experiences include the capture of Leipzig; and accepting Gen. SS, surrender and sword.

Married Martha (Jane) and has four children and eight grandchildren. Served as president of W.A. Hendrickson Co., an electronic manufacturing agent, until retiring in 1984.

BGEN FRANK SHERMAN HENRY was born in Cambridge in 1909, the worthy heir of great American families. His mother was descended from Gov. William Bradford of the "Mayflower". Young Frank may have inherited his military spirit from his paternal grandfather, James Alexander Henry, who served as an enlisted man in the 123rd New York Volunteer Inf. in the Civil War.

Sherm, as he was called, was too light to be more than a sub on the outstanding Cambridge football teams of the 1920s. He played well when called upon, but football was not his first sport. His first loyalty was to riding horses, a passion he inherited from his father. That passion included an ambition to become a cavalry officer, an ambition realized when he was appointed to the US Military Academy at West Point in 1929.

He graduated in 1933, and when duties with the 3rd Cav. Regt. in Ft. Myer, VA permitted, he participated in numerous equestrian events. It was obvious that Henry had a special talent.

Plans to compete in the 1940 Olympics were canceled by the coming of WWII. Henry graduated from the Command and General Staff School, and taught there for a period before assignment to the Joint Chiefs of Staff War Plans Committee. In 1945, he served in the headquarters of Gen. Douglas MacArthur.

The war over, Henry made the US Equestrian Team, and in the 1948 Olympic games in England, finally earned the recognition denied him by the war eight years earlier.

He won one gold and two silver medals. His record of three equestrian medals has been equaled only once. After the Olympics, Henry had many staff, command, and diplomatic assignments before retiring as chief of staff, III Corps at Ft. Hood, TX in 1963. Awards include the Legion of Merit w/OLC and the Korean Order of Service Merit, 3rd class.

His retirement years were spent as a judge for the American Horse Show Assn. and work with disadvantaged children. In 1989, Gen. Henry passed away.

Submitted by Joan H. Gooding

COL ALBERT L. HETTRICH was born Sept. 29, 1909, Gladstone, ND. Attended high school and one year of college in North Dakota. Enlisted July 21, 1931, in the cavalry and ordnance. He served six campaigns in Korea.

Served active service with Tp. B, 11th US Cav., 1931-40; 1940-44, instructor and branch chief automotive section, Ordnance School, AGP, MD; 1944-46, commanding officer of the 628th Ord. Bn., CBI Theater, Chabua, India; 1946-47, commanding officer, 328th Ord. Bn., Ft. Lewis, WA; 1947-49; member of the 6th Army Ord. staff, Presidio of San Francisco, CA; 1949-51, senior ordnance advisor on the Korean military advisory group staff, Seoul, Korea; 1951-53, commander, ordnance base shop, Atlanta General Depot, Atlanta, GA; 1953-55, Commandant Ordnance Automotive School, Atlanta General Depot, Atlanta, GA; and 1955-57, 46th Ord. Gp, Presidio of San Francisco, CA. He was often with Korean troops at the battalion level during battles both in the advances to Kunuri in North Korea and over the South Korean fronts in South Korea.

Memorable experiences include being a member of the KMAG from June 1949 to October 1950; being a member of the 11th Cav. Horse Show team, US Cav. Rifle and Pistol team at Camp Perry and the US Army 11th Cav. Provisional Plt.

Awards include the American Defense Service Medal, American Campaign Medal, Asiatic-Pacific Campaign Medal, WWII Victory Medal, National Defense Service Medal, Korean Service Medal, UN Service Medal, Armed Froces Reserve Medal, Distinguished Military Service Medal, ROK Presidential Unit Citation, Bronze Star, Legion of Merit and Meritorious Unit Commendation.

Married Katharine and has three children and six grandchildren. Worked as a cost accountant at the USAFB, Portland. Retired from the US Army July 21, 1957, and the civil service in 1973.

COL GEORGE F. HOGE

COL GEORGE F. HOGE was born Jan. 1, 1925, Alexandria, VA. Attended USMA, Naval War College, and received a MA in International Religion (GWU). Joined the cavalry armor on June 5, 1945. Stations included Korea; Hood; Europe, Vietnam, West Point and Ft. Leavenworth. Served with the 66th Tank, 14th ACR, 15th Armor.

Discharged on Aug. 1, 1975, with the rank of colonel. Awards include the Legion of Merit, Distinguished Flying Cross and Bronze Star.

Memorable experiences include being commanding officer of F Co., 14th ACR; 15th Armor; executive officer of 1st Sqdn, 14th ACR.

Married Gloria Bishop and has two children and six grandchildren. Served as Master of Foxhounds, Ft. Leavenworth Hunt, 1974-93. Retired on Aug. 1, 1975.

LTC LAWRENCE M. HOLMAN

LTC LAWRENCE M. HOLMAN was born April 1, 1912, Newton, KS; attended high school and six months of Business School, Wichita, KS. Joined the cavalry on Dec. 26, 1932. During WWII was stationed in France and with the Occupation of Army in Japan. Served with the MG Troop, 2nd Cav., Co. E, Troop 8th Cav.

Retired in 1957 with the rank of lieutenant colonel. He was awarded the Bronze Star.

Memorable experiences include serving as assistant chief of staff under Jumpin' Joe Collins with station at the Pentagon.

Married Elsie R. Holman, Feb. 6, 1936, and had one son, who was killed in an auto accident in his senior year at West Point. Worked for the US Army Security Agency, GS-14, for 10 years, until retiring in June 1967.

1ST LT EARLE T. HOLSAPPLE JR.

1ST LT EARLE T. HOLSAPPLE JR. was born Dec. 4, 1916, Troy, NY. Received MBA degree from Princeton University, Princeton, NJ. Joined the cavalry in January 1940. Stations included Ft. Devens, MA, 101st Cav., January 1940 to January 1942; Ft. Riley, KS, OCS, 1943; Camp Lockett, CA; North Africa, 1944; and Italy, 1944. Was held POW by the Germans, from April to May 1945.

Discharged in December 1945 with the rank of 1st lieutenant.

Memorable experiences were being taken POW in April 1945, in Bologna, Italy and being released by the Americans near Bolzano, Italy in May 1945.

Married Jane E. Holsapple and has three children and six grandchildren. Served as former chairman of the Board of American Diabetes Association, New Jersey affiliate; member of The National Board of The American Diabetes Association; board member and treasurer of The House of Good Sheperd, a non-profit home for the aging; trustee and chairman of The Development Committee of Centenary College, Hackettstown, NJ. Worked as president, CEO and served as chairman and consultant to Welsh Farms, Inc., Long Valley, NJ.

SP4 KENNETH P. HORNBY

SP4 KENNETH P. HORNBY was born July 22, 1960, Davenport, IA. Joined the US Army in June 1985, through the delayed entry program and entered active duty in November 1985. Trained at Ft. Knox, KY and was stationed at Bamberg, West Germany from April 1986. Served with H Co., 2nd Sqdn., 2nd ACR.

Discharged Nov. 11, 1987, with the rank of SP4. Awards include the Army Commendation Medal, Army Achievement Medal w/2 OLCs and Good Conduct Medal.

Memorable experiences include patrolling East German and Czech borders, which was fascinating. Aside from training (gunnery and maneuvers), this was their job. Of the 19 months he spent in Germany, something like 14 months were spent in the field. He would not trade his experiences for anything.

Married Janice A. Rieder in 1992. Presently works as a human resources generalist in St. Paul, MN and is a current member of the US Cavalry Association.

MAJ EDWARD M. HOUSE II

MAJ EDWARD M. HOUSE II was born Aug. 23, 1912, Houston, TX. Attended the University of Texas for three years; special assignments Exxon and real estate broker. Joined the 56th Cav. Bde., in 1932 and the 124th Cav. Regt., on Nov. 29, 1939. Attended Artillery School at Ft. Sill, OK, and served with the 264th Arty. Discharged in 1957 with the rank of major.

Memorable experiences include being platoon sergeant of the 124th; squadron bugler, 56th Brigadier School Troops Mtr. Officers, Ft. Sill, OK, S4, 264th FA.

Married Jerome and worked for Exxon. He retired in 1990.

COL HARRY JENKINS HUBBARD

COL HARRY JENKINS HUBBARD was born Dec. 1, 1909, Devisadero, El Salvador. Enlisted with the field artillery on June 12, 1934, West Point, NY. Served with D Btry., 82nd FA, August 1934 to March 1937. Participated in many artillery and cavalry exercises at Ft. Bliss and in the 1st Cav. Div. maneuvers in the Marfa, TX area in 1936.

Served as commanding officer of the 325th FA BN, 84th Inf. Div., June 1943 to April 1945; Div. Arty., S-3, 84th Inf. Div., April 1945 to September 1945; Rhineland, Ardennes-Alsace and Central Europe Campaigns. C and GSC, Armed Forces Staff College, AWC; artillery support for the 113th Cav. Gp. (Wm. S. Biddle), Nov. 25, 1944 to Dec. 20, 1944; artillery support for the 4th Cav. Gp. (John McDonald) Jan. 2 to 15, 1945; and artillery reinforcement for the 2nd Armd. Div. Task Force (I.D. White), Jan. 16 to 21, 1945.

Discharged July 31, 1958, Ft. Bliss, TX, with the rank of colonel. Awards include the Silver Star, Bronze Star, Legion of Merit and Army Commendation Medal w/OLC.

Married Charlotte Hanson and has five children: Harry J. III, Jeffrey H., Carolyn Chamberlain (Mrs. Craig R.), Bruce B. and Barbara McDonald (Mrs. Clement J.).

COL GEORGE BAIRD HUDSON

COL GEORGE BAIRD HUDSON was born Feb. 5, 1897, Portsmouth, OH. Entered West Point in 1915 and graduated three years later in June 1918 under the curriculum known as the War Emergency Course. Upon graduation he was commissioned in the Cavalry and was sent for training to the Infantry School of Arms at Ft. Sill, and on to the 7th Cav. at Ft. Bliss, commanded by Col. Tommy Tompkins. His service included occupation duty in France and Germany and subsequent cavalry troop assignments in the States with the 1st, 3rd, 7th and 8th Cavalry's.

The years just before WWII brought faster promotions and rapidly increasing responsibilities. In preparing for modern war, he commanded cavalry units that evolved into mechanized and tank destroyer units.

During the war, he served in England with the XXth US Army Corps as it prepared to open the second front in France. Postwar duties included occupation duty both in Japan and Germany and at Ft. Knox, KY, where he retired in 1953 after 35 years in the Army he loved. Medals and decorations include the WWI Victory Medal, Army of Occupation of Germany Medal-WWI, American Defense Service Medal, EAME Service Medal, American Campaign Medal, Asiatic-Pacific Service Medal, WWII Victory Medal, Army of Occupation Medal w/Clasp-Japan, Germany, WWII, National Defense Medal, Expert Marksmanship Badges for Rifle, Pistol-D, Pistol-M, Sword, Submachine Gun and Machine Gun.

Some of his most enjoyable professional experiences include the two times his troops won the Goodrich Trophy, 1919 and 1930, having been recognized as the best cavalry units in the Army. In 1927, Tp. E, 3rd Cav. was selected to lead the parade in Washington, DC welcoming Charles Lindbergh following his famous trans-Atlantic flight.

After retirement he was active in the El Paso area. He continued to serve his nation and his fellow man as a volunteer for the American Heart Assn., the School for Exceptional Children and the Humane Society. His ties to the Army were strengthened by his memberships in the West Point Society, the ROA, the Assn. of the US Army and the US Horse Cavalry Assn.

Married Lucie-Belle Snyder of Marfa, TX, on June 12, 1924, and had two children, six grandchildren and nine great-grandchildren. He passed away June 4, 1986.

SFC JAMES G. HUDSON was born Feb. 4, 1948, St. Louis, MO. Attended New York State and received an associate's degree. Joined the US Army Feb. 20, 1967. Stationed at Korea and Germany, three tours; Ft. Hood; Ft. Leonard Wood; and Ft. Bliss. Served with the 2nd/14 ACR; 2nd/64 Armor; 2nd/67 Armor and 3rd ACR/ and 2nd ACR. Discharged with the rank of sergeant first class.

Memorable experiences include all the places he served and side visits, each person he met, returning home and being inducted in 1978 into the Old Bill Assn. at Ft. Bliss, TX, 3rd Armd. Cav. Regt.

COL WILLIAM EUGENE HUDSON was born Nov. 9, 1913, Athens, GA. Graduated Athens High School, 1931; University of Georgia, BSLL, 1935; MSAE, 1938. Joined ROTC, graduated, 2nd Lt. Cav., Nov. 9, 1934, joining the US Army mechanized cavalry. Entered active duty March 2, 1942, joining the 15th Cav. Regt., April 10, 1942. Stations included Kansas, Texas, California, New York, England, France, Belgium, Holland, Germany and four campaigns in the ETO.

Discharged from WWII on Feb. 4, 1946; USAR, May 27, 1966, with the rank of colonel. Awards include the Bronze Star, French Croix de Guerre, ETO w/5 stars and Army Commendation Medal.

Memorable experiences include the Louisiana maneuvers, California desert; training overseas on the *Queen Mary*; combat in Brittany, France, Ruhr Valley and Germany; peace time at Ft. Leavenworth, KS; 50th anniversary trip back to Brittany, France.

Married Mary Virginia Aycock, June 1936, and has two children and three grandchildren. Worked as instructor, assistant professor, associate professor; professor director; campus planning, for the University of George. Retired on Dec. 31, 1981.

MAJ JAMES M. HUEY was born July 17, 1916, in Union, KY; and graduated Louisville Medical School in 1940. Entered service March 28, 1942, with 90th Inf.

Div., Camp Barkley, TX, transferred to 124th Cavalry, Ft. Brown October 1942. Served in border posts until going overseas July 1944. Served as squadron surgeon with Mars Task Force throughout Burma Campaign, then to China where unit was demobilized May 1945. Later served with 50th Portable Surgical Hospital Unit in 52nd Chinese army and in Internment Camp in Shanghai. Returned home as major, November 1945 and went on inactive status Feb. 28, 1946.

Awards include Bronze Star, Asiatic-Pacific Ribbon w/4 stars, Decorations from Chinese Combat Command, 52nd Army and Chinese government.

Most memorable experiences include march through Burma, carrying casualties on litters, wading the same river seven times one day; combat overlooking the Burma road where they had many casualties, including Jack Knight who was awarded Medal of Honor posthumorously, and his brother, Curtis, who was critically wounded but survived.

Married a nurse, Cordella Turner in 1940; and practiced medicine in Walton, KY, until 1989. Has two children and two grandchildren.

LTC FRED HUGHES JR. was born March 12, 1918, in Poolesville, MD. He graduated from the University of Maryland where he was active in the ROTC. Upon graduation he was commissioned a major in the US Army and assigned to Ft. Bliss, TX in 1940.

During WWII he served on the staff of Gen. Douglas MacArthur in the invasion of the Philippine islands. For Action in the Pacific he was decorated with a Silver Star for valor in the invasion of Leyte Island, with a Bronze Star for heroic

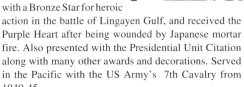

action in the battle of Lingayen Gulf, and received the Purple Heart after being wounded by Japanese mortar fire. Also presented with the Presidential Unit Citation along with many other awards and decorations. Served in the Pacific with the US Army's 7th Cavalry from 1940-45.

After the war in the Pacific, he resumed his civilian life and pursued his favorite activity, horses. He was a skilled rider and won many awards enjoying his favorite sport. He was active as a judge with the American Horse Show Association and was inducted into the Hall of Fame for the Maryland Horse Show Association in 1986.

It was through the love of horses and the cavalry that he met Mr. Busch of the Anheiser Busch Brewery in 1954. This friendship led to an opportunity for him to become the beer distributor for Anheiser Busch Company in 1970. At that time he founded H-H of Savannah, Inc., and has many awards of excellence from Anheiser Busch and the Savannah community. Mayor John Rousakis proclaimed Dec. 12, 1989, "Fred Hughes Day" in Savannah, GA. Over the years he has provided hundreds of jobs for Savannah residents and has always been there for his fellow veteran. The Vietnam veterans will always appreciate him for his support for the Vietnam Memorial on Bay Street, Savannah, GA.

It is with pride and great honor that the members of the Vietnam Veterans of America, Chapter 671, Savan-

nah, GA name their annual golf tournament "The Fred Hughes Golf Classic."

MAJ HUGH R. HUGHES was born Sept. 25, 1919, Cushing, OK. Attended high school; college; Cavalry School; and Communications School. Joined the cavalry in May 1940. Stations included the Southwest Pacific, New Guinea, North Britain and Philippines. Served with the 8th Cav., 112th Regt.

Discharged in November 1944 with the rank of major. Received the Combat Infantry Badge.

Memorable experiences include commanding the last regular line troop horse cavalry in New Caledonia.

Married and has one child and two grandchildren. Owned and managed a building supply company until retiring in 1987. His wife is deceased.

LTC WARREN E. HUGUELET was born Feb. 24, 1912, in Chicago, IL. Attended NMMI Jr. College along with Northwestern University and received a BS degree in 1934 and an MBA degree in 1934.

Drafted March 28, 1941, as 1st Lt. by 1st Armd. Div. (1AD), Ft. Knox, KY, May 1941 and promoted to captain's assistant S-3, HQs 1st Armd. Bde. On 1941 maneuvers, Louisiana and Carolina, developed liaison techniques, nicknamed Shadow. Initiated flank attack on 2AD as it neared Shreveport. Then declined a transfer to Army HQs. In a Carolina exercise, with number of future ADs (4-8) at stake, deploying and capturing Pee Dee bridge with just advance guard of 1AD tied up entire Army. Total of 16 ADs authorized. Rated S.

January/February 1942 acting executive officer, Combat Command A. Then recommended for major, GSC, Asst. G-3, Hqs 1 AD plus LO duty to V Corps, Ft. Dix, NJ. Also functioned as V corps assistant G-3 and their senior LO in Northern Ireland. Sole drafter of V Corps cross channel invasion plans (Operation Sledgehammer) August 21, 1942, which were tabled by Torch Div. LO to ports of Larne and Oran. Reported as Combat LO to HQs II Corps Jan. 21, 1943 for Operation Satin (Sfax) but situation became defensive. About 0800 hours, Feb. 23, 1943, put in charge of II Corps. Immediately ordered all of 1 AD to attack Kasserine Pass, and later XII Air Support Command to bomb Pass. Granted transfer HQs 1st Armd. Regt. (1 AR) March 1, 1943. Leading a CC A attack in vicinity Station de Sened March 22, 1943 jeep was demolished by anti-tank mine. Purple Heart awarded. Continued as S-3 to Tunis, then hospitalized. Elected to return to 1 AR and Italian campaigns. Regimental nickname Overlay Huguelet. Recommendations at Anzio Jan. 31, 1944 provided for timely defense of beachhead. Recommended use of four snakes in breakout May 23, 1944, by CC A. Objective taken on time, one killed, two wounded. September 1944 rotated to HQs the Armd. Center, Ft. Knox, KY. Became assistant G-3, Chief of Organization and Doctrine (Top Tactician), rated Superior, recommended for promotion to lieutenant colonel, earned Army Commendation Award and Victory Medals. Reverted to Reserves Dec. 16, 1945.

CPL ARTHUR B. HUNTER was born April 11, 1924, in Long Beach, CA. Grew up in Riverside county with his family moving quite a few times during his childhood. Coming from a family of six children during the great depression made education past high school unthought of. Was employed by Douglas Aircraft as an instrument installation assembler from 1942 until September 1944 when he was called to serve his country.

Reported to Ft. Ord, CA; was transferred to Ft. Riley for basic training and then back to Ft. Ord, CA; ordered to Ft. Hood, TX; Ft. Reno, OK, to break mules for packing; then after training the mules they were shipped to New Orleans, LA, and pastured in a pasture at Westwego awaiting orders. Orders came to ship mules to France; again, orders were changed. With the war ending in France, the mules and he returned to Ft. Riley, KS. He was ordered to report to Ft. Ord, then was shipped to Layta, Philippines and at that time was assigned to the 24th Div. FA BN. He also was shipped to Japan.

On Oct. 31, 1946, was honorably discharged from the US Army as a corporal, 63rd FA BN.

Retired from the Norwalk, LA, Mirada School District as bus driver and mechanic to purchase Hunter's Camp Williams. Moved from there to settle in the Kern River Valley in Kern County, CA, with his wife, Christine. They now run their business, the Hillside Horse Boarding Stables.

They have two sons Gary Arthur and Roy William; four grandchildren; and one great grandson. Just a small note, his father was also a cavalryman taking his cavalry placement training at Ft. Riley, KS, in 1904. He was a corporal of Troop E of the seventh regiment of the US Cavalry.

COL CLARK OSTROM IRVING

COL CLARK OSTROM IRVING was born Oct. 16, 1923, in Washington DC. He was raised on Army posts; graduated from high school at El Paso, TX; attended Texas A&M College for two years; received his BS from the University of Maryland; MS from Montana State University-Billings, and Certificate of Theological Study from Episcopal Theological Seminary Austin, TX. Had military schooling at cavalry, armor, infantry and airborne schools, Command and General Staff College, Armed Forces Staff College and the Army War College.

Received his commission from the Cavalry School Aug. 12, 1943, followed by service with the 115th Cav. Regt. and attendance at the War Department Military Intelligence School. Volunteered for service with the 1st Cav. Div. in the Admiralty Islands followed by the invasion of the Philippine Islands Oct. 20, 1944. He joined the 8th Cav. Regt. on Samar just prior to the Luzon campaign and served as a platoon leader in G Tp.

Led his platoon in the flying columhn as part of the 2nd Sqdn.'s run for Manila and was severely wounded the night of Feb. 3, 1945, but continued to fight until his wounds rendered him unconscious. He was evacuated back to Ft. Bliss where he was hospitalized for two years,

then returned to the 8th Cav. in January 1947 and served as a troop and squadron commander until 1949. He continued to serve in cavalry, armor, infantry and armored divisions primarily in command positions. He served in the Korean War as a tank company commander, regimental S-3, and as an infantry battalion XO, followed by staff and command positions in Japan, US and in Germany.

Served as division signal officer, staff officer at Dept. of Army level and commander of all signal troops in Alaska and as DCSOPS, USA Stratcom, Fort Huachuca, AZ at the time of his retirement in the rank of colonel. Awards include the Silver Star, Legion of Merit, two Bronze Stars, three Purple Hearts, Army Commendation Medal, WWII Victory Medal, American Campaign, AP Campaign, Philippine Liberation, Philippine Distinguished Service Star, Army of Occupation, National Defense w/OLC, Korean Service, UN Service Medal, Presidential Citation (US and Philippine), Vietnam Service and his most cherished awards, the Combat Infantry Badge 2nd Award and Parachute Infantry Badge.

He has been married to Aylett Griffin Irving for over 48 years, has five children (three deceased), and four grandsons. Civilian employment includes guide and outfitting, elementary country school teacher, an ordained deacon and priest in the Episcopal Diocese of Montana. He retired in 1989.

BG ALBIN F. IRZYK

BG ALBIN F. IRZYK graduated from the University of Massachusetts, 1940. Commissioned 2nd lieutenant cavalry and was a career Army officer. Served in 3rd US Cav. Regt. and commanded 8th Tk. Bn., 4th Armd. Div.; participated in five campaigns in Europ and was wounded twice. After the war, was G-1, G-3 and chief of staff, 4th Armd. Div.

Commanded the famed 14th Armd. Cav. Regt. along Iron Curtain during Berlin crisis, 1961. Headed the US Army Armor School, Ft. Knox, KY, 1965-67.

Served two years (seven campaigns) in Vietnam, 1967-69, the second as asst. div. comdr., 4th Inf. Div. Was deputy commander, Ft. Dix, NJ, and commanding general, Ft. Devens, MA. Graduate of the National War College and holds a master's degree in international relations.

Awards include Distinguished Service Cross, Distinguished Service Medal, Silver Star w/OLC, Legion of Merit w/2 OLCs, Bronze Star w/3 OLCs, Purple Heart w/OLC, Air Medal w/10 OLCs.

Married to Evelyn for 48 years. They have three children and five grandchildren.

SSG LEWIS G. JANACK

SSG LEWIS G. JANACK was born Dec. 28, 1953, Syracuse, NY. Attended the University of New York, receiving his AAS degree. Joined the USAF on April 28, 1977. Stations included RAF, Bentwaters, England, 81st Security Police Sqdn, 1977-79; F.E. Warren AFB, WY, 88th Missile Security Sqdn, 1979-82; Fairchild AFB, WA, USAF Survival School, 1982-83; Ellsworth AFB, SD, 45th Missile Security Sqdn., 1983-89; King Salmon AFS, AK, 5071 Cbt. Spt. Sqdn., Security Police, 1989-90; and F.E. Warren AFB, WY, 89th Missile Security Sqdn., 1990-93.

Discharged Sept. 1, 1993, with the rank of staff sergeant. Awards include the Basic Training Ribbon, Small Arms Expert Ribbon, Professional Military Education Ribbon AF Longevity Ribbon w/3 OLCs, AF Overseas Ribbon-Long Tour, AF Overseas Ribbon-Short

Tour, National Defense Medal, AF Good Conduct Medal w/4 OLCs, AF Outstanding Unit Ribbon w/3 OLCs and AF Commendation Medal w/OLC.

Most memorable experience was arriving at F.E. Warren AFB and joining the 5th US Cav. Organization. They participated in parades (local and in the states of Colorado and Nebraska). He has been with the organization ever since and is now the current commander of the 5th Cav. They strive to keep alive the history and spirit of this famous unit of the Indian War period by lectures to school children, tours of the veterans building on the base and through parades (including four Presidential Inaugural Parades).

SSG RAYMOND E. JACKSON

SSG RAYMOND E. JACKSON was born Oct. 25, 1922, Ada, OK. Attended high school and two years of Mechanic School. Enlisted in the US Army in Phoenix, AZ, Jan. 8,1941. Attended basic training with C Troop, 8th Cav., 1st Cav. Div., Ft. Bliss, TX. Was assigned to HQ Troop, 2nd Cav. Bde., Nov. 10, 1941—Jan. 31, 1942, Motor School, Ft. Riley, KS; January 1942—March 1942, Ft. Bliss, TX, HQ Troop, 2nd Cav. Bde.; March 22, 1942, 15th Cav. was activated but mechanized in Ft. Riley, KS; started a school to train recruits in basic rifle marksmanship maintenance and cavalry gunnery; Troop C, 15th Cav., 1942-43; 1943, Louisiana maneuvers, Camp Maxcy, TX; 1943-44, Desert Training Center, Mohave Desert, CA, in the M-5 Tanks; March 7, 1944, Gurrock, Scotland; July 1, 1944, Utah Beach in Normandy Invasion with Troop C, 15th Cav., Recon. Sqdn., and joined Gen. George Patton, 3rd Army, at Avaranches, France. Participated at Normandy and Brittany Peninsula.

Discharged at McClosky General Hospital, Temple, TX, April 5, 1945. Awards include the EAME Theater Medal, American Defense Service Medal, Purple Heart, Overseas Bar and Good Conduct Medal.

On Aug. 31, 1944, after taking one patrol, he took out another in Menez Non, one of many barren high hills in the Brittany Peninsula. He was seriously wounded in the right leg and pinned down by enemy machine fire with no chance of being rescued. He laid there thinking he was going to die, never to see his wife and baby son, whom he had never met. He prayed to God to help him. During the night a buddy crawled up the hill and carried him down to safety.

Married Jenny Rodriquez, May 5, 1943, and has four children and five grandsons. One son graduated from the Naval Academy in 1981 and is a commander in the Naval Air Force. Jackson owned and operated an auto truck garage for 31 years in Tucson, AZ.

PFC ALLAN J. JAY

PFC ALLAN J. JAY was born April 1, 1912, Boston, MA. Attended Mohegan and received an AS degree. Joined the 110th Cav., Jan. 10, 1930, and was assigned to HQ Troop.

Discharged on Jan. 10, 1933, with the rank of private first class. Received the Sharpshooter Award.

Memorable experience was being struck by a car while crossing the road in formation and killing his horse. Rode Three Fingers who had brands on her left flank (warning troopers).

Married and has two children and two grandchildren. Worked for the US Navy Department, fuel branch as a supervisor, retiring June 30, 1972.

CPT DONALD RAY JONES JR. was born July 31, 1955, Richmond, VA. Commissioned in the USAR, Richmond, Dec. 30, 1980. Was assigned to the Lima Troop, 3rd Sqdn, 11th ACR, Aug. 15, 1981—Jan. 15, 1984; HHT, 3rd Sqdn, 11th ACR, Jan. 15, 1984—Sept. 2, 1984; and HHT (squadron maintenance officer), 1st Sqdn., 4th Cav., April 30, 1985—present.

Military highlights include cavalry platoon leader, Aug. 15, 1981—Dec. 1, 1982; XO, cavalry troop, Dec. 1, 1982—Jan. 15, 1984; squadron signal officer, Jan. 15, 1984—March 30, 1984; AST S-3, March 30, 1984—Sept. 2, 1984; squadron maintenance officer, May 3, 1985—present.

Member of the Armor Assn.; ASA, Reserve Officer Assn.; Blackhorse Assn., AOBC, March 24, 1981—July 10, 1981; JOMC (by correspondence), December 1984; AOAC, Oct. 30, 1984—April 24, 1985; and was a history major in college.

COL EBEN R. JONES was born April 14, 1915, Richmond, VA. Received his LA degree from Virginia Military Institute, June 1937. Joined the US Army on July 1, 1937, and was assigned to Troop E, 3rd Cav. Regt., Ft. Myer, VA. Was stationed in the European Campaign with the 36th Cav. Recon. Sqdn., 1944-45. Served with the 188th Abn. Inf. Regt., 1952-54.

Discharged May 31, 1968, with the rank of colonel. Awards include the Legion of Merit, Bronze Star, Army Commendation and Senior Parachutist Badge.

Memorable experience was leading troops in the 36th Cav. Sqdn. when they approached the bridge on Elbe River at Wittenberge, Germany as Germans blew the bridge on the night of April 14, 1945. Ten days later the 6th Russian Cav. Div. arrived on the opposite bank of the river. There was much celebration.

Married Betty Williamson, March 7, 1942, in a traditional cavalry wedding at Ft. Riley chapel, KS. They have four children and six grandchildren. Worked as a special agent for Prudential, 1968-78. He retired in August 1978. Betty passed away on Aug. 16, 1993.

ALVIN A. JUNGHANS was born Oct. 24, 1911, Junction City, KS. He was drafted into Tp. B, 2nd Horse Cav. Regt. in March 1941 at Ft. Riley, KS. Within two weeks after Japan bombed Pearl Harbor, the 2nd Cav. Regt. was sent to Arizona to do guard duty at the reservoirs and rail stations. In June 1942 the 2nd Horse Cav. Regt. was deactivated and he was sent to Ft. Riley. He became a member of A Co., 19th Tk. Bn., 9th Armd. Div. and went overseas with the 9th Armd. Div.

Was wounded in the Battle of the Bulge and returned to Springfield, MO, O'Riley General Hospital in March 1945. After many surgeries he was discharged from the hospital and the Army on June 6, 1946.

Married Maxine Ascher in 1947 and has four children: Gary, Marsha, Joline and Lisa. He opened his own real estate sales business and has been a licensed real estate broker for 42 years. His son, Gary, has taken over the real estate business.

SSG VYRL W. JUSTICE was born on May, 20, 1920, in Iowa City, IA. Attended high school and Iowa University; enlisted in the 113th Horse Cav. in August 1939 in Iowa City, IA. Went on summer maneuvers at Camp Ripley, MN. Inducted into federal service in Iowa City, IA on Jan. 13, 1941. They took their equipment and horses to Camp Bowie, TX, by train. When they arrived the camp was not completed. Lots of rain and mud. They were to be there for one year but the bombing of Pearl Harbor took care of that. Went on maneuvers in Louisiana with our horses, what an experience that was. I was in machine gun squad, as gunner, and they had a pack horse that carried their 30 cal. machine gun.

In the spring of 1942, they turned in their horses and received jeeps and armored cars. They went on summer maneuvers in Louisiana and on the way had an inspection by Col. William Chase. He was the only one out of uniform and was broken from a T-5 to a private. After they got there the captain needed a driver, so they assigned him to the job. He was driving him through the forest and got lost. He asked the captain where he wanted to go and the captain replied "back from where we came", so he turned the jeep around and headed back which made the captain happy. The next day he was made a sergeant and given a section of men to command and did it. When maneuvers were over they left about 50 men there to run a truck company; he was in charge of the gas station, with three men under him. This lasted about two months. When he returned to Camp Bowie, they put him in charge of training 24 new recruits.

Their next move was to Camp Hood where they were school troops and used for the enemy. They attacked the tank destroyer and tried to get through the lines. From there they went to Camp Alexander, LA. They trained there for a short while and then to Camp Polk, LA which was in the fall of 1943. From there they headed north on the train. They knew they were going overseas; arrived in Chicago and turned east which told them that it was Europe. Went to Camp Milestanish, and sailed from Boston, January 1944 and docked at the Worth of Clyde, in Scotland.

From there they went by train through London to Salisbury to Camp Lobstom. The unit was reorganized into the 113th and 125th Sqdns., he was made staff sergeant in charge of the 2nd Plt. They arrived at Normandy Beach the 4th of July and went into combat soon after that. They were in the battle of Normandy, St. Lo, Mortain, Domfront, Franconville, Court-St-Etienne. He received

a medical discharge April 2, 1945, from a bullet wound he received in Belgium Sept. 6, 1944 east and south of Court-St-Etienne about eight forty five am, there mission for the day was to cross the Alberta Canal. He received the Purple Heart, and the Silver Star after he was discharged, for action in the town of Franconville, France.

Went back to work as a electrician in Iowa City, IA. Married Martha Dec. 29, 1945; they had a son David in January 1948. He and Martha moved to Cedar Rapids, IA May 1953. In 1961 he and Martha started the Justice Electric Company. Dave and his wife, Sherri, and there son Joe are in charge of it now. He has been active member in the St. Paul Methodist Church since 1954, member of Rotary, 32 degree mason, Shriner, Royal Order of the Jesters, the Cedar Rapids Country Club, Ft. Lauderdale Country Club. He was president of the Shine Drum and Bugle of North America in 1974, past director of St. Lukes Hospital Foundation, was chairman of the United Way yearly fund raising program, chairman of the Shrine Circus for two years, past director of the Cedar Rapids Chamber of Commerce, past treasurer of the Iowa chapter of the National Electrical Contractors Assn., president of the Cedar Rapids Div. of NECA, served on the apprentice committee for over 25 years, have attended eight NECA National Executive study programs plus seminars on estimating, overhead, labor relations, past director of jr. achievement program, VFW, American Legion, DAV, Elks, 32 year member of Iowa University I Club. He and Martha have been in charge of the last two Red Horse reunions plus help with many others. He submitted material of the 113th Cav., that was put in the corner stone of the battle of Normandy Foundation building in France. He was invited by the Vilna, group of the secret Army, of Belgium, who were surrounded Sept. 6, 1944, by the German SS troops, at a farm south of Ramillies his platoon freed them, they were celebrating 50 years of freedom. They reside in Pompano Beach, FL during the winter, and Cedar Rapids, IA, during the summer.

COL EVERETT H. KANDARIAN (KANDY), born Feb. 16, 1918, in Boston, MA; lived in Cambridge, MA 1925-39. Served in the 110th Cav. from 1935-39; 208th Coast Arty. (AA), 1940-42; Connecticut State Police, 1942-46, motorcycle section; Camp Perry, Ohio National Rifle Matches, 1939, 1986-94; 110th Cav. Regt. rifle champion; 43rd Military police, company CNG 1946-48; 1st Co. Governor's horse guards, Connecticut militia 1949-96; major commandant from 1955-84; Chief of Staff as colonel from 1985-96; Governor's (CT) military staff. Qualified as expert in rifle, pistol, sub-machine gun, and machine gun.

Life member NRA; American Horse Shows Association and served as a horse show judge and steward; US Cav. Assn.; Connecticut State Rep. Graduated as a diesel engineer in 1939. Employed by United Technologies for 39 years and retired as chief inspector on jet engines and rocket engines. Worked for the state of Connecticut for 12 years as senior design engineer.

Played polo for the 110th Cav. and 12 years for the Farmington Valley Polo Team; past-master of Wyllys St. John Lodge #4 AF&AM; active in the ancient accepted Scottish Rite, Royal Arch Order, Sphinx Shrine Temple-Desert (horse) mounted sheiks, Legion of Honor and Royal Order of Jesters; 1966 national commander of the Centennial Legion of Historic Military Commands and life director. Awarded 50 years long Military Service Medal from the state of Connecticut and Medal of Merit w/2 OLCs. He is member of the Americal Division Veterans Association; life member of the National Guard Assn. of Connecticut; and life member of the 100 Club of Connecticut.

Has been married to Thelma Dibble for 53 years and has three children and five grandchildren.

RICHARD TERRY KAUFFMAN,
of West Bloomfield, MI was born June 25, 1918, in McLean Co., IL. As a boy he fantasized riding with the historic cavalry heroes, and on Jan. 20, 1937, he joined the 3rd US (horse) Cav. Regt. and for the next 34 months rode with 20th century cavalry heroes, Cpt. Thomas Jon Hall Trapnell, Col. Jonathan M. Wainwright and George S. Patton Jr.

With the birth of the Arsenal of Democracy in 1941, Kauffman became a civilian engineering aide with the Army's Detroit Ordnance District which directed much of the War Department and Lend-Lease procurement in Michigan during those pre and post Pearl Harbor days with the automotive industry leading the way in production of wheeled and tracked vehicles for the mechanized cavalry, etc. During 1943-45, another sojourn in uniform took Kauffman to New Guinea, the Philippines and Japan (three Battle Stars).

In 1946 he resumed his career of defense quality assurance specialist (in 1948 became first resident inspector of ordinance in Michigan since WWII); later as assistant chief of Tank Section, Kauffman was concerned with contracts covering renovating and others for producing tracked vehicles; also the early research and development of those tanks and other armored fighting vehicles which the 3rd ACR rode during their February 1991 charge from the Saudi border to the Rumaylah oil fields through three Iraqi Republican Guard divisions ending Operation Desert Storm in 100 hours. Brave Rifles! Kauffman retired from the Defense Supply Agency in 1973.

Married Louise M. Melpolder of Washington, DC in 1941 and has three children, nine grandchildren and four great-grandchildren. Since retirement he has twice circumnavigated the earth and visited 84 countries. Avocations: national security and history. Memberships: American Defense Preparedness Assn. (life); American Security Council (since 1978) and their US Congressional Advisory Board (since 1981); Economic Club of Detroit; Nomads, Inc. (charter); US Cav. Assn. (charter)

CPL CLAUDE H. KENEASTER
was born Sept. 3, 1906, Gage, OK; and attended two years of college. Joined the 82nd FA in 1933 and served with the 1st Bn., 82nd FA. Discharged in August 1937 with the rank of corporal. He is widowed and retired.

1LT BURT KENNEDY
was born Sept. 3, 1922, Muskelon, MI; and attended high school. Joined the cavalry on June 23, 1942, was stationed in Leyte and Luzon and served with the 12th Cav. and 5th Cav.

Discharged April 1, 1951, with the rank of 1st lieutenant. Awards include the Silver Star, Bronze Star and Purple Heart w/cluster.

Memorable experience was getting prisoners out of Santo Thomas, Manila.

Has two children and five grandchildren. He is still working as a film director and writer.

E-5 LAWRENCE KENT
enlisted in the Regular Army on May 16, 1956, at Dayton, OH, for a six year obligation. Following processing at Ft. Thomas, KY and Ft. Leonard Wood, MO, he was assigned to the 508th Tk. Bn., 4th Armd. Div., Ft. Hood, TX and later to the QM School, Ft. Lee, VA. After overseas processing at Ft. Lewis, WA, he was to spend 467 days in Korea with the Finance Corps at Division HQ, first with the 24th Inf. Div., and then with the 1st Cav. Div., UN Forces, Pongilchoni, Korea. Returning Stateside March 5, 1958, he was processed at the Oakland Army Terminal, CA and Ft. Sheridan, IL. He then served with the Finance Section, 318th Sig. Co., XX Corps, Dayton, OH and Ft. Meade, MD.

Following promotion to E-5 and standby reserve service, he received an honorable discharge on Sept. 30, 1962. He holds the Good Conduct and National Defense Medals and is a member of the AMVETS, American Legion, VFW, 1st Cav. Div. Assn., 4th Armd. Div. Assn., 24th Inf. Div. Assn., US Cav. Assn., Military Order of Foreign Wars of the US, Sons of the Revolution, SAR, The Hereditary Order of the Descendants of the Loyalists and Patriots of American Revolution, General Society of the War of 1812, Descendants of Mexican War Veterans, Military Order of the Loyal Legion of the US, Sons of Union Veterans of the Civil War, SSMS, Military Order of the Stars and Bars, Sons of Confederate Veterans, Sons of Spanish-American War Veterans, and 14 additional hereditary societies.

He is founder of Presidential Families of America and has attained 51 degrees in freemasonry and four academic degrees: AA, BA, MA and Ph.D. In addition to banking, he enjoyed careers in local government, education, mental health, social services and is a professional writer. He resides in Orlando, FL.

PETER KING,
born Aug. 15, 1838, in Corballis, County Louth, Ireland. He immigrated with his family to Milton, VT, in 1847.

He enlisted in Co. B, 1st Vermont Cav. Regt. in October 1861 and participated in numerous battles and skirmishes in Virginia, particularly in the Shenandoah Valley. In June and July of 1863, he participated in the skirmishes with Confederate cavalry leading up to the Gettysburg Campaign. On the third day at Gettysburg, he took part in Farnsworth's ill-fated charge in the vicinity of the Round Trips. His horse was disabled by Confederate fire and he was rescued by his comrade and tent-mate, Francis Kinney.

In October 1864, he returned to Vermont and was mustered out, his term of enlistment having expired. He subsequently worked as a section hand on the railroad, married and purchased a farm. He was a life long member of the Reynolds Post, GAR, Milton, VT and served as commander of that post in 1899. He passed away in May 1900.

As destiny would have it, his grandson, Paul King,

joined the 172nd Inf., Vermont National Guard in 1941. He joined in the same town, St. Albans, VT, where his grandfather joined the cavalry 80 years previously. Paul King served three years as a platoon sergeant in the South Pacific (WWII). He was a member of the USHCA until he passed away in 1987. *Submitted by Mike King.*

SSG ROBERT P. KING,
was born Oct. 28, 1921, El Paso, TX. Attended grade and high school in El Paso, TX; Texas Western College, now known as UTEP, 1946-50; Biarritz American University, Biarritz, France, after the war with Germany was over. Enlisted in the 1st Cav., Ft. Bliss, TX, on Aug. 14, 1940. Was assigned to the 8th Cav. Regt., Vet Det. Transferred to USAAC in September 1941 and was stationed at Kelly Field, TX.

Went overseas June 1, 1943, aboard the *Queen Mary* and stationed in England in the 8th AAF Ground Crew; then sent to France in 1944.

Returned to the States on Sept. 12, 1945, and was assigned to Love Field, Dallas, TX. Discharged Oct. 5, 1945, from Roswell Air Base with the rank of staff sergeant. Awards include the American Defense, American Campaign, Good Conduct, and EAME w/Bronze Battle Star and WWII Victory Ribbon.

Married Erla Brawner, Feb. 14, 1959, and has two step-children, three grandchildren and two great-grandsons. Spent 31 years in the civil service with the last 27 years at White Sands Missile Range. Retired on Jan. 1, 1981, as a supervisor.

MSG CHARLES H. KLEIN,
served with the HQ Tp., 54th Cav. Bde., June 21, 1924. Discharged at ETS, June 20, 1927. Re-enlisted with Tp. K, 107th Cav., July 31, 1929. Transferred to NGR, Jan. 18, 1930; then to HQ Tp., 107th Cav., May 20, 1930; appointed master sergeant, discharged ETS, July 30, 1930; re-enlisted with HQ Tp., 107th Cav., July 31, 1930, discharged ETS July 30, 1931; re-enlisted HQ Troop 107th Cav. July 31, 1931; discharged ETS July 30, 1932; re-enlisted July 30, 1932; discharged ETS July 29, 1933, master sergeant.

Enlisted in HQ Tp., 107th Cav., OHNG, July 31, 1933, at Ravenna, OH, for a period of three years. Received honorable discharge on March 23, 1936, by reason of removal from station.

COL HANS ERNST KLOEPFER,
born Aug. 6, 1890, in Hildesheim, Germany. He came to America in 1909 and went to work as a hostler in a New York stable. He saved enough money to head west settling for awhile in Idaho where he worked as a cowboy, realizing his American dream.

He enlisted at Boise, ID, in the 1st Cav. on Aug. 28, 1912, rising quickly through the ranks, making sergeant in 1916 (unheard of then). He was commissioned at Ft. Riley in 1917, then posted to Ft. Bliss. From March 1918—December 1919, he commanded "M" Troop at Ruidosa, TX, where he led a successful raid into Mexico to rescue cattle stolen from a Texas rancher. By 1942 he had risen to the rank of colonel.

In his 34 year military career as a horse soldier, he was stationed in the Philippines and many other posts throughout the country: Ft. Bliss, Ft. Riley, Ft. Leavenworth, Ft, Meade (SD), Ft. Oglethorpe, Denver and New Guinea for seven months in 1944. Awarded the American Defense Service Medal, Asiatic-Pacific Campaign Ribbon and the American Campaign Medal. He retired for disability in 1946.

While at Ft. Bliss, he joined the polo team and that would remain one of his favorite pastimes throughout his military career. When there was no polo team to play on, he fox hunted. At Frankstown, PA he was the Master of Fox Hounds and also rode in the cavalry hunt at Ft. Riley and Ft. Leavenworth and again as Master of the Hounds with the Ft. Oglethorpe hunt. He retired to ranch in Colorado where he continued to fox hunt for many years with the Arapaho hunt.

Married Nancy Edwards in 1920 and has one child, Nancy Lee, and two grandchildren. Ever a cowboy at heart, he ranched until 1968 and passed away in El Paso Aug. 9, 1969. *Submitted by Mrs. Richard E. Sparks.*

MSG IRVIN D. KNIPP was born Dec. 7, 1910, Manitowoc, WI. Joined the cavalry and field artillery on April 4, 1931; stationed at Ft. Sheridan, IL; Ft. Bliss, TX; and Ft. Clayton, Panama; and served with the 14th, 8th Cav. and 2nd FA, Panama.

Memorable experience was parachuting from a disabled aircraft at San Pancrazio, Italy, April 1944. He had 300 combat hours in Asiatic Theater; completed 50 missions in European Theater; is a Pearl Harbor survivor, Hickam Field, HI, Dec. 7, 1941.

Retired as master sergeant, Nov. 30, 1955, after 25 years of active service.

HENRY JAMES KOENIG, born March 9, 1916, in Falls City, NE. He was raised on a farm and broke mules for extra money. Entered the US Army at Ft. Leavenworth on July 15, 1941. After basic training at Ft. Riley, KS, he was assigned to A Troop, 5th Cav., 1st Cav. Div., at Ft. Bliss, TX. He qualified with a six-shooter, mounted, and completed horse shoeing school at Ft. Riley, KS.

After Pearl Harbor he participated in mounted patrols along the Rio Grande and was later shipped off to Australia with the cavalry turned infantry for additional combat training.

Combat action throughout the Admiralty Islands and the Philippines combined to form the most vivid memories, the most memorable being the liberation of over 3,000 prisoners at Santo Tomas.

Besides the Combat Infantryman Badge, he was awarded the Purple Heart, Bronze Star, American Defense Service Ribbon, WWII Victory Medal, Asiatic-Pacific Campaign Medal, Philippine Liberation Ribbon w/2 Bronze Star Devices and one Bronze Service Arrowhead and the Distinguished Unit Badge. Discharged from the US Army at Ft. Leavenworth on Sept. 30, 1945.

Married Francis Wigand, parented two children and worked construction until his retirement on March 9, 1981. He is still very much active in community and cavalry association activities.

CPT WILLIAM S. KOESTER was born Nov. 14, 1919, Ft. Bliss, TX, son of 1st Lt. Fred W. Koester, 7th Cav. Raised on various cavalry posts, principally Ft. Riley, KS, Ft. Bliss and Ft. Robinson, NE QM Remount Depot. Attended the University of Kansas pre-WWII. Received a BA equivalent from the University of Southern California, post war.

Enlisted March 7, 1942, HQ Co., 4th Army, Presidio of San Francisco. Commissioned Oct. 4, 1942, 10th Cav., OCS, Ft. Riley; platoon leader and troop commanding officer, 124th Cav., Ft. Brown, TX, with DS as commanding officer, Eastern sub-sector, Southern Land Frontier at Eagle Pass, TX, April to October 1942; and commanded one of the Army's last horse mounted units.

Was ordered to Ft. Reno, OK, January 1944, as training officer, QM Pack Mule Operations School preparing units for Merrill's Marauders in CBI, also served as that post's assistant adjutant. In April 1944 he was sent to Italy, where he was eventually assigned to G-1 Section, HQ, 5th Army, under Gen. Lucian Truscott Jr. At Gardone, Italy, he was OIC of a detachment of German POWs and their captured horses, later serving in a similar capacity at the US Army rest center, Alassio, Italy, where he was assigned 120 Germany prisoners and 150 captured horses.

In September 1945 he went on TD with the 91st Inf. Div. for rotation back to the States. He was discharged as a 1st lieutenant on April 21, 1946, retaining his commission in the Army Reserve, joining the Armed Forces Radio Service as commanding officer, 205th AFRS Unit, Hollywood, CA. He retired from the Reserve as a captain in September 1961.

Most memorable experience occurred when as a buck private with duty as sentry on guard at the main entrance, HQ, 4th Army and admitted Gen. Jimmy Doolittle and Philippine President Manuel Quezon for meeting with the 4th Army CG John L. Dewitt, early in June 1942. This was a few weeks after Doolittle's Tokyo Raid and his award by President Franklin D. Roosevelt of the Congressional Medal of Honor and promotion to brigadier general.

Completed college at USC in May 1947, then went into broadcasting as a newscaster, writer and program producer. Later civilian employment includes advertising and sales promotion manager; advertising and PR director; account supervisor. He retired in 1981 as editor-in-chief, *Let's Live* magazine, and currently lives in Upland, CA, where he is a free-lance editor and publishing consultant.

Koester's father, the late Trooper F.W. Koester (Col., Cav.), was the inventor of the tattoo brand which replaced the Army's Preston brand in 1943, and was a co-founder of the US Army's War Dog Training Program (K-9 Corps).

He was married to Irma, who passed away in 1984, for 22 years and has two daughters.

1LT SAM A. KOURY, attended basic training, CRTC, Republican Flats, Ft. Riley, 1942. Entered the horse class at Ft. Riley in 1943; commissioned at Patton Hall, April 22, 1943; assigned to the 27th Cav., 2nd Cav. Div., Ft. Clark, TX, May 1943, as a weapons troop stable officer; and turned horses over to remount, December 1943.

Shipped overseas and turned troops over at Port Battalion at Oran and the officers eventually detailed in infantry. Served with the 88th Div. in Italy in the 349th Inf., H Co.

En route up the Italian boot, he "borrowed" a nice filly and was mounted most of the time until the 5th Army HQ caught up with him. Seems as how this was a horse of Savoy (Aristocracy) mare and they were trying to locate her from their records.

He was one of the few cavalry officers left in the infantry at the end of the war when they reached Brenner Pass, so they made him a livestock officer in charge of all the German horses. They processed 11,000 horses through the town of Bressanone. He had a German veterinary company under him to help gather the animals and dispose of them.

During WWII he received the Purple Heart, Combat Infantry Badge, three Battle Stars (Rome-Arno, North Apennines and Po Valley) and battlefield promotion to 1st lieutenant.

CLAIRE BLOSSOM LAIRD was born in December 1895, Algona, IA. Attended Algona High School; US Naval Academy Prep; Ground School, Austin, TX; and the University of Texas. He qualified for commission as a major of the cavalry in the IANG. Served with HQ, 57th Cav. Bde., 113th Cav. and HQ, 34th Inf. Div.

Retired Oct. 29, 1963, with the rank of colonel. He received the French Croix de Guerre Award.

Married Lucille Dailey and has two children and two grandchildren. Worked as an executive vice president and sales manager for Eagle Iron Works.

COL CHARLES GEST LAWRENCE was born March 31, 1874, Cincinnati, OH. Joined the cavalry, infantry and artillery in 1893. Was stationed in the Spanish-American War and the Philippine Insurrection. Served with the 6th Cav. for two years.

Discharged with the rank of colonel. He was awarded the WWI and WWII Victory medals.

Married Clara Peckham and has one child, Charlotte Fergusson and one grandchild. He passed away in 1963. *Submitted by MGEN R.G. Fergusson.*

T-5 ROBERT LEE LAWRENCE was born Dec. 3, 1921, Burden, Cowley County, KS. Enlisted July 9, 1942, at Ft. Levenworth, KS. Was assigned to Btry. B, 99th FA BN, 1st Cav., July 23, 1942 until Oct. 28, 1945. Promotions included private, medical basic training 657; private, animal packer 712, September 1942; Tec 5, truck driver, light 345; and corporal lineman, Field 641, November 1943.

Discharged Oct. 28, 1945, Ft. Logan, CO. Awards

include the Good Conduct Medal, Philippine Liberation Ribbon w/2 Bronze Service Stars Cir 136 WD 45; AP Service Medal and American Service Medal.

Memorable experiences were working with pack mules at Camp Hale, CO, and at the Donana Firing Range in New Mexico. Drove the only jeep with the American forces through the Luzon Valley during the Southern Philippines Luzon GO 67 WD45. He contacted malaria while serving in the Philippines, but finished his tour of duty. He left the States from Ft. Bliss, TX, for the Pacific Theater on July 3, 1943, arriving there on July 24, 1943. He departed the Pacific Theater on Oct. 8, 1945, arriving back in the States on Oct. 19, 1945.

Married Irma Dean Brashear and has two children, Robert Dean and Larry Lee. *Submitted by Robert D. Lawrence.*

CPT KERMIT R. LAY was born Jan. 30, 1916, Altus, OK. Joined the US Army Feb. 17, 1933. At the outbreak of WWII he was on Bataan, Philippine Islands. He was a survivor of the Bataan Death March and a Japanese POW for three and one-half years. He served in the 38th Inf.; 31st Inf. MP; 1st Inf.; F and G Troops, 14th Horse Cav.; and the 724th Avn. Ord. Co.

Awards include the Silver Star, Bronze Star w/ OLC, Purple Heart w/cluster, Infantry Combat Badge, POW Medal, Good Conduct Medal, American Defense w/Battle Star, Asiatic-Pacific Theater w/2 Battle Stars, WWII Victory Medal, Army Occupational Medal w/ Berlin Airlift Device, Humane Action Medal (Berlin Airlift), National Defense Medal, Army Forces Reserve Officers Medal, US Presidential Citation w/2 OLCs, Philippine Gold Cross, Philippine Defense w/Battle Star, Philippine Independence Medal and Philippine Presidential Citation.

After liberation he was stationed at the University of California, Berkeley, as ROTC instructor. Received a battle field commission from buck private to 2nd lieutenant, Infantry, on Jan. 25, 1942, on Bataan Peninsula. Retired from the US Army with the rank of captain.

Married Paula Adams, Aug. 19, 1946, and has two sons, Kermit Jr. and Lynn; three grandsons: Daniel, Scott and Jason. As a civilian he retired from Crocker National Bank on Jan. 30, 1981, as chauffeur to the president. After retirement he became involved in masonry; was investitured as a 32° Knight Commander Court of Honor in 1979; coronated a 33° in 1985; and received the National Sojourners, Inc. highest award, The Legion of Honor, in 1983. He is a member of many patriotic related and veterans organizations. He was commissioned as Kentucky Colonel in 1976; citizen of the day of San Francisco, CA, in 1967 and received the same honor from the mayor in Clayton, CA, 1989.

He and wife Paula moved to Clayton in 1987 to be closer to their sons and their families. They have been married over 48 years. He was the founding editor of *the Zentsujian* (ex-POW newsletter) in 1974, which is published on a quarterly basis, and distributed, to surviving members and widows of Zentsujians. He and Paula attended the Zentsujians' 8th Annual Reunion in Washington, DC, 1992, when they were selected to lay a wreath at the Tomb of the Unknown Soldier, Arlington National Cemetery.

LTC LEVIN LANE LEE II was born Aug. 4, 1916, Marion, AL, and raised on Breezy Point Farm, Hamburg, AL. After graduation from Perry County High School in Marion, he accepted an appointment to the USMA, West Point, NY. He graduated with the class of 1939 and was commissioned a 2nd lieutenant of cavalry. He joined the 12th Cav. at Ft. Bliss, TX, and subsequently served as a platoon leader and troop commander with the regiment at Ft. Ringgold, TX.

During WWII he participated in the Normandy Invasion with VIII Corps and in the Battle of the Bulge with the 14th Cav. Gp., earning the Bronze Star. He served 28 years in the Army and commanded the 1st Bn., 2nd Armd Cav. Regt. in Bayreuth, Germany, 1953-54. Retired from active duty in 1967 and worked as a traffic safety engineer for the city of El Paso from 1969-79. Helped found and develop the US Horse Cavalry Association and was named secretary-treasurer Emeritus of this organization. In 1980 he served as president, West Texas Council on alcoholism. He was active with the local West Point Society and the ROA.

He passed away Feb. 1, 1996, Sierra Medical Center, El Paso, TX. He is survived by his wife of 53 years, Dorothy Ann Lee of El Paso; three sons: Levin Lane III of El Paso, Frederick Gray Lee of Huntsville, AL, and James Manly Lee of Baton Rouge, LA; five grandchildren: Bryan Lane and Clinton John of El Paso and Ann Lafferty Lee, Thomas Bouie Lee and Catharine Prentiss Lee of Huntsville, AL; three sisters: Charlotte Vignes, Mobile, AL, Winifried Ash of Dallas, TX, and Sara Davis of Etowah, NC; and numerous loving nieces and nephews. He is buried at Ft. Bliss National Cemetery.

COL LEONARD L. LEWANE was born in 1928, in New Jersey. Graduated CMA and entered VMI in 1946. In 1950 he lettered varsity lacrosse; designated distinguished military graduate from VMI with BS degree pre-medicine and Regular Army commission as 2nd lieutenant, armored cavalry. From 1951-53, he served as commander, tank platoons and tank company with the 72nd and 64th Tk. Bn. of the 2nd and 3rd Inf. Div., respectively, on two combat tours during the Korean War; 1956-58, commander, armored cavalry troops in the 6th and 11th Armd. Cav. Regt., patrolling West German and Czechoslovakian border; 1966, commander, 1st Sqdn, 4th Cav., 1st Inf. Div., in Vietnam, during which time the squadron was decorated with the US Presidential Unit Citation for extraordinary heroism; 1972-73, commander, 1st Bde., 1st Armd. Div., in Germany; and 1973-74, chief of staff, US Army, Berlin.

Served as joint staff plans and operations officer at the US Joint Chiefs of Staff in the Pentagon; Far East Command in Tokyo; Military Assistance Command, Saigon, Vietnam; and STRIKE Command at MacDill AFB, Florida.

Graduate of the US Armored Company officer refresher course; armor officer advanced course; ranger course; airborne course; jump master course; Command and General Staff College; Armed Forces Staff College; and the Air War College. Graduate studies included George Washington University, MA degree in international affairs; and Auburn University, MS degree in political science.

Withdrew as colonel from active military service in 1976 and taught history and government at Culver Military Academy, Valley Forge Military Junior College, VMI and Temple University.

Awards include the Silver Star w/OLC, Distinguished Flying Cross for valor, Legion of Merit w/OLC, Bronze Star w/V device and OLC and Vietnamese Cross of Gallantry w/Palm.

Married in 1956 at Ft. Knox to the former Sara Sue McMillan and has twin daughters, another daughter and five grandchildren. He is currently teaching history at Blue Ridge Community College, VA.

1LT LESLIE R. LEWIS was born April 1, 1920, Dallas, TX. Graduated high school and joined the cavalry on Feb. 20, 1937; served in Rhineland and the ETO with the 101st Cav. Gp. He was injured in February 1945 and hospitalized until his discharge.

Discharged in August 1946 for six months limited service taken as a civilian, he went back to the hospital on Jan. 3, 1947, for re-examination and was finally discharged on March 2, 1947, with the rank of 1st lieutenant. Awards include the EAME Campaign Award, Silver Star, Purple Heart, American Defense, American Campaign, ETO Award and WWII Victory Medal.

Memorable experiences: (1) Being a member of a firing squad that was ready to honor Gen. Sheridan's body when he came through El Paso on the way to Arlington Cemetery. They made ready for about a week when finally told the general would live. He was a tough cavalry officer and lived until after WWII. (2) In 1939 the 8th Cav. passed in mounted review of the 7th Cav. while they received back their colors, lost at Custer's defeat at the "Little Big Horn."

He re-enlisted in 1940 and was made corporal and later sent to Ft. Riley, KS to CRTC to train recruits. He made sergeant and was sent to OCS in January 1942. He was happy to be reunited with his old commanding officer of Ft. Bliss, now Lt. Col. C.H. Valentine. They stayed in touch until his death 50 years later in Palestine, TX.

Married on April 27, 1943, and has nine children and 27 grandchildren. He owned an auto repair shop until retiring on June 30, 1983.

JACKSON LILE SR. was born Dec. 10, 1761, Hampton County, NC. Was drafted and served several terms of enlistment. In the first he fought at Camden, SC, Aug. 16, 1780; in the second he served as a dragoon, mounted soldier; and in the third he fought at Guilford Courthouse, March 15, 1781. In this battle he served in Capt. John Henderson's company of Granville County militia. This company was seconded by Sgt. Henderson. Granville Count was one of the suppliers of the North Carolina militiamen who fought in this battle. They served in the brigade commanded by Brig. Gen. john Butler, the same who, as a colonel, commanded Lile's company in his first enlistment. He served with the rank of private.

Married Elizabeth Hester on July 1, 1793, and had nine children: James Hester, Benjamine, Sally, William, Rebecca, Nancy, Clary, Elizabeth and Jackson Jr. He worked as a farmer.

COL SCHUYLER W. LININGER was born Oct. 29, 1923, Evanston, IL. Graduated from Tucson High School, 1940; entered the University of Arizona College of Business and Public Administration, September 1940; attended the University to Mary 1943, at which time he went into the military service.; and received his BS degree in business administration, University of Arizona, 1947. Enlisted in the Reserves in September 1942 and transferred to ROTC and was assigned to the cavalry in May 1943.

Served active duty as a private; attended basic training, Ft. Riley, KS; and OCS, Ft. Benning, GA, 1944. Was stationed at Ft. Riley, KS and Camp Fanin, TX, as a 2nd lieutenant in the cavalry, 1944-45; 1st Cav. Div., Tokyo, Japan, 1st lieutenant, 1945-46; USAR School; and USAR, 1946-77.

Retired as colonel in April 1977. Received the Asiatic-Pacific Service Medal and Campaign Medal. Retired Aug. 22, 1946, with the rank of colonel. Awards include the Army of Occupation Japan, WWII Victory Medal, American Campaign Medal and Asiatic-Pacific Service Medal.

Married Helen and has four children and seven grandchildren. Has been a resort hotel owner since 1947.

OMER LEE LONESS was born March 4, 1917, Esther, MO. He grew up and went to school in Annapolis. He started to help support the family at the early age of 13 by hewing a wagon load of ties and taking them to town every day. Drafted into the US Army, he entered service Jan. 22, 1941, at Jefferson Barracks, MO. Went to Ft. Leavensworth, KS, to Ft. Riley, then to Camp Funston, KS, Troop G, 2nd Cav.

Was shipped to Arizona when WWII started; then sent to Luke Field; by horses to Gila Bina; on to Ajo, AZ to patrol the borders of America and Mexico. They also made the Louisiana maneuvers then shipped back to Ft. Riley, June 19, 1942.

On returning to Ft. Riley they turned their horses and equipment in. On July 19, 1942, they were sent to Ft. Knox, KY; in August 1942 shipped to California on a cadre to form the 13th Armd. Div.; the shipped to Europe in 1945 and saw seven months of action there.

Received honorable discharge in October 1945. He returned to Missouri and worked for Wabash Drilling Company for 23 years before retiring in the fall of 1981.

His wife passed away in October 1977. He has two children, Omer Lee Jr. and Kelly Ann; three grandsons and one granddaughter. He married again in November 1982 and together they built a home on 10 acres in St. James, MO.

COL JOSEPH WILLIAM LONG (BILL) was born April 21, 1919, St. Louis, MO; attended OMA and the University of Oklahoma. Joined the cavalry and armor on June 1, 1940, stationed at Ft. Clark, TX; Ft. Hood, TX; and Ft. Bliss, TX and served with B Tp, 5th Cav., HQ Tp., 1st Cav. Div.

Was discharged in February 1970 with the rank of colonel.

Married Ada F. Long and has three children: Bill, Betsy and Bob.

1LT WILLIAM EDWARD LONG was born Dec. 1, 1912, New Harrisburg, OH. He was inducted into the US Army on May 21, 1942; sent to OTS and graduated in April 1943 as a 2nd lieutenant. He was assigned to the 89th Cav. at Ft. Clarke, TX, and shipped to North Africa where the 9th Cav. was disbanded and made into port battalions.

In early 1944 he was sent to Naples, Italy, to unload ships carrying ammunition and supplies, taking ships to Anzio and up and down the coast. In the fall of 1944 he was transferred to the 6742nd Remount Depot at Grosseto, Italy. The remainder of his time was served there and at Barbaracini (Pisa), until his discharge on Jan. 7, 1946.

Memorable experiences include several occasions being sent to a remount station north of Rome to bring back several hundred mules (by train) to transport ammunition up into the Apennine Mountains; and Sunday horse shows and jumping.

Married Elizabeth Fields and has two children and five grandchildren. He was owner of Ed Long, Inc., a farm equipment dealership, until he retired in 1984.

LTC KENNETH P. LORD III was born Sept. 30, 1942, Brooklyn, NY. Graduated Middle Tennessee State University, Murfeesboro, TN, with a MA degree, 1978. Served with the armor, 1966-72; and MP, 1972-94. Stations include Ft. Knox, KY, 1966; Ft. Bragg/Biggs Field, TX for advisory training and language (Vietnamese); Adv. Tm. 75 MACV, E/3/1st BCT Bde., Ft. Gordon, GA; Aide-de-Camp, CG Ft. Gordon, GA; E Tp., 1st Cav., 11th Bde., Americal; Bde. S4, 11th Bde. Americal; Sr. ROTC St. Lawrence Univ., Canton, NY; S1, 519th MP BN, Ft. Meade, MD, commander 293rd MP Co., Ft. Meade, MD; USAR duty with 2nd MTC, Jackson, MS; 87th MAC, Birmingham, AL; IMA DPM HQ USARJ/IXth Corps, Camp Zama, JA; Plans/Operations and S3, 220th MP Bde., Gaithersburg, MD; and commander, 304th MP BN, (EPW/CI), Nashville, TN.

Awards include several Bronze Stars, two Purple Hearts, two Meritorious Service Medals, three Army Commendations, Combat Infantry Badge and Cross of Gallantry (corps and division level).

Memorable experiences include being advisor, 2/6 Troop, RVN Cav., My Tho, RVN, 1967-68; Aide-de-Camp to the commanding general of Ft. Gordon, GA; then as commanding officer, E Troop, 1st Cav., 11th Bde.; culmination of 28 years of Active and Reserve came as battalion commander, 304th MP Bn.

Discharged May 16, 1994, Nashville, TN, with the rank of lieutenant colonel.

Married Martha Kinzer, Williamsport, TN, and has two children. He is currently employed as a special agent, Naval Criminal Investigative Service, specializing in white collar/procurement crime investigation.

COL SIDNEY L. LOVELESS was born Aug. 19, 1914, Hill County, TX. Received his BS degree in dairy manufacturing and BS in science in 1938. Was commissioned 2nd lieutenant on May 28, 1938, USAR, College Station, TX. Entered WWII at Ft. Riley, KS, on Jan. 27, 1942, with the rank of 12st lieutenant. He was assigned to HMS Dept. CRTC, Ft. Riley, 1942-43; and RSO regimental staff, 28th Cav., 1943-44. Went to California, then to the Mediterranean Theater of Operations.

Graduated Command and General Staff College, Ft. Leavenworth, KS, 1965; US Army Supply Management, Ft. Lee, VA, 1965; and was editor, Texas A&M College annual, the Longhorn, 1938.

Retired on Aug. 19, 1974, with the rank of colonel. Received the MTO, three Battle Stars and Legion of Merit.

Married Janet Micks and has four children: Joan Rogers, William E., Sidney L. Jr. and Robert A. He entered the life insurance business on March 1, 1938, while a student at Texas A&M University. Taught at the Texas A&M University, 1947-51; has written and had published several articles on life insurance agency management; served as president of You-Tomorrow, a non profit educational corporation for the benefit of youth. He has served in many civic organizations.

COL LAWRENCE LUSK was born June 19, 1919, Detroit, MI. Graduated Michigan State University, receiving his BA degree in business administration; and ROTC, Army, 2nd lieutenant. Reported for active duty July 14, 1941, with C Tp., 2nd Sqdn. (Horse), 4th Cav. Regt. at Ft. Meade, SD. During three active duty tours he also served with the 2nd AC Regt., HQ XII Corps, HQ 3rd Army and office chief Army Reserve at the Pentagon.

Primary assignments were recon and operations and planning in the United States, Europe and Korea.

Separated from active duty with the rank of colonel. Awards include the Legion of Merit, Bronze Star (two), Army Commendation (two), Purple Heart, French Croix de Guerre (two), Medal of Metz and Korean Presidential Citation.

Between active duty tours during WWII, Korea

and Vietnam, he was a Plymouth district sales manager, manager of a fishing tackle plant, manager of retail stores in Southern California and an analyst for the defense intelligence agency.

Retired from the military, Title III, as a colonel in 1979 and totally in 1980.

Married Norma Helen, Dec. 24, 1941, and has two children and three grandchildren

WO JESSE B. LYDICK was born May 14, 1914, near Erie, KS. In 1941 he was billeted to E Tp., 7th Cav., 1st Cav. Div. He then served as 1st sergeant and sergeant major of the 363rd Inf. Regt., 91st Inf. Div., in North Africa and Italy, with promotion to warrant officer and assistant ordinance officer, AFHQ-MTO. His unit coordinated in the capture of Livorno, Italy and the battle of the Gothic Line. Near Loiano he was wounded by artillery. Received various medals, including a Bronze Star and Combat Infantry Badge.

Married Anne Lucero, and has one daughter and one grandson. His civilian occupations include a bus business; dealership owner and fleet/truck sales manager for Ford Motor Company. Received Ford's national Grand Master sales award. He is presently a counselor for SCORE and serves on the executive board for the Memorial Medical Center Foundation, Las Cruces, NM. His autobiography, *One Man's Word,* is in its third printing.

MG JAMES M. LYLE was born June 11, 1940, Long Beach, CA. Attended the College of William and Mary, receiving his BA degree; and Lehigh University, receiving his medical degree. Joined the US Army on June 10, 1962, and was stationed in Vietnam from 1967-68 and 1970-71. Served with Troop C and D, 3rd ACR; HQ Tp., 3rd ACR; HQ 3/2 ACR; HQ 3rd ACR; squadron commander 2/2 ACR; C & C Sqdn, 2ACR; 61st COC, 3ACR; and advisor, 2/10 ARVN Cav. and 4th ARVN Cav.

Discharged June 30, 1996, with the rank of major general. Awards include the Distinguished Service Medal, Bronze Star Medal, Purple Heart, Legion of Merit, Meritorious Service Medal, Army Commendation Medal, Air Medal, Combat Infantry Badge and Joint Service Commendation Medal.

Married Carol Jaan Aug. 20, 1966, and has three children and two grandchildren. Superintendent, Fishburna Military School; retired June 30, 1996.

SFC ALLAN A. MACDONALD was born Oct. 14, 1923, in Kearny, NJ. Enlisted into the cavalry and assigned to Ft. Knox, KY. Later transferred to Ft. Riley, KS, assigned to 2nd Cav. for basic training. Transferred to Ft. Bliss, TX, assigned to HQ Tp., 1st Cav. Div., as colonels orderly. Sent to Tp. B, 5th Cav. Regt. and went to Australia to Camp Strathpine. After months of training went to Admiralty Islands then to Leyte and Luzon Islands, Philippines during WWII.

After Japanese surrender went to Japan and was stable sergeant for 1st Cav. Div., at Camp Drake, Japan.

In 1949 was sent by Gen. Chase, 1st Cav. Div. commander, on TDY to GHQ in Tokyo as stable sergeant for Gen. Douglas MacArthur. In 1950 when the Korean War broke out he went back to the division and went to Korea where he was wounded and Air Evac back home. Married Shizue Uchida in 1949 and had one daughter.

Came back to the US and assigned to Ft. Reno, OK, where he broke stud horses later shipped to Turkey. He made nine trips to Istanbul, Turkey with 1,200 horses or mules for the Turkish Army. After it closed down in 1954 was assigned to 35th QM Pack Mule at Ft. Carson, CO.

Another tour to Korea and Japan untill 1965 upon his retirement from the Army. Came to Ft. Ord, CA and worked with Post Maintenance, as a supply driver. In 1970 purchased a wild mustang and participated in change of command ceremonies for every commanding general incoming and outgoing till 1993. Participated for the 9th and 10th Cav. units at Ft. Ord, also the basic trainees, the basic combat support brigade and the Air brigade.

His horse, Comanche, died two days before the 7th Inf. Div. inactivation ceremony here at Ft. Ord in 1993 and is buried here at East Garrison, Ft. Ord, CA

Remarried another nice Japanese lady on Oct. 23, 1991. Has three children from first wife.

LTC LOUIS J. MACK, born Aug. 14, 1919, in Philadelphia, PA. Drafted into the US Army in June 1941 and assigned to Ft. Riley, KS. After completing basic training at the CRTC, he was transferred to Tp. B, 1st Sqdn., 2nd US Horse Cav. Regt. at Camp Funston, KS, and became one of the troop's buglers. Shortly after Pearl Harbor, the regiment moved by train to the West Coast where they successfully guarded bridges, dams and other vital structures. As part of this operation, his squad from the 3rd Plt. of Tp. B protected the bridge over the Colorado River near Blythe, CA.

In June 1942, he was selected to attend Infantry OCS at Ft. Benning, GA. After graduation he served with the 27th Inf. Regt., 25th Inf. Div. and participated in lengthy combat in the Luzon and Philippine Islands' campaign.

In 1952 he transferred to the Transportation Corps and retired as a lieutenant colonel in 1964. His military decorations include the Bronze Star Medal, Army Commendation Medal w/OLC, Joint Service Commendation Medal and the Combat Infantry Badge.

Following military retirement, he began a 20 year US Civil Service career which included transportation assignments with several Department of Defense agencies. Prior to his civil service retirement in 1983, he received the Navy Superior Civilian Service Award from the Naval Air Systems Command for distinguished and dedicated service.

He has been married to Catharine (Curry) Mack for over 47 years and has six children and 12 grandchildren. He resides in McLean, VA.

PVT JESS LESTER MALEN was born Nov. 4, 1920, Nebraska City, NE. Attended school through the

eighth grade, then rode race horses and gained a higher self-education because of his own experiences in life. Joined the US Army, Jan. 27, 1943, and was stationed in New Guinea, Admiralty Islands, Los Negros and Manas. Served with the 1st Cav. Div. 12th Regt. and Troop D, 2nd Plt.

Discharged May 18, 1945, with the rank of private. He was awarded the Combat Infantry Badge.

Married Candice (Caroll), a horsewoman, Oct. 27, 1979. Worked at Steeplechase as a jockey from 1939-46, and has trained thoroughbred horses since then. He has yet to retire.

LTC ELISEO V. MALLARI was born Sept. 8, 1910, Florida Blanca, Pampanga, Philippines; and received his bachelor's degree in agriculture. Joined the cavalry on Nov. 15, 1928, and was stationed in Luzon, Philippine Islands; Damortes, Binalonin; Taog; San Jose; Bagac; and Lamag. Served with Troop E., 2nd Sqdn.

Discharged on Jan. 31, 1957, with the rank of lieutenant colonel. Received the Silver Star, Legion of Merit w/Valor, WWII Victory Medal, American Defense Medal, Asiatic-Pacific Medal, Philippine Presidential Citation, National Defense Medal, Army Occupation Medal, Meritorious Service Medal and Purple Heart.

Memorable experiences consist of the first landing of the Japanese, his platoon was engaged with the enemy and withdrawal took place and the whole regiment delayed the enemy. He engaged 12 firing lines.

Married Maura G. Mallair and has 10 children and 11 grandchildren. He is engaged in the sugar industry and has a chief warehouse in California.

COL CARLYLE STEVEN MARCHEK was born Aug. 8, 1908, Carlyle, SD. Attended the University of Nebraska, receiving degree in 1926; Denver University, BS in law, 1961; and University of Denver, JD, 1962. Joined the Home Guard in 1918 and regular Army in 1926 and served with the 2nd, 9th and 13th Cav.

Retired Nov. 30, 1958, with the rank of colonel. He

was awarded the Commendation Ribbon w/Metal Pendant (2X).

Memorable experiences include being the evac officer at Valley Forge Army Hospital; spending four years in the surgeon general's office as assistant chief of operations; and commanding the medical depot in Hawaii, 1946-49.

Married Ellen and has three children, one of whom is deceased; 19 grandchildren; and 17 great-grandchildren. Worked as a pharmacist, 1928-37; practiced law, 1962-74; and was state court judge, 1973-79. His wife passed away in 1986.

2LT MARCEL MATHEVET was born July 22, 1921, Paris, France, and attended Paris University. Served from Aug. 20, 1944—Dec. 10, 1944, in the cavalry in France and Germany. He was assigned to the 5th Recon Troop, was a member of the French FFI and traveled with this organization as guide and interpreter.

Memorable experiences include the Moselle crossing; Metz storming; saving the life of his driver while surrounded near Nogent and Seine; knowing what was before them after interrogating the German prisoners; and only having two wounded during their march through France.

Married Jean Femling, a mystery writer, and lives in Laguna Niguel, CA. He works for the IRS as a tax examiner.

COL TOM MATLACK was born June 5, 1912, Philadelphia, PA. Attended Michigan State University; Cavalry School; Command and General Staff Order of Battle School, Ft. Leavenworth; and Grovner House, London, 1944. Joined the cavalry, July 1938, and was stationed in Normandy, France, Belgium and Luxembourg. Served with the 3rd, 4th and 6th Cav.

Discharged due to disability on July 6, 1946, with the rank of colonel. Awards include the Silver Star, Bronze Star, Combat Infantry Badge, Purple Heart, ETO w/5 stars and the American Defense Medal.

Married and has two children and three grandchildren. He retired on disability, July 6, 1946

LTC FRANK G. MAYFIELD, was born June 3, 1916, Osage County, OK. Moved to Stillwater, OK; graduated from city schools with perfect attendance for 12 consecutive years; and received commission as 2nd lieutenant 1938, at Oklahoma A&M College.

Entered active duty on Thomason Act, Dec. 1, 1939, with 1st Cav. Div., Tp. F, 5th Cav.; made all four Louisiana maneuvers with horses; promoted to captain, Oct. 22, 1943; and commanded Tp. G, Border Patrol (Tex-Mexico) Southern Defense Command. Shortly after the outbreak of WWII, they turned in their horses.

Transferred to Australia July 26, 1943, and was assigned to Co. G, Tp. 29 in February 1944. They were the first troop ashore on Momote Air Strip on Los Negros Island. Promoted to major, July 15, 1944; S-4, 5th Cav., landed in Leyte Oct. 20, 1944; assigned to 2nd Sqdn., November 6, fighting on Leyte; Feb. 1, 1945, with the Flying Column with orders, "Get to Santo Tomas in Manila to free the Internees." On February 16, with 2nd Sqdn., they took the Harrison Ball Park. When he hit the ground to rescue a wounded soldier a Nip bullet went through a metal pencil in his left jacket pocket (leaving

a perfect hole, he still has the pencil). Wounded on the evening of Feb. 22, 1945, outside the Manila Hotel.

Returned to duty at Ft. Riley, KS, Jan. 1, 1946; attended Staff and Faculty Ground General School, S-3; Germany, 1948-51; promoted to lieutenant colonel, Dec. 5, 1950; sub post commander, Ludwigsburg; 4th Army Commandant and commanding officer, special troops November 1951—July 8, 1955. Served same duties with the 8th Army in Seoul, Korea; return to HQ, 4th Army, January 1957; assigned to inspector general section, October 1957, TXNG advisor, New Braunfel, TX; then returned to IG Section, 4th Army.

Throughout his military career he attended 3rd Cav. basic 1941; the last advanced horsemastership and animal management course, 1948; and advanced armor course, 1952. Retired June 30, 1960, with over 20 years active service with the rank of lieutenant colonel. Awards include the Silver Star w/OLC, Bronze Star, Purple Heart, Presidential Unit Citation, Philippine Presidential Citation and Combat Infantry Badge.

Married Evelyn Rush, March 8, 1941, and both are life members of the US Cav. Assn. For several years he has served on Board of Governors of the 1st Cav. Div. Assn.

PFC ROBERT C. MCCORMICK, born July 21, 1924, Detroit, MI. Joined US Army March 22, 1943, in Detroit, and was sent to Ft. Riley, KS, for basic training at CRTC. Requested horse cavalry service and was transferred to Tp. A, 129th Cav. Sqdn. at Cavalry School in Ft. Riley, which was apparently the last active horse unit in US Army.

On Nov. 20, 1943, while participating in demonstration of horse cavalry tactics for Russian Cossack and other allied cavalry officers, he was dragged off

his horse by horses he was leading to the rear and suffered a badly broken ankle. The fine surgeons at Ft. Riley Station Hospital had to put a steel screw in his ankle so he could walk without a limp. While there he served as exercise instructor for patients in his ward.

Returned to duty, March 17, 1944, and served as cadre at Cavalry School until medical discharge at Ft. Sheridan, IL, Jan. 17, 1945, with rank as private first class.

Graduate with BA degree in journalism from Michigan State University in 1949 under the GI bill. Worked as reporter, columnist, and editor on newspapers in Michigan and Arizona. Retired from *Tucson Citizen* in 1989 after 17 years service.

LTG JOHN W. MCENERY was reared in the Army. His maternal grandfather had commanded the 2nd Cav. He graduated from West Point in 1948 where he was twice named All-American in LaCrosse.

Once commissioned in the cavalry, he eventually served in the 14th, 10th and 11th Cav. Regt. With the 11th he commanded the 3rd Sqdn. for a year in RVN, 1968-69. Later he formed and commanded the Army's first air cavalry combat brigade at Ft. Hood, TX. He subsequently commanded the 101st Abn. Div. and the

home of cavalry and armor, the US Army Armd. Center at Ft. Knox, KY. His last assignment was as a lieutenant general serving as the President of the Inter-American Defense Board in Washington, DC.

Awards include the Distinguished Service Cross, two Silver Stars, Bronze Star, Air Medal (26 awards) and the Purple Heart.

1LT JOSEPH M. MCKEON JR. was born Oct. 27, 1932, Bratenahl, OH. Attended John Carroll, 1954, BSBA; Case Western Reserve, 1971, MBA; Kent State, 1979, DBA; and CPA in Ohio. Joined the Regular Army, Aug. 19, 1954, with stations in Ft. Sill, Ft. Hood, Ft. Polk and Ft. Eustis, serving with the 1st Armd. Div., 27th AFA BN. Discharged Aug. 27, 1957, with the rank of 1st lieutenant.

Memorable experiences include Exercise Blue Bolt and Exercise Sage Brush; Col. Charles Elslander, ARTY, was a truly outstanding officer, mentor and person (he is now deceased).

Married on Dec. 27, 1954, and has three children and two grandchildren. Worked in various industrial and public accounting positions. From 1968-92 he was an accounting educator at several colleges, the last of which was Cleveland State University. Retired Dec. 31, 1992, as an associate professor emeritus, Cleveland State University. He is a member of the association because of his interest in military affairs and military history.

COL THOMAS L. MCKNIGHT was born March 16, 1917, El Paso, TX. He has received his BBA and MBA degrees. Joined the cavalry July 18, 1933, and transferred to the USAC, July 22, 1941. He served with Troop E, 7th Cav. and was discharged July 1, 1955, with the rank of colonel.

Married Ora T. and has two children and three grandchildren. Worked for Glenair, Inc. as president and retired Sept. 30, 1986.

CPT EDWARD G. MCNAMARA JR. was born Aug. 21, 1916, St. Ignace, MI. Attended high school at Culver Military Academy; Michigan State University; University of Detroit Law School; Command and General Staff School, Ft. Leavenworth, KS, 25th general staff class. Joined the armored cavalry March 28, 1941, and was stationed at Ft. Knox, Algeria, French Morocco, Tunisia, Naples, Foggia and Rome-Arno. Served with the 1st Armd. Div., 13th Armd. Regt.

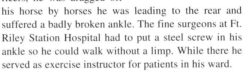

Separated from the service March 7, 1946, with the rank of captain. He received the standard campaign awards.

Memorable experiences include the visit of the Svc. Co., 13th Armd. Regt. kitchen display on field inspection of the 1st Armd. by the King and Queen (Queen Mum) of England. The mess sergeant offered the Queen a sample of the boiled potatoes hot off the stove, which she declined most graciously.

Married Margaret Hammond over 55 years ago. They have one son, E. Michael, an attorney at law.

CW4 LLOYD R. MCVAY, born Sept. 28, 1915, Quinlan, TX. Enlisted in the 13th Cav. at Ft. Riley, KS, April 6, 1934. Participated in campaigns at Rhineland, Ardennes, Central Europe, UN offensive, CCFINTERF, UN counter offensive, CCF spring offensive, UN summer offensive, 2nd Korean winter (total nine). Also served in Tp. E, 2nd Cav., from 1936-42; and the 83rd Inf. and the 75th Inf. Div.

Arrived in France with the 289th Inf. Regt., October 1944. From 1945-50, he was assigned to Rhode Island St. College, ROTC duty. At the outbreak of the Korean War he was assigned to 1st Bn., 38th Inf. Regt., 2nd Inf. Div.

Returned to the States Dec. 14, 1951, and retired June 1, 1964, with the rank of CWO4 and over 30 years of active duty. Awards include the Combat Infantry Badge w/star, two Bronze Stars for Valor, Bronze Star for Meritorious Service and Army Commendation Medal.

Married Iola M. Jacobson of Milford, KS, in July 1967 and has two children.

JOSEPH W. MERRIFIELD of Bethany, Harrison County, MO, joined the Missouri guards, by furnishing his own horse. He was sent to St. Louis where he was federalized, then sent to the front. Hw fell from his horse and was hospitalized with a bad leg; stayed in the hospital as long as he could, where he read to be a MD.

After he was separated from the service he came back to Missouri and opened an office in Pattonsburg, MO.

Married twice, his last wife was Amanda Belcher; they are interred at Memorial Gardens Cemetery, north of Pattonsburg. *Submitted by CW4 William H. Mott.*

LTC ROBERT H. MERSBACH JR, born June 24, 1924, Chicago, IL. He graduated from Bay Village, OH, high school in 1941 and attended the University of Illinois, graduating in 1948. On Dec. 12, 1942, he enlisted in the USAR and was called to active duty March 19, 1943, for basic training at CRTC, Ft. Riley, KS. He was then assigned to the 129th Cav. Sqdn. (mounted), the last regular horse cavalry unit in the US Army, of the 29th Cav. Regt.

When the 129th was dismounted in January 1945, he went to QM OCS at Ft. Lee, VA, where he was commissioned a 2nd lieutenant in June 1945. He was assigned to G-1, HQ, Alaskan Department, Ft. Richardson until placed in the inactive reserves. He graduated from the US Army Command and General Staff College in 1966 and retired from the reserves with the rank of lieutenant colonel in 1973.

He and wife Doris are retired and have two children and five grandchildren. He is a life member of the Reserve Officers Assn., and a member of the Sons of the American Revolution.

SSG EDWARD C. MERSKI was born July 20, 1921, Sayreville, NJ, and attended high school. Joined the 1st Cav. Div. in January 1943 and was stationed in

Admiralty Islands, Leyte and Luzon, serving with Troop B, 12th Cav.

Discharged Nov. 6, 1945, with the rank of staff sergeant. He was awarded the Purple Heart, Asiatic-Pacific Campaign Award, Bronze Star and Sharpshooter Award.

Has been married for over 48 years and has seven children and 11 grandchildren. Worked as a general building contractor until retirement on July 30, 1986.

COL ARCHIE MILLER was born in 1879, Highland Park, IL, near Ft. Sheridan. His military education began in high school at St. John's Military School, Salina, KS and he graduated in 1898 from St. Mary's College, KS. He was appointed 2nd lieutenant in the Missouri Volunteer Infantry. His outfit was mobilized and ordered to Puerto Rico, Cuba and the Philippine Islands.

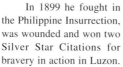

In 1899 he fought in the Philippine Insurrection, was wounded and won two Silver Star Citations for bravery in action in Luzon.

In 1901 he was given a regular commission, 6th US Cav. By 1905, he was ordered for duty to Ft. Meade, SD, near Deadwood. He married Madeline Whitside in Washington, DC, Oct. 5, 1905, and returned to Ft. Meade. His regiment was ordered to San Francisco by train to preserve order after the earthquake and fire devastated the city.

In 1907 ordered to Mindanao. The Morro Tribe, led by Jikiri, had pledged to behead 100 Christians for a better place in heaven. His first child, Samuel, was born Dec. 12, 1907, in Malabang, Mindanao. Madeline became ill and he was granted compassionate leave to return his family to Washington, DC.

Returned to Jolo in 1909, assigned the mission of capturing the Morro's, specifically the leader Jikiri. He was credited with killing Jikiri and later awarded the bolo knife used by the leader. He, his 1st sergeant, and two other officers were awarded the Congressional Medal of Honor in 1911 at the White House by President Taft.

In 1912, he was stationed to Ft. Des Moines, IA, with the 6th Cav., then stationed at Ft. Keough, MT, where his second child, Caroline McGavock Miller was born on Aug. 30, 1912. By 1917 he became adjutant of the 2nd Cav. at Ft. Myer, VA. He was then detailed to the air section of the Signal Corps, US Army, as XO. He quickly rose through the ranks to colonel. He founded numerous Army Flight Training Fields in Texas and North Carolina and Miller Field was named after him.

In 1918 he commanded Mitchell Field, Long Island, NY. He was to old to take flight training officially so he learned from his junior officers and got his wings. In 1919, he took command of all Army Air activities on Long Island and became one of the service's first senior pilots. The following year, he commanded Kelly Field and all the Army Air activities in Texas.

Between 1920 and 1921, he attended Army War College at Washington Barracks, now Ft. McNair, and became the first senior pilot chief of the USAAC.

On May 28, 1921, the day of graduation from the Army War College, there was an air show and races

being held at Langley Field, VA. He, along with some congressmen and senators, flew to the races in a converted hospital airplane, a Curtiss Eagle. Miller, his pilot Lt. Ames, and six members of the party decided to fly back in the Eagle, even though the weather had deteriorated. As the slow, lumbering plane crossed the Potomac into Maryland, a violent thunderstorm caught the Eagle and it plummeted into a farm near Indian Meade, MD. All were instantly killed. At that time, it was considered the worst air tragedy in history. He is buried at Arlington National Cemetery. *Submitted by Leslee Komlosy.*

T4 ROBERT A. MILLER was born March 14, 1912, Mineral Point, WI; and attended high school. Joined the cavalry Feb. 24, 1941, and was stationed in Normandy, Northern France, Rhineland, Central Germany and Ardennes, serving with Troop B, 106th Cav.

Discharged Sept. 24, 1945, with the rank of T-4. Awards include the Bronze Star, five Battle Stars and Good Conduct Medal.

Memorable experiences include being one of five who were the first American GIs to visit Hitler's Berghof, May 6, 1945; the barber for King Leopold and entourage while under their protection.

Married July 5, 1941, and has three children and eight grandchildren. Worked as a barber for 60 years and as a rural mail carrier for 23 years. He retired in 1992.

LTC SAMUEL WHITSIDE MILLER was born Dec. 12, 1907, Malabang, Mindanao, Philippines, where his father Archie Miller was fighting the insurgent Moro's. In keeping with a strong military tradition, he attended military schools in West Virginia and Virginia, entered West Point in 1925 and graduated in 1929.

He was commissioned in the infantry from West Point, later transferring to the 2nd Cav. at Ft. Riley, KS, where he graduated from the Cavalry School. He was then assigned to the 11th Cav. as unit instructor at Camp Seeley and Camp Lockett, CA. Upon deactivation of the horse cavalry in 1942, he attended and graduated from the Armored School, Ft. Knox, KY, and participated in the Tennessee War maneuvers. He was then assigned as commanding officer, 11th Armd. Regt., 10th Armd. Div., ETO, where he saw action in France, Belgium and Germany. His tours of duty took him to posts throughout the continental US, Hawaii and Alaska.

Retired in 1957, after 28 years of active service in the US Army. He was a third generation mounted officer. Awards include the American Defense Service Medal, American Campaign Medal, EAME Campaign Medal, WWII Victory Medal, Army of Occupation Medal and National Defense Service Medal.

Married Maxine Helen Kern in 1941 and has five

children, six grandchildren and one great-grandchild. He passed away July 7, 1994, and was buried at Ft. Huachuca, AZ, the cavalry post his grandfather Samuel Marmaduke Whitside founded in 1877. *Submitted by Leslee Komlosy.*

SP5 DAVID A. MITCHELL was born Feb. 10, 1947, Somerville, MA. He received his associates degree in business management; joined the US Army Oct. 16, 1967; and was stationed as security for Pamujon perimeter and DMZ, serving with B Troop, 4/7 Cav.

Discharged May 19, 1969, with the rank of SP5. Awards include the National Defense Service Medal, Good Conduct Medal and Armed Services Expeditionary Medal.

Memorable experiences include the people of South Korea and how they appreciated the Americans being there. The most memorable and scary experience was the release of the Pueblo crew.

Married Cynthia D. Shirey and has three children. He has worked for Xerox Corp since Nov. 3, 1969, as a senior technical representative.

LTC PERONNEAU MITCHELL, was born March 22, 1915, Forest, Bedford County, VA; and received his BS, VPI, Blacksburg, VA. Joined the infantry June 6, 1937, and served five campaigns in the ETO, with the US Rangers. He was discharged in July 1965 with the rank of lieutenant colonel. He was awarded the Bronze Star.

Memorable experiences include being adjutant, 3rd Army Ranger maneuvers; 2nd Cav. Regt. (horse); AP Hill Res., 1941; and the Carolinas maneuvers, 1941.

Married Betsie Lee Garbee and has two children and three grandchildren. Worked as manager of farm credit for 48 years. He retired in March 1985.

MAJ JOHN FOSTER MOALE SR. was born April 29, 1920, San Francisco, CA. Received his BS degree from the University of Nebraska; MS degree, Barry University, north Miami, FL; and attended the New Mexico Military Institute, 1940-42. Joined the CANG from 1936-39; and joined the US Army, cavalry, June 2, 1942. Served during WWII during the Pacific Theater and Korean Operations. Served with the 33rd and 27th Recon Troops.

Discharged on June 1, 1962, with the rank of major. Awards include the Bronze Star and Commendation Medal.

Memorable experiences consist of serving as a mounted scout with the 40th Inf. Div. (NG) versus the 14th US Cav. Regt. during summer training; spending two years of mounted cavalry ROTC at NMMI, 1940-42; desert training the Gen. Patton; and cave fighting in Okinawa, the final battle before the bomb.

Married Margaret (Peggy) and has four children and 10 grandchildren. Worked for 20 years as a teacher and retired in 1982. He is currently involved in community and youth activities.

TSG CURTIS O. MONTGOMERY was born Dec. 23, 1912, Houston, TX. He enlisted in the US Horse Cavalry on Feb. 16, 1934. He served three stints in the US Army at Ft. Clark, TX, assigned to Tp. B, 5th Cav. Div.

While on maneuvers in San Antonio, TX, the troopers were marching across a farmer's field when Col. Patton came by and commented that the smelly

SOBs should bathe in the creek. Trooper Montgomery replied, "Sir, the farmer wants a quarter a head," Patton flipped him and a couple of the other troopers a quarter and replied, "Carry on soldiers."

During his course of duty at Ft. Clark he had contracted tuberculosis just before the war and received excused orders from the War Department. He was transferred to Fitzsimons Army Medical Center in Aurora, CO, and discharged honorably with a medical, relieved of duties, July 24, 1943, and rank of technical sergeant. He received the Expert Rifleman Award.

Met his first wife on the post at Ft. Clark, Ella Lee Mathews. They married on Christmas Eve, 1935, in the officers mess hall. Their first son was delivered at the fort hospital in late 1936. He did recover from tuberculosis and settled in Colorado with his second wife. The couple had eight children and were married for 25 years. He was employed by the Defense Department of the Air Force as an instructor for over 23 years, receiving many outstanding awards. He retired in 1968. He moved to Sterling, CO, with his third wife, Roseleola, to be partners with her in a Merle Norman Cosmetic Studio. He was an accomplished guitarist and had a square dance band for over 25 years. He was an active life member in many associations and served as chief historian for the American Legion; chaplain, for the DAV; chief correspondent for the 40/8; and an active life member in the US Cavalry until his death in July 1991. *Submitted by his daughter Georgiana Montgomery.*

MAJ JOHN F. MONTGOMERY, was born Oct. 29, 1913, Newark, OH. Attended Denison University, receiving his AB degree. Joined the cavalry, March 14, 1941, and was stationed in the CBI Theater, North and Central Burma, 1944-45, serving with the 124th Cav. He was commissioned 2nd lieutenant, cavalry, OCS, December 1941; border service with the 124th Cav. and 56th Cav. Bde., in Texas, January 1942-May 1944; 124th Cav. Spec. in Mars Task Force, Burma, September 1944-May 1945; and engineer in China until October 1945.

Discharged Jan. 28, 1946, with the rank of major. He was awarded the Combat Infantry Badge.

Married Eva Fitch and has five children and six grandchildren. He was owner of a retail lumber company until retirement in October 1991.

MAJ PAUL BYRNE MORGAN was born Oct. 20, 1936, in New York, NY. Attended Xavier High School and Fordham University and received a BS degree. Enlisted in the US Army on Jan. 7, 1957, and served in the 82nd Abn. Div. for six years, one year in the US Army Special Forces, two years in Vietnam, two years in Germany and nine years in staff and school assignments. Received 22 awards and decorations and retired in 1976.

After retiring he organized and operated his own K-9 security company for 20 years. The highlight of his cavalry career was riding with the Union Cav. in the movie, "Gettysburg", on his horse Danny Boy.

Married Eileen T. O'Sullivan on April 23, 1962; they have two children and three grandchildren. They reside in New York State with their two horses, Danny Boy and Lewis.

COL JAMES L. MORRISON was born Dec. 16, 1923, Petersburg, VA. Commissioned in the cavalry on

graduation from VMI, he remained in the regular Army until retiring as a colonel in 1971.

While on active duty he attended the basic and advanced officers' courses at the Armor School, the Command and General Staff College, the Special Warfare School and the Defense Language Institute. He also obtained master's and Ph.D. degrees in history from the University of Virginia and Columbia University, respectively and taught that subject for 11 years at West Point.

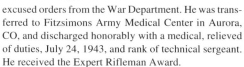

After retiring from the Army he joined the history faculty of York College of Pennsylvania. He published, *The Memoirs of Henry Heth* in 1974 and *The Best School in the World, West Point, The Pre-Civil War Years, 1833-1866* in 1986. The latter book describes the introduction of courses in equitation and cavalry tactics at the military academy.

Col. Morrison has also written articles for *Civil War History, Military Affairs,* (now called *The Journal of Military History*), *The Encyclopedia of Southern History, Against All Enemies,* and *Battles Lost and Won.*

He began his military career as a platoon leader in Co. B, 32nd Tk. Bn., 3rd Armd. Div.; subsequently, he held similar posts in the 18th and 45th Mechanized Cav. Recon Sqdns. and eventually commanded a troop in the 45th. While overseas in the early 50s, Cpt. Morrison served as tactics and gunnery advisor at the Japanese Armored School, commanded a company in the 56th Amphibious Tk. and Tractor Bn. and spent two years in the G-3 Section of the 1st Cav. Div. After two tours with the combat developments group of the Armor School and the history faculty at West Point, he was posted to Vietnam where he served in the J-1 Section, MACV and as the deputy senior advisor to the 22nd Inf. Div., ARVN.

His military decorations include the Legion of Merit, Bronze Star, Air Medal, Meritorious Service Medal, Army Commendation Medal, Gallantry Cross (RVN) and Honor Medal (RVN). Civilian honors include the York College Professional Service Award, Daughters of the American Revolution Medal of Honor and the designation, Professor Emeritus.

Married Carol and has three children and three grandchildren. He and Carol live on a farm outside Luray, VA. He is still an avid horseman, he keeps two geldings, Ringo Starr and Shenandoah Scout.

DALE W. MORSE, born Aug. 5, 1918, Norton County, KS. He enlisted in the horse cavalry on Jan. 27, 1941, and was sent to Camp Funston, KS. He was assigned to the Special Weapons Tp., 14th Cav., 2nd Cav. Div., where he stayed until Pearl Harbor. His outfit was then sent to Arizona to guard the Mexican border.

He was later transferred to HQ and HQ Co., 8th

Armd. Inf. Bn., 20th Armd. Div., as a technical sergeant training recruits for replacement.

In 1944 he was sent to West Point Academy on special duty and was assigned as instructor on small weapons. In March 1945 he sailed with the 20th Armd. Div. for France. They landed at LaHarue and worked their way north through Belgium. He was wounded April 9, 1945, on the bank of the Ruhr River at Julich, Germany, and was awarded the Bronze Star. He was discharged on Jan. 5, 1946, from HQ Hospital Center Camp at Edwards, MA.

Married to Marie Allen, Oct. 30, 1945, in Davidson County, TN. They have three children: James, Jack, and Mary Lou.

CPL SILAS SIMION MOTT,
born in Ohio in 1831. He was a blacksmith in his unit, wheelwright and ferrier. His family moved to Licking County, OH, and he joined the Indiana Volunteers at Ft. Wayne, IN, as a private of Cpt. Braden, in September 1861. He was promoted to corporal along with being a blacksmith. He served three years and was mustered out Sept. 29, 1864, by Maj. Carpenter, in Indianapolis, IN. Regimental clerk was Thomas Jones.

He was a prisoner at Andersonville, GA, and walked to his home in Indiana. He moved to Missouri.

Married Sarah Katherine Yetter from Montgomery County, IN. She was attended by his grandfather Merrifield, an MD who served in the Civil War. Correct records are few and far between. He died shortly after coming to Missouri and is interred at Webb Cemetery along with wife Sarah. The veterans administration furnished him a marker, but not his wife. Sarah raised a family alone in Missouri. Her cause of death was dropsy-dysentery. Morphine for treatment was given by great-grandfather Merrifield (Civil War). *Submitted by CW4 William H. Mott.*

CW4 WILLIAM H. MOTT
was born Dec. 10, 1911, Pattonsburg, MO; and graduated high school in 1930. Joined the US Army April 30, 1934, and served with many troops. Discharged Aug. 30, 1958. He received the same awards that the average soldier received.

Memorable experience was of a horse named Anti-Flow that scared the witts out of him every time he came near. It was a great big, tough, spooky, gelding bay.

Was married to Mary for 52 years until she passed away in 1995. They had one child and three grandchildren. Worked as an orderly in a civilian hospital until retirement on Aug. 30, 1958.

MAJ KENNETH B. MOUNTZ
was born June 14, 1908, in Breckenridge, IL. Enlisted Oct. 9, 1925, in the 106th Cav. ILNG, Springfield, IL, with no break in service to Nov. 25, 1940.

Entered federal active service on Nov. 25, 1940, as a 2nd lieutenant with Tp. A, 23rd Recon Sqdn., of the ILNG and served in a commissioned status until June 30, 1957. He enlisted on July 1, 1957, as a master sergeant in the Regular Army and served until his retirement, that became effective April 30, 1960, after more than 20 years active federal service. He attained his present grade in the US Army Reserve on Oct. 26, 1950.

Served in many and varied assignments in the continental US and overseas. Awarded the Bronze Star Medal, Commendation Ribbon w/Metal pendant, Good Conduct Medal, American Defense Service Medal, American Campaign Medal, Asiatic Pacific Campaign Medal, WWII Victory Medal, Army of Occupation Medal (Japan and Germany), Korean Service Medal w/Silver Service Star, National Defense Service Medal, United Nations Service Medal, Armed Forces Reserve Medal w/2 10 year Devices, Republic of Korea Presidential Unit Citation and Glider Badge.

Married and has one child and five grandchildren.

MG FRANCIS JOHNSTONE MURDOCH JR.
was born July 22, 1912, Tarboro, NC. Attended the USMA receiving a BS degree in 1935. Joined the cavalry June 5, 1935, and was stationed at Ft. Bliss, Ft. Riley, Ft. Clarke and Ft. Oglethorpe. He served with the 6th and 7th Cav., 1st and 2nd Cav. Div.

Discharged with the rank of major general. Received two Silver Stars, Bronze Star, Purple Heart, Legion of Merit and Distinguished Service Medal.

Memorable experience was serving in the 1st Inf. Div. as battalion and regiment commander with cavalrymen Terry Allen, Bill Wyman and Bob Porter.

Married Denzil Elizabeth Drew and has five children and three grandchildren. He retired in June 1970.

MAJ PAUL E. MULRENIN
was born Aug. 26, 1921, Joplin, MO, and lived there and in Kansas, Nebraska, Illinois and Kentucky where his father operated flour mills. He served with the 123rd Cav. in Kentucky and was inducted into federal service with the Indiana 38th Div. on Jan. 17, 1941. He reported to Kelly Field, TX, in April 1942 for pilot training and graduated from the USAAF Advanced Flying School in December 1942.

Entered combat with the US 8th AF in May 1943 and moved to Normandy in August 1944 with the US 9th AF and in support of Patton's 3rd, advanced to Chartres and then Laon/Rheims where he participated in the Battle of the Bulge.

Discharged Oct. 31, 1962, with the rank of major. Awards include the Distinguished Flying Cross, 10 Air Medals and the Distinguished Unit Citation, five Battle Stars for the Air Offensive Europe, Normandy Ardennes, Northern France and the Rhineland.

After WWII he commanded CE units throughout Europe, Africa and the Middle East and on Okinawa during the Korean action. He was awarded the Air Force Commendation Medal for effort in directing the ground engineering installations activities of the NAVAIDS and Flight Facilities in Spain 1957-60 in preparation for the Strategic Air Command operation REFLEX. Commanded an electronics squadron at Cape Canaveral, FL, in support of the launch of Shephard and Glenn into space.

Served as the historian of the 455th BS Assn. and has been the editor-in-chief and co-authored and published three history books about his squadron during WWII. Mulrenin is a life member of the US Cav. Assn.

FRANK NARDUCCI JR.,
was born April 3, 1929, Lansing, MI. Enlisted in the Michigan State Troops for one year, in early 1945, and was honorably discharged with the rank of corporal.

Entered the Last Mounted Horse Cavalry at Ft. Riley, April 4, 1946. He rode a horse named Chief for the entire 16 week course. At the end of the course he helped bury over 250 English riding saddles in a huge trench on the post along with the bridles, blankets and ditty bags. The grave was unmarked, but he knows where they are buried. The took the numbers off the horses necks and turned them loose in a large pasture.

From Ft. Riley he went to Japan with the 1st Cav. Div., 8th Cav. Regt., 4th District Nagano (CIC) Medical. He was hand picked from several divisions to be the combat aid man for the Counter Intelligence Corp. He saved many hundreds of men on the battlefield in Korea.

Entered into combat in the latter part of 1949 and spent one solid year in combat. The funeral patrol could not keep up with the dead. Over 30,000 soldiers lost their lives in the first year. He toe tagged many hundreds of the dead. He saved Father Capon, a recognized preacher at the time, and was put in to receive a Silver Star. Five major Battle Stars and three Bronze Stars were put in for the Silver Star, but the records were destroyed. He was offered the master sergeant position, but refused. Discharged Feb. 2, 1953, with the rank of sergeant.

He retired with 35 years of service with the government. His wife, Sally, retired at the same time with 21 years of service. Their ceremony took place on the same day. They have five children and eight grandchildren.

CPL ARTHUR A. NAULIN
was born Jan. 23, 1917, Kalamazoo, MI. Attended Shorewood High School and Beloit College, receiving his degree in 1939. Reported for duty as a one year volunteer, regular Army, in Milwaukee, WI, on Feb. 27, 1941. He was assigned to the Machine Gun Co., 11th Cav., at Camp Seeley, CA, where he completed three months basic training as a private and approximately three months as squad leader in the Machine Gun Co. as a private first class. Other stations were White Horse, Yukon and Detroit; and served with the 347th Ord.

Until late March 1942 he served in the office, first as mail and file clerk, then as assistant to the sergeant major, then as acting sergeant major. Most of this time he was a corporal. Until July 2, 1942, he attended QM OCS at Ft. Warren, WY. He was discharged to receive a commission. That ended his service as an enlisted man.

Memorable experience was serving before the war as an enlisted man in the 11th Cav., regular Army.

Married Verne Davis, Dec. 28, 1946, and has two children and three grandchildren. He worked in contracting, Jennifer Co., self-employed, 1961-71; and as a merchandise supervisor, Lucky American Stores, 1971-84. He retired in 1984.

COL JACK WALKER NIELSEN
was born June 3, 1924, Cincinnati, OH. Attended the University of Cincinnati, receiving his BBA degree in 1949; George Washington University, MSIA, 1970; and National War College, 1970. Enlisted in the US Army Nov. 16, 1942, and served five campaigns in the ETO and five campaigns in the RVN, with the 2nd AD; 3rd, 6th and 11th AC.

Retired Sept. 1, 1975, with the rank of colonel. Awards include the Silver Star, Purple Heart and Legion of Merit w/3 clusters.

Memorable experiences: being wounded on Siegfried Line in October 1944; Battle of the Bulge; being the first unit to enter Berlin in July 1945; TET 68, RVN, 1/11 ACR, squad commander; receiving the Presidential Unit Citation, Haunhia Prov, March and April 1968; BOE commander, 1970-72, Ft. Knox, KY.

Married Jane Ann, Aug. 7, 1948, and has four children and six grandchildren. Worked as a Realtor from 1976-87 and retired in June 1987.

E5 JIMMY H. NORTHCUTT

E5 JIMMY H. NORTHCUTT was born July 6, 1936. Enlisted in the US Army in November 1957. Although the horse cavalry was gone when he entered the Army, he still had admiration for them. After basic training in Ft. Carson, he was sent to Ft. Sam Houston, TX, for the Army Veterinary Food Inspection School. Went to Ft. Bliss at El Paso and after a short time received orders for Frankfurt, Germany, 97th Gen. Hosp. He arrived in Frankfurt, where later he was transferred to Munich, Germany, 483rd Med. Det. (VFIS) with duty stations in Stainach Stmk, Austria as a dairy products procurement specialist.

While in Austria he was fortunate enough to meet and become acquainted with Col. Alois Podhajsky, director of the esteemed Spanish Riding School in Vienna. Col. Podhajsky invited him to be a guest of the Reitschule in Vienna as well as the Piber Stutefarm (breeding farm of the Lipizzaners) in Piber, Austria. During the tour in Austria, Franz Bader (former Olympic horseman) of the St. Hubertus Reitschule in Salzburg gave dressage and jumping instructions to Northcutt as well.

Upon returning Stateside, he went to Quantico Marine Base for OJT Horse Shoeing School taught by the last official US Army Farrier, Sgt. Robert Bechtdolt. After completion of the OJT, he was assigned to the US Army Penthalon Team Stables at Ft. Sam Houston, where he was under the command of LTC John Russel. The Ft. Sam Houston stables were in the original cavalry buildings of the famous fort.

After an honorable discharge in June 1964 with the rank of E-5, he attended Texas Tech College (now university) in Lubbock, TX, where he received a BS in animal husbandry in 1968. After many years of working in medical sales, real estate, oil and gas exploration, he met the cavalry re-enactors of the 4th US Cav. Regt. memorial in Lubbock and joined the group in early 1989.

Moved to Amarillo, TX, where he founded Co. E, 4th US Cav. Regt. (memorial). He was able to participate actively in the filming of *Crossed Sabers*, in Ft. Davis, TX, for the US Cav. Assn. Currently, he is very active in presenting living history programs of the horse cavalry for various schools, civic organizations, Boy Scouts troops, as well as in PaloDuro Canyon and museums. He enjoys informing the school children as well as adults of the importance of Col. Ranald MacKenzies' 4th US Cav. Regt. in opening the Texas Panhandle and vast LLano Estacado to settlement.

He lives at the famous Creekwood Ranch, south of Amarillo, where he is active in the ranch's seasonal wild west show. He is a horseman who loves to ride the Texas plains of the famous LLano Estacado and bring the 1870s US Cavalryman to life for those that still hear the bugle call. He was recently elected to the 4th US Cav. Regt. (memorial) board of directors, which to him was a great privilege and honor. He is currently working for the

Texas Department of Health, supervisor of the enviro section, PHR-1, Canyon, TX. He has two children.

LT GEORGE MOSSE NORTON JR.

LT GEORGE MOSSE NORTON JR. was born May 16, 1912, Savannah, GA. AB degree, Milligan College, TN; and MS degree, University of Tennessee. Joined the US Army and served with Tp. A, 108th Cav. from May 26, 1930—July 20, 1932.

He then served the USN from July 27, 1943—April 16, 1946. His Navy service was spent entirely in the Bureau of Aeronautics, Washington, DC. Discharged from the USNR April 16, 1946, with the rank of lieutenant.

Married Adelaide Elaine Turner, Sept. 24, 1937, and has two children and three grandchildren. Worked as an accountant for General Motors, Corp., financial staff, New York City. He retired May 16, 1977.

LTC MYRON WILLIAM OPFERMANN

LTC MYRON WILLIAM OPFERMANN was born March 15, 1946, Audubon, NJ. Was commissioned, OCS, July 20, 1968. Served as training officer, HHC, 78th IN Div., 1968; traing officer, CO C, 2/309th, 1st Bde.(BCT), 78th IN Div., 1968-71; IRR, USAR Control Group Annual Trng. 1971; training officer, Co. D, 2/337th, 3rd Bde, AIT, 85th AR Div., 1971-72; commanding officer, CO A, 2/337th, 3rd Bde. (AIT), 85th AR Div., 1972-73; Ops. Officer, 85th AR Div. MTC, 1973-75; IRR, USAR Control Gp. annual trng., 1975; training officer, HQ 1st Army, Mobilization Designee (MOBDES), 1975-76; IRR USAR Control Gp. Annual Trng., 1976; Controller/Evaluator, Atlanta Detach., 2nd MTC, 1876-78; training officer, 139th Ammo Bn., 1978; IRR, USAR Control Gp. Annual Trng., 1978-80, AT Counterpart Tour: Asst. S-4, 2 Bde., 7th IN Div., 1979; Ops. officer, DPTS, Ft. McCoy (MOBDES), 1980-81; IRR USAR Control Gp. Annual Trng., 1981-82; Trng. Officer, HQ, 1st Army (MOBDES), 1982; IRR USAR Control Gp. Annual Trng., 1982-86; AT Counterpart Tour, Asst. S-3, 4th CST Bde. Ft. Jackson 1986; Ops. Officer, J3 AC Trng., FORSCOM, 1986-90, IMA; Ops. Officer, G3 Trng. Integration, FORSCOM (DIMA), 1991-present.

Awards include the Armed Forces Reserve Medal, Army Reserve Components Achievement Medal, Army Service Ribbon, Humanitarian Service Medal, National Defense Service Medal and Army Commendation Medal.

Education: high school graduate, Glassboro State Teachers College, Camden County College, DePaul University, University of Delaware, Univ. of California and Augusta College, Graduate BBA Acct. Worked 28 years as a controller for TTX Co. Hamburg Div. with time Illinois, Delaware and California. Present assignment: DIMA, Ops. Staff Officer, G3 Trng. Integration Div., FORSCOM, Ft. McPherson, GA.

Married Mary Louise Vandever on April 26, 1969, and has two children, Michelle Louise and William Myron.

PVT WILLIAM J. ORCHARD

PVT WILLIAM J. ORCHARD was born in England in 1835. Joined the US Army Dec. 31, 1863, in Framingham, MA, and was stationed in Hiltonhead, SC; Olustee, FL; Big Gum Creek, FL; and Richmond, VA. He served with Co. D, 4th Mass. Cav.

Discharged May 17, 1865, Beau Fort, SC, with the rank of private. He received the Civil War Medal.

Memorable experiences were of suffering from the

effects of exposure and sickness endured during the war, until his death in 1905. He contracted fever, ague, diarrhea and was in want of proper food.

Married Ellen Elizabeth Holtham and had six children. He worked as a machine operator. *Submitted by James Ditano, great-great-grandson.*

1LT EMIL H. OTTO

1LT EMIL H. OTTO was born Sept. 5, 1921, Milwaukee, WI. Attended Platteville State Teachers College, receiving his BS degree and Kansas State, receiving his MS degree. Joined the cavalry in October 1939 and was assigned to B Tp., 105th Cav., WNG. He also served with B Tp., 106th Cav. and E Tp., 4th Cav.

Retired Aug. 11, 1945, with the rank of 1st lieutenant. He was awarded the Purple Heart.

Memorable experiences were of landing on Utah Beach, June 12, 1944; being wounded near St. Lo, July 12, 1944; and retiring on Aug. 11, 1945.

Married and has four children and four grandchildren. Worked as a teacher for Milwaukee Public School for 28 years.

MAJ BENJAMIN P. OWEN (BEN)

MAJ BENJAMIN P. OWEN (BEN) was born Oct. 11, 1935, Ruston, LA. Graduated Hope High School, Hope, AR, 1954; played football; and received BA degree in economics, Ouachita Baptist College, 1958. Served four years in the ARNG and USAR, beginning in 1954; and 20 years on active duty as an infantry officer in the US Army, beginning in 1958. Served with Co. C, 1st BG, 38th Inf. (Mec); 1st, 2nd, 4th and 8th Inf. Divisions; the school brigade, Ft. Benning, GA; and in Balhomer, Germany.

Retired in 1978 with the rank of major. Awards include the Meritorious Service Medal, National Defense Service Medal, Combat Infantry Badge, two Silver Star Medals, Distinguished Flying Cross, three Bronze Star Medals w/V Device, two Army Commendation Medals w/V Device, seven Air Medals, two Purple Hearts, Vietnam Service Medal, Vietnam Campaign Medal w/6 Battle Stars, seven Vietnamese Cross of Gallantry Medals, five w/Palms, Silver Star, Bronze Star and three Vietnam Civil Action Honor Medals.

Married Janet Rae and has three children: Nancy, Gary and Laurie; and three grandchildren. Worked for the US Army, 1958-78; US Forest Service, 1980; and as a farmer, 1981-present. His travels include Germany, France, Canada, Mexico, Korea, Vietnam, China (Formosa), Thailand, Laos, Cambodia and Japan. He has lived and worked in 18 states of the US, with Arkansas being his home.

CPT MENANDRO BOCOBO PARAZO

CPT MENANDRO BOCOBO PARAZO was born March 4, 1919, in the Philippines, where he grew up. He left college in Manila in 1941 and entered the US Army on Feb. 10, 1941; and was stationed in Northern Luzon, Central Luzon and Bataan, Corregidor. He was assigned to the 26th Cav. Regt. of the Philippine Scouts. He fought the Japanese at Lingayen Gulf and continued delaying the enemy until his capture at the fall of Bataan. He was captured on April 9, 1941, and was forced to join the Bataan Death March. He was concentrated at Camp O'Donnell and later escaped and joined the guerrilla resistance movement. He was recaptured by the enemy and brutally tortured at Ft. Santiago. Escaped again and rejoined the US Army and participated in the liberation of Manila. He also served in Korea.

He received his direct commission in 1945 and

continued military service. His last duty was as military instructor at the Army Air Defense School, Ft. Bliss, for 12 years. His awards include the POW Medal, Bronze Star, WWII Victory Medal and Guerrilla Resistance Medals.

He received his BSME degree from Mapua Institute of Technology in Manila in 1949. After his retirement from military, he worked as a metrologist for RCA Corp. until second retirement in 1986. He is very active with veterans organizations and a past commander of Ex-POWs for the Department of Texas and presently president of the Gen. John J. Pershing Chapter of the Philippine Scouts Heritage Society in El Paso. He has been married to Teofila S. for 50 years and has four children who all earned their college degrees; 11 grandchildren; and four great-grandchildren.

COL GORDON MERRITT PARKS

was born July 28, 1916, of US parents in Davidson, Saskatchewan, Canada, and was raised and educated in Iowa. During his high school years, as a licensed radio operator, he enlisted in HQ Tp., 113th Cav. Regt. of the Iowa National Guard in Des Moines, IA, on May 22, 1934. He was the first enlisted radio operator in this "all horse" regiment.

On January 13th, 1941, the 113th Cav. (H-MECZ), with one squadron horse mounted, the other mechanized, was mustered into federal service and ordered to Camp Bowie, TX, for a "one year" training period. The Japanese attack on Pearl Harbor abruptly extended federal service "for the duration." During 1941 to 1943 the regiment dropped the (H-MECZ) designation for (MECZ) because they lost their horses, grew in size and became fully mechanized. He was promoted to master sergeant, then to warrant officer J. G. and later chief warrant officer as assistant regimental communications officer.

From Camp Bowie, the regiment moved to Camp Hood, TX, Camp Livingston and Camp Polk, in Louisiana and left Boston's port of embarkation for Camp Lopscomb Corners in southern England. There, on Feb. 6, 1944, the regiment was completely reorganized into a group headquarters, the 113th and 125th Cav. Recon. Sqdns.; and he became communications officer of the 125th Sqdn.

Landing in France shortly after D-Day, the group received its baptism of fire on July 4, 1944, and continued in combat for 309 days over a distance of some 800 miles. During combat in France, Belgium, Holland and Germany, he was reassigned to Gp. HQ as communications officer and received two battlefield commissions to 2nd and 1st lieutenant.

Returning to the US after the war, and deactivated at Camp Atterbury, IN, his interim CO of Gp. HQ Tp. had the honor of returning the regimental colors with its many battle streamers to the Adjutant General and the Governor of the state of Iowa.

After a brief civilian career on the engineering staff of radio station "WHO" in Des Moines, IA and being active in the post war National Guard, he returned to active duty and was assigned to the 1st Cav. Div. on occupation duty in Japan. As radio officer and later as assistant Div. Signal Officer, he received his third battlefield commission to captain during the Korean war. Subsequent duty stations were the Southeastern Signal School, Camp Gordon, GA; the Army Pictorial Center New York City; the Signal Corps Proving Ground, Ft. Huachuca, AZ; and the White House Signal Agency in Washington, DC. Retiring from active duty in 1963 with the rank of lieutenant colonel, he was later promoted to colonel and retired from the Iowa National Guard. Awards include the Bronze Star Medal w/OLC, the Commendation Ribbon with Metal Pendant, the Belgian Fourragere, and the Presidential Service Badge.

Appointed to the US Secret Service as its first communications officer, he modernized and expanded communications facilities to meet their growing mission. His service in the Washington, DC area, military and civilian, spanned service to Presidents Eisenhower, Kennedy, Johnson, Nixon and Ford, with final retirement in December 1976.

Currently active in the voluntary job of editing *The Redhorser Newsletter*, a quarterly publication for veterans of the 113th Cav., he and his wife Elizabeth are enjoying retirement in the western panhandle of Florida. They have eight children and fourteen grandchildren.

LTC JOHN C. PATTERSON

was born Sept. 9, 1918, in Okmulgee, OK, where he was raised. He graduated from Okmulgee High School and achieved the rank of Eagle in the Boy Scouts. After attending three years at Oklahoma Military Academy, Claremore, OK, he graduated from the University of Wyoming where he was an outstanding athlete on the football and baseball teams. He then completed his officer training at Ft. Riley, KS, and received his commission in the US Army in February 1942, after which he was assigned to the cavalry.

Only a few months later, he was de-horsed and assigned to a mechanized unit. Later it was as 1st lieutenant of Tp. B, 23rd Mechanized Recon Sqdn., that put him at the head of the first US troops into Pilzen, Czechoslovakia in 1945 at war's end. This action earned him the rank of captain, and he still saves an American Flag that his troops had made for him by a seamstress in Pilzen to fly over the occupation camp. During his tenure in Europe, he earned the Bronze Star as well as several ETO battle stars. He was assigned to Japan during the postwar occupation.

Patterson served in Korea and earned a star for the Korean Conflict. He then served in Special Services and later, the Nike Missile program from which he retired in 1962 with the rank of lieutenant colonel. He then was employed by General Electric in the Apollo Spacecraft program at NASA for the next ten years. During his military career, he achieved Expert status in rifle, pistol, carbine, 30 and 50 cal. machine guns as well as mounted pistol.

He married Dora E. Lebow on July 23, 1941, and has three children: Faye Ellen, John Clay Jr. and Douglas Edward. He is now retired and lives in Laguna Park, TX, near Lake Whitney, and has seven grandchildren and one great-grandchild. He enjoys his fishing boat and travels a great deal with his 30 ft. travel trailer, having completed a three month trip through Alaska in 1994.

E4 JAMES RAYMOND PAWLOWSKI JR.

was born July 10, 1969, Dunkirk, NY; and received his BA degree in history, cum laude, State University of New York at Fredonia. Joined the US Army, serving as a unit supply specialist (supply clerk); USAR, Oct. 1, 1987, to May 19, 1992; and active duty May 20, 1992, to April 21, 1995.

From June 1, 1992, to June 1, 1994, he served in Freidberg, Germany. Received honorable discharge on April 21, 1995.

In November 1994, started the civil war re-enactment; and May 1995, joined the 9th NY Cav. Reenactment Regt., Co. F. While in the USAR he served in the 120th Armd. Bn.

His lineage dates back to Buffalo, NY, militia, founded in the 1820s, and includes Civil War Service, including service in the Battle of Gettysburg.

COL GEORGE T. PITTS

was born Nov. 4, 1917, Beverly, MA; and graduated the University of Massachusetts in 1940 with a BS degree. Served in the USAR with the rank of 2nd lieutenant and joined the cavalry and armor in July 1940. Stationed at Guadalcanal, Korea, Ft. Ethan Allen, Ft. Myer, Ft. Meade and Ft. Knox.

He served with the 3rd Horse Cav., 43rd Sqdn., Mecz. Inf. Div.; Americal Div., 10th Corps HQ; 8th Army HQ; USARPAC, Oahu; Armored School; Defense Attache, Vienna, Austria; G2 MDW; 747th Amp. Tk. Bn; Aide-de-Camp, Lt. Gen. Patch, War Dept. Ops.

Retired May 31, 1970, as colonel. Awards include the Presidential Unit Citation (Navy), Asiatic-Pacific Campaign Medal, American Defense Service Medal, WWII Victory Medal, American Campaign Medal, National Defense Service Medal w/OLC, Korean Service Medal, UN Service Medal, Bronze Star Medal, Chungmu Distinguished Military Service Medal w/Gold Star, six Overseas Bars, ROK Presidential Unit Citation, Legion of Merit and Army Commendation Medal w/OLC.

Married Ruth Dailey in May 1943 and has four children and one grandchild. Director of security, Pan Am Airways, New York, Rome, Beirut.

GEN JAMES HILLIARD POLK

was born Dec. 13, 1911, of Army parents, at Batangas, Philippine Islands. After nearly 38 years of service he retired on March 31, 1971. He served in command positions of great responsibility, particularly in US Army Europe. He was involved in many major international assignments.

Graduated from the US Military Academy in June 1933, commissioned 2nd lieutenant of cavalry and was assigned to the 8th Cav. Regt., Ft. Bliss, TX. Prior to

1941 he served as a unit cavalry officer, as an instructor at West Point and attended command and general staff college. During WWII, he served in the ETO with the 6th Cav. Recon Sqdn., serving as executive officer of the 106th Cav. Gp. Mech., and commanding officer of the 6th Cav. Gp. Mech. and 3rd Cav. Gp. Mech. In early September 1944, he assumed command of the 3rd Cav. Gp., then in combat near Metz, France, and commanded this regiment for the balance of the war. He was three times decorated for gallantry and his regiment was authorized its own patch by Gen. Patton.

After brief occupation duty in Germany at the end of WWII, he returned to the States and became chief of tactics at the Ground General School, Ft. Riley, KS, and then attended the Armed Forces Staff College. In 1948 he was sent to Tokyo, Japan, and served in the G2 section of the US Far East Command for the next three years.

Early in the Korean War, he was assigned as assistant chief of staff, G2 of the X Corps and participated in a total of three campaigns. He later served on MacArthur's staff as the G2 of 8th US Army. Following duty in Korea, he returned home to attend the National War College and instruct at the Army War College. He was then assigned as chief of staff of the 3rd Armd. Div. at Ft. Knox, KY, and participated in the gyroscope movement of the division to West Germany. Following his promotion to brigadier general in 1956, he served as the assistant division commander. Following this tour, for two years, he served as assistant chief of staff for Plans and Operations, Land Forces Central Europe, North Atlantic Treaty Organization. Returned to Washington in July 1959 to serve on the staff of the assistant secretary of defense for International Security Affairs. Was promoted to major general in June 1961 and sent back to Europe to command the 4th Armd. Div. in West Germany. He became the US Commander, Berlin, Jan. 2, 1963.

Following his assignment as CG, V Corps, he was promoted to lieutenant general in September 1964. He then went on to serve as deputy, and then commander in chief of US Army Europe and 7th Army, and concurrently as commander Central Army Group, NATO. Retired from active service, March 31, 1971, after serving nearly 15 years as a general officer.

He was active in both national and local military and civic organizations. Gen. Polk authored a number of articles and book reviews for *ORBIS, US Strategic Review, Army, Armor and Military Review* magazines.

His citations and decorations include the Distinguished Service Medal w/OLC, Silver Star w/OLC, Legion of Merit w/2 OLCs, Bronze Star Medal, American Campaign Medal, EAME Campaign Medal, American Defense Service Medal, WWII Victory Medal, Army of Occupation Medal w/clasp for Germany and Japan, Korean Service Medal, Air Medal, Republic of Korea Presidential Unit Citation, UN Service Medal, American Forces Expeditionary Medal, Legion of Honor Commander, Croix de Guerre w/Palm decoration and Grand Cross w/Star and Sash.

Gen. Polk is survived by his wife, Josephine; his daughter, Josephine Schwartz; his son, James Hilliard Polk III; two brothers; and five grandchildren: Laura Smith, Jonathan D. Schwartz III, James P. Schwartz, Molly H. Polk and Anne M. Polk.

MSG MERRITT HARBER POWELL was born
June 20, 1933, Louisville, KY; graduated Clayton, MO High School, 1951; Vanderbilt University, 1951-53; University of Nebraska, 1956-62, BS and JD degrees; admitted Florida Bar, 1965; and practicing attorney. Served in the regular Army, 1953-56, with the 1st Bn, 2nd Armd. Cav., Bindlach, Germany.

Served in the USAR, 1956 until retirement in June 1984 with the rank of master sergeant.

Served in the positions of canoneer, fire direction, firing battery chief, tank crewman, turret and field artillery mechanic, infantry instructor, special forces weapons O&I and B Team sergeant major.

Awards include Master Parachutist, Good Conduct Medal, National Defense Medal, German Occupation Award, USAR Achievement Award and Organized Reserves Medals; and in 1959 the USAR NCO AKSARBEN Nebraska Award.

Served as adjutant general, Scottish American Military Society, 1985-92; Halifax Lodge 91, F&AM; St. Mary's Episcopal Church; Civil Air Patrol, 1948-1994, mission pilot, squadron commander and legal officer; USCGAux. 1975 to date, Vice Flotilla commander, aviator, AUXOP, Coxswain rated; USCG/USAF SAR School graduate, 1977; pipe major, Colonial Highlanders.

Married first time to Helga; and second to Rosalyn White. He has seven children (his, hers, ours) and one grandchild.

LTC VERNON LEE POYNTER was born April 7,
1922, in Wichita, KS. Leaving school at age 17, he joined the Army at Ft. Riley, KS in January 1940 and was assigned as a private to Btry. C, 3rd FA., 2nd Cav. Div. He attended Cavalry OCS in 1942 and was assigned to the Armd. Cav. Sqdn. at Camp Barkley, TX which later became the 36th Cav. Recon Sqdn., 11th Cav. Gp. When the reorganization took place they activated an assault gun troop. With his experience in "C" Btry. with 75mm Howitzers, he was the logical choice for the commanding officer assignment. He was promoted to captain and remained in this role as troop commanding officer for the rest of WWII. The squadron entered combat in December 1944 just prior to the "Battle of the Bulge". Starting on the N flank of III Corps they crossed the Rohr, the Rhine and the Elbe; from there they were called back, although they were just minutes from Berlin.

He was awarded the Bronze Star and Purple Heart and reassigned to the Cav. School at Ft. Riley after electing to remain in the service. While on assignment as an instructor in the Dept. of Tactics, he attended Liaison Pilot Training in 1947. Liaison pilots later became Army Aviators in Army Aviation as we know it today.

After graduating from Liaison Pilot training his assignments were Aviation Officer 1st Constab. Bde. Wiesbaden; commanding officer 7th Army Flight Detachment, Stuttgart; aviation officer III corps, Ft. Hood, TX; aviation officer and company commander 1st Cav. Div. Inf. Korea.

While commanding officer of 7th Army Flt. Detachment, he was called on in 1953 to organize and command the air evacuation of tidal wave victims from the lowlands of Holland. With 8 Army H-13s, two AF H-19s and a Dutch and British helicopter, his small group of pilots evacuated 878 people from the flooded area to safety in a three day period. He also assigned one of his pilots to fly Prince Bernhard on a daily basis to work with the village mayors where it was possible. For this action he was awarded the "Order of the Orange Nassau" by Queen Juliana of Holland.

Between Europe and Korea he attended C and GS at Leavenworth, KS. He was promoted to lieutenant colonel while in Korea and retired in February 1960 at Ft. Hood, TX.

He was married at Camp Barkley, TX to Bobbie Jean who was with him through his entire Army career and mother of his five children. Bobbie Jean passed away in 1972. He later remarried Jean and now has 10 grandchildren, one of whom served in the Gulf War.

He is still active in the plastics molding business as a sales executive.

CPL LAWRENCE A. PREUSS (LARRY) was
born Jan. 7, 1918, North St. Paul, MN, and attended three and one-half years of high school and ICS structural engineering. Joined the cavalry, Oct. 31, 1936; was stationed at Ft. Meade, SD; and served with Tp. A, 4th Cav.

Memorable experience was making hike in July 1938 from Ft. Meade to Pole Mt., WY for war maneuvers. He spent 14 months in Veterans Hospital due to a jumping accident and received disability discharge, Oct. 20, 1939, with the rank of corporal. Received shooting, rifle, machine gun and pistol medals.

Civilian Employment: 1942 asst. chief guard, Anniston Ord. Depot, Anniston, AL; 1943 electrical engineering Dept., Oregon Ship Yard, Portland, OR; 1944-46, Engineering Dept., Gunderson Bros., Engineering Corp., Portland, OR; 1965-78, had his own business design: construction. He retired in October 1978. Widowed after 51 years and has no children.

SSG RICHARD C. QUINT was born July 22, 1922,
Winnebago, Faribault County, MN; and attended Eastern Illinois University, Charleston, IL, receiving his BA degree. Joined the US Army, May 23, 1939, Ft. Snelling, MN, and was assigned to Btry. F, 14th FA BN, a horse mounted unit. They moved to Ft. Jackson, SC, and became motorized in July 1941 as Btry. B, 45th FA BN, 8th Inf. Div. Stations included Omaha Beachhead, Battle of the Bulge and Remagen Bridgehead.

Transferred to the 96th Replacement Bn., shipped overseas on the *Queen Elizabeth* in September 1943; and shipped to Omaha Beach on D-Day plus six on HMS *Mecklenberg*. Requested combat duty in the fall of 1944 and was assigned temporarily to Co. C, 26th Inf., 1st Div., and saw combat as a medic at Hurtgen Forest near Aachan, Germany. He then transferred to Co. B, 27th Armd. Inf. Bn., 9th Armd. Div. prior to their capture of the Ludendorf Bridge at Remagen, Germany. Following cessation of hostilities their unit occupied the village of Ebermannstadt, Germany.

Discharged July 10, 1945, with the rank of staff sergeant. Awards include the Bronze Star and Combat Infantry Badge.

Married Jean Morton, June 18, 1960, Kell, IL, and has two children and four grandchildren. Worked as a machinist instructor and instructor supervisor at Chanute AFB, IL, Metals Technology Field. He retired in July 1978.

LTC EDWIN PRICE RAMSEY was born May 9, 1917, in Carlyle, IL. At age two his family moved to Wichita, KS, where he grew up and was educated until completing his junior year, then his senior year and two years college at Oklahoma Military Academy, Claremore, OK. He later received his BA and LLB degrees from the University of Oklahoma and graduated from the Industrial College of the Armed Forces. Upon turning 21, he received his ROTC commission in May 1938. He entered active service February 1941 with the 2nd Sqdn., 11th Cav. and two months later volunteered for duty in the Philippine Islands with the 26th Cav. Regt. of the Philippine Scouts, arriving there in June 1941.

On Jan. 16, 1942, at the Battle of Moron, he led the last horse cavalry charge in US Army history. They continued to fight the Japanese until the surrender of Bataan. He escaped through the Japanese lines where he began to organize and later command 39,000 Philippine guerrilla troops in the Philippine Islands.

He was put on inactive status Dec. 12, 1946, with the rank of lieutenant colonel. He received the Distinguished Service Cross (awarded by Douglas MacArthur, himself), Silver Star w/OLC (awarded by Gen. Wainwright), the Philippine Legion of Honor, Degree of Commander, and many other awards and decorations for his honorable service.

He has been married to Raquel R. Ramsey, Ph.D., for 14 years, and has four children from a previous marriage and four grandchildren. His civilian employment includes: Vice-President, Far East Area for Hughes Aircraft; Director of Satellite Communications Systems for Hughes International; President, Ralph M. Parsons Electronics Corporation; Chairman and President, Ramsey's Industries Tiawan, Managing Director Intercane Pacific and Chairman for R&R International in Manila and Hong Kong, until his retirement in February 1986.

Jan. 16, 1991, he published his story entitled *Lt. Ramsey's War*, which was republished in May of 1996.

BG HORACE RANDAL, West Point graduate and confederate brigadier general in the Civil War, son of Sarah McNeil (Kyle) and Dr. John Leonard Randal (QV), was born Jan. 4, 1833, in McNairy County, TN. In 1838 the family moved to Texas, locating near San Augustine. In 1849 he and James B. McIntyre were the first Texas appointees to the US Military Academy. He spent five years at the academy because of a deficiency in mathematics and English and thus was the second Texas graduate from West Point.

Graduating on July 1, 1854, he was commissioned brevet 2nd lieutenant in the 8th Inf. On March 3, 1855, he was transferred to Co. G, First Dragoons with the rank of 2nd lieutenant. He subsequently served continuously on frontier duty in the Indian territory, Arizona, New

Mexico and at Ft. Bliss and Ft. Davis (QQV) in Texas. He resigned from the US Army on Feb. 26, 1861, went into the confederate service and was commissioned a 1st lieutenant in the cavalry on March 16, 1861. He first served in Gen. Bragg's QM Corps at Pensacola, FL and later transferred to the Army of northern Virginia where on Nov. 16, 1861, he was appointed Aide-de-Camp to Maj. Gen. Gustavus W. Smith. On Feb. 12, 1862, he was commissioned a colonel of cavalry and recruited the 28th Texas Cav. Regt. (dismounted) in and around Marshall, TX. He recruited his father, brother and brother-in-law as members of his regimental staff. On July 9, 1862, the regiment of twelve companies paraded through Marshall and left for Little Rock, AR to join in what later became the 2nd Bde. of Gen. John G. Walker's (Greyhound) Div. As a colonel, he was appointed brigade commander on Sept. 3, 1862, and served in Arkansas and Louisiana. He led the brigade at Milliken's Bend, June 1863, during the Vicksburg Campaign and in repulsing N.P. Bank's (QV) Red River Campaign (QV) in the spring of 1864. He was appointed brigadier general by Gen. E. Kirby Smith on April 8, 1864; but his promotion was never confirmed by the confederate government since later that month he died of wounds received at the Battle of Jenkin's Ferry, Arkansas on April 30, 1864. He was first buried at the hamlet of Tulip, AR, near the battlefield; and later his remains were removed and reburied in the Old Marshall Cemetery at Marshall, TX. A state marker was erected at his grave in 1962. Randall County was named for him.

He was first married to Julia S. Bassett on June 2, 1858 in New London, CT. She accompanied him to the southwestern frontier and was living with him in 1860 at Ft. Buchanan in New Mexico territory, 50 miles southeast of Tucson. Julia was unable to withstand the rigors of frontier life and died in the fall of 1860. They had no children. His second marriage was to Nannie E. Taylor on July 8, 1862, in Marshall, TX, the eve of his departure with his new regiment. They were the parents of one son, Horace Jr., born in December 1863 in Ft. Worth, TX.

COL THOMPSON LAMAR RANEY was born March 13, 1920, in Fresno, CA. Enlisted in the 6th Cav., Ft. Oglethorpe, GA, March 13, 1939, and assigned to HQ TP with duty as radio packhorse driver. First fatigue detail: unloading a gondola car full of coal along with a garrison prisoner. Qualified expert with the 1903 Springfield for which he received $6.00 extra per month for six months. Reorganized as a horse mechanized regiment in 1940, and in February 1942 they moved, "less animals and equipment pertaining thereto," to Camp Blanding, FL.

Commissioned 2nd lieutenant from Cav. OCS July 1942 and assigned, with 14 classmates, to the 823rd TD Bn. Went to England April 1944, then to Normandy June 24, 1944. This great outfit knocked out 124 tanks and SP guns; the second highest in the ETO, ending the war on the Elbe.

In Korea as XO 64th Tk. Bn. January 1952—March 1953; CO, 3rd Sqdn., 12th Cav., 3rd Armd. Div. July 1959—July 1961. and USAWC 1962. Two tours in Vietnam as CO 1st Bde., 1st Armd. Div. August 1966—July 1968. G-3, VII Corps 1968-71.

Married Marianne Hofmeister in 1947 and has three children and five grandchildren. Retired as colonel in 1975 after 38 plus years of continuous service.

CPT RONALD WILSON REAGAN was born Feb. 6, 1911, Tampico, IL. Enlisted in the Reserve

Corps, April 29, 1937, as a private. Joined the US Cavalry, June 18, 1937, Ft. Des Moines, IA, with the rank of 2nd lieutenant.

Joined the 323rd Regt. June 18, 1937, and was classified limited service because of his vision. Called to active duty in April 1942, during WWII, and was assigned to PT&O, Ft. Mason, San Francisco, CA. Transferred to 1st Motion Picture Unit, USAAC, Los Angeles, CA. His first assignment was recruiting for direct commission motion picture directors, writers, camera men, etc. Post was established in Culver City, CA, and he became personnel officer, later adjutant and executive officer. Discharged in 1953, with the rank of captain, Los Angeles, CA.

Married Nancy Davis and has four children: Maureen Elizabeth, Michael Edward, Patricia Ann and Ronald Prescott.

1ST SGT GEORGE ALBERT REEVE was born Dec. 14, 1920, Springdale, IA. Graduated West Branch High School and joined the Horse Cavalry Unit of the IANG in 1938. In January 1941 it was federalized. After training in Texas and Louisiana, Tp. B, 113th Cav. Regt. (Mecz), he was transported to England for further training.

On July 3, 1944, Tp. B landed on Omaha Beach as a reconnaissance squadron operating in Normandy, Northern France, Rhineland and Central Europe.

Discharged in October 1945, with the rank of 1st sergeant. Served in combat earning a Bronze Star, Purple Heart, five Battle Stars and the Belgian Unit Croix de Guerre.

Married Lorna T. over 23 years ago and has three sons from a previous marriage, three step-daughters and six grandchildren. Has lived in the Iowa City and Cedar Rapids area since his discharge, retiring in 1983 from his plaster contracting business. One of his numerous interests was being the editor of the *Red Horser Newsletter* for many years, and he and Vyrl Justice were organizers of the biannual Red Horser reunion. He was elected a member of the US Horse Cav. Assn. Board of Trustees in 1986 and enjoyed that honor until ill health made it necessary to resign. He has been living at the Iowa Veterans Home in Marshalltown since November 1994. *Submitted by Lorna T. Reeve*

GABRIEL RENVILLE, born in 1825, was a mixed blood Dakota. He was chief of the Sisseton-Wahpeton tribe and signed the 1867 treaty establishing the Lake Traverse Reservation in South Dakota.

He opposed the Dakota uprising of 1862 and served Gen. Henry Sibley as chief of scouts under the command of his white brother-in-law, Joseph R. Brown. He picked the Indians to be enrolled as scouts, assigning them to a line of camps sending out mounted surveillance patrols. The scouts are credited with protecting frontier Minnesota settlement from hostile Indian attacks. He never learned English.

Renville passed away at the home of his nephew, Samuel J. Brown, at Browns Valley, MN, in 1892.

COL ROBERT M. REUTER was born Oct. 18, 1928, New York, NY. He was commissioned in 1951; earned his BS degree from New Mexico Military Institute; and MS from Shippensburg State College.

Following a series of troop command and staff assignments and Aviation School, he commanded the UTTH Co. in 1963 (the Army's first armed helicopter company in Vietnam) and the 7/17th Air Cav. Sqdn. in Vietnam in 1968. A graduate of the C&GSC and the USAWC, he served on the faculty of both institutions, and as an area commander, and chief of staff of the 4th ROTC Region at Ft. Lewis, WA. In addition, he served with the 31st Inf. Regt. in Korea; 1st, 6th and 13th Cav.; and the 1st, 2nd and 3rd Armd. Divisions.

Retired in 1980 with the rank of colonel. Decorations include the Legion of Merit w/4 OLCs, Distinguished Flying Cross w/2 OLCs, Bronze Star, Army Commendation Medal, Air Medal w/20 OLCs and the Combat Infantry Badge.

Married Lucy Hudson, June 13, 1953, and has two children and six grandchildren. Resides in Olympia, WA.

T/5 CHARLES H. REW was born Oct. 2, 1918, at northern Otter Tail County, MN. His family moved to a farm near Frazee in 1931; graduated from Frazee High School, 1938; and was drafted into service March 19, 1941, Ft. Snelling, MN. He was stationed at Ft. Meade, SD, 4th Cav., Tp. C. The 4th Cav. was dismounted in the spring of 1942; Tp. C was dismounted; and they were left at Ft. Meade. They received mules and were in a number of camps learning mule packing. Departed New Port New, MD, April 23, 1944, and spent 30 days on a ship going to Bombay, India, around South Africa.

Landed in Bombay, India, and went to northern India and into Burma. Arrived in Myitkyina as replacement 31 QM Pack. Saw combat in Burma and went to combat in China by way of Ledo Road.

When the war was over he flew back to India over Hump, took a train to western India and a ship to New York. Discharged Nov. 9, 1945, at Camp McCoy, WI. Awards include the American Defense Service Medal and APTS Medal.

He semi-retired in October 1983, and continues to work as a farmer.

COL EDWIN M. RHOADS (ROCKY) was born

Aug. 18, 1919, in Douglas, AZ, while his father, 2nd Lt. Mark Rhoads, was serving in the 10th Cav. at Ft. Huachuca. Early years as an Army brat included stations at the cavalry posts of Ft. Ethan Allen, VT, and Ft. Bliss, TX. While a student at the University of Denver, he enlisted in the CONG in 1938 and was assigned to the 45th Div. Tk. Co., attaining the rank of sergeant.

Appointed to West Point in 1940, he graduated in June 1943 as 2nd lieutenant of cavalry, regular Army. His first troop assignment was the 124th Cav. Regt. (horse), Ft. Brown, TX. In June 1944 the regiment was transferred to Ft. Riley, KS, from POM where the unit's horses were turned in, and proceeded by ship, rail and river steamer to Camp Ramgarh, India. Now dismounted, the regiment was flown to Myitkyina, Burma and brigaded with the 475th Inf. to form the Mars Task Force. This unit, complete with pack mules, continued the mission of Merrill's Marauders in the Central Burma Campaign which ended in June 1945. During this action he served as 3rd Sqdn. I&R platoon leader, commanding officer, I Tp. and Sqdn. S-2. The regiment was then flown to Kunming, China for deactivation; he was assigned to a small detachment in Sichang, western China with the mission of procuring pack horses for the Chinese Nationalist Army.

Following V-J day, he was assigned to HQ, China Theater Command in Shanghai as assistant construction engineer until August 1946. Subsequent assignments included commanding officer, F Co. (Tk), 3rd Cav. (Mecz), Ft. Meade, MD, 1947-48; executive officer and commanding officer, 6th Tk. Bn., 24th Div., Korea, 1955-57; Combat Development Center, Ft. Ord, CA, 1957-59; MAAG, Germany, 1963-66; R&D Division, Army Material Command, Alexandria, VA, 1966-68; and commanding officer, US Army Arctic Test Center, Ft. Greely, AK, retiring June 30, 1971, in the grade of colonel.

Awards include the Legion of Merit, Silver Star, Purple Heart, Combat Infantry Badge, American Campaign Medal, Asiatic Pacific Medal w/3 stars, American Defense Service Medal, National Defense Service Medal and four Overseas Bars.

Rhoads married Irene E. Rogers on Aug. 8, 1943, and they moved to their present home in Fairbanks, AK, in October 1971. He received degrees of MS, 1973, and Ph.D., 1986; in northern transportation at the University of Alaska, Fairbanks and established a consulting business in transportation planning. He is active in the Fairbanks Chamber of Commerce, and as an officer in the 124th Cav. Explorer Post, a senior level organization of the Boy Scouts of America which is patterned on the post-Civil War cavalry in the West. The Rhoads have two daughters, five grandchildren and one great-grandchild.

CPT MARK RHOADS was born Sept. 9, 1897, Edge Hill, PA. He was appointed to West Point in 1916, graduated Nov. 1, 1918, and commissioned 2nd lieutenant of the cavalry.

Married Esther W. Buckman of Philadelphia. His first troop assignment was the 10th Cav. Regt. stationed at Ft. Huachuca, AZ. While there, their first child, Edwin Milton, was born. He was the godson of the class of November 1918.

Served in the Panama Canal Zone and the 3rd Cav. Regt. at Ft. Ethan Allen, VT, prior to attending commu-

nication classes at Yale University and the US Army Signal School. In 1924 he was assigned to the Signal Section, HQ, 2nd Bde., 1st Cav. Div., and transferred to the Sig. Corps in 1927. During this period, the couple had three other children: Esther Marcetta, Elizabeth Ann and Mark Charles. Edwin and Mark went on to West Point and careers in the Army.

Rhoads became a cryptographer in the Signal Intelligence Agency, War Department, under William Friedman in 1932, and was transferred to radio intercept duty in the Philippine Islands in 1935. There he contracted tuberculosis and after hospitalization at Fitzsimmons General Hospital, Colorado, was retired in the grade of captain in 1937.

His family moved to Arvada, CO, where he became a successful business man. In 1944 he went back to the War Department as a civil servant, again under William Friedman. He retired in 1951 and was awarded the Decoration for Exceptional Civilian Service. He and his family moved to Daytona Beach, FL, where he went to Fiddler's Green on Oct. 18, 1967.

PVT GEORGE B. RICHARDS was born Jan. 2, 1903, Cleveland, OH, and attended Purone University, receiving his BS of mechanical engineering degree. Joined the 107th Cav. in 1935. Discharged in 1938 with the rank of private.

He is a widower and has one adopted child and two grandchildren. Worked as a paymaster and retired in January 1967.

WILLIAM A. RICHARDSON, born Jan. 28, 1921, Salida, Co. Assigned to F Troop, 7th Cav. (1st Cav. Div.), Ft. Bliss, TX, for recruit training and duty. Rode in the last mounted parade of the 1st Cav. Div. Promoted to warrant officer, September 1942. Served with 7th Cav. Regt. in SW Pacific from Australia, July 1943 to the occupation of Japan in October 1945.

Returned to the US and civilian duty in October 1945. Re-enlisted in the US Army in July 1946 for 1st Cav. Div., Tokyo, Japan. Assigned to 7th Cav. Regt. and given a field commission in December 1946. Continued to serve in the 7th Cav. Regt. until reassignment to the US in June 1949. Served at Ft. Hood, TX, and in Europe with the 2nd Armd. Div. and in Arlington, VA, and in Korea with the US Army Security Agency. Retired from the Army with rank of major in February 1961.

Worked as Dept. of the Army civilian for the US Army Security Agency from April 1961 until retired in April 1984. Married to Miss Eva Ulias, El Paso, TX, April 2, 1942. They have two daughters (one was born in Tokyo, Japan), four grandsons and two great-grandchildren.

Charter member of the 1st Cav. Div. Assn., charter member of US Cavalry Assn., past-president of 7th Cavalry Assn. and since August 1996 president of 1st Cav. Div. Assn.

SGT DALE RICKARDS was born June 29, 1921, Wichita, KS. Enlisted in Tp. E, 114th Cav., KSNG at Wichita, KS, in the spring of 1939. He made the summer maneuvers at Ft. Riley, KS. He was on the boxing team and fought middle weight. Made it to the finals before being eliminated. He was also on the horse jumping team with a horse named Ranger.

Made the summer maneuvers at Ft. Snelling, MN. Was on a 12 man detail to the stockyards at Kansas City. They picked up about 1,000 head of horses the French government had purchased. When France fell, the horses were turned over to the US. He had his pick and chose a big bald face bay with four stockings. He was so good that the 1st sergeant took the horse from him. The stable sergeant gave Rickards a three-fourths thoroughbred remount from Montana; green broke. The maneuvers lasted seven days and that horse was still bucking until the very last day. Sleeping sickness hit the horses causing 70% of their troop's horses to get sick.

One highlight was that they had an all Indian troop in their regiment, and a number of them were good bronc riders. He recalls one Indian trooper getting bucked into a tree and breaking his arm. The Indian trooper unbuttoned his shirt, stuck his arm in a sling, crawled back on the horse and rode him to a stand still.

They were called into active service in December 1940. They lost their horses and were made an artillery unit. Their unit was 7th Corps, 1st Army, 195th FA, all through five campaigns in Europe. He was recalled during the Korean War and met his old chaplain, Col. Hilliard.

Married and has three children and three grandchildren. He was a Los Angeles policeman at the time of the Korean War. He returned to the LAPD and worked 20 years as a mounted policeman. He has his own business renting western props for the movie business.

1LT CLAUDE R. RIGSBY was born May 19, 1920, Tallassee, AL. He graduated high school; joined the NG in November 1939 and served with the 112th Cav. He was inducted into federal service and active duty Nov. 18, 1940, with first station at Ft. Bliss, TX; then 1941 Louisiana maneuvers; to Ft. Clark, TX. Departed Ft. Clark in early July for San Francisco, CA.

On July 17, 1942, sailed for overseas: New Caledonia, Australia and made first combat landing on Woodlark Island, July 4, 1943. Woodlark is where they got most of their jungle training. Made combat landing at Arawe, New Britain, December 1943. He was wounded in January 1944, returned to his unit in July at Drinimore River, Aitape, New Guinea. Moved to Leyte Island then to Luzon. War ended Aug. 7, 1945.

Memorable experience was being in Tokyo Bay and seeing Gen. MacArthur and the Japanese sign the peace treaty. Served overseas 38 1/2 months. Returned to the States Oct. 8, 1945 and was discharged in November 1945 with the rank of 1st lieutenant. Awards include two Bronze Stars, one Purple Heart, Good Conduct Medal, Asiatic-Pacific Medal and four stars, WWII Victory Medal, one star and Combat Infantryman's Badge. Married to Naomi Marie Harris for over 50 years and has three children and three grandchildren. Worked for Braniff Airways as a mechanic. Retired May 12, 1982, and moved to Chandler, TX.

AH-RE-KAH-RARD (RUSH ROBERTS), was a private in Capt. North's Bn. of Pawnee Scouts, US Army (Northern Cheyenne and Sioux Campaign) of 1876. Barely 17 years of age, he was the youngest of the Pawnee scouts in Gen. Crook's campaign.

He charged hostile villages with MacKenzie's cavalry. For this action he was given his father's name "Fancy Eagle." He later became chief of the Skedee, Pawnee Tribe. "Fancy Eagle" was born in Nebraska in 1859 and died at Pawnee, OK in 1958. He was buried with full military honers.

On Veterans Day 1982, at a war dance at round house, Pawnee, OK, a name giving ceremony was performed at request of Aunt Lena Tafoya, giving Col. Templeton the Indian name of his late grandfather Rush Roberts Sr., Latakuts Kalahar (Fancy Eagle). Col.

Templeton's extensive military service began at an early age and included OKNG, Pawhuska, from age 13-20; 5 years at Oklahoma Military Academy, Claremore (to name a few) spending his last 3 years of active service as an instructor to the Oklahoma Reserves at Lawton, then retiring as Colonel, USA, Fort Sill, June 30, 1959, with over 25 years active service. Colonel Templeton is the nephew of Lena Roberts Tafoya and son of the late Nellie Roberts and C.K. Templeton

SSG RC ROZELLE (ROZY) was born March 25, 1915, Illion, NY; graduated high school, Wauchula, FL, and joined the 3rd Cav., Ft. Meyer, VA, April 16, 1941. Was stationed at Ft. Oglethorpe, GA; Ft. Benning, GA; Ft. Meade, MD; Central Europe; Rhineland; Camp Edwards, MA; Woodrow Wilson Hospital, Stanton, VA; and finally Camp Butner, NC, for separation, Oct. 13, 1945. Served as supply sergeant, then platoon sergeant of the 104th Timber Wolves Inf. before being promoted to staff sergeant. He was awarded the Combat Infantry Badge, European Ribbon w/2 Battle Stars and Purple Heart.

Married Margaret J. Henkel, March 4, 1944, and has two daughters, four grandchildren and one great-grandson. Spent 25 years after his discharge in retailing, first as buyer, then merchandise manager for a chain of discount stores. In 1973 he was made vice president of a short lived (18 months) import firm in Chicago. From 1973 he was employed as consultant for various manufactures and sales representatives.

Retired again in 1995 and has taken it easy since. His merchandising endeavors required travel through the Far East markets such as Japan, Taiwan, Hong Kong, Korea, Philippines, Singapore, main land China and Bangkok. As a consultant took a trip to London, Brussels, Cameroon, Gabon, Nigeria, Ghana, Ivory Coast and Liberia. Not a pleasant trip because of a revolution and some countries less than cordial treatment of Americans.

1SG JAMES A. RUOTSALA, was born Feb. 17, 1934, in Juneau, AK. He joined the US Navy at the age of 17 and served in the Korean War. He was honorably discharged in 1956.

On Feb. 7, 1958, he joined the US Army. Served first with CO C, 3rd Med. Tk. Bn. (Patton) 69th Armd. and then transferred to HQ TP, 3rd Recon Sqdn., 4th Cav. on July 5, 1960. He left the Army in December 1963 but remained in the Army Reserve and retired in February 1994 as a 1st sergeant from a career that spanned 42 years.

Awards include the Meritorious Service Medal w/ OLC, Joint Service Achievement Medal, Army Achievement Medal w/3 OLCs, Korean Service Medal w/2 Bronze Stars, Korean Presidential Unit Citation, United Nations Service Medal, Armed Forces Expeditionary Medal (Vietnam), Vietnam Presidential Unit Citation, and the Vietnam Cross of Gallantry.

He is married to Janet and has five children, six grandchildren and one great-grandchild.

LTC JOSEPH R. SAIN was born Nov. 10, 1916, Clymer, PA; earned his BSEE degree and attended Command and General Staff College. Joined the US Army on Jan. 21, 1942, and participated in five campaigns in Europe and Vietnam in 1963. Served with the 3rd Cav., 6th Cav. and 38th Cav.

Discharged in May 1967 with the rank of lieutenant colonel. Awards include the Silver Star, Legion of Merit, Bronze Star w/4 clusters, Air Medal, Purple Heart, French Croix de Guerre w/L argent, Belgium Croix de Guerre, Presidential Unit Citation and European Campaign Ribbon w/5 stars.

Memorable experiences include commanding B Tp., 38th Cav. Recon Sqdn. in the Battle of the Bulge at Monschua, Germany and along with the rest of the squadron and attached units beating a larger German force, December 16-18, 1944. Also, conducting airborne operations against the Viet Cong in 1963 and surviving two helicopter crashes.

Married Dorothy and has two sons and four grandchildren. He is a real estate broker in Maryland.

SAMUEL B. SANDERS was born March 1, 1821, in Edmonson County, KY. He joined for duty and enrolled on Aug. 20, 1862, in Edmonson County, KY and mustered in on Nov. 17, 1862, at Owensboro, KY. He was wounded in action Jan. 16, 1864, and was hospitalized. He mustered out on Aug. 23, 1865, in Louisville, KY. He was granted a pension of eight dollars a month which he received from Louisville until March 4, 1876. Then his records were transferred to Topeka, KS when he moved to Chanute. His request for the change was dated June 5,

1876. Those dates provided the information that placed the family move into that three month time period. He and the other men in the family did some small scale farming in Kansas but to no great extent.

He married Ellenore Morgan on Jan. 15, 1845. They had nine children; Sarah Jane, Georgeann, Decatur James Lee, Martha Carolina, Henry Clay, Stephen Morgan, Amanda Frances, Mary Angeline, and Melvina Ellen. He lost to death a son in 1880, a daughter in 1881, and his wife in 1882. They and another son and two infant grandchildren are all buried in old Greenwood cemetery. He passed away on May 12, 1903, and is buried beside his son-in-law and war partner, Thomas Andrew Jackson Denham. Four of the children continued the family's westward migration by moving to Idaho. His paternal ancestors were William P., Samuel III, Samuel II and Samuel Joseph from Scotland.

LTC GEORGE E. SAPORA was born Nov. 28, 1908, in New York City. Shortly thereafter, his family moved to Renovo, PA, where he graduated from high school in 1926. He left the employment at Paramount Pictures in New York to enter the University of Illinois in 1927. He received his BS degree in 1933 and a commission in the Cav. Reserve in 1933.

While employed at Paramount in 1935, he volunteered for six months EAD in the CCC program, serving in Washington State. In 1936 he was ordered to duty for a year with the 6th Cav. Regt. at Ft. Oglethorpe, GA, with the first Thomasson Act group. In 1938 he re-entered CCC duty in New Jersey. He served in a civilian status from Oct. 1, 1939 to Sept. 29, 1941. On Sept. 30, 1941, he volunteered for EAD for one year. Being too old for duty with troops as a 1st lieutenant, he was assigned to the Reception Center at Camp Upton, NY.

When ordered overseas in 1942, he served over three years in the services of supply at various bases in Australia, New Guinea and Leyte, PI, earning an arrowhead for the Leyte landings. He was ordered to Ft. Riley in November 1945 as commander of the Student Officers Detachment and later he served as Executive Officer of the Department of Horsemanship. On Sept. 30, 1946, he was ordered to Michigan State College as assistant PMS&T. For his last three years there, he was branch chief of the Armd. Cav. Branch, ROTC.

While he was on "delay en route" to Yokohama, the Korean war broke out. He was assigned to the 7th Inf. Div. where he earned the Combat Infantry Badge, to add to his 15 medals and awards. Sometime after his retirement in 1958, he was a security specialist at Inspector of Naval Materiel, and later with DOD, both in the Los Angeles area, retiring in 1973. There he was active in the Reserve Officers Association and the Retired Officers Association.

Married Margaret Kelly of Shamokin, PA, in 1938. They now live in Brookings, OR. While he was serving in Munich, Germany, they adopted twin boys and have one grandson. Since 1973 he has been active in politics, serving eight years as county GOP Committee chairman and as an officer in the Congressional District Committee. He also is active in Elk Lodge activities.

SSG S. SANDY SATULLO was born July 19, 1923, Cleveland, OH. He graduated high school; joined the US Army in 1941 and was stationed at Ft. Riley, Ft. Bliss, Australia, New Guinea, New Britain, Admiralty Islands,

Philippines, Leyte, Japan, and Luzon. He served with G Tp., 7th Cav. Discharged in November 1945.

Memorable experience was presenting Adm. Halsey with the white horse in Japan in 1945.

Has three sons and two grandchildren. Worked as a hotel manager and retired in July 1974.

PFC STUART J. SATULLO was born July 19, 1923, Cleveland, OH. He attended high school; joined the US Horse Cav. on Dec. 7, 1942, and was stationed at Ft. Brown, TX. He served with the SQ HQ, 124th Cav.

Memorable experience was the Mexican border patrol. Received medical discharge Dec. 21, 1944, with the rank of private first class.

Active in AMVETS and served as post, district, state and as national commander, 1957-58; Greater Cleveland Veterans Council, past president, 1951; DAV; Ohio Soldiers' and Sailors' Home, member of board of trustees; PANCO, past national commanders orgainization and US Council of the World Veterans Federation. He is also a member of numerous professional and fraternal organizations.

Married Eleanor and has one daughter, Jan, and two grandchildren, Toni and Nikki. He is the owner of his own business, Satullo Appraisals. He retired in July 1986.

1LT GERALD A. SCAGLIONE was born Sept. 19, 1918, New York, NY. He attended one year at Fordham College. Joined the cavalry Feb. 13, 1941, and was stationed at Cassino, Rom and Bolonga.

He served with the 12th, 8th and 27th Cav. and 91st Cav. Regt. Sqdn. Discharged in February 1946.

Scaglione is a widower and has three daughters and 10 grandchildren. He retired in February 1946.

LTC JOHN J. SCANLAN attended the US Military Academy, 1973; FAOAC; Command and General Staff College. Entered active duty and served with the 6th Cav., 14th FA, 1st Armd. Div., FRG; and 1st Cav., 92nd FA, 2nd Armd. Div., Ft. Hood.

Served Reserve duty with the 39th Inf. Bde., Arkansas ARNG; 95th Div., USAR; 3rd Cav., 83rd FA, USAR; and currently serving as inspector general, 87th Div. (Ex).

Works in business development, Vector Moncy Management, Inc., Vice President, Jackson, MS.

TSG JOHN HYMER SCHEIDEGGER was born July 27, 1910, in Winchester, TN. He enlisted in the Army on July 2, 1931, 25 days before his birthday when his parents agreed to sign for him. He was sworn in by Col. Hardy, Chattanooga, and assigned to Ft. Oglethorpe, GA. He worked in Machine Gun Tp., 6th Cav. where he stayed for 12 years. While there he was awarded the Sharpshooter Medal.

Scheidegger attended Winchester Normal, Winchester, TN; City High, Chattanooga. At Ft. Oglethorpe he worked on small arms and went on cadre to form the Air Force Ord. Co. Assigned to McDill AFB, Tampa. Transferred to London where he was in the blitz. Stationed at Bury St. Edmonds; this unit was transferred to Air Force.

Awards include the American Defense Service Medal, Campaign and Service Victory Medal, WWII Victory Medal. He retired on Sept. 30, 1956, at Tyndall AFB, Florida, as a technical sergeant.

Married twice, has three children and six grandchildren. As a civilian worked at Pratt-Whitney, West Palm Beach, FL; Chrysler Space Div. in New Orleans, LA; Chrysler Missile Div. at Cape Canaveral AFB, FL, where he was coordinator between design engineering and operational engineering on missile stands.

MG LAWRENCE EDWARD SCHLANSER was born July 21, 1912, in Honolulu, HI. His military career demonstrated the versatility and adaptability traditionally associated with the troopers of the US Cav. He progressed from the horse cavalry at Ft. Riley, KS, to adapting computers to coordinate the many phases of the combat service support system in the 7th Army.

At one time or another, after graduating from the US Military Academy, he served with no less than six cavalry units: the 13th Cav. and the 2nd Cav. at Ft. Riley; the 3rd Cav. Bde. of the Western Defense Command; commander of the 19th Cav. Recon Sqdn. on coastal patrol in Maine. 1944; November 1944 he led his squadron which went overseas with the 16th Cav. and engaged in the Rhineland and Central European campaigns.

After WWII he returned with the 19th Cav. to Ft. Campbell, KY, where it was deactivated in 1945. In October he was assigned as XO of the Communications and Electronics Test Section of Army Field Force Board #1 at Ft. Bragg, NC. In 1946 he returned to Ft. Leavenworth and took courses in the Command and General Staff College. In 1950 he was assigned to the Office of the Assistant Chief of Staff, G-1, Department of the Army, in the Pentagon, Washington, DC.

In 1954 he proved his versatility as chief of staff of the 24th Inf. Div. in Korea, and later became operations officer, G-3 Section, of the 8th Army in Seoul.

He was named chief of the Combat Development Group at Ft. Knox, KY, in 1955. In 1959 he became regimental commander of the 2nd Armd. Cav. Regt. Two years later he commanded the 7th US Army Training Center in Germany. Upon promotion from colonel to brigadier general in 1962, he was assigned as deputy commanding general, US Test and Evaluation Command at Aberdeen Proving Ground, MD.

He returned to Korea in 1965 as chief of staff of the 8th Army. He was promoted to major general in 1967, the rank he held at retirement.

In 1970 he was awarded the Distinguished Service Medal by President Nixon. The citation accompanying the award said, in part: "His outstanding accomplishments have been truly remarkable and without precedent, and will have a profound and lasting impact upon the logistical posture of the US forces committed to NATO."

WILHELM SCHOEPFLIN was born Jan. 25, 1845, in Lahr, Baden, West Germany on the edge of the Black Forest. He arrived in New York and enlisted June 1863 in the 15th New York Heavy Artillery, originally the 3rd Bn. German Heavy Artillery. In March 1864 he transferred to B and L batteries, 2nd US light artillery, which were horse batteries.

He served under Gen. Sheridan during Grant's spring campaign pushing through the Shenandoah towards Richmond, VA, and saw action in Rapidan, Wilderness, Brock Rd., The Furnaces, Todd's Tavern, James River, Ground Squirrel Church, Yellow Tavern, Trevillian Station, Brook Hanovertown, Crumps Creek, Haw's Shop, Totopotomoy and Cold Harbor. Wounded in Cold Harbor he returned to Washington and was later discharged in August 1865.

He moved to Cincinnati, OH, married Alvina Schlandt and had six children. He was a woodturner and said to have voted twice for Abraham Lincoln. He passed away in 1937 at the age of 92. *Submitted by Ronald A Zerges.*

MGEN HENRY C. SCHRADER was born Jan. 5, 1918, Chicago, IL; attended the University of Illinois, receiving his BSCE in civil engineering, 1940, and MSCE in structural dynamics, 1958. Joined the Corps of Engineers in 1941, Co. B, 14th Horse Cav., Ft. Sheridan, IL; was battalion commander, 53rd Engr. Bn., 8th Armd. Div. during WWII; participated in Korea; and in Vietnam where he was commander of the 18th Engr. Bde., 1970-71.

Retired June 1, 1973. His awards include the Distinguished Service Medal w/cluster, Legion of Merit w/3 clusters, Air Medal w/2 clusters.
Married Marium in 1942 and has two children and two grandchildren. Vice president URS Consultants from June 2, 1973 to present.

MAJ HUGHES SEEWALD was born April 17, 1919, Amarillo, TX; graduated from Amarillo public schools; and served in the National Guard while still in high school. Graduated from Texas A&M University with a degree in zoology. He was in the cavalry at A&M and received highest honors in military science. He was one of two in the class of 1942 to receive a regular Army commission.

Entered the Army immediately and attended the Cavalry School at Ft. Riley, KS. He completed the course of instruction Sept. 26, 1942. From there he went to Ft. Bliss, TX, and joined the 1st Cav. Div. He served in the division throughout WWII in Australia, New Guinea, the Admiralty Islands and the Philippines. He was wounded at Cabanatuan on the flying column push

to Manila. He commanded G Tp. of the 5th Regt. at the time. Among other medals he received was the Silver Star for bravery and distinguished service. He was a major. After two years in Army hospitals, he took medical retirement.

Married Katherine Lynn and had two children and one grandchild. He was in the oil and gas business and the cattle business. He raised and showed Morgan horses and was a member of the National Board of Directors of the Morgan Horse Club. He died April 5, 1995.

MSG MIKE SEWICK was born Nov. 1, 1914, New York City, NY; attended school through the eighth grade and received his GED. Joined the service Jan. 14, 1938, serving in the infantry, cavalry and artillery. He was stationed in Hollandia, Biak Island, New Guinea, Leyte, Luzon and the Philippine Islands. He served with the 41st Inf., 1st Cav.

Discharged Aug. 17, 1968, with the rank of master sergeant. Awards include the Bronze Star and Purple Heart.

Memorable experiences include joining the 117th Inf., Machine Gun Tp., 109th Cav., TNNG, FYFFE Stables, Chattanooga, TN, Jan. 14, 1938; and making maneuvers at Biloxi, MS, 1938 and Louisiana, 1939-40.

Married Estelle C. Scott, Jan. 11, 1941, and has two children and three grandchildren. Worked for the US Forest Service as a mechanic, 1935-41. He retired Aug. 17, 1968.

SGT CHARLES SHENLOOGIAN was born Sept. 9, 1916, Union City, NJ. He graduated high school; inducted March 14, 1941, Newark, NJ; and sent to Ft. Riley, KS. One of the first ones at CRTC, sent to 11th Horse Cav., Camp Moreno, CA, in July 1941.

Moved to Camp Lockett, CA. July 1942 went to Ft. Benning, GA; cadre for 10th Armd. Div., 11th Tk. Bn., Ft. Knox Tank Maintenance School, October 1943, Camp Gordon, GA, September 1944, Cherbourg, France, England General Hospital, Atlantic City, NJ, August 1945.

Discharged Nov. 21, 1945, with the rank of sergeant. Awards include EAMETO Ribbon w/3 Battle Stars, American Theater Ribbon, WWII Victory Medal, American Defense Medal, Good Conduct Medal, Silver Star Medal, Distinguished Unit Badge, Purple Heart w/2 OLCs.

Married Eleanor April 16, 1950, and has two children and five grandchildren. Worked as an embroidery foreman until retiring in March 1979. He has been on tours to Europe three times with the 10th Armd. Veterans Assn., visiting old battle grounds.

JOSEPH H. SHIELDS, born June 5, 1928, Chillicothe, OH; was educated in Chillicothe schools; and attended technical college. Entered the US Army in 1951 and was assigned to F Co., 2nd Bn, 3rd Cav. Regt., Ft. Meade, MD. Attended radio school at Ft. Knox, KY, and returned to F Co. as commo chief.

In December 1952 F Co. won the honor to take part in President Eisenhower's inauguration parade. On that day in January 1953, they could feel the presence of all the old troopers riding with them. Cavalry spirit and pride were at their highest as they received a salute from Ike. He was assigned to Active Reserve from 1953-57.

Married Nancy C. Tyo, June 5, 1955, and has one son, Joe Jr., and two grandchildren, Tonya and Heather.

He retired June 5, 1993, from the Ohio Department of Transportation, Highway Design Department.

COL MOYERS SIDNEY SHORE was born June 19, 1906, San Angelo, TX; received AB degree from the University of Arizona in 1911 and was a honor graduate from NMMI. Served the cavalry from 1931-46 and joined the Regular Army Infantry in 1947. He was stationed in New Guinea, Admiralty Islands, Leyte and Luzon; and served with the 8th Cav.

Discharged Sept. 7, 1950, with the rank of colonel. Awards include the Asiatic-Pacific Campaign Medal w/Arrowhead and four Service Stars, Combat Infantryman Badge, American Campaign Medal, American Defense Service Medal, Legion of Merit, Bronze Star Medal w/1st and 2nd OLCs, Philippine Presidential Unit Citation, WWII Victory Medal, Army of Occupation Medal, Air Medal, National Defense Service Medal, Armed Forces Reserve Medal, USAF Commendation Medal, US Army Commendation Medal and Philippine Liberation Ribbon w/2 Service Stars.
Married Mary Arntzen in 1931; she passed away in 1973. Remarried in 1976 to Waunette Collins. Has three children, nine grandchildren and three great-grandchildren. Works as a rancher and farmer. Retired on Sept. 1, 1961, with 30 years of credited service.

AL SHRAWDER was born in Bridgeton, NJ, in 1919. Drafted into the Army on June 17, 1941, and sent to Ft. Riley, KS, for 13 weeks of basic in the US Horse Cav., Tp. A, 2nd Sqdn, CRTC. After basic he was sent to Tp. F, 3rd US Horse Cav. Regt. at Ft. Myer, VA. The 3rd Cav. was the presidential guard regiment.

In 1942 he went on the Carolina maneuvers. The regiment was sent to Ft. Oglethorpe, GA, where it was dismounted and disbanded in June 1942. He was then sent as cadre to Co. D, 331st Inf. Regt., 83rd Inf. Div. at Camp Atterbury, IN. After training the 83rd Div., landed in France and was in all five campaigns.

He was awarded the Combat Infantry Badge, Bronze Star w/cluster and five campaign stars.

Now livinf in Evansville, IN, he became widowed in 1989 and has four children and seven grandchildren. He retired in 1983 as an executive with Atlas Van Lines.

COL LOWELL G. SIDWELL was born March 7, 1918, Clarinda, IA. Attended the University of Iowa and received his BS degree; George Washington University, MA degree. Joined the US Army July 2, 1937, and was assigned to the Horse Cavalry, serving with Tp. F, 14th Cav. After pilot training he spent all of WWII in B-26 airplanes with the 587th BS and 394th HQ.

After WWII he was assigned to Strategic Air Command for eight years; five years in B-29 and B-50 squadrons and wings; and three years in SAC HQ. Graduated from Air War College in 1957. He was assigned to the Pentagon for three years as chief of the USAF Military Personnel Enlisted Assignment Division.

Retired May 31, 1960, with the rank of colonel. Awards include the Distinguished Flying Cross, Air Medal w/8 OLCs, Distinguished Unit Badge (394th BG), French Croix de Guerre w/Etoile de Vermeil, ETO Campaign Medal and various campaign medals.

Worked for Lockheed-Georgia Co. for eight and one-half years in the C-5 airplane program.

Married Laura Lee Lane and has four children and seven grandchildren; and works as a cattle rancher.

CPL SAM SILVERMAN was born Nov. 27, 1916, and attended high school. Drafted into the US Army in 1941; trained at Ft. Riley, Horse Cavalry; and was assigned to the 11th Cav., Tp. F, 2nd Sqdn., at Moreno Lake. The 1st and 2nd Sqdn. combined at Camp Lockett on Dec. 9, 1941. The cavalry was dismounted in July 1942. The 11th Cav. became the 11th Tk. Bn., 10th Armd. Div. He was stationed in Europe and participated in the Battle of the Bulge.

The 11th Tk. had been together four years before going into combat. They captured Metz early in December 1944. On December 16, the Germans made the big break through, the Battle of the Bulge. They were in the 3rd Army, and Patton sent them to Luxembourg City. They arrived the morning of December 17 and saved the southern flank from Echternach, Berdorf and Bastogne. He was wounded on Dec. 18, 1944, when Panzerfaust hit his tank in Berdorf.

Discharged in 1946 with the rank of corporal. Awards include the Purple Heart, American Campaign Medal, EAME Medal, WWII Victory Medal, Good Conduct Medal and American Defense Medal.

Memorable experiences include the 11th Cav. and 11th Tk. being together five years and developing a great feeling of camaraderie.

Married Mildred and has one son and two grandchildren. Worked as a photographer for the National Institute of Health. He retired in January 1971.

TSG DONALD NESTOR SMELTZ (JACK) was born Sept. 27, 1919, Harrisburg, PA, and attended high school. Joined the USANG, 104th Cav., Oct. 14, 1940. They were on maneuvers in North Carolina and on their way home when they heard about the disaster at Pearl Harbor. Entered active duty Feb. 17, 1941, and served with the 6th Cav., Tk. Div. He drove tanks throughout WWII and lost two by direct hit of enemy fire. He was stationed at Normandy, Ardennes, Northern France, Central Europe and Rhineland. They were in the Normandy Landing, D+5 days organization, C Tp., 104th Mecz. Cav., RCM Sqdn, from Oct. 14, 1941, to Oct. 24, 1945, almost four years to the day.

Discharged Oct. 31, 1945, with the rank of technical sergeant. Awards include the Good Conduct Medal, American Defense Medal, EAME Campaign Award w/ 5 Bronze Stars.

Memorable experiences were of landing in Normandy; being a tank driver and getting hit twice; going into Berlin with Patton's 3rd Army; and meeting his brother, Bob, in Ireland.

Married Betty A. Tritt-Smeltz, and has three children and five grandsons. Worked as a driver for Stroehmanz Baker. He retired in October 1982.

PFC BUELL BERNARD SMITH was born Oct. 21, 1926, Hamilton County, IL, and received his master of commercial science degree (accountant). Joined the US Army, cavalry, June 8, 1945, and served with King Tp., CRTC, June 25, 1945 to Oct. 20, 1945; Saddlers School, CRTC, Nov. 26, 1945, to Feb. 15, 1946; and Service Tp., Horse Plt., 6th Constabulary Regt., Weiden and Bayreuth, Germany, March 30, 1946—Dec. 6, 1946.

Discharged Dec. 6, 1946, with the rank of private first class. Awards include the WWII Victory Medal, one Overseas Service Bar and Army of Occupation Medal-Germany.

Memorable experiences were of Saddlers School when the class had a contest to see who made the best bridle in class and got to keep it. He made the best bridle, kept it, and in 1991, donated it to the USHCA to be displayed in the Cavalry Museum at the 1991 Bivouac in Ft. Riley. They were training to invade the Pacific Islands on Mainland Japan when President Truman had the atomic bomb dropped on Hiroshima and Nogasaki, and the war ended. They were then sent to Germany where their outfit rode border patrol on horseback where the border terrain was too tough for military vehicles, out of Weiden, Germany.

After discharge he received his GED. In 1947 he went to work for the FBI, Washington, DC, and attended night school at Strayer College of Accountancy. Received his bachelor of commercial science degree in 1954 and master of commercial science degree in 1955. He resigned from the FBI and went to work for a CPA firm. He took the CPA examination twice before passing, and received his certificate on Aug. 6, 1963, in the state of Virginia. Was employed by a CPA firm for approximately 10 years as an auditor and tax accountant; then went to work for the IRS as an accountant in the Financial (Fiscal) Branch, three years; transferred to the General Services Administration to get a salary increase and worked in the accounting systems section for about three years. He then transferred to the Small Business Administration and worked principally as a systems accountant and budget officer until he retired.

Married Grace E. Revercomb, Aug. 24, 1952, and has one son, Kevin Ashley Smith and two grandchildren. Retired July 29, 1989. Over the past 50 years most of his time has been spent in and around Washington, DC. As a result, he has not been able to keep up with his high school classmates. However, he always looks forward to the class reunions. It is good to get back to where he grew up and spent many happy days in school and in other activities related to school and to meet a lot of his classmates who shared in those happy-go-lucky times.

MAJ EMMET C. SMITH was born Jan. 3, 1928, Columbus, OH. Attended Ohio State University, receiving his BS degree in agriculture in 1950; and Kenyon College Seminary, 1954. Joined the cavalry in December 1949 and was stationed at Ft. Knox and Ft. Benning, serving with the 7th Inf. Regt., Tank Co.; 325th Tank Co.; and 761st Tank Co.

Retired in 1974 with the rank of major and chaplain. Awards include the Combat Infantry Badge, Bronze Star and Korean Corp w/3 stars.

Married to Joyce Crutchfield and has two children and two grandchildren. He is rector of Episcopal churches in Ohio and Florida. He retired in 1983 after 38 years of service.

MG JAMES C. SMITH was born into the 6th Cav. Regt. on Sept. 5, 1923, at Ft. Oglethorpe, GA. Received his BGE degree from the University of Nebraska at Omaha and enlisted in the US Army in June 1942. He was commissioned from OCS, Cav. School in January 1943 and served in seven cavalry regiments: 1st Cav. 6th Cav. (twice), 9th Cav., 11th Cav., 14th Cav. (twice), 16th Cav., and 29th Cav. all of them either mechanized or armored cavalry. He also served in five divisions: 1st Cav. (twice), 1st Armd.  (twice), 3rd Inf., 7th Inf., and 101st Abn. He served in three wars: WWII, Korea and Vietnam. He is a qualified Army aviator and parachutist. He is probably best known for having formed the horse cavalry platoon in the 1st Cav. Div. in 1971; it is currently an official ceremonial unit in the Army.

Served on active duty for almost 39 years, and has many medals and awards, retiring as a major general in March 1, 1981.

Married Doris Lewis and has seven children and 10 grandchildren. Currently, he is an officer on the Board of the US Cav. Assoc.

LTG JEFFREY G. SMITH, was born Oct. 14, 1921, in Ft. Sam Houston, TX. Graduated from the Virginia Military Institute on May 22, 1943 with a BS degree and commissioned 2nd lieutenant of cavalry, Jan. 15, 1944. Transferred to infantry in 1946; received MS degree in 1949 from the Johns Hopkins University; MA degree in 1964 from George Washington University and graduated from Army Command and General Staff College, Armed Forces Staff College and the National War College.

Began 36 year Army career with 124th Cav. Regt. at Ft. Brown, TX, serving with the regiment in Burma and China until near VJ day. Subsequent assignments in Alaska, US, Korea, Germany, and Vietnam, including command of 2nd Inf. Div. and 1st US Army before retiring as lieutenant general Oct. 1, 1979.

Decorations include Distinguished Service Medal, Silver Star, Legion of Merit w/3 OLCs, Distinguished Flying Cross, Bronze Star w/V device and two OLCs, Air Medal w/12 OLCs, Purple Heart w/OLC and two awards of the Combat Infantryman Badge.

Joined the Ethyl Corporation in January 1980, retiring as a vice president Dec. 31, 1993.

He and his wife, the former Jane Holland, live in Alexandria, VA, and have six children and 12 grandchildren.

SGT RAYMOND G. SMITH, was born July 4, 1912, in Farley, IA. Enlisted in Tp. B, 13th Cav., Ft. Riley, KS, in 1929. Promoted to Corporal and re-enlisted in HQ Tp., 14th Cav., Ft. Des Moines, IA, in 1932. Graduate, Radio Electricians Course, Signal School, Ft. Monmouth, NJ. Promoted to sergeant and chief operator, Ft. Des Moines Post Radio Station, WZT. Honorably discharged in October 1936.

In 1940 selected for civil service position with FAA, the start of a 33 year career in airway facilities communications, maintenance, installation and engineering, including two year assignment as airways facilities consultant to Taiwan; three years in Hawaii as deputy chief, Electronics Engineering Branch; and 12 years at FAA's Washington, DC HQ as chief, Airway Facilities Evaluation Staff, responsible for evaluation of airway facilities establishment and maintenance nationwide.

Awarded Medal of Merit by Taiwan's Minister of Communications. Upon retirement, was presented Distinguished Career Service Award by FAA.

Married Anna L. and they has two sons, Ralph and Douglas. Retired 1973. Lifetime member IEEE.

LTC DONALD C. SNEDEKER, was born July 16, 1946, Brooklyn, NY. Grew up as an Army brat, following his cavalryman father, George, across the US and to Europe. Graduated from Xavier University in February 1969 and commissioned a 2nd lieutenant, US Cavalry. After Airborne School he joined the 3rd ACR at Ft. Lewis, WA.

Deployed to Vietnam in December 1969, where he joined the 2nd Sqdn., 1st Cav. in Song Mao, II Corps.

Served as an armored cavalry platoon leader with C Tp., and then as the blackhawk long range reconnaissance patrol platoon leader. Finished his tour in October 1970 with a Bronze Star w/V and a Purple Heart.

While attending the armor advanced course, worked on the armored reconnaissance scout vehicle task force which selected the M-3 Bradley as the Army's scout vehicle. Assigned in December 1974 to the 11th Armd. Cav. Regt. in Fulda, Germany. Served as the regimental S-3 training officer, 1st Sqdn. S-2, and Bravo Troop commander.

Later assignments included tours of duty as executive officer, 2nd Bde., 3rd Armd. Div.; speechwriter for the chairman of the joint chiefs of staff, Adm. William Crowe and Gen. Colin Powell; instructor at the German Army Officer's Academy; and chief of inspectors conducting arms control inspections in the former Warsaw Pact and USSR. Graduated from the Army War College in 1992.

Retired as lieutenant colonel in 1992 and is now residing in the Washington, DC area. Past president and vice president of the Washington Chapter of the Blackhorse Assn.

GEORGE SNEDEKER was born June 14, 1911, Brooklyn, NY. Joined the 101st Cav., NYNG, in 1935. When the regiment was federalized in 1940, he went to Camp Devans, MA, and then to Ft. Irwin, CA. Attended Cavalry Officers Candidate School in late 1942 at Ft. Riley, KS, and commissioned a 2nd lieutenant in February 1943.

Joined the 17th Cav. Recon Sqdn., 15th Cav. Gp. and served with it throughout WWII in England, France, Belgium and Germany, winning a Bronze Star. Left the Army in 1945 and returned to Brooklyn. Re-entered active service in 1947 and was assigned to the 2nd Armd. Div., Camp Hood, TX. Served as battalion adjutant and company commander with the 89th Tk. Bn., 25th Inf. Div., in Korea in 1950-51, winning another Bronze Star.

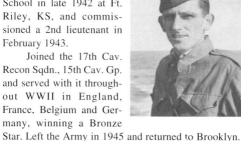

Further assignments included duty as regimental adjutant of the 11th Cav. Regt., at Camp Hood, TX, 1951-54; CCA and assistant division IG, 2nd Armd. Div. in Germany, 1954-57; 1st Tng. Bde., Ft. Knox, KY, 1957-59; and Hanau Military Community, Germany, 1959-62. Retired from active service as a lieutenant colonel, May 31, 1963.

Married Gladys Muriel Knapp, Dec. 24, 1941, and has three sons: George K., who served as an air cavalryman and air traffic controller and died on active service as a 1st sergeant in 1981; Robert, who died less than one year after birth in 1943; and Donald C., who served 23 years as a cavalryman and now lives in the Washington, DC area. George passed away April 2, 1973, and Gladys passed away May 19, 1990. Both are buried in Arlington. *Submitted by Donald C. Snedeker.*

CPT CHARLES H. SODEMAN was born March 26, 1913, Trimble, Clinton County, MO, and attended college receiving his BS degree. Entered service Jan. 11, 1941, and was sent to the Special Weapons Troop, 2nd Cav., 2nd Div. at Ft. Riley, KS. Was with the cavalry in the Louisiana maneuvers in 1941 and in Arizona when the horses were taken away. He was sent to the 83rd Inf. Div. and from there to OCS at Ft. Benning, GA.

Commissioned 2nd lieutenant, infantry on Jan. 8, 1943, and was then sent to the 44th Inf. Div. Served in the ETO with this division from September 1944 to VE-day.

Discharged Nov. 25, 1945, with the rank of captain. In the ETO he was in the campaigns of Northern France, Rhineland and Central Europe. He received three Bronze Stars.

Married Mary L. McBurney and has one child. Worked as a school teacher, bank president and farmer after the service. Retired March 1, 1978.

DR. ALBERT C. SPANNAUS was born in Arlington, MN. After graduating from Arlington High School, he attended the University of Kansas, graduating as a veterinarian.

He enlisted in the cavalry in 1918 and was stationed at Camp Green Leaf, GA.

Upon discharge he practiced at Waconia, MN, until the 1970s. *Submitted by Sibley County Historical Society.*

RICHARD EDGAR SPARKS was born Nov. 24, 1918, Yuma, AZ, but lived in Texas most of his life. He graduated from high school in Fabens, TX, and went on to college at Texas A&M where he graduated with honors as a 1st lieutenant in 1940. He returned home to ranch with his family and in July 1941, married Nancy Kloepfer, to whom he would remain devoted for the rest of his life. He began his active duty at Ft. Bliss on Aug. 5, 1941.

Served in the 82nd FA, 1st Cav. Div., in WWII. He was in Australia for six months on training maneuvers before going into action in the South Pacific. He saw his first action in the Admiralties and was involved in many campaigns, which included the Bismarck Archipelago, New Guinea, Leyte, Luzon, the liberation of the Southern Philippines and the Japan Occupation. He was awarded several medals among which were the Silver Star for bravery on the Flying Column to Manila, WWII Victory Medal, American Defense Services Medal, Air Medal, Asiatic-Pacific Campaign Ribbon w/4 Bronze Stars, Air Medal, Asiatic-Pacific Campaign Ribbon w/4 Bronze Stars and Philippine Liberation Ribbon w/2 Bronze Stars.

He resigned his active duty as major after the war and returned to ranch with his family outside of El Paso. He farmed and ranched from November 1945 until August 1964, when he began a new career as a civil engineer in El Paso. He had a great love for mathematics and the sciences and was an amateur astronomer. He had two daughters and two grandsons, in whom he infused a great love of the land, history and a great and lasting love of knowledge. He continued engineering until his death on July 24, 1992. *Submitted by Mrs. Richard E. Sparks.*

CPL CARLTON B. SPRAGUE SR. was born

May 8, 1925, Gardner, ME; and attended 15 semesters of high school and college. Joined the military on June 3, 1943; assigned to G Tp., 7th Regt., 1st Cav. and participated in campaigns in New Guinea, Admiralty Islands, Leyte, Luzon and Korea.

Memorable experience was being submerged in a rotten river in daylight for three days. Discharged in January 1948, re-enlisted same month and serving until June 2, 1952. He attained the rank of corporal.

He is divorced and has one son. He worked as a policeman, chemical worker, retiring on June 15, 1981.

COL JAMES R. SPURRIER entered a cavalry ROTC military school, the Oklahoma Military Academy in 1932. He earned his commission as a 2nd lieutenant, Cavalry Reserves, 1939.

Graduated from Pennsylvania Military College in 1940, BS degree, and became one of the outstanding intercollegiate polo players in the nation.

He requested and was accepted for active duty with the Regular Army. First duty station was 2nd Sqdn., 12th Cav. Regt., Ft. Ringgold, TX. The 12th Cav. was a horse regiment and remained as such, until Feb. 28, 1943. Participated in major Army maneuvers in Louisiana in 1940, 1941 and 1942. Was appointed, as 2nd lieutenant, to captain the regimental polo team, was placed in charge of the polo and jumping stable. Applied for and received his Regular Army appointment in October 1942.

When the regiment was dismounted and became foot soldiers, he was shipped to Australia. His first combat engagement was in Admiralty Island where he made an amphibious landing and earned a Bronze Star. Made initial amphibious landing on Leyte and earned a Silver Star. Moved to Luzon, Philippine Island, where it played a major role in the liberation of Manila. He received the Purple Heart and was awarded the Combat Infantry Badge. Following the surrender of the Japanese, his regiment moved to Japan and became a part of the Army of Occupation.

Completed three years overseas in August 1946, returned to the States and was assigned to the Cavalry School, at Ft. Riley, KS, as XO, Department of Horsemanship. Received orders to attend the Armor Advanced Class, Fort Knox, KY, then sent overseas to Germany where he joined the 2nd Bn., 14th Armd. Cav. where he spent four years.

Returned to the States and assigned to the Command and Staff Department, the Armor School, Ft. Knox, KY, for the next four years. Was active in the development of tactics for armor cavalry units and the writing of field manuals, for which he received the Army Commendation Medal. Had short overseas assignment with the MAAG in Taiwan; assigned to the Pentagon with the deputy chief of staff for operations, Department of the Army; assigned to the officer of International Security Affairs, Department of Defense; then served a short tour with the Combat Development Command, Ft. Belvoir, VA, from where he retired in 1963.

After retiring he purchased a horse farm in Virginia and organized his own polo club, the Reston Polo Club,

and fox hunted with the Fairfax Hunt Club. In 1976 and organized a group of old cavalrymen in El Paso, TX, to escort wagon trains across the country in celebration of the bicentennial of the United States celebration. He then organized the US Horse Cav. Assn. and became the first chairman of the board of trustees and its first president. He remained at the helm for almost 20 years, until age and other considerations, required that he ask for the resignation as its president. He was then appointed president emeritus and remained on the board. He was designated the outstanding alumni at the Oklahoma Military Academy; received the Cavalry Medal and the Order of the St. George, Gold Medallion.

He has remained married to a cavalry brat, Lucile G. Lafferty, since 1941. They have three daughters: Patricia S. Bright, Lucile S. Christie and Sarah S. Stewart.

CPL HOWARD KENNETH STACEY was born July 18, 1920, Osage, OK. Joined the 1st Cav., 12th Regt., March 19, 1939. Was stationed in New Guinea, Bismarck, Philippines, Luzon, Leyte and Australia. Served with E Tp. and Weapons Tp.

Discharged Aug. 20, 1945, with the rank of corporal. Awards include the Purple Heart, Philippine Liberation Medal w/2 Bronze Stars and the Defense Service Ribbon.

Memorable experience was being wounded in 1945 while in the Philippine Islands.

Married Marie Luensmann and has two children and four grandchildren. Retired in 1973 from the civil service at Kelly AFB.

GEN DONN A. STARRY, USA, RET, enlisted in 1943; commissioned USMA 1948; commanded armor units platoon through battalion, US Army Europe; G2 Staff, 8th US Army, Korea, 1954-55. Commanded 11th Armd. Cav. Regt. in Vietnam, 1969-70, led his regiment into Cambodia in 1970 and wounded leading the assault on Snuol, May 5, 1970. Commanded Armor Center and Fort Knox, 1973-76, V Corps US Army Europe, 1976-77, TRADOC, 1977-81; US Readiness Cmd., 1981-83.

As commander, TRADOC, principal architect of AirLand Battle doctrine so successful in Desert Storm, 1991. Graduate of Army War College, MS International Affairs George Washington University. Retired in 1983. Ford Aerospace Corp. VP/General Manager Space Missions Group and corporate executive VP, 1983-87. Retired industry 1990.

Member Defense Science Board, 1985-93; inducted Fort Leavenworth Hall of Fame, 1993; Order of Aaron and Hur 1982; charter member Friends of the 5th of May; trustee, Eisenhower Foundation, 1994; and chairman of the Board, US Cavalry Foundation, 1994. Married 46 years to Letty Gibbs and has four children and seven grandchildren.

CARL A. STEFAN, was born June 16, 1918, Chicago, IL; and completed the ninth grade of school. Joined the US Army in July 1936 and was discharged in December 1939, with the rank of corporal. Served with Tp. B, 14th US Cavalry. Spent 13 months as a recruit instructor at Ft. Sheridan before transferring to the USN.

In April 1944 he joined the USN and was discharged in December 1945 with the rank of S1/c. Boot camp was only five weeks, and when the drill instructor of Co. 938 was suddenly transferred, Stefan was called

upon to lead his company through the two weeks of boot that were left before graduation. Then, fresh out of recruit training, he took a company of 140 men through boot camp as a S1/c. He then volunteered and was accepted for the submarine service. He served aboard the USS *Proteus* AS-19, a submarine tender at Guam, and aboard the USS *Thornback* SS418 in the South Pacific and back to the States for discharge.

Awards include the American Defense Medal, Asiatic-Pacific w/star, American Campaign Medal and WWII Victory Medal.

Married Edna E. Ratsch and has two children, six grandchildren and eight great-grandchildren. Worked as an over-the-road semi driver. He retired in November 1978.

WILLIAM F. STEFURAK

CPL R. MURREL STEPHENS was born June 11, 1896, Worthington, WV; graduated high school and attended college course work. Joined the US Army on Jan. 19, 1914; served with the 13th Cav., M Tp., 4th Cav. HQ; stationed in El Paso, TX and Columbus, NM.

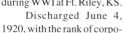

He was involved in skirmishes in Mexico. After the Mexican War, during which Pancho Villa was never captured, he served during WWI at Ft. Riley, KS.

Discharged June 4, 1920, with the rank of corporal. He was awarded the Sharpshooter Award.

Married Lucille Moder and has four children, seven grandchildren and two great-grandchildren. Worked as a business proprietor and retired in 1964. He and Lucille have made several trips to the Middle East. *Submitted by David L. Stephens.*

MSG ALLAN STEPP was born Oct. 19, 1888, Hastings, Dakota County, MN. Enlisted on Feb. 19, 1911, Ft. Slocum, NY. He was stationed at Curtis Bay Ord. Depot, Curtis Bay, MD, from 1930-42. Curtis Bay was not a large Army post, but it had open space to pasture retired US Cavalry horses. The men of the post had a day of duty occasionally. On these days they rode one of the retired horses around the perimeter of the post to exercise the horse and to check the condition of the fence surrounding the post. He served with the American Embassy in China; in the Philippines on the Mexican border and a score of Army posts in the States. He served under Gen. Pershing in the Mexican border Campaign.

Discharged on April 30, 1943, at Camp Pickett, VA, as master sergeant. He was issued a Bronze Victory Button on July 3, 1920.

Married Anna Mae Low and had four children: Velma, Billie, Allan Jr. and Norma. Worked in the rail transportation office of the Induction Center at Greensboro, NC. He died Nov. 20, 1972. *Submitted by Velma Stepp Wilson.*

1SG RAYMOND STILL was born March 25, 1917, Camp Creek, TX. He went to school in Normangee, TX. Joined the 5th Cav., Tp. B, in April 1937 and participated in campaigns in North Africa, Sicily and Italy.

Wounded June 8, 1944, during the heavy fighting north of Rome. Received the Purple Heart and Commendation Medal. Discharged Feb. 2, 1965, with the rank of 1st sergeant.

Married Hildegard Grasse of Berlin, Germany. They have one son, Tom, and one grandson, Justin. He worked in civil service for the USAF and retired in February 1985.

JOHN C. STRADER was born Oct. 27, 1917, at Harrodsburg, KY. Moved to Canadian, TX in 1930. At age 19, in 1937, he enlisted in the US Cav. at Ft. Bliss, TX. After six weeks of recruit training, was sent to Tp. A, 8th Cav. The four years he spent in the cavalry were very good years, riding and drilling with the horses and then to the detail of recruit training. He instructed the new men for six weeks, turned them to duty and then had 30 more to instruct. This job he didn't like. He wanted something with a lot of "action," so he volunteered to go to the Philippine Islands and soon discovered plenty of action - a little more than he asked for. WWII started and he was thousands of miles from home. Was sent to Bataan to fight the Japanese, then to surrender to be a prisoner of war for three and one half years. Looking back down memory lane includes 50 years married to Goldie and three children; John Jr., Beverly and Rochelle.

"After all is said and done, he still loves those Cavalry Hay Burners."

1LT LEE WILSON SWIFT JR. was born Nov. 14, 1924, Orange, NJ. Graduated Lafayette College, AB degree, 1951 and ROTC distinguished military student. Joined the armor in July 1951. Performed duty patrolling Czechoslovakian border, HQ Regensburgh, Germany.

Served with G Co., 3rd Bn., 6th Regt.; 76th Tk. Bn., 11th AB Div., Ft. Campbell, KY, November 1951— November 1953; USMCR, private, 1944-46, training in the States and Pacific with service in China, which included being a member of the 1st Tk. Bn., 1st Marine Div.; qualified as a cadet trooper, Essex Troop of Cavalry, Cadet Sqdn., sponsored by the 102nd Cav. Regt.

He recalls a surprise inspection of his company bade by Lt. Gen. George H.L. Decker while training in Regensburg, Germany. Discharged on Oct. 17, 1956, with the rank of 1st lieutenant. Awards include the China Service and German Occupation Awards.

Employed as US Dept. of Commerce official; rose in rank to become joint chief of staff during the Kennedy administration, 1961-63. Retired in 1979. Married Peggy and has three children.

SGT ROBERT F. SWIFT was born Dec. 8, 1920, in Detroit, MI. In September 1942, he left Junction City destined for the CRTC at Ft. Riley, KS, and arrived in a horse van. He participated in basic training and horsemanship and enjoyed early Sunday morning "joy rides," including riding the artillery range.

By January of 1943 he was one of 11 slated for Cav. School. A stroke of ill luck countered his chances, and he was not included in the school's selection. He was dismounted in April of 1943, and, by that time, had become cadre and platoon sergeant. He left the cavalry in September 1943 to become a cadet in the US Air Corp.

He married Josephine Bonnaventura on Aug. 28, 1943. They have two children; Janice and Robert James, and two grandchildren, Natalie and John Robert. Worked in sales, drug store designer; as vice president, Vi-Pann Chemical; vice president, IXL Glass until present time. To this day, the fondest and proudest memories of his service will always be the US Horse Cavalry.

TSGT JAMES T. SWINDLE was born Oct. 29, 1925, Norman, AR. He graduated high school and joined the US Army April 12, 1945; was stationed in Leyte, Luzon and Camp Robinson, AR. He served with Tp. B, 12th, 1st Cav.

Discharged May 5, 1946, with the rank of technical sergeant. Awards include the Bronze Star, Asiatic-Pacific Medal, WWII Victory Medal, Combat Infantryman's Badge and Philippine Liberation Medal. Married Patricia Sue Watkins and has two children and four grandchildren. He was self-employed in the pipeline construction business. He retired in July 1979.

COL DALE W. TAYLOR was born Aug. 3, 1918, Wooster, OH; attended Wooster High, Ohio State University, Maryland University and Kansas University. Enlisted in the US Army in March 1941 and sent directly to Ft. Riley, KS, for basic training in B Tp., 1st Cav. Sqdn. for horsemanship.

Left Tp. B to attend the 15th OCS class at Ft. Riley; graduated as 2nd lieutenant in December 1942; and

assigned back to the Cavalry Replacement Training Center to continue to train the horse cavalry 13 week program. Sent to Europe during WWII and assigned to the Recon Tp., 28th Inf. Div. Received the Bronze Star, four Battle Stars and several other medals.

Returned to the States in December 1945 with assignments at the Army General Ground School, Ft. Riley; Army Aviation School, Sheppard Field, San Marcos, TX; Artillery School, Ft. Sill, OK, graduating as liaison pilot in October 1946. Assigned to HQs, 15th Cav. Gp. at Ft. Meade, MD; (1947) to TRI Partite HQ in Vienna, Austria; April 1948, 2nd Constabulary Bde., Munich, Germany.

Sent back to Ft. Knox, August 1950, for Advanced Armor School; transferred to Ft. Hood and 1st Armd. Div. and one year later became a pilot in the 1st Armd. Div. flight section. Transferred to 1st Army HQ as a pilot and aid to the deputy army commander Maj. Gen. E.B. Sebree; 1953 transferred to Taiwan and military assistance advisory group for two years.

Returned to the States and the Command and General Staff College. Assigned to the 2nd Army HQ, Ft. Meade, MD, as the aide-de-camp and pilot for Lt. Gen. George Reade. Transferred in 1960 to Schwabach, Germany, 4th Armd. Div.; Ft. Leavenworth, KS, and assigned to Command Arms Gp., Doctrine Div. for three years; 1966, Ankars, Turkey and the Central Treaty Organization as a US representative in the operations division, writing defense plans for Turkey, Kran and Pakistan. Returned to the States and Hunter AAF, Savannah, GA, where they were training Vietnamese pilots for the Ft. Ruck School.

Retired in February 1971 as an colonel after 30 years of dedicated years and service. His last decoration was the Legion of Merit.

Memorable experience was his first observation mission when he left his jeep to observe German w/d, and a Germany mortar hit the middle of the jeep.

Went to work for the Trust Co. Bank, Savannah, GA, and became manager of the Garden City Branch for 11 years.

Married to Shirley and has three children: Richard, Ronald and Susan, and 10 grandchildren. He retired in February 1983.

KENNETH W. TIEMAN enlisted May 26, 1939 O.N.G. He was commissioned to Federal Service March 5, 1941 and served with Troop B, 107th Cavalry during W.W.II. He was discharged Dec. 10, 1945.

PVT GEORGE E. TOBIAS was born Oct. 26, 1846, Jennings County, IN. Joined the cavalry on Dec. 17, 1863, and participated in the Civil War, serving with Co. K, 120th Regt. Discharged Jan. 8, 1866, in Raleigh, NC.

Memorable Experiences: marching with Gen. Sherman through Georgia to the sea; making the 1889 "run" into Oklahoma with two beautiful black mares of race horse stock and filed a claim in what is now Kingfisher County, OK.

Married Roxie (Emmaline) Townsend on Jan. 26, 1876. They have nine children: Roxy, Jessie, Fannie, Mattie, Anna, John, Edna, Eddie and Willie; and 14 grandchildren. He worked as a farmer until he passed away on May 26, 1931.

MGEN W. RUSSELL TODD was born May 1, 1928, Seattle, WA. Attended Norwich University receiving his BA degree and the University of Alabama receiving his MBA degree. Joined the US Army, cavalry, June 15, 1950. Was stationed in Korea with the 2nd Inf. Div. and received five Battle Stars; in Vietnam with the 25th Div. and received five Battle Stars. Discharged June 30, 1982, with the rank of major general.

Memorable experience was starting his career as 2nd lieutenant, 3rd Armd. Cav. (light) and ending as commanding general, 1st Cav. Div.

Married Caroline Foster Wyeth and has three children and nine grandchildren. He was president of Norwich University until his retirement June 30, 1992.

CPL HAROLD HAAKON TOLLEFSON was born March 26, 1922, Rudyard, MN; and attended college. In 1939, while a junior in high school he read an article entitles, *The Rape of Poland*. At that time he was determined he would join some branch of the service. When he graduated in 1940, he tried to enlist in the USN, but was turned down do to an overbite. Looking across the Post Office building in Great Falls, MT, he saw the sign "Uncle Sam Needs You" next to an Army recruiting officer. He had no idea what branch of the Army he wanted to get into and had no idea what they had. When he was asked if he could ride a horse - that was it, the Horse Cavalry. He joined the 11th Cav. on Sept. 3, 1940, and was assigned to Troop E, at the Presidio of Monterey.

He was given meal money for the two day trip but soon lost the money in a crap game and arrived in Monterey hungry and wiser. As luck would have it, he and another recruit were assigned to KP duty to peel 200 pounds of potatoes—food at last. They wore their civilian clothes as no Army clothing was available for several days.

He was assigned a horse called Popeye which looked pretty mean to him. Popeye had never let them clip his head which was shaggy and gave him a rather individual look, which he exercised on their first jumping assignment. They raced toward the 2 1/2 foot jump and Tollefson was thinking what a great choice he had made - $30 a month, a horse, good food, when the horse applied all four brakes and he sailed over his head and made the jump all by himself.

In the spring of 1941 they patrolled the Mexican border and the cavalry began to build in both manpower and horses. He was assigned to the remount detail. On their first shipment of halter broken horses, four of them would draw four numbers and ride those horses until they were satisfied they would be a good cavalry horse. His favorite was So High. He would let you ride until you felt comfortable, then buck, usually leaving you in front

of him with the reins between your legs. Another technique was to turn around and grab the back of your foot.

In the fall of 1941 he put in for a short discharge and wanted to re-enlist in the 26th in the Philippines. Two choices had to be listed and he was assigned to the 501st Coast Arty. in Puerto Rico.

Discharged on Oct. 10, 1945, while with the 9th Service Command on the West Coast. Awards include the American Defense Medal, American Theater Award and Conduct Medal.

Married and has two children and two grandchildren. Worked as a supervisor of claims for Farmers Insurance. Retired on Sept. 1, 1994.

COL STANLEY W. TYLER was born Oct. 24, 1911, Lynn, MA; attended Massachusetts State receiving his BS degree and Staley College receiving his BA, MA and DA degrees. Joined ROTC at the University of Massachusetts and was assigned to the cavalry in June 1929. Stations included Ft. Ethan Allen, Ft. Bliss, Ft. Leavenworth, Africa, Sicily, Italy, France and Germany. He served with the 3rd Cav. Discharged Feb. 28, 1976, with the rank of colonel.

Married Irene in 1934 and has two children and nine grandchildren. Worked as a chief research chemist for N.E. Grain Products Co., until retirement on Feb. 28, 1976.

COL CHARLES HOWARD VALENTINE was born Aug. 15, 1901, Palestine, TX. He received his BS degree in 1925 from Texas A&M; joined the cavalry on

Sept. 7, 1925, and served three campaigns in Europe during WWII. Served with the 5th Cav., Ft. Clark, TX, 1925; 26th Cav., Ft. Stotsenberg, Philippine Islands; 8th Cav., Ft. Bliss, TX; 9th Cav., Ft. Riley, KS; 80th Inf. Div., C/S, Camp Pickett, VA; 28th Inf. Div., C/S, Europe, WWII; 3rd Cav. Co., Ft. Meade, MD; US Constabulary, 7th Army, Germany; and 4th US Army, Ft. Sam Houston, TX.

Discharged on Oct. 30, 1955, with the rank of colonel. Awards include the Legion of Merit, Bronze Star Medal w/OLC, Legion of Honor Chevalier (France), Croix de Guerre w/Palm (France), Order of Leopold w/ Palm (Belgium) and Croix de Guerre w/Palm (Belgium).

Memorable experiences consist of convoying the first four Recon jeeps to Ft. Riley in 1940; polo player, student officer pilot training, Brooks Field, TX. Was released for a physical disability and transferred to the cavalry.

Married Iona Underwood and has two children and six grandchildren. He worked as a rancher and was an avid hunter. He passed away Oct. 16, 1991. Submitted by Col. William D. Wooldridge, USA (RET).

R. THOMAS VAN KLEECK was born in 1919 in a Colonial Dutch region of New York State - Albany, Hudson River, Manhattan. Dutch progenitor original settler 1652 when still a Dutch trading colony.

Enlisted pre-WWII to achieve three goals: be a horse cavalryman, earn a commission and complete a

university education. All achieved! Short RA, discharge got a transfer to 1st Horse Cav. Div., TX. Commissioned in 1942 at Ft. Riley and assigned to Tp. A, 10th Horse Cav. Regt. - famed Buffalo Soldiers.

Overseas duty evasive. Achieved via Mtn. Pack School begetting orders for Bureau. Short-stopped Philippine Islands as replacement body in Leyte action. Luck rejoined 1st Cav. after Luzon action, did V-J Day landing in Yokohama only two thirds combat loaded after steaming past big MO as Gen. Mac signed pact with Japanese. Erie, Erie!

Opted for career when transferred into 8th Army HQ. Attended University of Idaho as physical rehab, earning MA degree in 1953. Last assigned D/A Pentagon as general staff action officer. Retired 1975 after passed over twice for star promotion. A mustang cannot compete at this level against pointmen. Overall, rewarding, regardless.

Retired 1980 from 2nd career with Federal Bureau of Land Management, administrating 405 million acres of public domain - also, a rewarding career. Army experience and education productively applicable.

Several marriages sired several broods of children; most are successful and happy. Sign of the times, he has some grandchildren. Life is what one makes of it - a lost proverb. The Father continues to bless me in all ways. I'm happy and rich - especially in values of other worth.

COL FRANK VARLJEN was born Dec. 19, 1929, in West Winfield, PA. Enlisted in December 1950; attended basic training at Ft. Knox, KY.

Served as company clerk; Camp Gordon, GA; Armor/Cavalry OCS, Ft. Knox, KY; and commissioned May 1952. During 30 years service he served in several armored cavalry units: 14th ACR, Fulda, Germany; 2nd Sqdn., 8th Cav., Ft. Lewis, WA; 3rd Sqdn, 8th Cav., near Mannheim, Germany; 2nd Sqdn, 4th Cav., Schwabach, Germany; and 11th ACR, Vietnam.

Two highlights of cavalry service were commanding 3rd Sqdn, 11th ACR in Vietnam and performing border duty along entire US sector of East-West German border. Retired 1980 with rank of colonel.

Since retirement, worked in defense industry, VP, with current focus on mine clearing. Married Luise Lehner on May 21, 1955, and they reside in Manassas, VA. They have two children and three grandchildren. One son currently USA LTC commanding signal battalion in Belgium; other son Army veteran of Desert Storm, managing restaurants in Dallas, TX, area.

SGT HERMAN FREDERICK VOIGT was born Aug. 14, 1836, in Halle, Saxony, Germany. In 1852 he came to the US and arrived in Hastings, MN, in 1857. Went to St. Louis, MO, and in 1861, enlisted for 90 days in Co. B, 1st Regt. Missouri Volunteer Inf. under Capt. M. Lathrop. After fighting battles in Camp Jackson and Boonville, MO, he was wounded at Wilson Creek. His 90 days were up.

After recovering from his wound, he went to Cairo, IL, where Gen. Grant was organizing a regiment of Illinois volunteers. He enlisted in Co. B, 16th Regt. Illinois Volunteer Cav. under Capt. Thielman. After the capture of Ft. Henry, Ft. Donelson and Shiloh, he was promoted to sergeant. His company fought many battles in Tennessee, Mississippi, Georgia and Virginia.

At Vicksburg there is a marble building housing the war memorial to the Illinois troops who fought there in 1863. Voigt is listed on a bronze plaque as part of Gen. Sherman's HQ Cav. Tp. and personal bodyguard, 2nd Cav. Thielman's Cav. Bn., Co. B. He was honorably discharged Nov. 25, 1864, at Springfield, IL.

Returned to Hastings, MN, and married Wilhelmenia Smith. They had two children, two grandchildren and three great-grandchildren who loved to hear his stories about the Civil War. He and his brother bought a saw mill in Beldenville, WI, and later purchased the Ramsey Mill in Hastings, MN. He retired to a farm on Lake Isabel in Hastings. The whole town came out to celebrate his 100th, 101st and 102nd birthdays, on Nov. 19, 1938, he passed away at the age of 102. *Submitted by his great-grandson, Frederick Herman Voigt.*

T/5 EDWARD ALAN WADE was born Feb. 10, 1922, Newburg, Phelps County, MO. Attended 11 years of school; joined the US Army on March 17, 1941; was stationed in North Burma, China and New Guinea and served with Merrill's Marauders.

On Sept. 16, 1940, the 116th Cav., IDNG became the 183rd FA Regt. and was called to service on April 1, 1941. Between those dates he enlisted and took basic to the tune of cavalry jargon, saddle soap, uniform and all sans the horse. Eleven months later a bad case of misjudgment coupled with allegiance to a good friend who was in conflict with the 1st sergeant, he volunteered to transfer to the 98th FA BN (Pack). In September 1943 while in New Guinea that friend?, plus others, persuaded him to volunteer for a hazardous mission which turned out to be Merrill's Marauders in Burma.

Upon returning to the States in November 1944, he was eventually to find a home with the 611th FA BN (Pack) at Ft. Riley, KS. On Feb. 6, 1945, the 611th was disbanded with enough of them to form a gun battery, transferred to the Cavalry School (school troops). They were to support the fire direction and observation classes in the school troops.

He still wears the scarlet piping (artillery) on his overseas cap, the cavalry insignia on the lower part of his lapel and below that the Combat Infantry Badge. Discharged on Aug. 26, 1945, with the grade of T/5. He was awarded the Bronze Star.

Memorable experiences were being run over by a mule (plug 188-B); and writing a story, *Personality Profile of an Army Mule."*

Married Della Lorene Wiley on Nov. 3, 1947, and has two children and two grandchildren. Still working as tractor driver for a farm cooperative.

CPT DONALD S. WARNOCK was born Aug. 5, 1916, in Northampton, MA. Attended college for two years; joined the cavalry on Oct. 1, 1940, and stationed at Forts Jackson, Knox and Campbell and overseas in Rhineland and Central Germany. Served with 102th Horse Cav. 88th Recon. 33rd Armd. Recon Sqdn. and 20th Armd. Div.

Led small task force of cavalry, infantry tanks and engineers into Dachau. Had a small fire fight before

breaking into camp. From records later released, they must have entered from the side or rear. Reported conditions to squadron HQ, gave out all of their food and continued on their mission to circle Munich. He did not know what Dachau was or the importance of the camp until after the war ended. Later, Dachau was released by troops from 20th Armd. Div., 42nd and 45th Div. They had released British, Canadians, Army ground troops and Air Force officers from four POW camps prior to Dachau. Awarded eight medals and was discharged in March 1946 with the rank of captain.

Married Virginia Bittles and has two children and five grandchildren. Worked as a sales executive for Springs Mills and Fieldcrest Mills; retired in 1976 due to health. Co-founder of Warnock Automotive Group in Hanover, NJ, and active as secretary-treasurer.

LTC WILLIAM H. WARREN SR. was born Feb. 18, 1911, Holdenville, OK; received his BA degree from Oklahoma University and JD degree from Samford, AL (Cumberland, TN Law School). Joined the USAAF and was stationed at Kelly AFB, San Antonio, Goodfellow and San Angelo. Served with the AAF BU.

After 20 years service, including Reserve, he retired March 30, 1946, with the rank of lieutenant colonel. Awards include the American Defense Medal w/Bronze Star, American Theater Ribbon and WWII Victory Medal.

Married Florence Cardwell (deceased) and has two children and five grandchildren. He is an attorney.

LTC PHILIP T. WEISBACH JR. was born Nov. 19, 1916, in Chicago, IL. Joined the US Army Sept. 2, 1941, and was stationed in New Guinea, Admiralties, Leyte and Luzon. Served with the 12th Cav. 1st Med. Sqdn.

Awarded the Bronze Star w/OLC. Discharged on April 20, 1946, with the rank of lieutenant colonel, M.C.

Married Maymie Nelda Pruitt and has four children and eight grandchildren. He is a physician in private practice, 1946-present.

CPT ADDISON I. WEST was born Oct. 1, 1918, in McPherson, KS. Inducted July 14, 1941, and assigned Tp. C, 4th Sqdn. Cav. Replacement Center, Ft. Riley, KS. Later assigned as troop clerk, then assigned battalion sergeant major, 4th Bn. MP Training Center, Ft. Riley.

Graduated 2nd lieutenant, Administrative OCS Fargo, ND, December 1942; assigned assistant post adjutant, Camp Atterbury, IN; August 1944 sent to Hollandia, New Guinea and assigned as adjutant 470th AA AW Bn. and made invasion of Philippines on islands of Luzon, Panay and Negros. Placed on inactive status November 1945 as captain, AGD.

Married to Betty McKee, Dec. 13, 1942, and has two children and four grandchildren. Received JD degree, University of Michigan and has been assistant US attorney and corporation counsel and manager legal staff of Boeing Company, Seattle; retired November 1981 as assistant general counsel, Northrop Corporation, Los Angeles.

His grandfather, William West, Ashtabula, OH, was a cavalry trooper of Co. F, 2nd Regt., Ohio Volunteer Cav. known as the "Black Horse Sqdn.," Sept. 9, 1861. He was wounded in action in southern Missouri and his leg was amputated. He was discharged from US Army hospital in St. Louis, MO, in December 1862.

LTC LESLIE M. WESTFALL was born March 31, 1917, in Lisbon, ND. Attended the University of Arizona from 1938-42 and joined the cavalry in May 1942. Served with the HG&HG Tp., 100th Cav. Discharged in May 1946 with the rank of lieutenant colonel.

Married with four children and eight grandchildren. Retired from the Westfall Stevedore Co. Dec. 30, 1986, as president.

COL JOEL CHESTER WHITE JR. was born July 2, 1921, and grew up in Hope, AR. In September 1936, his family moved to Tucson, AZ, where he attended public schools. His first military experience was in junior ROTC at Tucson High School. At age 17, still in high school, he enlisted in Co. H (MG Co.) 158th Inf. AZNG, which was part of the 45th Div., headquarters in Oklahoma.

In September 1939, age 18, he enlisted in RA at Ft. Bliss, TX; assigned to the 7th Cav. Regt, 1st Cav. Div.; transferred to 8th Corps area headquarters, Ft. Sam Houston, TX, in November 1940. Served as staff sergeant, military secretary to Maj. Gen. Richard Donovan, CG, 8th Corps until July 1942, when he entered the Air Corps at Randolph Field, TX, as an aviation cadet, pilot trainee; "washed out" due to physical disability in December 1942. Retained in the Air Corps, he served in the campaigns of New Guinea, Leyte, Luzon, and Okinawa, as a crytographic specialist with the 5th AF.

After WWII he enrolled in the University of Arizona, graduating in 1951 with BA degree in history. Later earned a master's degree in education. Attended ROTC, but dropped it when he received a direct commission as 2nd lieutenant of infantry, and assigned to AZARNG. Served in AZNG as company commander, battalion staff officer, battalion commander and brigadier XO.

Transferred to Army Reserve in 1969; promoted to colonel in spring of 1970 and assigned to Army C&GS college, summer school facility, University of Nevada, Reno, for three years. Assigned to Army Intelligence

Center, Summer School Faculty, Ft. Huachuca, AZ for three years. Transferred to Retired Reserve, 1974, with rank of colonel, Military Police.

Completed Infantry, Armor and Army Intelligence schools, and graduated from the US Army Command and General Staff College, 1966. Completed two year extension course, Industrial College of the Armed Forces in 1972.

Received Meritorious Service Medal w/4 Campaign Stars (New Guinea, Leyte, Luzon, and Okinawa) Philippine Liberation Medal, Philippine Presidential Unit Citation, and a number of NG and Army Reserve service medals.

Taught 23 years at Tucson High School, retiring in 1982, as Chairman, Social Studies Department. Has served as volunteer Docent (AZ) Historical Society Museum, Tucson, for the past 10 years.

Married Jean Baker, Tucson High School teacher, 1977. Second marriage for both. Between them, they have seven children and 17 grandchildren. They live in Tucson, AZ. Jean is also a volunteer at the Arizona Historical Society Museum.

SAMUEL M. WHITSIDE served as a commissioned officer of the US Army from Nov. 4, 1861 to June 9, 1902. He enlisted Nov. 10, 1858 at New York City and was assigned as a private to General Mounted Service. He was appointed 2nd Lt. , Troop K, 6th Regt. of Cavalry, Nov. 4, 1861.

He served with the Army of the Potomac in VA Nov. 1861-Sep. 1862, as ADC to Gen. Banks (Defenses of Washington) Sep. 1862-Nov. 1862, on the staff of Gen. Martindale June 1863-Nov. 1863, as ADC to Gen. Pleasanton to March 1864, as Mustering and Disbursing Officer March 1864-March 1865, and as Commissary of Mustering to Sep. 1865.

He established Fort Huachuca, AZ on March 7, 1877.

T-4 JOE J. WIELAND was born on July 24, 1920, Des Moines, IA. He graduated high school; joined the 113th Cav. in October 1940 and was called to active duty on Jan. 13, 1941. Participated in Germany, Northern France, Normandy and Ardennes campaigns. He served with F Tp., 125th Cav. RCN Sqdn., 113th Cav.

Discharged on June 28, 1945. Re-enlisted in RA, Ft. Monmouth, NJ, April 28, 1948. Discharged on June 3, 1952, with the grade of T-4. Awards include four Bronze Stars for Germany, Northern France, Normandy, Ardennes campaigns per Ltr ETOUSA, Good Conduct Medal, American Defense Service Ribbon, EAME Theater Campaign Ribbon and two Overseas Bars.

Married JoAnne L. and has five children and 10 grandchildren. Worked as a purchase agent for Wanamaker Rent. He retired in July 1986.

CPL JAMES KING WILCOX was born Feb. 25, 1843, Ursa, IL. Joined the cavalry on Aug. 5, 1862, participating in the Civil War. He served with Co. D, 118th Regt. Discharged on Oct. 1, 1865.

Memorable experience was locating his brother,

Stephen Franklin Wilcox, who died at Andersonville Prison and buried in the Louisiana National Cemetery at Baton Rouge and bringing his personal effects home.

Married Lucinda Pomery Campbell on May 8, 1866. They had 10 children and 43 grandchildren. Worked as a farmer and breeder of horses. He passed away on June 15, 1918, in Quincy, IL.

COL DONALD H. WILLS was born May 23, 1918, Lynchburg, VA. Graduated from VMI in 1940 with BS degree in chemistry. Joined the cavalry June 15, 1940, and ended up in the 14th Cav. Asked for and was transferred to the Philippines.

Fought in the Battle of Bataan and struggled to survive imprisonment by the Japanese. The story of his service is told in his book, *The Sea Was My Last Chance*. He became a POW when Bataan fell in April 1942. Eventually was sent to the infamous Cabanatuan prison camp where the death rate was high, food was scarce and disease and brutality were widespread. Prisoners spent most of their time trying to find food and ate whatever they could get, from worms to boiled grass and caribou eyes.

When the Japanese wanted volunteers to do farm work on Mindanao, Wills decided to go. The situation was better, although difficult; he remained in Mindanao's Davao prison until June 1944. By then, the American Army was drawing close to the Philippines and the Japanese wanted to send American prisoners by ship to Japan where they would be put to work.

He was determined to find a way to escape and his opportunity came within days of being loaded onto a prison ship. He jumped into the sea and, luckily, was not hit by rifle or machine gun fire and swam four miles to safety. Once ashore, he ran into guerillas, refused evacuation and stayed with them to help destroy enemy garrisons.

Returned to the States in May 1945 and was discharged in October 1945 with the rank of colonel. Awards include the Silver Star, Distinguished Flying Cross, Air Medal w/cluster, Bronze Star, Purple Heart, Philippine Gold Cross, Medal of Merit and Silver Wings.

Married Mary over 49 years ago. They have two children and three grandchildren. Worked for P&G for 18 years; then self-employed in real estate in Dallas. Retired on May 23, 1978.

COL GARNETT H. WILSON (BILL) was born Feb. 22, 1896, in Waco, TX. While his early education was in mining and chemical engineering (Los Angeles and UW/Seattle), he later took a degree in commerce and finance at Seattle University, where he became an assistant professor after his retirement from military service.

He joined the USMC in 1913 and saw military action in 1914 at Vera Cruz. Also, at the time "underweight and underage," he was the featherweight boxing champion of the Sixth Fleet.

Just prior to WWI, as a very young National Guard captain in Douglas, AZ, he led a notable mounted action against a tough demonstration of IWW "Wobblies."

In 1917 he was commissioned lieutenant (ORC), serving two years with the 6th Cav. Regt. in France. In 1920, after a brief but memorable stint as a mining engineer in Sonora with Mina Mejico, he was recommissioned in the Regular Army, assigned to the 8th Cav. at Ft. Brown, TX. He served with the 12th Cav. (Ft. Brown-

Ft. Ringgold, 1922-24); 2nd Cav. 1929-33 at Ft. Riley, where he had also completed the basic and advanced Cav. School courses. After a second tour with the 6th Cav. at Ft. Oglethorpe, GA, 1935-38, he was assigned to the 26th Cav. (PS) at Ft. Stotsenburg, PI, 1938-40, serving as regimental adjutant. He also served as XO of the 4th Cav. at Ft. Meade, SD, 1941.

In January 1942 he was assigned to the 115th Cav. as XO and in June, at Ft. Lewis, WA, was promoted to colonel and assumed command of the regiment. He took the 115th, now mechanized (light tanks) and reorganized as a cavalry group to combat duty in the ETO, January 1945. After the close of hostilities, Wilson, with his HQ Gp., set up and ran the Weihenstephan Agricultural and Technical College, a subsidiary of the University of Munich at Freising, Germany.

After brief duty with the Dachau War Crimes commission, he became commandant of Stuttgart Post. From 1950-52 he was the first commanding officer of Ft. Richardson, AK, then commanding officer of Ft. Lawton, WA until his retirement from active duty in August 1953. His medals and decorations included the Bronze Star, European Campaign w/3 Stars, WWI Victory Medal, Mexican Border Service (US Army), and USMC Mexican Campaign (Vera Cruz 1914).

While in the Philippines, Wilson, accompanied by daughters Sally and Jane, climbed Mt. Pinatubo during the memorable expedition of April 1939. The quintessential horseman and dedicated rider was a fine polo player and raked in the silver at many horse shows over the course of his career. In 1936 he was instrumental in helping reorganize the Ft. Oglethorpe Foxhunt, first acting as Whip, then as Joint MFH. In Germany, after hostilities ceased in 1945, he organized a number of theater-wide horse shows and prevailed on his friendship with Herr Alois Podhajsky of the Vienna Reitschule for that gentleman to serve as judge. After retirement, he rode almost daily, well in into his 77th year. He also rode with the Ft. Leavenworth Hunt, with daughter Nan, and taught equitation to his grandchildren and other Army Brats. He was a grand raconteur and knew "more songs than anyone".

He married the former Durrett Oglesby of Louisville, KY, in 1922; his three daughters, Sally Janis, Jane Cooper and Nan Olson, are members of the US Cav. Assoc.

MAJ LEWIS H. WINNE was born Oct. 25, 1918, Poughkeepsie, NY. He graduated high school, OCS, Knox tank tactics and Ins. School, NY. Joined the cavalry on March 13, 1941; stationed at Ft. Riley, Ft. Picket, Camp Forest, Ft. Oglethorpe, etc.; and served with the 104th Cav., 16th Cav. and 19th Cav.

He participated in the ETO. Memorable experiences include draftee, OCS, Ft. Riley; coastal patrol, Canada to Rhode Island, looking for submarines; Ft. Knox Tank School; *Queen Elizabeth* to Scotland; English Channel to Le Havre, through France, across Rhine under smoke to Weisbaden.

Discharged in March 1946 with the rank of major. Awards include the ETO Award and American Defense Medal.

Married Jean, a 1st lieutenant Army nurse in the Bulge. He and Patton liberated her. They have one son, Philip, who is a college professor. Winne is owner of four offices of independent claims adjusters. He retired in 1951.

LTC W. B. WOODRUFF JR. enlisted in the H/S Btry, 612th FA Bn. (Pk) 1943-45, enlisted in the L Co., 35th Inf. Div., Korea 1951-53, officer, Tk. Bn., 1st Armd. Div., Berlin and Cuban Missile Crisis. Served reserve duty in the 90th Div., US Army, 49th Armd. Div., Texas ARNG.

Attended Texas A&M College and the University of Texas School of Law, Armor AOC, C&GSC. He is a retired attorney, active author and historian and resides in Decatur, TX. *Submitted by John J. Scanlan.*

LTG W.H. STERLING WRIGHT was born Oct. 29, 1907, Duluth, MN; graduated USMA, 1930 and NWC, 1950. Joined the cavalry and armor on June 12, 1930. Participated in action in North Europe during WWII and in Korea, 1950.

Was tactical officer, USMA, West Point; assigned various Army staff positions, Pentagon, including Joint Chiefs of Staff, 1942-56; miliatry aide to Honorable Henry Stimson, 1942-44; staff planner, Normandy Invasion, 1944; and landed on Omaha Beach, D-day, 1944. Participated in military ops. as staff officer in France, Belgium and Germany, 1944-45, and celebrated V-E Day in Weimar Geramy, 1945.

Staff officer planning invasion of Japan, 1945; chief Korean MAG at outset of Korean Conflict, 1950; commanded 2nd Armd. Div., Fort Hood, TX, 1960-63. Retired in 1965 as lieutenant general. Decorations: Distinguished Service Medal, two Legions of Merit, French

Croix de Guerre and Legion of Honor, and various foreign decorations including Russian Order of Fatherland's War Memorable experience was being a member of the US Equestrian team 1937-40; and US Olympic Equestrian Team, 1947-48.

Married Matilda Thayer Basinger in 1937 and has three sons and five grandchildren. Matilda passed away in 1981. He married Gibson Dey Eppler in 1983.

SGT PAUL STANLEY ZERGES was born Sept. 4, 1896, in Cincinnati, OH, the son of German immigrants. In 1913,t age 16, he enlisted in the US Army and joined F Tp., 12th Cav. in Ft. Robinson, NE.

In 1914 he went to Louisville, CO for eight months to control a miners strike, then to Columbus, NM. He was in camp the night of Pancho Villa's infamous raid, and participated in the "Punitive Expedition" into Mexico pursuing Pancho Villa. He served under Gen. Pershing at various posts and outposts; Del Rio, Ft. Brown, Ft. Clark, and Ft. Columbus until his discharge in 1926.

He was a muleskinner, mess sergeant, and supply sergeant. He qualified expert with .45 cal. pistol mounted and dismounted and expert swordsman. He also was an

expert horseman and performed what was called "monkey drills" with four horses at a time.

He returned to Cincinnati, married Myrne Schoepflin, had five sons and one daughter. He passed away Dec. 17, 1975. *Submitted by Ronald Zerges*

LTC LAWRENCE J. ZIELINSKI was born April 10, 1917, in Menasha, WI. Attended St. Mary High School, graduated in 1935; joined the US Army March 17, 1941, OCS graduate, Ft. Riley, KS, Oct. 17, 1942. Other stations include Ft. Bliss, TX; Ft. Campbell, KY and participated in the ETO. He served with CRTC, E Tp., 5th Cav.

Memorable experiences include the conversion from citizen to horse soldier in 13 weeks; combat through the Vosage Mountains, France; break through the Siegfried Line.

Discharged as lieutenant colonel. His awards include the Bronze Star, EAME Theater Medal w/2 Bronze Stars, American Theater Medal, WWII Victory Medal and the French Victory Medal.

Married Dorothy Hemes (deceased) and has three children and seven grandchildren. Retired June 1 1982, as paper manufacturing superintendent.

Index